Lowestoft, 1550 – 1750

Development and Change in a Suffolk Coastal Town

Lowestoft, 1550–1750

Development and Change in a Suffolk Coastal Town

David Butcher

THE BOYDELL PRESS

First published 2008
The Boydell Press, Woodbridge
Paperback edition 2023

ISBN 978–1–84383–390–1 hardback
ISBN 978–1–83765–076–7 paperback

The Boydell Press is an imprint of Boydell & Brewer Ltd
PO Box 9, Woodbridge, Suffolk IP12 3DF, UK
and of Boydell & Brewer Inc.
668 Mt Hope Avenue, Rochester, NY 14620–2731, USA
website: www.boydellandbrewer.com

A CIP catalogue record for this book is available
from the British Library

Designed by Tina Ranft
This publication is printed on acid-free paper

Contents

Illustrations

Plates 4, 6, 8, 11, 18, 19, 23 and 24 form part of the Isaac Gillingwater collection of illustrations and are reproduced by kind permission of the Suffolk Record Office (Lowestoft)

LIST OF MAPS

LIST OF TABLES

To the memory of the Reverend John Tanner (1684–1759)

parish priest and antiquarian

Foreword and Acknowledgements

In the preface to *An Historical Account of the Ancient Town of Lowestoft* (1790), Edmund Gillingwater claimed that 'perusal of works which are in general of a local nature is apt to be unpleasant, and is seldom entertaining, to the generality of Readers'. His principal reasons for writing a history of the town were as follows: the regard he had for his birthplace (he had, for a number of years, resided in the Norfolk town of Harleston); the desire to provide information and entertainment for the merchants and other inhabitants; and the wish to recover 'from the hands of all-devouring Time, and transmitting them to posterity, the best accounts and modern state of the town' that he was able to find. The writer of this present volume is unable to subscribe to the first statement cited above and cannot claim family ties with Lowestoft. He can, however, find common ground with his predecessor in wishing to provide the place's inhabitants with information (if not with entertainment!) and to do something in the way of recording its history, using appropriate sources.

In essence, the purpose of this book is to give an account of everyday life in the town of Lowestoft during the early modern period, based mainly on surviving documentary evidence of the time and, to a lesser extent, on the topographical study of existing physical features. The whole work is underpinned by full family reconstitution of the parish registers and is the product of twenty-five years' ongoing research. In its early stages, it was influenced in both form and focus by A. Hassell Smith of the University of East Anglia and the writer acknowledges the importance of the perceptive and well-directed guidance received. At the pre-publication stage, considerable assistance and support were forthcoming from Carole Rawcliffe of the same university, for which sincere thanks are expressed.

There is also a debt of gratitude to be recorded to various other individuals who have facilitated the process of research. Over the years, members of staff in both the Norfolk and the Suffolk record offices have been of assistance in making a wide range of documents available for scrutiny. Especially helpful are a number of people who have worked in the North Suffolk Record Office, located in the town of Lowestoft itself: Rosemary Rogers, Gwenn Stearn, Paul Brough, Gordon Reid, David Wright, Kerry Meall, Kate Chantry, Louise Clarke, Bill Wexler and Brenda Gower. Thanks are also due to the parish rector of the time, the late Alan Glendining, who approved access to the early register books of St Margaret's Church, while they were still lodged in the building, and to Pat King-Gardiner, who gave generously of her time in the cold confines of the crypt while the work of transcription took place. This exercise was the first stage of a family reconstitution of the registers, backed by the Cambridge Group as part of its extensive programme of population studies. Both Tony Wrigley and Roger Schofield offered a great deal of support and sound advice, not only concerning the mechanics of reconstitution but also on its usefulness as a means of re-creating past societies.

Further assistance in the task of historical reconstruction has also been received from various other people. Over the years, Peter Northeast has been very kind in providing probate material relating to Lowestoft citizens in the fourteenth and fifteenth centuries, while the late Eric Porter was equally helpful in revealing eighteenth-century references drawn from contemporary local newspapers. Paul Durbidge has been the writer's archaeological mentor for a long period of time and has, through work of his own on the face of the cliff in the old part of town, been able to confirm an early fourteenth-century date as the starting point of Lowestoft's development on a new site. Ivan Bunn not only helped to prepare a number of the maps and plates used to enhance the text, but has also been a valued collaborator of long standing on a number of projects aimed at re-creating aspects of Lowestoft's past. Finally, my wife, Ann, has been consistent in encouraging the writing of this book (and the research which preceded it) and has used her digital skills to format many of the illustrations which embellish its pages. While, at the Boydell Press, Caroline Palmer, Anna Morton and Vanda Andrews have been both helpful and professional.

This history of Lowestoft has a dual identity. It stands on its own as a sequence of events which happened in a particular location as the result of various contributory factors; but it also has wider significance as part of a national pattern, whereby certain communities grew larger than others in their respective neighbourhoods and became important as focal points of economic and social activity. The study of urban societies has occupied a significant place in the sphere of academic history for the last thirty or forty years, with much of the debate focusing on the nature of urbanity itself. A wide-ranging discussion has taken place regarding the elements that are required to make a town, how large a settlement has to be in order to be considered 'big' or 'small', and what influences are required to create civic identity. Attention will be given to this ongoing discussion, where it is felt to be appropriate, and an attempt made in the final chapter to place Lowestoft in a national context. The town of today is Suffolk's second largest community – the result of continuous growth from the middle of the nineteenth century – but its earlier core is still easily identifiable and has a fascinating story to tell.

This volume has been published with the support of the Centre of East Anglian Studies and the School of History of the University of East Anglia, and with the aid of a grant from the Ann Ashard Webb Bequest. Ann Ashard Webb (1902–1996) made her bequest to the School with the express purpose of funding an accessible series of works on the history of Suffolk which would appeal to a wide readership. In addition to the main volumes in the series, it is intended to produce a number of more specialised titles, of which *Lowestoft 1550–1570: Development and Change in a Suffolk Coastal Town* is one. Others which have already appeared with support from the bequest are:

JUDITH MIDDLETON-STEWART *Inward Purity and Outward Splendour: Death and Remembrance in the Deanery of Dunwich, Suffolk, 1370–1547*

CHRISTOPHER HARPER-BILL, CAROLE RAWCLIFFE, R.G. WILSON (eds) *East Anglia's History: Studies in Honour of Norman Scarfe*

CHRISTOPHER HARPER-BILL (ed) *Medieval East Anglia*

MAIN SERIES

MARK BAILEY *Medieval Suffolk: An Economic and Social History, 1200–1500*

LUCY MARTEN *Late Anglo-Saxon Suffolk* (forthcoming)

Abbreviations

AHR	*Agricultural History Review*
BA	British Academy
BL	British Library
CPR	Calendar of Patent Rolls
CRS	Catholic Record Society
CSP	Chetham Society Publications
CSSH	*Comparative Studies in Sociology and History*
CTB	*Calendar of Treasury Books*
DNB	*Dictionary of National Biography*
EHR	*Economic History Review*
HJ	*Historical Journal*
HMC	Historical Manuscripts Commission
HR	*Historical Research*
HWC	Heritage Workshop Centre, Lowestoft
IMR	Infant mortality rate
IJLP	*International Journal of Law and Psychiatry*
JBS	*Journal of British Studies*
JHG	*Journal of Historical Geography*
JIH	*Journal of Interdisciplinary History*
JSA	*Journal of the Society of Archivists*
JSPMA	*Journal of the Society for Post-Medieval Archaeology*
JUH	*Journal of Urban History*
LA&LHS	Lowestoft Archaeological and Local History Society
LH	*Local Historian*
LPFD	*Letters and Papers, Foreign and Domestic* (published)
LRS	London Record Society
MCA	Magdalen College Archives, Oxford
MM	*Mariner's Mirror*
NCC	Norwich Consistory Court
NH	*Northern History*
NNGS	Norfolk and Norwich Genealogical Society
N&Q	*Notes and Queries*
NRO	Norfolk Record Office
NRS	Norfolk Record Society, or Navy Records Society
NS	*New Scientist*
OU	Open University
PCC	Prerogative Court of Canterbury

P&P	*Past and Present*
PS	*Population Studies*
PSIA	*Proceedings of the Suffolk Institute of Archaeology*
RHS	Royal Historical Society
SAC	Suffolk Archdeaconry Court
SANUT	Society of Antiquaries of Newcastle-upon-Tyne
SCC	Suffolk County Council
SGB	Suffolk Green Books
SP	State Papers (original documents)
SPD	*Calendar of State Papers, Domestic* (published)
SR	*Suffolk Review*
SRO(I)	Suffolk Record Office (Ipswich)
SRO(L)	Suffolk Record Office (Lowestoft)
SRS	Suffolk Records Society
SS	Selden Society
TIBG	*Transactions of the Institute of British Geographers*
TNA: PRO	The National Archives at the Public Record Office, Kew
TNNNS	*Transactions of the Norfolk and Norwich Naturalists' Society*
UHY	*Urban History Yearbook*
VCH	*Victoria County History*
WDC	Waveney District Council
WEA	Workers Educational Association
WRS	Wiltshire Records Society

A Note on Dating and Transcription

In all cases, the year has been taken as beginning on 1 January, not 25 March. Wherever original material has been reproduced, spelling has been modernised but original grammatical forms and usages retained. People's forenames and surnames are reproduced in their original spelling throughout, in both text and notes.

– 1 –

Origins and Influences

Introduction

The town of Lowestoft is, and has been for centuries, England's most easterly settlement. It occupies a coastal site with a configuration of sandbanks and channels favourable to maritime activity (Map 1) and with a fertile hinterland of varying soil types. It is one of twenty-five ancient parishes which constitute the Hundred of Mutford and Lothingland (Map 2) and, for at least 500 years, has been the dominant community in this area. It did not always enjoy a position of pre-eminence, however, and before any discussion of its early modern history can begin a summary of its antecedents needs to be presented.

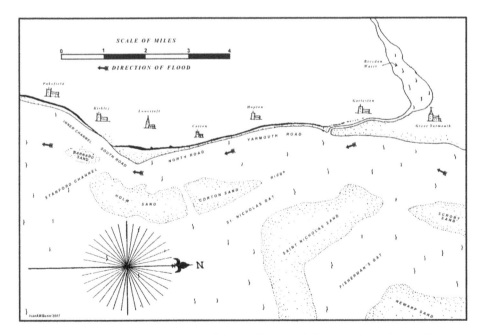

Map 1. *The local coastline: the position of the sandbanks and channels (shown here as they were at the end of the eighteenth century) remains basically the same today. The usual approach to Lowestoft was through the Stanford Channel, but navigation between the Holm Sand and Corton Sand was possible – as was a more circuitous route using the St Nicholas Gat.*

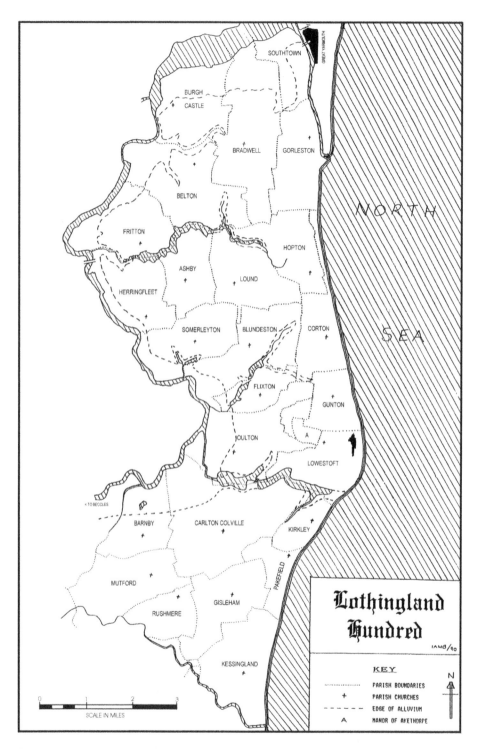

Map 2. *Mutford and Lothingland hundred. Known alternatively as Lothingland (or Lothing) Hundred, this group of twenty-five parishes was bounded by water on all sides: Breydon Water to the north, the rivers Hundred and Waveney to the south and west, and the sea to the east. The uneven split into two distinct half-hundreds (two-thirds and one-third of the land-mass, respectively) was caused by the physical location of Lake Lothing and of the broad at Oulton.*

The name Lowestoft itself is Scandinavian in origin and may be translated as *Hloðver's toft* – 'the homestead of Hloðver'.[1] A number of the place-names in the local hundred are of similar derivation and probably date back to the period of invasion during the 860s, when the Danish forces of Ivor the Boneless and his brother, Halfdan, controlled many of the eastern parts of England. It is likely that an existing Anglo-Saxon settlement was taken over and renamed by a dominant incomer and his dependents rather than a new community being established where nothing had previously existed.

By the time of the Domesday Survey (1086), Lowestoft is described as 'an outlier' (to the paramount manor of Gorleston), with 450 acres of arable land and a head-count of sixteen adult male inhabitants: three villagers, ten smallholders and three slaves. There were two demesne plough teams and three belonging to the men, enough woodland to sustain eight pigs, and five acres of meadow. The livestock consisted of eight cattle, eleven pigs and 160 sheep.[2] A decline since the reign of Edward the Confessor was recorded in terms of population, ploughing capacity and livestock,[3] and the settlement was one of about eight or nine in the hundred which occupied what may be described as a 'middling' position in the local hierarchy. Six other communities were much larger in terms of both cultivated land and population.[4]

Close to Lowestoft, on its north-western perimeter, was the small manor of Akethorpe (Maps 2 and 3). Its name combines Old English and Danish elements, with the first syllable deriving from *ac* (meaning 'oak') and the second from *þorp* (meaning 'farm'). With the latter also meaning a settlement that had its origins in a larger, nearby community,[5] it is possible that Akethorpe developed from Lowestoft itself. The first element probably related to the type of tree found growing on the heavier clay in that location – as opposed to the lighter soils which prevailed elsewhere in the area. Domesday Book records Akethorpe as consisting of eighty acres of arable land, with four adult male inhabitants: a freeman (Aelmer the Priest) and three smallholders. There was one demesne plough team and half a team belonging to the men, sufficient woodland to support five pigs, and one acre of meadow. The livestock totalled three pigs and forty-eight sheep.[6]

If the adult males living in Lowestoft and Akethorpe are added together and regarded as family heads (with the exception of the priest, who may well have been single), a figure of nineteen is the result. Applying a multiplier of 4.75 per household to this number, in order to arrive at a notional population, produces a total of 90

---

[1] E. Ekwall, *Concise Oxford Dictionary of English Place Names*, 4th edition (Oxford, 1960), p. 305.

[2] A. Rumble (ed.), *Domesday Book, Suffolk: Part One* (Chichester, 1986), 1 (33).

[3] There had been five villagers and five slaves thirty years previously, five plough teams belonging to the inhabitants, and fourteen cattle.

[4] Carlton (Colville), Flixton, Gorleston, Kessingland, Lound and Mutford.

[5] Ekwall, *English Place Names*, p. 468.

[6] Rumble, *Domesday*, 1(56). The history of Akethorpe is traceable in the records of Magdalen College, Oxford, to which institution it belonged from 1479–1960; it was progressively sold for building development during the twentieth century.

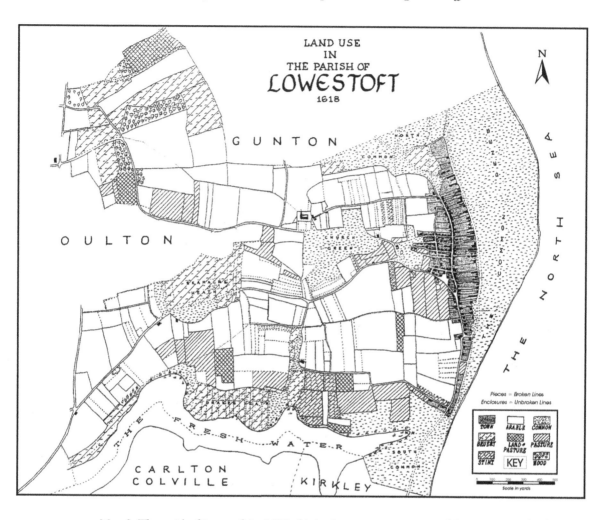

Map 3. *The parish of Lowestoft in 1618: this land-use map was constructed from a manor roll of that year. Vestiges of mediaeval strip farming can be seen in certain locations, on both north–south and east–west alignments. The manor of Akethorpe occupied the area in the top left-hand corner, to the west and north-west of the parish church. Lowestoft itself was originally located due south of the church, at the meeting point of trackways below Church Green.*

people.[7] The sum total of inhabitants may have been greater than this, or less, but the figure arrived at serves to create an impression, at least, of a body of people sufficient to form a community, with most of the members concentrated in one particular area.

---

[7] The multiplier used strictly applies to a period stretching from the late sixteenth to the early twentieth century – see P. Laslett and R. Wall (eds.), *Household and Family in Past Time* (Cambridge, 1972), p. 126 – but it has also been used for earlier epochs.

The likely location for the core settlement is the area of convergence of roads and tracks half a mile or so south of the church (Map 3).[8] The presence of a priest in Akethorpe at the time of Domesday implies that there was also a church, but without sufficient assets to be taxable. This building (or a later one) then became the parish church of Lowestoft, with the dedication to Saint Margaret of Antioch suggesting a renaming of the early Norman period. Such antecedents explain why this site is three-quarters of a mile removed from the cliff-top position where the town was to develop during the fourteenth and fifteenth centuries. The earlier location was concentrated in the vicinity of what is now the traffic roundabout where Rotterdam Road, St Peter's Street and Normanston Drive all converge. Thus it was well placed at the point where two of the common fields joined (the South and South-west). Furthermore, the church was conveniently situated nearby; a local high point (now Hill Road) provided a suitable site for the construction of a windmill; and just over half a mile to the south supplies of coarse fish, wildfowl, reed and peat were available from Lake Lothing.[9] In addition to available topographical evidence, a number of sporadic finds of pottery sherds dating from the Anglo-Saxon period serves to confirm a concentration of human activity in the vicinity (Plate 1).

Plate 1. *The original site of the town: a view looking northwards. The traffic roundabout referred to is in the foreground and marks the junction of the former South and South-west open fields. St Margaret's Church stands impressively at the top of the hill.*

[8] This map was developed from a manor roll of 1618: SRO(L) 194/A10/73. A transcription and translation of the document is available in published form: D. Butcher, *The Lowestoft Manor Roll of 1618* (Lowestoft, 2004).

[9] This stretch of water is an old outlet of the River Waveney, blocked during the final period of glaciation and left landlocked after the ice-melt. It has formed Lowestoft's inner harbour since the 1830s. During the sixteenth and seventeenth centuries, it was always referred to as 'The Fresh Water'.

Evidence of Lowestoft's existence during the twelfth and thirteenth centuries is sparse, but a Lothingland hundred roll of 1273–4 names twenty-six chief tenants of the manor (which was still in the possession of the Crown, as it had been at Domesday) holding a total of 289¼ acres.[10] It is not known whether the arable land had increased in extent from the 450 acres recorded in 1086, but even if it hadn't the area of demesne under cultivation was still in excess of 160 acres. Topgraphically, the most interesting reference in the roll is the name of one of the tenants: Thomas of the Cliff. This suggests that the settlement was still nucleated in the area referred to in the previous paragraph, it being unlikely that someone would be described as 'of the cliff' if a whole settlement were located there.

In terms of the hierarchy of communities in the Hundred of Mutford and Lothingland, based on subsidy returns, Lowestoft still occupied a comparatively modest position during the first half of the fourteenth century. The subsidy of 1327, which was levied at a rate of one-twentieth on movable goods of 5s or more in value, shows the town in fourteenth place out of twenty-one settlements (there are three instances of two parishes combined as one and Barnby is not listed). Twenty-nine of its inhabitants made contributions totalling £1 9s 6d.[11] In first place was Gorleston, with seventy-six people paying £7 6s 7½d. The 1334 taxation list shows Lowestoft ranked twelfth in the local order, but with a different calculation in operation as to how the assessment was made.[12] Two hundred years later, a profound change had occurred. The 1524 Lay Subsidy shows 170 Lowestoft townspeople paying a total of £35 18s 7d – three and a half times as much as the £9 18s 4d contributed by ninety-eight residents of nearby Pakefield.[13] Its ascendancy is confirmed by the 1568 Subsidy, in which 111 people are seen to have paid the sum of £34 19s 8d – four and a half times the amount collected from twenty-eight inhabitants of Carlton Colville.[14]

There is probably no single reason for Lowestoft's rise to pre-eminence, but maritime activity (especially herring fishing) may well have been an important factor. It is noticeable that, as the fourteenth century progressed, Great Yarmouth became increasingly concerned about its own position as the dominant town on a large sector of the East Anglian coast. This was partly due to continuous silting up of its haven mouth, but it also viewed the commercial activities of neighbouring communities with some degree of alarm – especially the fishing enterprise conducted at Lowestoft, some eight miles to the south. Eventually, it

---

[10] Lord John Hervey (ed.), *The Lothingland Hundred Rolls, 1273–74* (Ipswich, 1902), pp. 8–9.

[11] S. H. A. Hervey (ed.), *Suffolk in 1327*, SGB, ix (Woodbridge, 1906), 95. Only seven places had a greater number of taxpayers, but a further six, with fewer contributors, are seen to have paid more.

[12] R. E. Glasscock (ed.), *The Lay Subsidy of 1334* (Oxford, 1975), p. 290. Lowestoft's contribution was £3 15s 2¼d. Former crown demesne paid one-tenth on movable goods; all other communities were assessed at one-fifteenth. Most settlements in Mutford & Lothingland Hundred fell into the former category, but some in the Mutford half were in the control of more than one lord.

[13] S. H. A. Hervey (ed.), *Suffolk in 1524*, SGB, x (Woodbridge, 1910), 242–7 and 261–3.

[14] S. H. A. Hervey (ed.), *Suffolk in 1568*, SGB, xii (Bury St. Edmunds, 1909), 186–9 and 197.

succeeded in persuading Parliament – largely because of the number of ships it contributed to Edward III's navy in times of trouble – to pass the Statute of Herrings (1357), one of the effects of which was to give it control of the local autumn herring trade within a seven-league distance of its quay.[15] In the case of Lowestoft, if fishing and associated trades were becoming increasingly important, re-locating the centre of population to a more convenient position would have made good sense.

The edge of the cliff, slightly less than a mile east-north-east of the original settlement, was a bleak and exposed site, but one better suited to maritime activity because of its proximity to the sea. The cliff itself had been stable for many centuries, as a result of the width of beach beneath it (as much as 300 yards) – a stretch of sand and shingle covered in tough grass and scrub vegetation. As well as keeping the sea at bay, this area (known as The Denes) was also important as a source of rough grazing and as an area where fishing nets could be spread out for drying and repair, where vessels could be beached, and where cargo could be stored awaiting transhipment.[16] Equally important, both for its own craft and for passing ships, was the anchorage offered by the haven. The inshore reaches at Lowestoft were known respectively as the 'North Roads' and the 'South Roads' and, once either of the channels through the outlying sandbanks had been negotiated, there was easy mooring available in three to eight fathoms of water at low tide (Map 1).

From the circumstantial evidence cited in the two preceding paragraphs, it would appear that Lowestoft's physical shift from one site to another occurred during the early years of the fourteenth century. There is now archaeological proof to support this supposition, in the form of mediaeval potsherds which have been found during the course of excavations to the rear of Nos 74, 75, 76, 77–79 and 80, High Street – the earliest of which date from about 1300.[17] Further evidence is to be seen in the oldest surviving mediaeval building on Lowestoft High Street – a vaulted cellar beneath No. 160, the masonry of which is datable to the first half of the fourteenth century and is similar to that in the undercroft of St Olaves Priory, Herringfleet, some seven miles to the north-west.[18] It seems that the move to the new site was largely completed by about 1350, because it was in that year that William Bateman, Bishop of Norwich, sanctioned the licensing of a chapel-of-ease on the High Street. The building was to be used during the winter months, at times when bad weather made access to the parish church difficult.

Another factor in the town's moving from one location to another may have been the sale of the manor, because in 1306 it passed from the Crown into the possession

---

[15] The distance of the *leuca*, or league, was not defined. Three centuries of argument ensued between Great Yarmouth and Lowestoft as to whether it was one, two or three miles.

[16] R. Reeve, 'A History of Lowestoft and Lothingland', 4 vols (c. 1810), iv, 203 (SRO(L), 193/3/4).

[17] P. Durbidge, 'A Second Limited Excavation in the Grounds of the John Wilde School, Lowestoft', LA&LHS *Annual Report* 37 (Lowestoft, 2005), 30–1.

[18] N. Pevsner, *The Buildings of Suffolk*, 2nd edition (London, 1974), p. 267. The dating placed on the St Olaves Priory undercroft is c. 1300.

of John de Dreux, Earl of Richmond.[19] Never, in the whole of its history, did the manor of Lowestoft have a resident lord (at least, not until the second half of the nineteenth century), which meant that the conduct of affairs lay in the hands of the steward and the chief tenants – with the latter probably having considerable autonomy. Whether the sale resulted in looser control than had previously been the case can only be speculated upon. It is, however, an interesting coincidence that, at a point of fundamental change in the town's economic and topographical development, the manorial title should have changed hands. It is also interesting (and may perhaps appear to be contradictory) that, at the very time when the two subsidies of 1327 and 1334 showed Lowestoft's communal wealth to be un-exceptional within the context of its own area, there should have been such effort and expense invested in the establishment of a new town site.[20]

Perhaps the most significant visible evidence of an upturn in Lowestoft's status and position locally is to be seen in the architecture and construction of the parish church. St Margaret's is one of the ten biggest and finest Perpendicular buildings in Suffolk, with a beautifully integrated nave and chancel, elegant north and south aisles and a superb south porch. All of this dates from the second half of the fifteenth century, but the extremities are over a century older. The tower has a late fifteenth-century parapet and spire, but the rest of it was built some time after 1300; both the scale and the decoration are impressive for the time.[21] Sixty yards to the east there is a fine early fourteenth-century crypt beneath the high altar. It would seem that the townspeople of Lowestoft felt able to embark upon a bold scheme of reconstruction at about the same time as they were relocating their community. Presumably, the earlier church (or, at least, part of it) was left standing as the new building was begun, and the answer to the question of why work came to an end probably lies either in an insufficiency of funds or in the ravages of the Black Death. Given the devastating effects of this disease, it is entirely possible that it was another 100 years before the inhabitants of Lowestoft were able to resume work on St Margaret's and produce the building which stands today (Plate 2).

If some of the wealth for building a grand new parish church, in both phases of its construction, derived from fishing and maritime activity, it is also worth noting that Lowestoft had a rich and productive agricultural hinterland. However, the Island of Lothingland, which constituted one half of the Hundred of Mutford and Lothingland, had strategic significance as well.[22] This is no doubt why, in 1539, three earth redoubts were constructed at Lowestoft to guard the sea

---

[19] W. A. Copinger, *The Manors of Suffolk*, 7 vols (Manchester, 1905–11), v, 53–4.

[20] The assessment for the 1334 subsidy was made on the basis of a negotiated sum for each community, not on the sum total of individual levies (see Glasscock, *Lay Subsidy*, p. xiv). Perhaps Lowestoft's leading citizens were able to negotiate a lower sum than should have been paid.

[21] The tower is out of proportion with the rest of the building simply because of the fifteenth-century construction work's scale.

[22] The area remains an island and one of four bridges has to be crossed in order to leave it. Lothingland is twice the size of the Mutford half of the hundred, with twice the number of parishes.

Plate 2. *A view of St Margaret's Church from the east end: this picture gives a sense of the building's Perpendicular strength and elegance. All buttresses on the south and east elevations have flushwork panels set within ornate stone canopies.*

approaches, with three or four small cannon in each and three gunners appointed from the royal arsenals in London to take charge of operations.[23]

---

[23] J. Gairdner and R. H. Brodie (eds.), *LPFD, Henry VIII*, vols xiv (i), xv, xvi, xvii and xx (i) (London, 1894–1905). Nos 655 (vol. xiv), 196 (vol. xv), 1391 and 1488 (vol. xvi), 220 (vol. xvii) and 717 (vol. xx) give the information. Nicholas Sendall, James Haymys and Simon Legge were chosen to serve, each at a wage of 6d a day. The guns mounted were slings, which fired a stone shot of 2½ inch calibre and 2½ pounds' weight a distance of some 1,100 yards.

Forty years on from this work of fortification a number of Lothingland's leading inhabitants and landowners (including members of the Baspole, Bedingfield, Hobart, Jernegan, Jettor and Wentworth families) were deemed sufficiently suspect in loyalty to the Crown, because of Roman Catholic sympathy or practice, for the authorities to fear that a Spanish invasion from the Netherlands might be launched at a point somewhere between Lowestoft and Gorleston. A defence survey of June 1584 describes the island as being 'very fertile' and able to yield 'store of corn, cattle and other victual able to maintain itself and to help others, so as the strength is greater to the possessor'.[24] Such agricultural productiveness was due in part to soil quality in the area, which mainly varied from medium loam to lighter types – thereby enabling those who worked the land to avoid the difficulties of ploughing and cropping such ground as the heavy clay of High Suffolk and to escape the problems of having to make a living from the infertile sands of much of much of the county's coastal fringe. In addition to the advantages of having reasonably tractable and fertile soils over much of the island, there was the added bonus of extensive grazing marshes alongside the River Waveney.

The seventeen parishes of Lothingland Half-hundred helped to provide Lowestoft with the prosperous rural hinterland identified as being of crucial importance in the location of a market town.[25] For this is what Lowestoft had become during that important phase of its development, in the first half of the fourteenth century, within a mere two years of the manor passing from royal control into private hands.[26] The fact that the town developed in the extreme south-eastern corner of the island, rather than in the middle, undoubtedly owed a good deal to the previously outlined maritime advantages. But it was also partly the result of Great Yarmouth serving the five or six northernmost parishes; this factor removed about 9,500 acres from Lothingland's total of 25,000 as a potential market district, but it was partly compensated for by the addition of the Mutford sector of the Hundred. Most of the eight parishes lying in this southern area looked to Lowestoft as their local centre, thereby adding upwards of 7,000 acres to the 15,500 which remained after Great Yarmouth's influence had been allowed for. Thus, with an area of around 22,000 acres or more, Lowestoft's hinterland conformed to the Suffolk pattern of marketing areas averaging less than 30,000 acres – while the town's ten-mile distance by road from the two nearest markets (Great Yarmouth to the north and Beccles to the west-south-west) observed the average spacing for such communities.[27] Finally, the statement that, during the pre-industrial era, the average small market town in the south and east of England

---

[24] TNA: PRO, SP 12/171/61, 62i and ii, 63.V. B. Redstone, 'The Island of Lothingland, 1584', *PSIA* xx (Ipswich, 1928–30), 1–8, provides a transcript of the documentation and a facsimile reproduction of the accompanying map. The latter identifies all suspect gentry in the various parishes.

[25] P. Clark and P. Slack, *English Towns in Transition, 1500–1700* (Oxford, 1976), p. 18.

[26] A market was granted to the lord of the manor in 1308: TNA: PRO, Charter Rolls, C53/95.

[27] A. Everitt, 'The Marketing of Agricultural Produce', in J. Thirsk (ed.), *The Agrarian History of England and Wales*, iv (Cambridge, 1967), 496 and 498.

relied largely on custom generated within a five- or six-mile radius means that Lowestoft once again reflected the accepted norms.[28]

As a last word in this over-view of the town's mid/late mediaeval history, it is worth commenting on how surface geology influenced its development. Apart from the beach and The Denes (about 210 acres in extent), the parish as a whole is largely covered by Pleistocene sands and gravels, with a belt of chalky boulder clay running across the middle on a west-north-west/east-south-east alignment.[29] These surface deposits resulted in the presence of a good deal of low-grade agricultural land – a fact reflected in the amount of common and heath which once existed: about 205 acres out of a total area above the cliff of 1,275 acres (Map 3).[30] One of the largest pieces of manorial waste had originally been situated along the edge of the cliff itself, and it seems that the town's shift from its earlier location was facilitated by a new and more productive use being given to land that had previously been devoted largely to rough grazing. Throughout most of the early modern period, the area covered by dwellings, yards, other buildings and streets was about sixty acres. The two maps used in the next chapter to demonstrate the physical extent and location of house-building in the century between 1618 and 1725 clearly shows a remnant of common pasture (Goose Green) which had not been built upon to the west of the town. By the time that the tithe map was drawn, in 1842, these ten acres had almost been completely covered with houses.

---

[28] C. G. A. Clay, *Economic Expansion and Social Change*, 2 vols (Cambridge, 1984), i, 171.

[29] Geological Survey, *Quarter Inch Geological Survey Map* (London, 1931).

[30] The areas given in this paragraph have been calculated with the assistance of the Manor Roll of 1618 and the parish Tithe Apportionment of 1842. Walking and measuring various boundaries and perimeters has also been carried out.

− 2 −

Topographical Features of the Town

Terracing the cliff

The major task facing the people of Lowestoft, on moving to the new site some time after 1300, was making the face of the cliff usable. A slope of up to 60° or more, composed of stratified glacial deposits, did not lend itself to easy management. Intervention was necessary, therefore, in order to create viable house-plots along the edge of the cliff itself and to provide convenient access to the shoreline. The latter requirement was fulfilled partly by nature, in the form of gullies created by the grooving action of surface water draining down the face. These were known as *scores*, a word deriving from the Old Norse *skora*, meaning 'to cut' or 'to incise', and they were regularly spaced along the length of cliff chosen for re-development. Some were suitable for footways, others for use by carts, and their presence was (and still is) one of the defining features of Lowestoft's urban topography (Plate 3). Their function was assisted by the building of retaining walls along their length, while their surfaces were levelled and consolidated, and, in the case of the footways, stepped and paved for easy passage.[1]

The terracing of the cliff was a considerable undertaking in terms of scale and therefore also of the labour required. No estimate can be made of the time it took to accomplish, but it was certainly a matter of years rather than of months. It may have been carried out and completed before dwellings were built along the cliff-top itself. A great deal of communal effort and co-ordination must have been required for the operation, which would have had to be carried out in addition to the agriculture, fishing and various other trades by which the inhabitants sustained themselves. Investigation of the structure of the terraces shows that the engineering was not a piecemeal exercise, but one that was pre-conceived and integrated. The general north–south alignment of the various levels is consistent and unbroken – detectable even where the scores cross the terraces at right-angles – and the landscaping is impressive both in terms of conception and execution.

---

[1] The scores have been constantly remodified over centuries and over time were known by different names, reflecting local conditions and personalities. The three footways which best reflect their original alignment and ancient appearance are Mariners Score, Crown Score and Maltsters Score.

Plate 3. *Crown Score: a view taken in the 1930s. Named after The Crown inn, which stands opposite, this footway was known as George Rugge's Score in the 1590s – after a man who lived in a house on its top, left-hand corner adjoining the High Street. He features in manor court indictments for verbal abuse of fellow townspeople.*

Altogether, about 1,000 yards of cliff were terraced, with four stages over most of the length (the first being the top of the cliff itself) – diminishing to three and then to two in the last 300 yards at the southern end, as the ground level sloped downwards and eventually finished just a few feet above sea level. This was effectively the end of what may be called the built-up area, and all that remained to the south of it were four houses strung out along the roadway which led southwards

Plate 4. *A late eighteenth-century view of the town from the sea. Richard Powles' ink-and-wash drawing shows not only the basic topography, but various types of vessel associated with Lowestoft (including three-masted herring boats). The craft nearest the viewer is the revenue cutter,* Argus.

to Kirkley and Pakefield, finding its way over the shingle bank which separated Lake Lothing from the sea. By the time that Edmund Gillingwater came to describe the terraces in his history of the town, in 1790, they had been in existence for over 450 years and were reckoned to be one of the finest and most distinctive local features in terms of amenity and appearance, providing the beholder with a particularly fine prospect from the sea (Plate 4).[2]

In practical terms, the work of creating the terraces consisted mainly of digging and levelling and of building retaining walls to hold back the stratified sands and clays. Originally, most (if not all) of the dwelling plots were roughly the same width, but as the years went by subdivision occurred, leading to many becoming narrower than they had once been. In the first phase of construction, timber may have been used for some of the retaining walls, but the earliest ones now identifiable (dating from the sixteenth and seventeenth centuries) show a combination of brick and cobbled flint. The latter material was readily available from the beach, while there were pockets of suitable clay for making bricks scattered over much of the parish. During the summer of 2000, while work was being carried out to the rear of No. 80, High Street, leading to the building of a new retaining wall between the first and second terraces, an interesting discovery was made (Plate 5). At the bottom of the trench in which the footing of the new wall was to be placed, a layer of clay was found which had nothing to do with natural stratification. It had been introduced artificially – almost certainly with the intention of providing a firm foundation on which to build the original retaining wall.[3] The material was undoubtedly dug from

[2] E. Gillingwater, p. 50. The writer describes the view in complimentary terms, referring to 'very beautiful hanging gardens'.

[3] The writer took part in the excavations.

close at hand and simply reconstituted with the addition of water, before being laid as a base course. Extrapolating from this one piece of evidence and assuming that the introduction of clay was the method employed to foot terrace walls up and down the length of the cliff is not a flight of fancy. The method employed was both structurally sound and made good use of a plentiful local resource.

Once established, the terraces became an important part of each dwelling plot. The first one, on which the house stood, was customarily used for the storage of household goods and materials – sometimes under the cover of lean-to buildings. The second one, immediately below, was a multi-purpose area, often planted with fruit trees (apples and pears, mainly) and sometimes with a summerhouse built on it for the residents' enjoyment.[4] Ironically, perhaps, it was also used as a dumping-ground for all kinds of domestic waste – though people's sensitivity towards rubbish and the smells it produced would, at the time, have been far less than that evident

Plate 5. *Cliff terracing to the rear of Nos 77–79 and 80, High Street. This photograph was taken from the third of the four terraces and shows how the cliff's slope was managed and made usable. The retaining wall referred to in text is uppermost of the two shown; that nearest the camera dates from the 1950s.*

[4] The planting of small orchards and the construction of summerhouses seems to have been a feature of the seventeenth and eighteenth centuries – evidence, perhaps, of growing refinement in society.

today.[5] The third and fourth terraces were mainly used for the siting of the buildings associated with the conduct of fishing and other maritime enterprises: curing houses, net-stores, tackle-sheds, stables, etc. And it is interesting to note that the lowest of these, and even the one above it, are sometimes referred to in probate inventories as 'The Mount' – presumably because of the rise in ground level from the beach area itself.

The stratification of glacial sands and clays (a feature both of the natural cliff-face and of its terraced successor) had further significance in Lowestoft. It played a crucial role in determining the availability of water for both domestic and industrial uses. Any precipitation filtered through the light topsoil which covered much of the parish, finding its way down to an impervious layer of clay. From there, a good deal of it worked its way to the cliff, following the slope of the land from west to east and emerging as a series of springs. All houses along the cliff-top had either individual wells or ones that were shared with adjacent properties, and this was largely the case with the dwellings on the west side of the High Street.[6] However, the smaller houses in the side-lane area were not as generously endowed with wells and many of their inhabitants drew water from the Green Well, which stood at the junction of Back Lane and Frary's Lane – its name probably harking back to a time when residential plots had not spread so far westwards and the Goose Green area had been more extensive.

The town in 1618: physical configuration and street map[7]

The main built-up area of Lowestoft (Map 4) was about 1,000 yards in length (north–south) by approximately 370 yards in width (east–west). It was essentially linear in shape, but with a block of residential development protruding westwards. Broadly speaking, it was the existence of a cliff-line on the eastern extremity and the presence of a piece of manorial waste immediately adjacent to it which largely determined the shape of the town. The former provided a well-defined limit, with the terracing of its slope providing viable dwelling-plots; the latter, lying as it did between two areas of better-quality agricultural land to the north and south, allowed housing to spread in a westerly direction. It did not cover the whole of the waste,

---

[5] Archaeological work to the rear of Nos 74–80, High Street, has produced an assortment of broken pottery and glass, butchered animal bone, shellfish remains and metal artefacts. See P. Durbidge, 'A Limited Excavation of the Drying Area at Wilde School, Lowestoft, Suffolk', LA&LHS *Annual Report* 36 (Lowestoft, 2004), 16–33, and 'Second Excavation', 21–43. It appears that the second terrace was used for temporary deposition of rubbish before it was disposed of elsewhere. The dumping of waste generally must have polluted water supplies.

[6] There are frequent references in the court baron records to shared wells, with stipulated rights of access. Wells at the top of the High Street had to be dug deeper than those at the southern end because of the slope of the land southwards.

[7] Both maps reproduced in this chapter were developed by the writer and his fellow researcher, Ivan Bunn, using the manor roll of 1618, manor court records and the parish tithe map of 1842. The last document has an inset of the town's built-up area, which was still largely confined within its ancient limits at the time the survey was carried out.

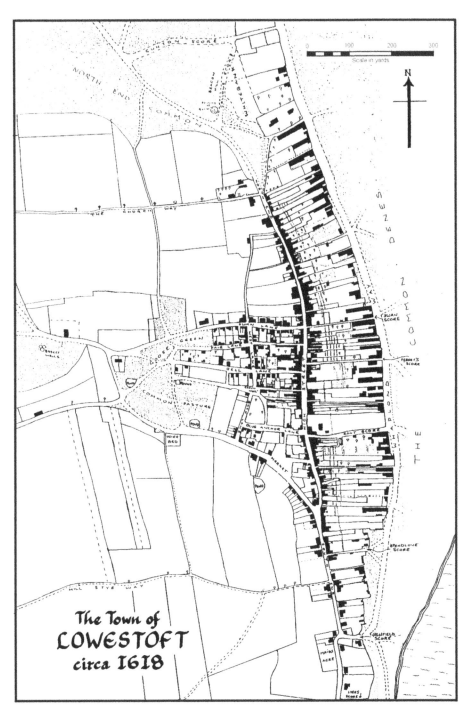

Map 4. *The town in 1618: this reconstruction of Lowestoft's urban topography derives from the manor roll of that year, which gives detailed description of messuages in the built-up area. The use of an area of cliff-edge waste to create a new settlement is plain to see, as is the westward growth onto Goose Green between higher-quality agricultural land to the north and south.*

however; a portion was retained as one of the parish common-grazing areas.[8] At the bottom of the cliff, and lying between the various fish-curing premises and net-stores and the shoreline itself, was the largest common green of all – The Denes.[9]

As suggested in the previous chapter, a local manorial dimension was of considerable importance in the overall development of the town. Surviving court baron records clearly demonstrate that the main residential area grew up on land that was of lesser value than the arable acreages which lay to the north and the south of it.[10] The expression 'a messuage (or cottage, or tenement) from the waste of the lord' is used a sufficient number of times in the manor court minute books, concerning the sale and transfer of residential plots, to leave no doubt as to the previous use of the land on which the town grew up. At least thirty examples of the phrase are in evidence (fifteen of which refer to properties on the High Street), and it was obviously a time-honoured one because it was used over and over again as successive transactions on the particular houses were recorded.

The means by which manorial waste was released in order to allow the town to develop physically had one obvious advantage for the lord. The sale of each plot was made subject to customary (or copyhold) tenure, thus enabling it to produce a triple income. First, there was the money deriving from the sale of the land itself, then the lord's rent payable each year on the plot, and lastly the entry fine imposed on a new owner each time the property changed hands. The money generated from the two latter charges was not spectacular, but it provided a steady trickle of cash into the manorial coffers. The Lowestoft copyholders had good security of tenure and appear to have been free from exploitation by their non-resident lord, whoever he may have been and however far away he lived.[11] The manor roll of 1618 specifies an annual

<hr>

[8] It was variously called Fair Green, Goose Green and Pound Green, these names reflecting its different uses. Part of it, known as St Margaret's Plain, remains today – occupied largely by a car park and children's play area.

[9] The name is a variant of 'dunes', describing the beach's natural state before it became covered with vegetation. No houses were sited there before the later years of the eighteenth century and widespread construction did not take place before the middle of the nineteenth. This comparatively late development resulted from the area's use for rough grazing and as an open-air wharf. Once the harbour was opened in 1831 and further developed during the 1840s, The Denes were no longer needed for the passage or storage of cargo.

[10] There are two sets of records which provide information: SRO(L) 194/A10/5–17 and 454/2. The former are manor court minute books covering the period 1616 to 1734; the latter is a series of extracts from them, giving details of sale and transfer of practically every copyhold house in town. It was compiled between 1720 and 1725 by the vicar, Rev. John Tanner. Two other communities which grew up on manorial waste close to the sea were Whitehaven and Deal, but their development as new towns of the late seventeenth and early eighteenth centuries was different in essence from that of Lowestoft. See C.W. Chalklin, 'The Making of Some New Towns, c. 1600–1720', in C. W. Chalklin and M. A. Havinden (eds.), *Rural Change and Urban Growth* (London, 1974), pp. 238, 241 and 243.

[11] Under the custom of the manor, the only way a copyholder could forfeit a house was by reversion to the lord – usually if the property had been allowed to fall into serious disrepair. The security offered by copyhold tenure during Tudor and Stuart times has been noted by various writers. One of them has pointed out how copyhold by inheritance (the Lowestoft type) was as good as freehold tenure. See B. A. Holderness, *Pre-Industrial England* (London, 1976), p. 76.

rental value of £4 14s 10½d deriving from 203 copyhold messuages in the main built-up area of the town – 149 of which were houses. Just over 100 years later, in 1725, when the Rev. John Tanner (incumbent of the parish) had compiled his listing of the customary properties and property owners (he recorded 256 premises in all), there was very little difference in the two amounts.[12] Any subdivision of plots which had occurred between the two documents' compilation simply resulted in the lord's rent being split according to the size of the new messuages created.

Lowestoft High Street extended over a total length of about 1,000 yards, with a drop of some fifty feet from north to south – a slope still most pronounced in the last 300 yards southwards. In addition to this marked fall, there is a far less noticeable gradient from west to east, and the two of them together were enough to make surface-water drainage a matter of some complexity.[13] The street itself assumed a slight sinuosity through following the line of the cliff and it was met at regular intervals on its western side by five cross-lanes, which were named, from north to south: Swan Lane, Fair Lane/Tyler's Lane (the latter being the eastward section), Bell Lane, Frary's Lane (too narrow to name on the maps) and Blue Anchor Lane. On the eastern side lay the scores, giving access to The Denes, and at the bottom of the cliff (running parallel with the High Street) was Whaplond Way.[14]

According to the 1618 manor roll, there were 211 houses in the parish as a whole (including inns), of which 194 were located in the main, built-up, area of town. Of this number, 149 were built on copyhold land, the other forty-five on two areas of freehold land to the west of the High Street.[15] The physical constraints placed upon building by the limited amount of land available resulted in two distinctive types of house plot. The ones on the east side of the High Street, which belonged for the most part to the wealthier members of local society, were long and narrow (anything between 350 and 500 feet), taking advantage of the terracing of the cliff.[16] Those in the side-street area, to the west of the main

---

[12] SRO(L) 454/1. This document accompanies the one referred to in n. 10, above.

[13] The leet court minutes record fines imposed on High Street residents who allowed culverts to block or otherwise caused local flooding. Cellars were particularly vulnerable and some of them had wells built to collect surplus water, before it was emptied (and later pumped) into the street. A surviving example, dating from the late sixteenth century, lies below No. 149, High Street – the former *Bell* inn.

[14] The five cross-lanes are now called Mariners Street, Compass Street/Dove Street, Crown Street, Wesleyan Chapel Lane and Duke's Head Street. Whaplond Way has long been called Whapload Road.

[15] The first of these areas lay at the north end of town between Church Way and Swan Lane (now St Margaret's Road and Mariners Street); the second was situated further to the south, downhill from the market place and on the opposite side of the road. The agricultural land owned by the lord of the manor seems to have been progressively sold off from an early stage, because by the time that the roll of 1618 was compiled only sixty-eight acres of demesne remained.

[16] Messuages of this shape are usually called *burgage plots* – a term originally used to describe tenements in urban areas held for a specified annual rent. Because house-plots in such communities were often long and narrow, and stood at right angles to the street, it has become generic for all plots of this nature.

thoroughfare, tended to be much smaller and were largely square or rectangular in shape. It is possible that some of these smaller plots (particularly those to the east of Back Lane and West Lane) had originated from subdivision of large messuages fronting the High Street. The freehold area north of Swan Lane also suggests this process. A number of large plots are visible there, with some evidence of subdivision having already begun – especially along the north side of Swan Lane itself, where the line of houses can certainly be interpreted as back-land development of the yard of the dwelling on the corner.

The arrangement of house plots at right angles to the one long main street was typical of many mediaeval and early modern settlements. In Lowestoft, about half the houses on the High Street had plot widths in the range of thirty to fifty feet, the other half being somewhere between fifteen and twenty-five (some of these latter probably being the result of earlier subdivision). The wider plots had dwellings fronting the street lengthwise, while the narrower ones resulted in gable ends providing the elevation.[17] In the side-street area, the individual messuages were generally much smaller, with an average size of about twenty to thirty feet wide by about fifty to sixty feet long.[18] The five cross-lanes, along with their crossings with West Lane and Back Lane (aligned north–south), created a tight little gridiron which did not lend itself to generously sized curtilages.

The market place and the fair-stead

Once the new manorial lord had received approval for a market in Lowestoft (1308), the town was provided with a positive force for growth and influence in its own area. It is not known whether the award reflected a developing local situation or whether it was sought to increase the status and value of the manor, but either way it would have had a beneficial effect. A scrutiny of the High Street reveals that it was probably sufficiently wide between Swan Lane and Blue Anchor Lane (about thirty to thirty-five feet) to have accommodated market stalls, but the place chosen was on the south-western edge of town, not far from where it joined the main roadway bringing traffic in from the west. There was also a separate area specifically used for trading in corn, which stood on the same site as the chapel-of-ease. This latter was located on the west side of the High Street, between Swan Lane and Tyler's Lane, and there are suggestions that the building may have served more than one use from quite early on in its existence.

---

[17] Seven of the former type are still easily identifiable on the east side of the High Street today: Nos 27, 31–32, 75–77, 78–79, 80, 81–83 and 102–104. On the west side are Nos 139–140, 147 and 148–149. All of them date from before 1650.

[18] Useful comparisons with Lowestoft's house plots may be found in two of Michael Laithwaite's studies: 'Totnes Houses, 1500–1800', in P. Clark (ed.), *The Transformation of English Provincial Towns* (London, 1984), p. 65, and 'The Buildings of Burford: A Cotswold Town in the Fourteenth to Nineteenth Centuries', in A. Everitt, *Perspectives in English Urban History* (London, 1973), pp. 62–5. Vanessa Parker, *The Making of King's Lynn* (Chichester, 1971), p. 36, also offers a perspective.

Plate 6. *A late eighteenth-century study of the Town Chamber. Richard Powles' drawing clearly shows the ground-floor arcading, where corn trading took place, with civic meeting room above. The rearward section was an Anglican chapel-of-ease.*

The whole complex was rebuilt in 1698, on funds collected by public subscription, and the resulting structure was also multi-purpose in nature (Plate 6).[19]

The main market area was about half an acre in size and surrounded by houses on three sides. Far from being the determining factor in the overall layout of the town, as has been suggested for many other market places,[20] the one at Lowestoft

---

[19] The Town Chamber (as it was called) of the sixteenth, seventeenth and eighteenth centuries served as corn cross, chapel-of-ease, meeting room and (for a time) grammar school. The subscription lists for its rebuilding may be seen in NRO PD 589/112 ('The Lowestoft Town Book'), pp. 55–7 and 67–8.

[20] Clark and Slack, *Towns in Transition*, p. 18. P. Corfield, *The Impact of English Towns, 1700–1800* (Oxford, 1982), p. 18, states that market towns 'physically, as well as economically, centre on a large market place or broad-based commercial area in the main street'. More recently, P. Borsay, 'Early Modern Urban Landscapes, 1540–1800', in P. Waller (ed.), *The English Urban Landscape* (Oxford, 2000), p. 114, has identified market places as a 'core feature'.

seems to have been allotted a convenient situation on the edge, where no building had hitherto taken place. The very irregularity of its shape suggests that, by the early seventeenth century, domestic messuages had begun to encroach onto its trading area – a process that was to accelerate noticeably after 1650. One very singular feature of the Lowestoft market place is that, on its south-western side, it faced out across the roadway onto a meadow with a large pond in it. This piece of land had no houses built where it met the street, opposite the market, and presumably the space had been left free to facilitate the grazing and watering of livestock being traded. It is not known whether Lowestoft market had movable stalls or permanent ones, or a combination of the two. Nor has any information come to light regarding the respective sizes of individual booths.[21]

The original grant of the Wednesday market was made on 15 November 1308. As well as this privilege, a fair was authorised to be held on the eve of the Feast of St Margaret of Antioch (the parish's patron saint), on the feast day itself (20 July) and for six days following. After a re-grant of 15 December 1445 to the lord of the manor of the time, William de la Pole, Duke of Suffolk, the annual fair was expanded into two events and the date was changed.[22] No longer was St Margaret commemorated, and both fairs became seven-day occasions. The first was based on the feast day of St Philip and St James (1 May), with three celebratory days either side of the actual festival, while the second one was an identical event centred on the feast of St Michael and All Angels (29 September).

At some point, a misunderstanding arose concerning the siting of both market and fair in Lowestoft. Edmund Gillingwater, in his history of Lowestoft, either through an error of his own or by continuation of a mistake made by someone else, says that both were originally held 'below the town' – meaning on The Denes.[23] This notion is the direct result of a mistranslation of the phrase *infra villam*, which should be rendered as 'within the town', not below. The fairs were held on the common green immediately to the west of the built-up area, as the names Fair Lane and Fair Green suggest. However, this particular stretch of waste was also known as Goose Green, a name which designates another use very clearly – though, given the way that they foul any location frequented for any length of time, it is to be hoped that the geese were taken off their pasture well before the fairs were held![24]

---

[21] C. Barringer and F. Macdonald, *Aylsham in the Seventeenth Century* (North Walsham, 1988), pp. 18ff, has interesting information regarding market stalls in a small Norfolk community.

[22] TNA: PRO, Charter Rolls, C53/188.

[23] E. Gillingwater, p. 55.

[24] A leet court minute of 1582 shows Goose Green to be the only area of common where geese were permitted. A fine of 2d per bird was imposed on anyone breaking the rule. See SRO(L) 194/A10/4.

The town in 1725: physical configuration

A cursory perusal of Lowestoft's topography in 1725 (Map 5) may seem to suggest that little change had taken place in the previous hundred years. The physical boundaries of the town remained the same as they had been in 1618 and the street plan had undergone no alterations. Moreover, as mentioned earlier in this chapter, the annual rental value of the copyhold messuages had not increased – a fact which may initially appear to imply no increase in the number of customary properties. Yet, it is known that the number of dwelling houses did increase and that the population grew from something below 1,500 to about 1,850. How, then, was this expansion managed?

The answer may be found in the use made of existing dwelling plots situated within the confines of the town. Close study of the manorial records between 1618 and 1725 shows that there was systematic and steady exploitation of yards and gardens offering sufficient space on which to build.[25] Altogether, eighty-three new plots were developed (seventy-five copyhold and eight freehold) and 153 houses provided. Added to this were another twenty-nine copyhold dwellings that were built, for which no details of plot-provision exist. The grand total of 182 houses is reduced to 170 because of twelve units which were lost for one reason or another during the overall period of re-development. This means that, in the century covered, Lowestoft's housing stock increased by 87% in the built-up area of the town and by 80% in the parish as a whole.[26]

With all the extra dwellings (and any accompanying outbuildings) being accommodated within the town's existing boundaries, a mode of expansion had been found that was both convenient and economical in terms of the amount of space available. The town stayed within its limits; the integrity of Goose Green (or Fair Green) was maintained; and there was no encroachment onto the arable land to the north-west or south-west. The availability of plots suitable for development also probably meant that there was no compelling need to subdivide existing houses in order to cope with a growing population – a practice that was adopted in some larger urban communities where the available space had already been intensively exploited.[27] There were examples of subdivision to be found, but this was not widespread.

The relatively restricted amount of land taken up by the town (sixty acres) was not sufficiently small to ensure that all (or even most of) the houses were built gable-end on to the street. But neither was there enough room to allow each dwelling to

---

[25] One great benefit of copyhold tenure is that every individual transfer was supposed to be recorded in the court baron minutes. This makes tracing sequence of ownership possible. In Lowestoft, about 80–85% of the houses in the built-up area were copyhold, the other 15–20% freehold.

[26] For a full break-down of the construction which took place in different parts of the town, see D. Butcher, 'The Development of Pre-Industrial Lowestoft, 1560–1730' (unpub. MPhil thesis, University of East Anglia, 1991), pp. 35–9.

[27] See A. D. Dyer, *The City of Worcester in the Sixteenth Century* (Leicester, 1973), p. 164.

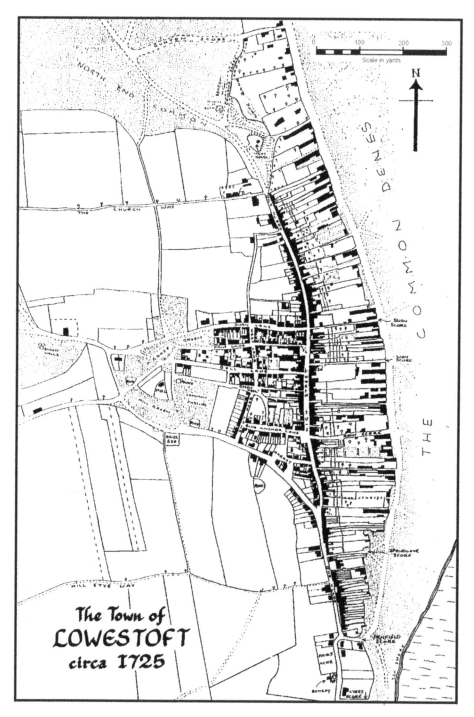

Map 5. *The town in 1725: the increase in house-building over a hundred-year period is clearly seen – particularly in the side-street area west of the High Street, at the southern end of the High Street itself and on the freehold land north of Swan Lane. The town was to keep this configuration mainly intact until the arrival of the railway in 1847.*

have a generous amount of space on either side. Many of the houses fronting onto the High Street (mainly the larger, better-quality, ones) shared gables with each other and had access to their yards provided by occasional entry passages and by the scores.[28] It can be clearly seen in Maps 4 and 5 that the linear nature of plots to the east of the High Street would allow easy development to take place only where there was sufficient space onto the roadway to allow insertion of a dwelling. Once this space had been taken up, no further building was convenient. Back-land development off the scores onto the terraces did not take place because the people who owned the messuages (merchants and substantial tradespeople, mainly) required their yards and gardens for the siting of ancillary buildings, for the storage of goods and for personal amenity. The most densely built-up part of the High Street was the southern end – especially below Spendlove Score, where seven plots were intensively developed.

The other heavily exploited part of town was the side-street area to the west of the High Street. The configuration of lanes and back-ways resulted in the plots being much smaller rectangles (some were even square) and much more accessible on all sides. The yards and garden spaces in this vicinity lent themselves more readily to development, which resulted in some plot widths being as little as ten or fifteen feet, though overall lengths of somewhere between thirty and sixty feet were maintained. A majority of the new houses in Lowestoft between 1618 and 1725 were built in this locality – especially between 1650 and 1700, when most of the spare capacity on the High Street had been taken up.

The pattern of urban growth within existing limits is not without parallel elsewhere,[29] but one noticeable effect of plot-infill to the west of the High Street was that the market place became less open to view. Up to about 1650 it was easily visible from the main thoroughfare, but the following fifty years resulted in its becoming more and more hemmed in as plots to the north and east of it were developed. The final phase of this infilling came after 1700, when messuages on its western edge were further subdivided and a block of seven houses was constructed at its widest point adjacent to the highway, opposite the meadow and pond.[30]

It is possible that the gradual closing-in of the market made use of the site increasingly inconvenient, because in 1703 a new market place was provided about 300 yards to the north, at the southern junction of Tyler's Lane with the High Street. An inn called *The New White Horse* was demolished and a space of about 900 square yards created by its removal. This was a good deal smaller than the original market area, but the two spaces together seem to have been sufficient to meet the needs of the community. The creation of the new market place came only five years after

---

[28] D. W. Lloyd, *The Making of English Towns* (London, 1984), p. 48, identifies houses directly abutting onto each other as a feature of the mediaeval period.

[29] See Parker, *King's Lynn*, p. 81. During the period 1560–1700, the revamping of mediaeval houses in the Norfolk town saw the old pattern of dwellings standing at right angles to the street, with space to spare on the frontage, replaced by units built across the total width of the plot.

[30] The release of land for this latter development occurred on 22 January 1707, when it was acquired by Francis Adams (fisherman). See SRO(L) 194/A10/14.

reconstruction of the Town Chamber, which stood a few yards further to the north and needed to be made larger because of its multi-purpose use: corn cross, chapel-of-ease, civic meeting place and free grammar school.[31]

Industrial zoning

The most obvious example of buildings and equipment concentrated in one location because of the particular requirements of a trade is maritime activity – especially fishing. The lower terraces of the cliff, The Denes and the shoreline itself all showed their connection with the dominant industry and the visual impact created at the time must have left no room for doubt that here was an essential part of the local *raison d'être*. Traces of it can still be seen today. The line of substantial merchants' houses along the top of the cliff is still there, many of the terraced gardens remain (although much neglected) and at the bottom of the slope are the smoke-houses and net-stores.

Most of these service buildings are of late nineteenth- and early twentieth-century construction, and they have largely been converted to other uses. However, they are the lineal successors to buildings which feature on late eighteenth- and early nineteenth-century prospects of the town and whose earlier antecedents can be seen on an Elizabethan map-maker's impression of the local coastline drawn in about 1580.[32] In this illustration, the residences along the cliff-top are represented by about a dozen buildings of various shapes and sizes, behind which the spire of the Town Chapel (or, to be accurate, the spire which is used to indicate its presence) is plainly visible. Below the dwellings lies a line of eight buildings, rather square in appearance, which is clearly and specifically labelled 'Laystofe Fish Howses'. None of the shapes is probably accurate in strict architectural terms, but the overall topographical impression conveyed is certainly realistic (Plate 7).

The Lowestoft merchants, many of whom had a direct interest in fishing and fish-processing, lived close to their work premises, almost certainly thinking it no disgrace to do so. A sense of social refinement which made a man aware of the vulgarity of the environment from which he derived his wealth and therefore wish to be removed from it was not a feature of the sixteenth and seventeenth centuries. Such sensitivity was to develop out of the growing politeness of Georgian times. The buildings used for curing the catches and servicing fishing gear were sited on the lower terraces and at the base of the cliff, because such a position put them nearest to where the fish were landed (on the shoreline) and could be most conveniently handled, and where the vessels themselves were easily accessible for the transporting of equipment. Furthermore, The Denes themselves provided an ideal area for spreading out fishing nets for inspection, as well as for drying them off prior to, and

---

[31] The work took place over fifty years after the end of a period identified as notable for the construction or conversion of town halls (1500–1640). See Borsay, 'Early Modern Urban Landscapes', in Waller, *English Urban Landscape*, p. 112.

[32] BL Add. Mss. 56070; SRO(L), 368. The latter is a copy of the original document.

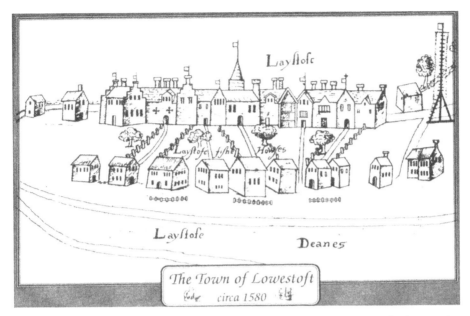

Plate 7. *A diagrammatic view of the town and its fish-houses, c. 1580: a stylised, somewhat military-looking representation, which gives no indication of the cliff's terracing. The ladder-like structure on the right-hand edge represents a beacon erected in 1550 to warn of coastal attack.*

after, preservative treatment against the rotting effect of salt water. The townspeople were allowed the privilege of net-drying without charge, but the manor imposed a seasonal payment of 2s 8d on foreigners and 1s 4d on English fishermen from anywhere outside Lowestoft.[33]

It was also in this particular area where shipbuilding and boat repair and maintenance took place. Vessels under construction were set up on stocks just above high-water mark, while those requiring attention were simply beached and pulled ashore. No pictorial evidence of such practices during the sixteenth and seventeenth centuries has come to light, but material from the eighteenth and nineteenth certainly confirms the practice (Plate 8). Most charming of these views is the scene depicted on a blue-and-white-ware flask produced at the town's soft-paste porcelain factory in 1780.[34] One side of the piece shows a vessel under construction, with a man using a large hammer visible amidships; the other reveals a three-master (presumably, the completed ship).

In topographical terms, it is interesting and probably significant that a family of shipwrights based in Lowestoft during the second half of the sixteenth century and the first part of the seventeenth (the Barnards) owned two residential messuages on

[33] Reeve, 'Lowestoft and Lothingland', iv, 203 (SRO(L), 193/3/4). The writer (steward of the manor during the late eighteenth and early nineteenth centuries) was drawing on material from the minute books. There are references to these charges in the proceedings of courts held in September 1631 and April 1672. See SRO(L), 194/A10/6, p. 313, and 194/A10/12, p. 1.

[34] G. A. Godden, *The Illustrated Guide to Lowestoft Porcelain* (London, 1969), plate 158.

Plate 8. *A late eighteenth-century view of the Low Lighthouse: Richard Powles' study of 1784 shows fishing vessels under construction or repair close to the light itself. Also visible are bathing machines, first introduced to the town in 1768 and modelled on those at Margate.*

the east side of the High Street, with yards which ran right down to The Denes.[35] Another shipwright, called Thomas Hawes (whose father had been vicar from 1610 to 1639), who was plying his trade in the middle of the seventeenth century, had a house and yard situated in the same location as the Barnards' properties.[36] Prior to the harbour works and improvements of the nineteenth century, the sea came in quite close to the cliff-line at the southern end of town – a factor which was convenient for the construction of ships and smaller boats. In the absence of specific records, it is not possible to give the size of craft built at Lowestoft, but a comment made by a leading maritime historian (concerning small-scale shipbuilding in England) can probably be taken as appropriate: 'Small vessels, up to a few score tons, could be and were built in any sheltered waters, and by any competent carpenter'.[37]

Apart from specific maritime industries, there was no other clear industrial zoning in Lowestoft of any topographical significance, except perhaps for the production of leather. Both of the town's largest tanneries stood next to each other, below the cliff, at the northern end of the built–up area, beneath the site where a lighthouse has stood since 1676. Plentiful water was available there from a spring-line which is traceable today, and thus a major requirement for the treating of hides was met. Other important activities in the town's economy showed no significant concentration in any one area. The four or five breweries were not grouped together, nor were the malt-houses which supplied them – though there was a tendency for the latter to be located on the cliff-face rather than on the west side of the High Street. Indeed, there are one or

[35] The first of these occupied the site of what is now No. 87, High Street, while the other, larger, one was the second plot south of Spendlove Score (now incorporated in a divisional police headquarters).

[36] Now Nos 105 and 106, High Street.

[37] R. Davis, *The Rise of the English Shipping Industry in the Seventeenth and Eighteenth Centuries* (Newton Abbot, 1962), p. 55.

two examples to be found in the manor court records of malt-houses having been converted from fish-curing premises. Four of the windmills which served the parish at varying times during the period under review stood well out of town, occupying suitably elevated positions, while a fifth one was built on the common green just to the west of the side-street housing area (Maps 4 and 5) – leading to this area being sometimes called Mill Green, as well as Goose Green and Fair Green. All the other many trades and occupations which contributed to Lowestoft's economic and social structure were spread over various parts of the town.

Conclusion

The intention of this chapter has been to show both the geographical relationship of Lowestoft to its particular neighbourhood and to trace its physical development over a designated timespan. Two of the best-known commentators on urban history have said that a major aspect of continuity in the development of towns between 1500 and 1700 is topography, in that although their appearance changed considerably during the time their basic layout did not.[38] The comment may be applied to Lowestoft both in the period covered in the pages of this book and in succeeding centuries. The town, as seen in the tithe map inset of 1842, was essentially the place of 300 or 400 years before – except for development which had taken place on Goose Green. The population had increased from around 1,500 to 4,600 or so, and the number of houses in the parish had risen from 200 or more to just over 1,100.[39] But the physical boundaries of the town had scarcely altered. Obviously, a good deal of intensive development (both new building and the subdivision of existing houses) had taken place in order to provide accommodation for a growing population, but the basic ground-plan remained much the same as it had been for three centuries and more.

Even today, the basic layout of the mediaeval/early modern town can still be ascertained without undue difficulty – and this in spite of a modern relief road that was constructed through part of the old quarter during the late 1970s. Houses were demolished to make way for the motor car, but that was about as far as the alterations went: Jubilee Way, as it is called, simply followed the north–south alignment of three of the former back-ways: Back Lane, West Lane and Turnpenny (or Flies) Lane. Thus, the shape of the town (as seen in the maps used in this chapter) remains essentially the same today – although completely surrounded on the landward side by nineteenth- and twentieth-century commercial and residential building and, on the seaward side, by post-war industrial and holiday development on The Denes. The town started its rapid growth towards being Suffolk's second-largest community during the 1840s, after the harbour began its expansion under the influence of Samuel Morton Peto and after the rail link with Norwich (Peto again) was opened. Since then, construction has never ceased and the whole parish of Lowestoft is now largely covered by brick and concrete.

[38] P. Clark and P. Slack (eds), *Crisis and Order in English Towns, 1500–1700* (London, 1972), p. 6.
[39] The Census Return of 1841 gives a specific population count of 4,647.

– 3 –

Historical Demography

Introduction

The information in this chapter derives from a full family reconstitution of the Lowestoft parish registers carried out twenty years ago under the guidance of the Cambridge Group for the History of Population and Social Structure. Selected data, along with material drawn from twenty-five other English parishes, has helped to form the most comprehensive statement made yet concerning English population characteristics between the Elizabethan period and the end of Georgian times.[1] The intention here is not to give a detailed account of more specialist aspects of population study (especially that regarding human fertility), but to present aspects of human existence in the very basic matters of being born, growing up and marrying, producing and raising children, growing old and dying. The journey from womb to grave is one that every human being makes, be it long or short, and the people whose lives feature in the following pages were probably much more aware of the fact than many of us living today.

The Lowestoft parish registers date back to the year 1561 and, for the whole of the 200 years covered in the pages which follow, have entries which show little interruption or dislocation (apart from the period 1640–63) and which go well beyond the bare minimum of information required for official purposes.[2] The wealth of detail concerning people's relationships to one another, their occupations and their social status means not only that the reconstitution exercise was facilitated and made more interesting, but that the means of getting to know the community

---

[1] E. A. Wrigley et al., English Population History from Family Reconstitution (Cambridge, 1997).

[2] NRO, PD 589/1, 2 and 4. Each volume contains baptisms, marriages and burials. Transcriptions were reproduced between 1895 and 1898 in the parish magazine and published in book form in 1899. Errors are present and all references to illegitimate children were omitted. The registers themselves have remarkably little disruption in the entries, with even the Civil War and Commonwealth period showing continuation of the registration process – albeit of a more chaotic nature than was customary and with a certain degree of under-registration. The defective years are as follows: marriages 1640–5, 1651–3, 1658–62; baptisms 1644–5, 1651–3, 1658–63; burials 1643–6, 1649–50, 1651–3, 1658–63. The under-registration is commented on in Wrigley et al., pp. 84–7.

more intimately than might otherwise have been possible were provided. This is not the place to consider various caveats that have been raised over the years concerning the value of family reconstitution, particularly those made in the first decade after it had been pioneered in this country.[3] Suffice it to say that, having carried out the exercise, the writer is convinced of its worth as a means of becoming familiar with a pre-industrial society and of creating a body of information which can be used to form cross-references with data drawn from other contemporary documents. It is the latter function which underpins much of the material presented in this book.

Size of population

Three suggested methods, based on parish register material, were used to estimate Lowestoft's population between 1561 and 1750. The first involved taking the average number of baptisms over a given period, dividing an accepted crude birth-rate figure by this number, and then dividing 1,000 by the answer. The second was an identical calculation using burials and an accepted crude death-rate figure, and the third used marriages in exactly the same way.[4] A crude birth-rate of thirty-four per thousand, a crude death-rate of thirty per thousand and a crude marriage-rate of eight per thousand were adopted.[5] The register averages of the number of births, burials and marriages were worked out in blocks of twenty-five-year duration from 1561 down to 1750 (the first block of all being only fifteen years, of course) and the calculation which gave the most consistent estimate, in the sense of its being least susceptible to fluctuation, was the crude death-rate method. Thus, the figures produced by this means are the ones which have been adopted. According to the calculations, the population of Lowestoft remained at about 1,500 between 1561 and 1675 (though it dropped for a time as the result of heavy mortality in 1603 and 1635), rose to about 1,650 between 1676 and 1700, increased further to about 1,850 between 1701 and 1725, and continued the upward trend to just short of 2,000 in the year 1750. Twenty-five years later, a population count of 8 August 1775 (carried out by the minister and churchwardens) gave the number of inhabitants as 2,231.[6]

---

[3] For a discussion of these, see Butcher, 'Lowestoft', pp. 54–9. E. A. (Tony) Wrigley carried out the formative study on the Devon parish of Colyton during the early 1960s, using the work of the French demographers M. Fleury and L. Henry as his inspiration.

[4] A. MacFarlane, *Reconstructing Historical Communities* (Cambridge, 1977), p. 165, recommends the use of crude birth-rates and crude death-rates. D. E. C. Eversley, 'Exploitation of Anglican Parish Registers by Aggregative Analysis', in E. A. Wrigley (ed.), *An Introduction to English Historical Demography* (London, 1966), p. 54, discusses the possible use of crude marriage-rates.

[5] E. A. Wrigley and R. S. Schofield, *The Population History of England, 1541–1871* (London, 1981), pp. 174 and 182, offered the guidance required on crude birth-rates and death-rates. Eversley, 'Exploitation', in Wrigley, *Historical Demography*, p. 55, did the same regarding crude marriage-rates.

[6] See E. Gillingwater, p. 54. The writer probably drew his information from the memorandum book of the Rev. John Arrow (incumbent of the time), where the census details are recorded. See NRO, PD 589/92. The number of houses in the parish is also given: 445.

Marriage and remarriage

Altogether, 1,870 marriages were solemnised in Lowestoft between 1561 and 1730.[7] Of these, 144 (7.7%) were the unions of people where one partner or both had their origins outside the parish and did not settle in the place where they were married. A further 301 (16.1%) were between couples who, though identified as parishioners in the registers, did not stay in town after their marriages had been conducted.[8] Thus 445 (23.8%) of all marriages which are recorded did not lead to family units being created in Lowestoft. The 301 sets of married couples that moved out of town soon after the ceremony consist, in approximately equal numbers, of those people whose families were living in town (nearly all of them women) and those for whom there are no apparent blood-ties within resident family groupings. It is likely that these latter consisted mainly of men and women who had been working locally for a period of time (e.g. journeymen, labourers, live-in servants), but who were not part of its family structure. Once such people had married, if opportunity for employment locally was not favourable, they would have moved on elsewhere. As will be demonstrated later, a substantial proportion of Lowestoft's population was transient, so a marked degree of 'marrying and moving out' should come as no surprise.

Of the 1,425 marriages which are left once the 445 accounted for above are eliminated, 317 (22.2%) produced no children. There is no evidence of deliberate family limitation being practised, as detected elsewhere,[9] but childless couples did represent a substantial minority of married people in the town. In nine cases, the wife died soon after the marriage ceremony, leaving no time for children to be born, and in another nine instances she was too old to bear children at the time the marriage took place. This leaves 299 marriages out of the 317 where, in theory, children could have been produced, but were not. The 1,108 fertile unions of the people who married in Lowestoft, and who lived there for at least some of their time together, represents 77.7% of the total of 1,425 marriages whose partners were resident in the town.

Pre-nuptial pregnancy is detectable, with 127 brides being at varying stages of the condition and a further thirty-eight who had possibly conceived by the time they were married. The former number represents 8.9% of the total of 1,425 marriages, while the latter is 2.7%: a combined figure of 11.6%. Taken as a proportion of the 1,108 fertile marriages, the two figures became 11.5% and 3.4% respectively,

---

[7] The registers were fully reconstituted between 1561 and 1730, with a further 'run-on' period of twenty years created to observe at least some of the registration events affecting later cohorts of marriage partners. Because of all the other lines of research undertaken, there was not enough time to reconstitute all marriages up till 1750 and allow a twenty-year 'run-on' to 1770.

[8] Removal from Lowestoft after a marriage had taken place is assumed from the fact that no further registration events (i.e. baptisms and burials) are recorded for that particular couple.

[9] E. A. Wrigley, 'Family Limitation in Pre-Industrial England', *EHR* 2nd series 19 (1966), 82–109; E. A. Wrigley, 'Marital Fertility in Seventeenth Century Colyton: a note', *EHR* 2nd series 31 (1978), 419–28.

combining to produce an end result of 14.9%. In neither case does the percentage approach the 20% cited as being that which applies to pregnant brides, as a proportion of the whole, for pre-1700.[10] There is closer correlation with the 11–12% adduced for Bedfordshire during the late seventeenth century.[11]

The place of origin of marriage partners who came from outside the town is often revealed in the parish registers. A majority (83%) of the 162 people named as coming from other communities emanated from within a fifteen-mile radius of Lowestoft, thereby serving to confirm the conclusion of at least one commentator, who identified this particular distance as being the one which would account for nearly all the places of origin of marriage partners in any pre-industrial community.[12] Mainly, it was a case of the bridegroom originating from outside Lowestoft and marrying a local woman (129 examples), but there are instances where local men married women from beyond the parish (33 examples). Of the eighty-eight outside partners from Suffolk (sixty-six men, twenty-two women), seventy-eight lived in communities within a fifteen-mile radius of the town (sixty men, eighteen women) and forty of that seventy-eight (thirty-two men, eight women) within five miles. It was not geographically possible for any Norfolk community to lie within a five-mile radius of Lowestoft, but of the forty-six outside partners from that county (thirty-five men, eleven women) thirty originated from places within a ten-mile distance (twenty-three men, seven women) – and, of that thirty, twenty-five came from Great Yarmouth (nineteen men, six women).

Maritime links of some kind would seem to be in evidence regarding the connection with Yarmouth and probably also with four other towns (Southwold, Ipswich, Felixstowe and King's Lynn). In addition to these places, there were also men (one in each instance) from Colchester, Eltham, London and Newcastle who married in the town between 1561 and 1600 (maritime connections are again possible in three cases), from London and Hereford between 1676 and 1700, and from Southwark between 1701 and 1730. In addition to these seven, twenty 'sojourners' and one 'stranger' (to use the register's terms) also married Lowestoft women between 1701 and 1730, but no parish of origin is given for any of them.[13]

As well as the 1,870 marriages that took place in the parish church of St Margaret, there were another 2,163 marital partnerships which manifest themselves

---

[10] P. Laslett, *The World We Have Lost*, 2nd ed. (London, 1971), p. 302. The work referred to was carried out by P. E. H. Hair on seventy-seven parishes in twenty-four English counties. Wrigley *et al.*, table 7.27, p. 421, gives a figure of 22.36% for pre-nuptially conceived first births for the period 1538–1700.

[11] J. D. Chambers, *Population, Economy and Society in Pre-Industrial England* (Oxford, 1972), p. 75. The author drew upon the work of N. L. Tranter, 'Demographic Change in Bedfordshire, 1670–1800' (unpublished PhD. thesis, University of Nottingham, 1966).

[12] D. E. C. Eversley, 'Population History and Local History', in Wrigley, *Historical Demography*, p. 22. N. Evans (ed.), *Beccles Rediscovered* (Beccles, 1984), pp. 76–7, shows a similar pattern of out-of-town marriage partner distance to that of Lowestoft. Beccles, too, was a market town and was situated about eight miles to the west-south-west of Lowestoft.

[13] Sojourners were temporary residents, usually doing work of some kind before moving on.

largely by children's baptismal and burial entries. These unions represent either the marriages of Lowestoft's transient population or the ones contracted by townspeople with partners from outside the parish, which led to the ceremony being conducted elsewhere. Whether the majority of these latter would have taken place within a five-mile radius of the town (this distance suggested as the key one within which to find such marriages) is a moot point.[14] A scrutiny of the parish register of the village of Corton, just to the north of Lowestoft, between 1580 and 1728, revealed only three or four marriages of Lowestoft people.[15] The records of Pakefield, to the south, showed eight for the period 1697 to 1726.[16] Even with another fifteen parishes within the five-mile radius, if the two places observed provide any kind of guidelines regarding numbers it is doubtful whether the 354 marriages which are known to have been contracted by Lowestoft people outside the parish (and are included in the total of 2,163 above) could have been wholly accommodated within such a limited area.

At least one commentator has observed that there was a restricted geographical range for the lower orders of society within which to choose marriage partners, and a much greater choice for those higher up the social scale, but no specific distances are given.[17] It may well be that that even lesser folk travelled further to find spouses than has been presumed – especially men. Indeed, in the case of labourers and servants, who tended to move from place to place as part of their employment pattern, relationships may well have been established in previous places of work.

The great majority of the 354 marriages where identifiable inhabitants of Lowestoft married someone from outside the parish are those of men (339 instances), with a small minority of cases involving women (fifteen in all).[18] A number of the people are recognisable as being members of merchant families, but there are also those who belonged to the maritime and artisan fraternities, as well as a lesser number from the labouring section of the population. Nonconformity is another factor to be considered, with certain of the known local Dissenting families (Kingsboroughs, Landifields, Mewses, Neales, Pacys, Risings and Wards) noticeable in their tendency to wed outside the parish – perhaps as a way of avoiding too many marriages made within too limited a circle of acquaintance and propinquity.

Finally, there are seventy-six examples of couples from the town getting married in other places, with thirteen of the unions entered in the Lowestoft registers (eleven of them between 1669 and 1678, the other two in 1698 and 1708 respectively),

---

[14] Eversley, 'Population History', in Wrigley, *Historical Demography*, p. 22.

[15] NRO, PD 564/1. There is a major gap in transactions between 1657 and 1698.

[16] NRO, PD 551/1. No registration details earlier than 1697 have survived.

[17] L. Stone, *The Family, Sex and Marriage in England, 1500–1800* (London, 1977), pp. 61–2.

[18] This figure represents 16.6% of the 2,137 marriages involving Lowestoft people known to have taken place inside or outside the parish. J. D. Chambers, 'Three Essays on the Population and Economy of the Midlands', in D. V. Glass and D. E. C. Eversley, *Population in History* (London, 1965), p. 329, cites a figure of 10.8% for marriages where there was one extra-parochial partner. The statistic was derived from a survey of nine Nottinghamshire parishes between 1670 and 1700.

presumably at the request of the people themselves.[19] The other sixty-three have no official acknowledgement in the home parish's records and venues for them are largely unknown.[20] Indeed, in most cases, the wives' maiden names have only been discovered through information revealed in wills. If the documents had not survived, the female pedigree would have remained unknown. Most of the couples who got married out of town were from merchant families and from among the better-off tradespeople and mariners. Pre-marital pregnancy does not seem to have been a factor in their choosing to become man and wife in a parish removed from their own, but Nonconformity was a likely reason in certain families – especially after The Declaration of Indulgence in 1672, when Nonconformist places of worship were officially recognised and licensed.[21]

The mean age at first marriage (each partner) for the period 1600–1750, in both exogamous and endogamous unions, was 25.2 years for men and 24.8 for women, and small differences are noticeable within subdivisions of the overall timescale.[22] For 1600–1649, the average age was 24.5 years for men and 24.6 for women; from 1650–1699, it was 25.7 and 24.7 respectively; and from 1700–1749, 25.3 and 25.2.[23] Teenage marriage was uncommon, especially for men – a characteristic noted in other English communities during the pre-industrial era.[24] With only five bridegrooms under the age of twenty out of a total of 317 whose ages at marriage are known, the proportion (1.6%) is consistent with the observation that teenage grooms never exceeded 4% of the total number before 1750.[25] The number of teenage brides was thirty-one, out of a total of 335 whose ages at marriage are known – a proportion of 9.3%, which is a little below the 11%–13% noted in other English parishes.[26]

With regard to age-difference between spouses, out of 224 first-time marriages where the age of both partners is known, 169 fall within a ten-year range, which extends from the man being six years older than the woman to the woman being four years older than the man. Within this group, 106 marriages show the man being older than the woman and sixty-three the reverse. The tendency for a husband to be

[19] With the exception of one in Norwich, all were solemnised within a ten-mile radius of Lowestoft: four in Great Yarmouth, three in Beccles, two in Oulton and one each in Gunton, Pakefield and Kessingland. Nearly all of the people were from either merchant or maritime families.

[20] A very small number manifests itself in the Corton and Pakefield registers. Scrutiny of other local parish records would undoubtedly reveal further examples.

[21] Lowestoft did not have a purpose-built Nonconformist chapel until 1697, but it is known that the Independent Chapel in Great Yarmouth was important to Dissenters in the town.

[22] An exogamous marriage is one where the date of the partnership's termination is not known; an endogamous one is where the terminating date is known.

[23] Wrigley *et al.*, pp. 184–5, table 5.18.

[24] E. A. Wrigley and R. S. Schofield, 'English Population History from Family Reconstitution: Summary Results, 1600–1799', *PS*, 37 (1983), 166.

[25] *Ibid.*, 166.

[26] *Ibid.*, 166.

older than his wife is also evident in the total number of 224 first-time marriages referred to above, where there are 133 cases of the husband being older and ninety-one instances of the wife's age exceeding that of her partner.

Once a couple had become man and wife, there was only a one in four chance that their marriage would survive for more than five years. It has been said that most couples in pre-industrial England could expect to spend twenty years together and that the duration might stretch to thirty years for 20%–25% of the partners.[27] This is not true of Lowestoft. As Table 1 shows, out of a total of 1,049 marriages, where both the date of the wedding ceremony and of the death of one or other of the spouses is known, 284 (27%) lasted five years or less.[28] Only 133 marriages (12.7%) were of sixteen to twenty years in length and a mere sixty-one (5.8%) lasted between thirty-one and thirty-five years.

Table 1. *Length of marriage in Lowestoft, 1561–1750*

Length of marriage	Number	Percentage
0–5 years	284	27.0
6–10 years	191	18.2
11–15 years	157	15.0
16–20 years	133	12.7
21–25 years	82	7.8
26–30 years	74	7.1
31–35 years	61	5.8
36–40 years	27	2.6
Over 40 years	40	3.8
	1049	

With so many marriages ending comparatively early because of the death of a partner, it is not surprising that remarriage was a pronounced feature of conjugal life. At no point did the number of remarriages in Lowestoft, as a proportion of the whole, fall below 27.8% – and this during a twenty-five-year period in which there was defective registration, meaning that the number of remarriages was almost certainly higher than the total recorded.[29] The neighbouring market town of Beccles has had its pattern of remarriage examined, with the following percentages revealed: 22.7% for 1608–41, 26.4% for 1662–1700 and 21.2% for 1701–54.[30] Thus, even the largest proportion recorded is short of Lowestoft's smallest.

[27] P. Laslett, *Family Life and Illicit Love in Earlier Generations* (Cambridge, 1977), p. 184.

[28] The figure includes remarriages.

[29] Laslett, *The World We Have Lost*, p. 103. It is stated here that remarriages constituted about 25% of all marriages during the seventeenth century.

[30] Wrigley and Schofield, pp. 258–9 n. 101.

Table 2. *Remarriage in Lowestoft, 1561–1750* [31]

Period	No. of marriages	No. of remarriages	Remarriages as % of the whole	Situation
1561–1575	212	70	33.0	12 widower & widow 17 widower & single 41 widow & single
1576–1600	312	134	43.0	58 widower & widow 29 widower & single 47 widow & single
1601–1625	295	122	41.4	58 widower & widow 35 widower & single 29 widow & single
1626–1650	177	68	34.2	28 widower & widow 20 widower & single 20 widow & single
1651–1675	212	59	27.8	20 widower & widow 24 widower & single 15 widow & single
1676–1700	239	83	34.7	30 widower & widow 28 widower & single 25 widow & single
1701–1725	335	105	31.3	37 widower & widow 28 widower & single 40 widow & single
1726–1750	361	112	31.0	36 widower & widow 50 widower & single 26 widow & single
1561–1750	**2143**	**753**	**35.1**	**279 widower & widow** **231 widower & single** **243 widow & single**

Though it is not indicated in either Tables 1 or 2, part of the pattern of remarriage in Lowestoft was the length of time taken for people to find new partners after the death of a spouse. It is evident from those marriages solemnised in St Margaret's Church that Lowestoft people took less time to form fresh alliances than was customary for the country as a whole. During the seventeenth century, Lowestoft men had an average inter-marriage interval of 15.2 months and women 27.9, as opposed to 23.0 and 36.5 nationally, while during the first half of the eighteenth it

---

[31] Note that there was defective registration from 1640–5, 1651–3 and 1658–62, meaning that fewer marriages were recorded than took place. Thus, under-registration is a feature of 1626–1650 and 1651–1675. The high percentages for 1576–1600 and 1601–1625 were partly the result of high mortality years caused by epidemics.

was 21.6 and 30.5 months compared with 26.3 and 47.6.[32] The incidence of rapid remarriage was also more pronounced for men than the national figures show, with 41.4% of widowers remarrying within six months of the death of a partner during the sixteenth and seventeenth centuries, compared with 33% nationally. Women, however, showed even less of a tendency to remarry quickly than the national figure of 15% established for their gender, with only 11.4% of them taking new husbands within a six-month interval.[33]

The male proportion of the remarriage data is 62% of the whole, and that of women 38%. However, in spite of this disparity, a perceived common problem faced by both sexes at the time, when seeking to remarry, must have been the presence of under-age children (ten years being the normally accepted upper limit to define 'under age'). In fact, the information available shows that this situation made little difference to men.[34] During the seventeenth century men without children had an average inter-marriage interval of 13.1 months, while for those with young families it was 17.3. For the first half of the eighteenth century the length of time was 21.8 and 21.4 months respectively. In the case of women, however, under-age children seem to have been an impediment to remarriage, probably because of financial responsibility for them devolving upon new husbands. The mean intervals cited for men in the previous two sentences are seen to be as follows for women: 23.9 and 31.9 months for the seventeenth century and 26.5 and 34.5 months for the eighteenth. As a final word on remarriage, it might be presumed that seafarers with under-age children would be soonest to find themselves new spouses – but the figures do not suggest this. Men who made their living on the waves were no more likely to remarry quickly than those working on land – which means that they must either have come ashore and changed their occupation or left their offspring in the care of relatives while at sea.

One area in which maritime activity did influence the pattern of marriages and remarriages in Lowestoft was that of seasonal distribution. This is noticeably different from that observed by historians over England as a whole. The peak time for marriages in the eastern and southern parts of the country, generally speaking, was October and November, while in northern and western regions it was April, May and June.[35] Lowestoft shows a departure from the norm for the southern half of the country by having its marriage peak in November, December and January – a factor which was probably due to the local herring fishing season being in full swing during the month of October, thereby leaving a substantial number of adult males no time to spare for setting up home. Up until 1675,

---

[32] Wrigley *et al.*, p. 172, table 5.14.

[33] *Ibid.*, p. 177.

[34] *Ibid.*, p. 177. This is also the feature observed nationally.

[35] Wrigley and Schofield, pp. 303–4. The difference was due to agricultural practice, with harvest and early autumn ploughing delaying marriage in corn-growing areas and with the cutting and drying of hay resulting in an earlier marriage peak in pastoral regions.

March was always the month with the lowest number of marriages (this being the result of Lenten observance and abstinence), but October was low also because of the practical considerations referred to in the previous sentence. The noticeable increase in marriages taking place in each of these months after 1675 may have been due in part to a decline in traditional Lenten observance in post-Restoration England and to Lowestoft's economy being less reliant on herring fishing after the granting of port status in 1679.[36]

Table 3. *Marriages per month in Lowestoft, 1561–1750*

Period	Jan	Feb	March	April	May	June	July	Aug	Sept	Oct	Nov	Dec
1561–1575	30	7	4	18	22	8	19	14	31	6	32	21
1576–1600	30	31	6	26	26	23	29	20	30	10	48	33
1601–1625	39	34	11	30	25	17	13	27	30	14	32	23
1626–1650	37	14	7	14	21	9	7	9	9	15	22	13
1651–1675	24	9	6	11	12	12	13	13	20	11	30	51
1676–1700	26	12	19	17	11	14	9	19	10	15	54	33
1701–1725	51	23	19	22	16	21	18	18	21	29	47	50
1726–1750	61	24	10	27	21	15	25	21	18	30	40	69
1561–1750	**298**	**154**	**82**	**165**	**154**	**119**	**133**	**141**	**169**	**130**	**305**	**293**

It is worth noting that the October figure overall is inflated in the last two twenty-five year periods by a substantial number of males from outside the parish getting married in town during that particular month. If they are removed from the reckoning, October marriages add up to a total of twenty-one for 1701–1725 and seventeen for 1726–1750, making a total of 109 for the overall timespan. There is also some distortion of the figures for 1626–1650 and 1651–1675 because of the under-registration of marriages for 1640–5, 1651–3 and 1658–62. Apart from these statistical considerations, the only other necessary comment is that the relatively low rate of marriages during the three summer months of June, July and August was probably as much the result the result of men being absent on seasonal fishing voyages as being involved with agricultural activities. Indeed, the slight rise detectable in marriages during the month of September may reflect the practice, on the part of some fishermen, of getting married in the lull between the end of the North Sea second cod voyage and summer mackerel-catching and the beginning of the autumn herring season.

---

[36] The autumn herring voyage remained important, but general maritime trade increased in volume and was less influenced by seasonal factors than fishing.

Mobility of population [37]

References in the previous section to the mobility of marriage partners raise the question of the mobility of people generally. This is seen at its most obvious in the 2,163 family reconstitution forms which exist for those people who married outside the parish and who were either natives of the place or, much more numerously, who were migrants into it. 554 of these seem to belong to families who were resident in the parish for only a limited length of time. However, the total of 1,870 marriages solemnised in St Margaret's Church also includes 373 unions which seem to have been of a short-stay nature,[38] as well as 144 which are best discounted because one partner, or both, were from out of town and did not stay for any length of time after the ceremony. Thus, out of an overall total of 3,889 marriages, 981 (25.2%) seem to be those of people who stayed less than three years in the town – the evidence being based mainly on just one or two baptismal (and sometimes burial) entries in the registers for each family unit.[39] If the period of residency, using the same number of family reconstitution forms, is extended to twelve years, the percentage rises to 33.5%, which is not far removed from what has been observed elsewhere.[40]

This mobile element of the population, on the evidence of occupational references in the parish registers, seems to have been largely composed of labouring people and lesser tradesfolk and artisans. It also contained a small number of gentry (especially between 1560 and 1650), though the men in question had no ascertainable connection with the handful of lesser gentry established in the town. A study of urban residents in the dioceses of Bath and Wells, Exeter, Norwich, Oxford and Salisbury found that between a half and two-thirds of the people who featured in ecclesiastical court depositions were migrants, and the tendency to migrate was greatest among men and women under the age of twenty-five years and also pronounced in the age group from the mid-twenties to late thirties.[41] If child-bearing evidence is to be believed in the case of Lowestoft (in that most of the data

---

[37] Further information may be found in D. Butcher, 'Aspects of Population Mobility in Pre-Industrial Lowestoft', in A. Longcroft and R. Joby (eds), *East Anglian Studies: Essays Presented to J. C. Barringer on his Retirement* (Norwich, 1995), pp. 41–52. This includes tables showing places of origin of outsiders.

[38] This includes forty-eight couples who have just a single baptism entry in the registers, usually within a year to eighteen months of their marrying. This is probably the result of the custom of mothers returning to their parish of origin to have the first child baptised.

[39] A three-year residency was chosen to represent short stay because this is what the registers indicate as being the significant period. There is a noticeable demarcation at the three-year point in baptisms and burials, when the entries as a whole are studied, with nearly all of the short-stay families falling within this timespan.

[40] Laslett, *Family Life and Illicit Love*, p. 65. The Nottinghamshire parish of Clayworth has two listings of inhabitants, for 1676 and 1688, which have survived. The documents show that 37.9% of the people had moved out of the community between the first and second count.

[41] D. Souden, 'Migrants and Population Structure of Later Seventeenth Century Provincial Cities and Market Towns', in Clark, *Transformation of Towns*, p. 139.

which suggests a pronounced degree of population mobility takes the form of baptismal entries in the registers), then the transient members of the community were very largely in the second age group identified above. Burial entries also occur from time to time for 'a single man' or 'a single woman', and it may well be that at least some of the people thus classified were in the under-twenty-five-years age group previously referred to.

It has been stated that population mobility was a pronounced feature of the sixteenth and early seventeenth centuries, and that most urban growth was the result of migration, not natural population increase.[42] In Lowestoft's case, the regular influx of people from outside probably helped to keep the population at a fairly constant level between 1560 and 1650 (though major epidemics in 1603 and 1635 would have had a marked diminishing effect at the time they occurred). The motivation behind migration into the parish cannot be unequivocally identified, but it was probably a combination of what has been described as the 'subsistence' type and the 'betterment' type.[43] It was almost certainly the former of these which made itself felt during the 1580s, to the point where the leet court of 1582 felt compelled to make the following pronouncement:

> *First we do ordain that forasmuch as Daily have & Do recourse unto this Town many & sundry poor people out of other Towns & do hire Cottages of the inhabitants here bringing w[i]th them many children to the great Burden of this Town & impoverishing the same if remove be not provided, That therefore none of the Inhabitants of this Town shall let at any time hereafter any Cottage or Tenement to any any such poor p[er]son unless the same owner shall enter first under to the churchwardens of Lowestoft getting first the consent of the most p[ar]t of the same Towne upon pain to forfeit for every time so letting to the contrary to the Lord of this Leet xxxixs xid.*[44]

Whatever brought people into Lowestoft at any time over the 200-year timespan considered in this book, one thing is certain: at least a quarter of them did not stay in the place for very long.

The parish registers give no clue as to the places of origin of the families that arrived in town, though the parishes of incomers who married townspeople are usually recorded. It is almost as if the ministers and parish clerks of the time regarded family groups as inhabitants of the place as soon as they were resident there. However, it is possible to trace the parishes of origin of most of the people coming into town between 1698 and 1769 because of the survival of a book recording

---

[42] P. Clark, 'The Early Modern Town in the West', in P. Clark (ed.), *The Early Modern Town* (London, 1976), p. 26.

[43] Clark and Slack, *Towns in Transition*, p. 93. The terms are largely self-explanatory, with the first meaning migration forced on people in order for them to survive and the second implying a deliberate attempt to improve economic opportunity and living standards.

[44] SRO(L), 194/A10/4, p. 14.

settlement orders.[45] A study of its first three decades reveals that, up until the end of 1730, 144 orders were made for the following combinations of people: parents (both) and children, seventy-three; women with children (including one widow), four; married couples without children, thirty-three; widows, four; single men, twenty-six; single women, four. The great majority of them (136) refer to people from Suffolk and Norfolk, but there were six sets of incomers whose places of origin were as follows: Colchester (married couple), Harwich (parents and children, single man) and London (three lots of parents and children). Two further entries mention parents and children from Hevingham and a married couple from Sutton. The former might refer to Heveningham in Suffolk or Hevingham in Norfolk, while the latter could have been in either county.

The most obvious feature of this inward migration is the way that the great majority of newcomers (110 out of 136) originated from places within a fifteen-mile radius of Lowestoft, with the strongest influence exerted by the town on Suffolk parishes lying within a five-mile radius. No genuine long-distance migration is revealed – and even if the six examples mentioned in the previous paragraph are cited, it remains a minor factor at best. A notional maritime connection is possible with the incomers from Colchester, Harwich and London, and the same kind of association is detectable in some of the other communities named: Hollesley, Southwold and Woodbridge in Suffolk, Cromer, Great Yarmouth and King's Lynn in Norfolk.

It is possible through family reconstitution data to attach occupations to thirty-three of the 132 men who are named in the settlement orders between 1698 and 1730. There were ten labourers, six mariners/fishermen, two bakers, two cordwainers, and one shoemaker (a newer term at the time than the more traditional 'cordwainer'), brickmaker, mason, house carpenter, glazier, gardener, maltster, keelman, barber-innkeeper, surgeon, arrerer, chimneysweep and fiddler. Thus, it can be seen that the concentration of occupations, where known, was largely in the labouring, maritime and artisan elements of the population.

Family reconstitution also enables assessment of these incomers' length of stay. Nine of the ten labourers settled (remained in the town until they died) and the last stayed for six or seven years. All six mariners/fishermen settled, as did the two cordwainers. One of the bakers remained, but the other one seems to have moved out soon after arrival because he does not feature in any parish register entries. The brickmaker, mason and house carpenter all settled, and the glazier was resident for six or seven years. The gardener and the maltster became permanent residents, but the keelman stayed for only four or five years. The barber-innkeeper, surgeon, chimneysweep and fiddler settled, but the arrerer seems to have moved on soon after arrival because he is not detectable in the registers (he and one of the bakers are the only people to have their occupations specified in the settlement orders). Table 4 gives details concerning how long all 144 people remained in Lowestoft after their arrival.

---

[45] SRO(L), 01/13/1/3. The Settlement Act of 1697 prohibited strangers from residing in a parish unless they provided a certificate (usually presented to the churchwardens) showing that they could return to their parish of origin should they become dependent on poor relief. The Lowestoft settlement book also records details of the apprenticing of poor children.

Table 4. *Length of stay: people named in settlement orders, 1698–1730*

	Do not feature reconstitution	Short stay – 1 to 3 years	Medium stay – 4 to 8 years	Settled in town	Total
Families	30	7	6	30	73
Women with children	2			2	4
Childless couples	12	6	3	12	33
Widows	4				4
Single men	12	2	2	10	26
Single women	2	1		1	4
Total	**62**	**16**	**11**	**55**	**144**

A further reminder of the general mobility of population in the pre-industrial period is to be found in the Lowestoft burial entries, where there are frequent references to outsiders who died in the parish. There are 284 of these altogether between 1561 and 1750 (226 males and fifty-eight females), and the people do not feature at all in the family reconstitution material. They probably represent, in the main, men and women (children being no more 5% of the whole) who had come to the town on business of one kind or another or who were just passing through – rather than genuine migrants who came into the parish to settle. For the most part, the outsiders can be classified in three broad geographical categories: people from Suffolk (seventy-four) and Norfolk (sixty-eight), with 87% of the combined total emanating from within a fifteen-mile radius; people from other parts of England (102); and people from Scotland, Ireland and the Continent (40). Maritime connections are clearly discernible in all three groups and the number of women dying in the place increased noticeably after 1700.[46] In addition to outsiders whose geographical locations are given, there is also a substantial minority (19%) who simply bear the title of 'stranger' in the burial entries (often in addition to their names) and whose places of origin are not therefore known.[47]

Included in the people cited above, there were two burials of unlocatable inhabitants of Norfolk: a boy with no home parish specified (1565) and a man from Copstead (1706), a place which it has not been possible to identify. Between 1726 and 1750, eighteen of the twenty-one Great Yarmouth people buried in Lowestoft had originated from there (five men, seven women, four boys and two girls), and there is evidence that some of the other local burials were the result of family

[46] The registration details also show a reduction in the number of outside contacts which took place during the first half of the seventeenth century particularly, in a period of maritime decline. The increased presence of women after 1700 (especially from Great Yarmouth) may be a reflection of the upturn in maritime activity resulting from the granting of port status.

[47] Of the 284 outsiders buried in Lowestoft between 1561 and 1750, 80% have both their names and places of origin recorded, 15.5% their names only, 2.5% their places of origin only, and 2.0% neither names nor places of origin.

connections with the town. The term 'Western man', which is encountered from time to time, was generally applied to anyone from the south coast, and various maritime occupations and ranks are referred to among deceased male strangers, as well as among the men from places that are named ('sailor' and 'fisherman' being the most common). In the final period, 1701–1750, there are fifteen burials of men who had died, or been killed, on passing ships.

Burial of people from the European mainland (especially the Low Countries) seems to have resulted largely from their being temporarily based in town while engaged either in fishing or other commercial activity. The subsidies of 1524 and 1568 show that Lowestoft had foreign residents – a feature also detectable in neighbouring communities (Corton, Kirkley, Pakefield and Kessingland). The earlier return shows two Dutchmen assessed on goods worth £7 and £12 respectively, while four Dutchmen, four Frenchmen, one Breton, two Channel Islanders and four Scotsmen were each assessed on £1 wages.[48] The two merchants and fifteen wage-earners were probably connected with the fishing industry, which had wide geographical connections at this time in relation to the catching, curing and export of herrings. A maritime association is also visible in the 1568 subsidy, for among the denizens of the town are two 'Iceland boys' in service with local innkeepers (the connection here being cod-fishing, not the herring industry) and a Dutchman and a Frenchman working as servants for two local merchants.[49]

The parish registers, especially between 1561 and 1583, contain a substantial number of references to foreigners – a feature which is most noticeable between 1571 and 1574, when at least twelve Dutch families were resident in the town. This particular three-year period is the only occasion that people from overseas came into the town in such numbers and lived there – albeit for a limited period. Their arrival was probably due to the Duke of Alva's suppression of Protestants in the Low Countries, but the decision to come to Lowestoft may have been influenced by links established through herring catching and processing. After 1600 the registers contain far fewer references to people from outside, whether foreign or English, distant or local. There are 166 such entries for 1561–1600, but only thirty-eight for 1601–1650. It is as if the town withdrew into itself for half a century or more, before becoming more open again in the post-Restoration period and particularly in the early decades of the eighteenth century (at least, so far as inhabitants of other English towns were concerned). The period of reduced links with outside communities resulted from a combination of factors: England's own political troubles, wars abroad on land and sea, and a decline in traditional herring and cod fishing enterprises.

---

[48] SGB, x, 243–7. The man assessed on £7 goods, Martin Cornelius, settled in the town and the family lived there until a grandson or great-grandson (also called Martin) moved out some time after 1596.

[49] SGB, xii, 186–9.

Births and family size

During the pre-industrial era, the rate of conceptions in England is generally acknowledged as having been highest from April to July and lowest from August to November.[50] Lowestoft did not conform to this pattern. Table 5 shows that it had its peak from November to February, while the low point occurred between June and September. The pattern was subject to fluctuations within certain of the twenty-five year blocks, but over the period as a whole it can be seen to have been maintained – especially during the first half of the eighteenth century. This departure from the norm may well have been the result of maritime influences on the community's sexual behaviour.[51] As was noted earlier, the town's marriage peak occurred from November to January to synchronise with the autumn herring season and this would then have had a knock-on effect with regard to conceptions and births. The winter lull in fishing activity was used as a period of preparation for cod voyages to Iceland and Faeroe, as well as in the North Sea, and trading operations were often reduced because bad weather kept vessels confined to local waters. This meant that mariners had their longest period on land out of the whole twelve-month cycle.

Considering that the peak time for conceptions occurred between November and February, it may appear surprising that this is not reflected in a corresponding peak for baptisms during the period February to May. Table 6 clearly shows that baptisms were distributed evenly across all the four-month periods adopted. It has been claimed that the birth of a child was followed very closely by baptism in the

Table 5. *Conceptions by four-month periods, 1561–1750*

Period	April–July	June–September	August–November	November–February
1561–1575	235	232	291	280
1576–1600	370	394	422	405
1601–1625	337	280	332	361
1626–1650	331	288	286	363
1651–1675	280	284	270	333
1676–1700	434	475	459	477
1701–1725	415	387	475	583
1726–1750	425	391	401	534
1561–1750	**2827**	**2731**	**2936**	**3336**

[50] Wrigley and Schofield, p. 291.

[51] There was no distorting under-registration of births in Lowestoft because of Nonconformity until about 1710. Up till then, most nonconformist children were baptised in the parish church and some of them were even identified by the parish clerk during the first decade of the eighteenth century.

Table 6. *Baptisms/births by four-month periods, 1561–1750*

Period	January–April	March–June	May–August	February–May
1561–1575	235	232	264	237
1576–1600	370	394	422	394
1601–1625	337	350	322	353
1626–1650	331	288	286	322
1651–1675	300	284	270	293
1676–1700	434	475	459	453
1701–1725	415	387	475	402
1726–1750	425	391	401	415
1561–1750	**2847**	**2801**	**2899**	**2869**

pre-industrial period (a few days at most), but the limited evidence available in the Lowestoft registers suggests this may not have been the case. There are only twenty-six instances where both birth and baptismal dates are recorded and the difference between them ranges from four days to a month, with the majority concentrating around an interval of ten to fourteen days.[52] Any baptisms occurring weeks (rather than days) after the babies had been born would serve to obscure the pattern of births. Furthermore, given the fact that Lowestoft was a maritime community, it is possible that baptisms in seafaring families may not have taken place until the father had completed a fishing season or trading voyage.

One of the most obvious features revealed in an overall analysis of births/baptisms is the excess of male births over female ones. This can be seen clearly in Table 7 and works out very close to the ratio of 105:100, which has been identified as being typical of all populations.[53] Other aspects of the overall view include the number of illegitimate children baptised, as well as those of parents from outside the local community, who either happened to be staying in town at the time of birth or who were temporarily resident there. These latter consisted partly of the Dutch refugees referred to in the previous section, and sixteen of thirty baptisms of outsiders recorded between 1561 and 1600 were of their children. The other fourteen were of the offspring of people from nearby parishes (five examples) or from further away (nine examples). The pronounced drop in the number of outside baptisms after 1600 may be further evidence of Lowestoft becoming much more isolated from the wider world in the manner referred to at the end of the previous section.

Another aspect of family structure detectable in the baptismal entries in the parish registers is the birth intervals between children. These are broadly in line with what has been previously observed in the early modern period and may summarised

---

[52] Laslett, *The World We Have Lost*, p. 147, says that the average interval between birth and baptism in the pre-industrial period was about fourteen days.

[53] Wrigley *et al.*, p. 298; Chambers, *Population, Economy and Society*, p. 48.

Table 7. *Baptisms/births in twenty-five-year periods, 1561–1750*

Period	Legit. M/F	Illegit. M/F	Totals Legit/Illegit.	No gender given	Out-siders	All baptisms	Av. baptisms per year
1561–1575	380/341	11/9	721/20	0	15	756	50.4
1576–1600	614/537	7/10	1151/17	0	15	1183	47.3
1601–1625	547/467	6/5	1014/11	7	2	1034	41.4
1626–1650	528/455	7/8	983/15	5	0	1003	40.1
1651–1675	445/417	0/3	862/3	5	0	870	34.8
1676–1700	702/620	2/1	1322/3	23	0	1348	53.9
1701–1725	710/653	21/12	1363/33	8	4	1408	56.3
1726–1750	691/636	17/17	1327/34	0	3	1364	54.4
1561–1750	**4617/4126**	**71/65**	**8743/136**	**48**	**39**	**8966**	**47.2**

thus: a period of fourteen to eighteen months between marriage and first child, twenty-five to thirty-three months between subsequent children born before the penultimate one, and thirty-one to thirty-seven months between the penultimate child and its predecessor and between it and the last child of all. These intervals are of a generalised nature and do not take account of the many factors considered by the Cambridge Group in arriving at more sophisticated and detailed statistics,[54] but they will serve as an indicator here. So will the data, reproduced in Table 8, showing the average age of mothers at the time of their last child being born.

Table 8. *Mean age of mothers at birth of last child, 1561–1750*

Period	Age at marriage	Mean age at birth of last child (years)
1561–1600	29 years and under	36.6
	30 years and over	42.0
	All ages	37.1
1601–1650	29 years and under	37.5
	30 years and over	40.1
	All ages	38.2
1651–1700	29 years and under	36.5
	30 years and over	41.4
	All ages	37.4
1701–1750	29 years and under	39.0
	30 years and over	41.2
	All ages	39.5
1561–1750	**29 years and under**	**37.3**
	30 years and over	**41.3**
	All ages	**38.1**

[54] Wrigley *et al.*, pp. 430–49.

Table 9. *Illegitimate births per twenty-five-year periods, 1561–1750*

Period	Male/Female	Total	Total baptisms	Percentage of the whole
1561–1575	11/9	20	756	2.6
1576–1600	7/10	17	1183	1.4 (3.8)
1601–1625	6/5	11	1034	1.1 (3.6)
1626–1650	7/8	15	1003	1.5 (2.6)
1651–1675	0/3	3	870	0.3 (1.4)
1676–1700	2/1	3	1348	0.2 (1.8)
1701–1725	21/12	33	1408	2.3 (2.3)
1726–1750	17/17	34	1364	2.5 (2.9)
1561–1750	**71/65**	**136**	**8966**	**1.5 (2.6)**

A further body of information made available by the parish registers is the rate of illegitimacy. This was low throughout the whole period of study, with only 136 baptisms of bastard children recorded out of an overall total of 8,966 (1.5%) – though the proportion increases slightly to 1.7% with the addition of thirteen children born out of wedlock who were buried without having been first baptised. In overall terms, illegitimacy was less marked in Lowestoft than in the country as a whole – at least, up until 1700. Table 9 presents the details, with the national percentage appended in brackets in the right-hand column for the purposes of comparison.[55]

Finally, there is the matter of family size to be considered. Taken as a unit with both parents and children, it averages out at about 4.5, which is what is generally accepted as being typical of the pre-industrial era. But there should be no cosy comparison with the much cited '2.4 children' situation of modern times. In early modern Lowestoft, before a marriage had reached ten or fifteen years' duration, there was a one in two chance of either partner being dead, and a one in five chance of each of the three or four children who would have been born not reaching the age of one year. Such are the stark realities which lie behind the pages of parish register data.

Mortality

Infant mortality rates in Lowestoft for children in their first year are among the higher ones recorded for parishes which have been fully reconstituted.[56] Table 10 shows a breakdown for individual fifty-year blocks of time, leading to an overall rate

---

[55] Wrigley *et al.*, p. 219, table 6.2. The information given here regarding illegitimacy derives from R. L. Adair, 'Regional Variations in Illegitimacy and Courtship Patterns in England, 1538–1754' (unpub. PhD thesis, University of Cambridge, 1991), table 2.1, p. 63. The percentages are given to two decimal points, but have been rounded up to one.

[56] *Ibid.*, p. 217. Gainsborough has the highest IMR recorded.

Table 10. *Lowestoft infant mortality rates, 1561–1750*

Period	Male rate per '000	Female rate per '000	Combined rate per '000
1561–1600	155	197	178
1601–1650	192	150	172
1651–1700	177	191	189
1701–1750	248	283	265
1561–1750	**193**	**206**	**201**

for the whole 190 years of 201 per thousand.[57] These levels of infant death probably reflect the urban nature of the parish (albeit of modest scale), for it is generally accepted that areas of higher population density frequently suffered from greater mortality than did rural areas.[58] However, part of the wood-pasture belt of central Suffolk, within a twenty-mile radius of the town (the South Elmham group of parishes) had an infant mortality rate of 155 per thousand between 1550 and 1640, which is not significantly less than Lowestoft's during the same timespan.[59] Illegitimate children fared far worse than those born in wedlock and the Lowestoft registers show that, out of a total of 149 children (136 definitely base-born and thirteen strong possibilities) between 1561 and 1730, sixty-five (44%) died within a year.

One interesting feature of the figures in the table above is the fact that, apart from during the period 1601–1650, there was a better survival rate for male infants than for female ones. This is contrary to accepted trends and there is no ready explanation for it.[60] One possibility is that in a coastal community, where boys and men were of prime importance in crewing fishing boats and trading vessels (as well as providing the workforce for onshore trades), more care may have been devoted to their nurture than to that of female children. The only fifty-year period in which girl infants had the better survival rate was between 1601 and 1650 – a period of severe maritime depression for the town when the fishing industry was in decline and, on the evidence of occupational data in the parish registers, many local men reverted to agriculture as a way of maintaining themselves and their families.

With a high incidence of infant mortality recorded, it comes as no surprise to find that Lowestoft also had quite a high rate of maternal mortality:[61] 23.4 deaths per

---

[57] Wrigley *et al.*, p. 217. A rate of 215 per thousand is cited as the Lowestoft figure for the period 1561–1730 – the timespan of the reconstitution undertaken for the Cambridge Group. The slightly higher figure is probably the result of adjustments made to the data in order to produce the most accurate result.

[58] Wrigley and Schofield, p. 178–9; Wrigley *et al.*, p. 217.

[59] N. Evans, 'The Community of South Elmham, Suffolk, 1550–1640' (unpub. MPhil thesis, University of East Anglia, 1978), p. 129.

[60] Chambers, *Population, Economy and Society*, p. 48; Souden, 'Migrants and Population Structure', in Clark and Slack, *Transformation of Towns*, p. 151; Wrigley *et al.*, p. 298.

[61] Wrigley and Schofield, 'English Population History', 181.

thousand births for the period 1561–1600, 15.5 per thousand for 1651–1700 and 14.3 per thousand for 1701–1750 – the second and third sets of figures being ones which do not differ greatly from what has been observed elsewhere. A study of thirteen fully reconstituted English parishes established rates of 17.5 per thousand for 1650–1699 and 12.9 per thousand for 1700–1749,[62] while a much more comprehensive survey has arrived at around 16.3% and 12.8% for the same fifty-year periods.[63] As the great majority of maternal deaths occurred soon after the baby was born, the child was deprived of its mother's milk from early on.[64] There is little tangible evidence from pre-industrial England regarding the practice of wet-nursing, other than literary references, and no documentary proof has come to light in Lowestoft concerning its use in the wealthier levels of local society or further down the social scale. However, it may have been carried out in order to rear babies that had lost their mothers.

The writer has neither the expertise nor the desire to present a detailed account of human mortality across the whole spectrum of gender, age range and social groupings. The paragraphs above were simply meant to convey some sense of the fragility of life at the earliest and most critical stage. It might well be argued that life was fragile at all stages during the early modern era (with average life-expectancy of thirty to thirty-five years), and some sense of this is certainly conveyed in the Lowestoft burial registers. The town suffered badly from epidemics of one kind or another, with six of the nineteen decades between 1560 and 1750 showing an excess of burials over baptisms (1581–90, 1601–10, 1611–20, 1631–40, 1721–30 and 1741–50). This is worse than the average ascertained in a study of 404 English parishes, but not as bad as the worst rates prevailing in some urban areas located close to marshland.[65] Table 11 shows those years in the demographic history of Lowestoft which may be regarded as crisis ones, in that the general mortality rate was at least twice the average for the period considered (the period, in this case, being a span of twenty-five years).[66]

In addition to the years indicated above, 1602 and 1610 (with eighty-one and eighty-two burials respectively) would also have qualified as crisis years had not the extremely high mortality in 1603 raised the average for the period 1601–1625. During the eighteenth century, smallpox caused high mortality at certain times, but the epidemics do not show as crisis years simply because the average burial rates for the two periods, 1701–1725 and 1726–1750, was relatively high anyway. Table 12 shows those years of high mortality in Lowestoft which do not technically constitute crisis years. It is to be noted that, from 1676 onwards, and especially after 1700 there were more burials being carried out and registered in the town because of an increasing population.

[62] Wrigley and Schofield, 'English Population History', 182, table 16.

[63] Wrigley *et al.*, p. 313, table 6.29.

[64] Data from Sweden for the mid-eighteenth century to the mid-nineteenth has shown that 45% of maternal deaths following a live birth occurred within four days and 75% within two weeks.

[65] Wrigley and Schofield, p. 116.

[66] MacFarlane, *Reconstructing Historical Communities*, p. 169. A mortality crisis year is defined as one where the death-rate was more than double the average for the overall period.

Table 11. *Mortality crisis years*

Period	Year	Number of burials	Average number of burials for period	Comments
1576–1600	1585	129	46.44	Plague year
	1588	95	46.44	Probably plague; high female death-rate
1601–1625	1603	310	51.8	Plague year
1626–1650	1635	170	34.12	Plague year
1651–1676	1669	84	31.0	High child death-rate in the spring

Table 12. *Other years of high mortality*

Period	Year	Number of burials	Average number of burials for period	Comments
1561–1575	1573	74	44.3	
1576–1600	1592	82	46.4	High autumn mortality
1601–1625	1602	81	51.8	High adult mortality, Jan to Apr
	1610	82	51.8	Highest rate, Jan to Apr
1676–1700	1680	74	50.8	
	1681	76	50.8	
	1683	74	50.8	
	1684	78	50.8	
1701–1725	1707	76	56.2	
	1710	97	56.2	35 smallpox (36.1%) – Nov & Dec
	1718	71	56.2	14 smallpox (19.7%) – Oct to Dec
	1719	98	56.2	7 smallpox (7.1%) – Jan to Feb
	1721	75	56.2	
	1724	77	56.2	19 smallpox (24.7%) – Jan to Sept
1726–1750	1729	89	58.4	
	1738	102	58.4	34 smallpox (33.3%) – all year
	1748	109	58.4	48 smallpox (44.0%) – last 6 months
	1749	83	58.4	34 smallpox (41.0%) – first 3 months

Tables 11 and 12 show that epidemics in Lowestoft reflect the national trend, in that plague afflicted it during the later sixteenth century and the first half of the seventeenth, and smallpox became the main menace during the first half of the eighteenth.[67] It has been said that plague outbreaks were most frequent and heavy

[67] The word 'plague' is used because that is the conventional term. Research carried out in recent years suggests it may not have been Bubonic Plague (*Yersinia pestis*), but a haemorrhagic virus such as Ebola. See D. Mackenzie, 'Ring a ring o' rosies', *NS* 172, no. 2318 (November, 2001), 35–7. This article draws upon material published in S. Scott and C. Duncan, *Biology of Plagues: Evidence from Historical Populations* (Cambridge, 2001).

in London and the larger urban areas, and less common in smaller towns (with the notoriety of Eyam, in Derbyshire, tending to obscure the latter fact), but if Lowestoft's situation is anything to go by that statement may need qualification.[68] The 1603 outbreak was particularly severe, with 280 people dying between May and September (234 of them in June, July and August), which was about 19% of the population – a proportion comparable with that of the Sussex coastal town of Rye a generation earlier.[69] With so many corpses to dispose of, the question of burial is an interesting one. St Margaret's churchyard was not large at the time and could not have accommodated so many dead in so short a period; nor has a plague pit of any kind ever been discovered in a parish now almost totally built over. There is a strong possibility, therefore, that the bodies were taken out in ferry boats beyond the offshore sandbanks and committed to the sea, any liturgical considerations regarding burial having to give way to necessity.

The 1603 epidemic seems to have formed part of a wider pattern of infection. The town of Southwold, ten miles further down the coast, suffered even more, with 373 burials recorded during the year. This was the reason given for its minister not submitting a communicants' return in response to a demand from Norwich diocese on behalf of the Canterbury province.[70] Great Yarmouth, some seven or eight miles to the north, was also afflicted, reputedly via Amsterdam.[71] The seaside parish of Corton, just three miles north of Lowestoft and only five to the south of Great Yarmouth, had lost thirty-three of its 140 or so inhabitants (23%) to plague in the previous year, the sickness lasting from the beginning of August to the beginning of November (the register identifies the specific cause of death). And, finally, the inland market town of Beccles had outbreaks of the disease in 1602 and 1603, though mortality there was of lesser degree than that suffered by Lowestoft in either the 1603 pestilence or the one which followed a generation later, in 1635 (170 deaths).[72]

The other chief identifiable killer, smallpox, is specifically named in the Lowestoft registers. It seems that the vicar of the time, John Tanner, wished to record it for some reason and therefore appended the details in his own hand. According to one modern study, 10% of the deaths recorded in London mortality bills during the

---

[68] D. Palliser, 'Dearth and Disease in Staffordshire, 1540–1670', in Chalklin and Havinden, *Rural Change*, p. 67. A. G. E. Jones, in 'Plagues in Suffolk in the Seventeenth Century', *N&Q* CXCVIII (1953), 384–6, says that Lowestoft suffered as severely from plague during the first half of the seventeenth century as any community in England. J. F. D. Shrewsbury, *A History of the Bubonic Plague in the British Isles* (Cambridge, 1970), pp. 212 and 372, makes reference to this article.

[69] S. Hipkin, 'The Economy and Social Structure of Rye, 1600–1660' (unpub. PhD thesis, University of Oxford, 1985), p. 7. The epidemic of 1563 killed between 16% and 23% of the population, that of 1579–80 about 20%.

[70] 'The Communicants' Return of 1603 – Archdeaconry of Suffolk', in C. H. E. White (ed.), *PSIA* vi (Ipswich, 1886), 367–8. This printed version derives from BL, Harleian Ms. 595 no. ii, folio 168.

[71] F. P. Wilson, *The Plague in Shakespeare's London* (Oxford, 1963), pp. 85–6.

[72] Evans, *Beccles*, p. 30. Ninety-two burials were recorded in 1602, 72 in 1603. With the loss of so many people in 1603, Lowestoft's population might still have been around the 1,200–1,300 mark in 1635, which would have made the 170 fatalities that year about 14% of the inhabitants.

Table 13. *Burials per selected four-month periods, 1561–1750*

Period	January to April	August to November
1561–1575	226	235
1576–1600	337	470
1601–1625	365	434
1626–1650	249	335
1651–1675	268	297
1676–1700	397	480
1701–1725	433	512
1726–1750	480	532
1561–1750	**2755**	**3295**

eighteenth century were attributed to smallpox, while a census of the deaths which occurred in thirty communities during the 1720s gives 16.5%.[73] Lowestoft's smallpox death statistics may be seen in Table 12 and, generally speaking, they are much higher than the ones cited. It may be that the growing number of people coming into the town during the first half of the eighteenth century (to say nothing of increasing contact with crew members from ships involved in coastal trade) increased the risk of infection. The 191 deaths recorded above split almost equally between adults and children (ninety-one and one hundred respectively), with females generally having lower fatality than males. Thirty-three women died from the disease and fifty-eight men; thirty-nine girls succumbed and fifty-four boys (there being seven deaths where the child's gender was not recorded).

Various other epidemics are suggested in the registers in the high mortality rates encountered at certain times of the year or in the ones which can be seen as primarily affecting either children or adults. There are also cases where particular families were struck down by sickness, without any evidence of what the fatal illnesses were.[74] The peak time of year for burials in pre-industrial England was January to April, with a high point being reached in the latter two months of the four.[75] Once more, Lowestoft does not conform to the pattern. Its burial peak (shown in Table 13) was from August to November throughout the whole period of study. There is no ready explanation for the phenomenon, but it may have resulted yet again from a maritime factor: the autumn was the time of the local herring season and many of the town's seafarers (who would have been absent at other times, engaged upon different activities) would have been present for the main fishing enterprise.

[73] T. McKeown and R. G. Brown, 'Medical Evidence Related to English Population Changes in the Eighteenth Century', *PS* ix (1955), 126; P. E. Razzell, 'Population Change in Eighteenth Century England: a Reappraisal', *EHR* 2nd series xviii (1965), 323–4. Both articles are reproduced in M. Drake (ed.), *Population in Industrialisation* (London, 1969), pp. 40–72 and 128–56.

[74] Heavy winter mortality may have resulted from the so-called 'sweating sickness' (influenza).

[75] Wrigley and Schofield, p. 295.

Table 14. *Burials in Lowestoft, 1561–1750*

Period	Men	Women	Children Male/Female/Unknown	Strangers Male/Female	All burials	Average no. per year
1561–1575	119	156	161/163/1	52/12	664	44.3
1576–1600	260	314	271/273/8	30/5	1161	46.4
1601–1625	314	361	328/277/3	10/2	1295	51.8
1626–1650	222	281	174/164/3	8/1	853	34.1
1651–1675	194	233	178/139/15	16/0	775	31.0
1676–1700	341	376	280/219/9	25/2	1252	50.1
1701–1725	312	396	325/283/36	37/16	1405	56.2
1726–1750	316	397	361/319/0	46/22	1461	58.4
1561–1750	**2078**	**2514**	**2078/1837/75**	**224/60**	**8866**	**46.7**

Table 14 provides a summative statement concerning burials in Lowestoft over a period of nearly 200 years. The overall trend is seen to be an upward one, which probably reflects the town's gradual increase in population. The two twenty-five-year periods which show a fall both had their figures affected by faulty registration during the period of the Civil Wars, during the last year of the Protectorate and during the Restoration. But another factor also has to be considered: the town's population was probably still suffering at this time from the effects of two severe epidemics in 1603 and 1635. A further feature of interest is the marked number of adult female deaths over and above the male total; this is probably the result of women's susceptibility to sickness and death in their child-bearing years, because later on in life women had a better survival rate than men.[76]

The opinion has been expressed that a high level of widowhood might be expected in a seafaring town or city.[77] Loss of life at sea was certainly a feature of maritime communities, but in Lowestoft's case the exact degree cannot be ascertained. The possibility of the deaths of drowned mariners being entered in parish registers has been speculated upon,[78] but this was not the practice in Lowestoft. The loss of fourteen fishermen is recorded in the vicar's day-book at one point, but the drownings are not written in the register entries themselves.[79] Presumably, the circumstances were exceptional in some way, because nowhere else in the surviving parochial documentation is such loss at sea mentioned. Four of the men died in 1714 and ten in 1716, and it may have been the case that two individual storms were responsible for their deaths. Out of the ninety-one Lowestoft mariners

[76] Wrigley *et al.*, p. 302.

[77] Souden, 'Migrants and Population Structure', in Clark, *Transformation of Towns*, p. 153. The remark was made with reference to Bristol.

[78] Hipkin, 'Rye', p. 7.

[79] NRO, PD 589/3. Day-books are comparatively rare. They were kept by incumbents and clerks to record events as they occurred, prior to entry in the registers. They often contain more detail than registers and are a source of useful information.

whose wills have survived for the period 1560–1730, forty have no burial entry in the registers and may well have been lost at sea. Of this forty, twenty-nine had wives who were alive when the document was drawn up. Altogether, forty-four of the wills were made by testators in a state of good health, which suggests that the men themselves knew only too well the risks involved in making a living on the oceans.[80]

From time to time in the Lowestoft registers, there are details of death caused by accident. Such fatalities constitute only a tiny proportion of the total number, but they serve to give a sense of what life at the time was like. Drownings in wells are recorded, as in burial entries of 5 August 1561 and 29 October 1589. In the former case, Alice Fraunces, a servant of Thomas Jeggell, died in her master's well (she may have been quite a young girl), while in the latter an unnamed boy met his end somewhere else in town. The vulnerability of the young is well illustrated on a number of occasions. There is the case of ten-year-old John Grudgefield (a merchant's son) and his companion, Robert Heasell, who were drowned in Lake Lothing and buried on 15 August 1580. There is that of John Postle, aged two years, who perished in one of his father's leather-tanning vats and was buried on 7 September 1655. And there is that of five-year-old William Pilot, who was crushed to death by a cart in Rant Score and buried on 10 November 1715.

Accidents at work are mentioned too. An unnamed man (an outsider, probably) was buried on 25 March 1581, having been killed while engaged in building work on the *White Horse* inn. Thomas Cudden met his end in the collapse of a clay-pit at Gunton and was buried on 28 January 1702. And there are cases of men drowning while coming ashore in small boats from the larger vessels which lay offshore. Most graphic of all these maritime mishaps, and one that has a certain degree of grim humour about it, is the one which involved Henry Blackman, a fishing-boat master. His burial entry of 12 May 1706 reads thus: 'Henry Blackman, who joking with the next person following under sail in the North Road both fell overboard into earnest eternity (a fair cavett to others not to do the like). They were taken up the week following and buried etc'. Neither man would have been able to swim, in typical fashion of the time, and a few days had obviously elapsed before the bodies were washed ashore.

Death by violent means of one kind or another occurs only very occasionally. The first case is that of Anthony Debdall, who was buried on 22 September 1564, having been killed by a firearm. The entry does not say whether his decease was the result of an accident or whether it was an act of murder. There are just two definite cases of homicide evident in the registers, a lower incidence than that documented elsewhere.[81] The first is that of Frances Bates (whether male or female is not

---

[80] In the pre-industrial era, the great majority of wills were made by testators who were sick. In Lowestoft, the average interval between making a will in a state of poor health and being buried was five to six days.

[81] P. Razzell (ed.), *The History of Myddle* (Firle, 1979), p. xvi. The introduction of this edition of the work states that there were ten specific cases of murder mentioned. With a population of about 600 people, Myddle was less than half the size of Lowestoft. Richard Gough wrote the book in 1700, and revised it the following year, drawing upon long-established family connections with this Shropshire parish, seven miles to the north of Shrewsbury.

Table 15. *Lowestoft baptisms and burials, 1561–1750*

Period	Baptisms	Burials	Natural increase	Comments
1561–1575	735	600	135	
1576–1600	1162	1126	36	
1601–1625	1026	1283	-257	Effect of 1603 plague
1626–1650	997	844	153	
1651–1675	864	759	105	
1676–1700	1342	1225	117	
1701–1725	1398	1352	46	
1726–1750	1355	1373	-18	Effect of smallpox
1561–1750	**8879**	**8562**	**317**	

known), who was buried on 10 September 1663, having been killed with a mace. No assailant is named. Nearly two years later, on 22 July 1665, Ann Bolden was buried, having been shot dead by Thomas Base. None of these people feature in the family reconstitution material.

Finally, only two instances of suicide are detectable.[82] The first is that of an outsider, John Horning, from Thurlton in Norfolk, 'who w[t] [sic] a knife wilfully ended his life, yet lived a short time and repented'. His burial is recorded on 26 November 1567. The second concerns Ann Butt, wife of Thomas, who drowned herself (there is no information as to where and how) and was buried on 14 June 1669. As a daughter, Susanna, was baptised the following day, the death was possibly caused by post-natal depression.

Conclusion

A comparison of the overall numbers of baptisms and burials of Lowestoft people during the period 1561–1750, as shown in Table 15, enables an opinion to be formed as to whether urban recruitment was necessary to maintain the population level.[83] Certain adjustments needed to be made in order to keep the calculations pertinent to the town. Thus, anyone who featured in the baptism and burial registers without having a true residential qualification was disregarded. Among the people eliminated from the reckoning were those who were just passing through, those returning to have a first child baptised,[84] and those temporarily living in the place

---

[82] Razzell, p. xv. Myddle, too, had only two cases of suicide mentioned in its registers, with one further possible or 'open' case.

[83] F. Braudel, 'Pre-Modern Towns', in Clark, *Early Modern Town*, p. 59, says that inward migration was required to keep population levels up.

[84] It was customary at one time to have the first child baptised in the mother's parish of origin.

because their business had taken them there for a short period of time. This removed eighty-seven baptisms from the overall total of 8,966 and 284 burials from the 8,866 recorded, making respective totals of 8,879 and 8,562.

Apart from two twenty-five-year periods, when epidemic had an adverse impact, it can be seen that Lowestoft's population achieved a small overall increase – at least, in the simplistic sense that the number of baptisms totalled more than the number of burials. This was the result of the procreative output of people indigenous to the town and of those incomers who settled there. There was never a large degree of inward migration into Lowestoft, but that which did take place undoubtedly helped to ensure that the population level recovered from periods of high mortality (especially the two plague outbreaks of 1603 and 1635) and helped it to grow once the balance had been restored. None of the statistics presented in this chapter has the ability to comment on the essential transience of the human condition as eloquently as James Rous, the vicar, did in a written comment placed at the end of the first register book in February 1650: 'Thus one generation passes and another succeeds in its place like bubbles in the water one breaking to make way for another'.

– 4 –

Occupation and the Local Economy

Introduction

The creation of an occupational structure involved using and cross-referencing as wide a variety of suitable sources as possible.[1] This produced a total of 140 occupations, parochial offices and social rankings for the period 1561–1750, which was reduced to 125 after the removal of designations having no connection with a craft or trade (e.g. constable, overseer) or that showed status in a calling (e.g. apprentice, master to sea).[2] Arguably, this number could be further reduced to 106 by treating as one occupation those areas of work which had alternative names (e.g. cordwainer and corviser, reeder and thatcher). This was not done, in order to allow the full variety of terminology to manifest itself. But even if it had been, it would still have resulted in a total number of occupations far in excess of what has been claimed for the last thirty years or more as typical for small towns of the early modern era (twenty to thirty). Therefore, it would seem that a number of historians, in commenting on occupational structures, need to revise their figures upwards – and, even more pertinently, to investigate as many sources as they can, rather than relying on one or two alone.[3] At least one other East Anglian commentator has demonstrated the complexity which existed in two Suffolk market towns (Beccles and Halesworth) within a fifteen-mile radius of Lowestoft, using parish register evidence only and still identifying seventy-six and seventy-nine occupations respectively.[4]

---

[1] Parish registers and probate documents were the dominant primary sources.

[2] The one exception (in the former case) was 'gentleman', because the small number of gentry resident in the town needed to be represented in its overall socio-economic structure.

[3] Clark and Slack, *Towns in Transition*, pp. 5 and 28; J. Patten, *English Towns, 1500–1700* (Folkestone, 1978), pp. 252, 254, 273 and 283; Clay, *Economic Expansion*, i, 180; S. M. Jack, *Towns in Tudor and Stuart Britain* (London, 1996), p. 66. These publications put the number of occupations in pre-industrial small towns in the range cited in-text. Over the years, some researchers have used will registers as a convenient way of collecting information, but the source is unreliable as register copies may not include the various testators' occupations as stated in the original wills themselves.

[4] Evans, *Beccles*, p. 75. N. Evans, 'Occupations in Parish Registers: A Note', *LH* 15, vi (May 1983), 361. Nesta Evans carried out the work in both towns with WEA classes that she was tutoring.

Table 16. *Documentary sources of Lowestoft occupations, 1561–1750*

Period	Source	No.of refs	Period	Source	No.of refs
1561–1600	Parish register	399	**1651–1700**	Parish register	229
	Probate documents	91		Probate documents	135
	1584 muster roll	38		Tithe accounts	50
	Leet court minutes	14		Woollen burials	41
	1568 lay subsidy	8		Leet court minutes	12
		550		Parish accounts	5
				Treasury Books	3
				Court baron minutes	2
				Quarter sessions	2
				State Papers Domestic	1
					480
1601–1650	Parish register	398	**1700–1750**	Parish register	486
	Probate documents	125		Tithe accounts	137
	Leet court minutes	37		Probate documents	115
		560		Apprenticeship/settlement	14
				Court baron minutes	10
				Parish accounts	7
				Leet court minutes	4
				Treasury Books	1
					774

Having established the number of occupations available in the various documentary sources, as outlined in Table 16, it was then necessary to devise a system of classification able to reflect the complexities of Lowestoft's economic structure.[5] Twelve main categories were devised, and three subsidiary ones – the latter consisting of a level of society whose members did not have to work (gentry), a class of workers who often functioned in different areas of occupation (labourer) and another which tended to reflect a phase in the life-cycle as much as an occupation in its own right (servant).[6] These were then used in each of the four individual sub-periods that acted as subdivisions of the overall period. The classification proved equal to the task and was able to show changes which occurred within the town during its pre-industrial past.

The respective numbers of people classified within the various headings in the tables which follow can be taken as representing the relative importance of their

[5] Among the various occupational structures devised over the years by historians which deserve attention are the following ones: D. Hey, *An English Community: Myddle under the Tudors and Stuarts* (Leicester, 1974), p. 53; W. G. Hoskins, 'English Provincial Towns in the Early Sixteenth Century', in W. G. Hoskins, *Provincial England* (London, 1963), p. 80; A. L. Beier, 'The Social Problems of an Elizabethan Country Town: Warwick 1580–90', in P. Clark (ed.), *Country Towns in Pre-Industrial England* (Leicester, 1981), p. 52; M. Reed, 'Economic Structure and Change in Seventeenth Century Ipswich', in Clark, *Country Towns*, p. 102; J. Pound, 'The Social and Trade Structure of Norwich, 1525–75', *P&P* 34 (1966), 49–69.

[6] Servants were often younger men and women living in with their employers and sometimes being trained in different crafts and trades. At some point in their mid-twenties many of them would have hoped to marry and establish homes of their own.

trades and occupations to the economy of the town. There are very few documented references to dual occupations, in the sense of a man practising two different trades concurrently, and there are not many examples of change of occupation during a man's working life. What is suggested at times (especially in probate material) is that people seem to have had interests subsidiary to their primary occupation – a feature to be discussed later. The family reconstitution exercise reveals that the individual occupational references drawn from the various sources used add up to about 60% of the town's adult male population. The great majority of these men (57%) were heads of household, and it is pleasing to note that both figures remain consistent across the total timespan investigated. Thus, with three-fifths of the town's adult male population classifiable in terms of the occupations followed, the relative importance of each individual occupation as a proportion of the whole can be accepted as valid. There is no reason to suppose that the remaining 40% (were the information available) would show any substantial deviation from the pattern established.

Occupational groups, 1561–1730

Altogether, 550 occupational and social references were collected for the period 1561–1600 – a figure that was reduced to 515 once the necessary omissions had been made and the number of people referred to in more than one source considered. This resulted in a total of sixty-two individual occupations. Table 17 presents the information, using the classification system explained above.

The importance of maritime trades, which total one quarter of the mainstream occupations recorded, can be seen immediately. Interestingly, the term 'fisherman' is found only once, in the inventory of John Harborne (February 1592), with all the other references being to 'mariners' or 'sailors'.[7] This contrasts with a survey of maritime personnel undertaken in 1566, which credits Lowestoft with twenty-seven fishermen and eighty-seven mariners.[8] The reason for the differences in terminology probably lies in the dual use of vessels at this time, whereby a number of them were employed on both fishing and trading voyages, according to the particular time of year and to the owners' wishes. Local merchants were much involved in the catching and curing of fish (especially herrings), in the export of them, and in the handling of various kinds of merchandise in both coastal and overseas trade.

Apart from men who went to sea, the other large category is servants.[9] Most references to them occur in parish register burial entries (forty-five) and in a 1584

---

[7] In order to prevent a plethora of end-notes in this chapter, and in succeeding ones, references to individual probate documents will not be given. All of them can be traced in SRO(L), in the research material deposited there by the writer.

[8] TNA: PRO, SP 12/39/17.1.

[9] 'Servant' in this case does not necessarily mean a domestic helper (though some of the women probably did fulfil that function). It refers to a person who was hired to assist with a particular kind of work – what Adam Smith referred to as a 'productive' employee. See A. Kussmaul, *Servants in Husbandry in Early Modern England* (Cambridge, 1981), p. 4.

Table 17. *Occupations, 1561–1600*

Category	Occupations and the number of people involved	Total	% of the whole
Maritime (at sea)	Fisherman (1) Mariner (43) Sailor (52)	96	18.6
Maritime (on land)	Cooper (14) Hook-maker (1) Hoop-maker (1) Roper (3) Shipwright (12)	31	6.0
Agriculture	Husbandman (6) Neatherd (3) Shepherd (1) Yeoman (1)	11	2.1
Retail & Distribution	Draper (5) Fishmonger (1) Goldsmith (1) Merchant (22) Merchant tailor (1)	30	5.8
Food & Drink production	Baker (8) Brewer (5) Butcher (27) Miller (10)	50	9.7
Leather Trades	Cobbler (1) Cordwainer (5) Currier (2) Glover (3) Knacker (2) Shoemaker (5) Tanner (3) Tawer (1)	22	4.3
Clothing	Hatter (1) Tailor (36)	37	7.2
Textiles	Dyer (1) Weaver (9)	10	1.9
Building	Carpenter (9) Glazier (1) Joiner (4) Mason (11) Sawyer (2) Thatcher (2)	29	5.6
Metalwork	Blacksmith (3) Pewterer (1) Smith (10) Tinker (2)	16	3.1
Professional & Services	Barber (4) Innkeeper (3) Minister (7) Nurse (1) Proctor (2) Schoolmaster (1) Scrivener (1) Surgeon (1) Victualler (1)	21	4.1
Miscellaneous	Carter (4) Chimneysweep (1) Fletcher (1) Gunner (1) Ostler (1) Singing man (1)	9	1.7
		362	
Gentry	Gentleman (12)	12	2.3
Labourer	Labourer (36)	36	7.0
Servant	Maidservant (6) Servant (99: 79 male, 20 female)	105	20.4
15 categories	62 occupations	**515**	

Muster Roll of able-bodied men in the Hundred (thirty-three).[10] Their prominence may reflect the buoyant state of the fishing industry (especially herrings) in the late sixteenth century, for it is noticeable that many were employed by the town's merchants and mariners. Their surnames suggest that a majority (about 65%) were either from the town itself or from neighbouring parishes, but there is no information as to their age, the ways in which they were hired, or how long they stayed with an employer.[11] It has been estimated that, from the late sixteenth century to the early nineteenth, servants constituted about 60% of the national population in the fifteen to twenty-four-years age group and comprised as much as 56% of the hired labour in some parishes.[12] Nothing much is known about servants in Lowestoft, other than their names, but their considerable presence in town shows that they were an important part of the workforce. Their almost total absence from

---

[10] E. Powell, 'Muster Rolls of Territorials in Tudor Times', in *PSIA* xix (Ipswich, 1925), 65–70.

[11] Kussmaul, *Servants*, p. 51 and pp. 59–63. The information here, concerning the second and third matters, largely deals with the second half of the eighteenth century and first part of the nineteenth.

[12] *Ibid.*, p. 16.

the family reconstitution material appears to suggest that they were members of the age group referred to in the previous sentence and this means they had not reached the typical age of marriage and set up households of their own.

The Clothing category is dominated by the presence of thirty-six tailors – a relatively large number, which seems to reflect a trend of the time.[13] Their presence was in no way the result of a large-scale local textile industry (nor is there evidence of a single dominant employer controlling a number of people), but the town may have served as a workshop for the surrounding area, with its craftsmen making garments for people who lived in the outlying parishes. Butchers, too, constituted a sizeable group within the Food and Drink classification – a feature which has been observed in larger towns such as Worcester and Leicester.[14] In the case of Lowestoft, there was good cattle-grazing country on the marshes in its hinterland, sheep were kept by some of the neighbourhood's farmers, and there were pigs in many of the town's back yards.[15] The supplies of meat thus available not only kept the land-based population supplied, but were also used to provision trading ships (including those engaged in coastal traffic) and fishing vessels.

The importance of maritime activity in the town can also be detected beyond the seafaring element. Seventeen of the twenty-two merchants had interests connected with fishing or seaborne trade. Even the sole goldsmith, William Rogers, had to be included in the Retail & Distribution category, because his inventory shows clearly that he was really a merchant, involved in brewing, fishing and fish-curing (there is no evidence of his working in precious metals). It is arguable, too, whether the two sawyers would have worked exclusively for the building trade; in a maritime community, their skills would undoubtedly have been used in the construction of ships, as might those of carpenters and joiners – to say nothing of the various smiths. The difficulty of categorising trades in the sixteenth and seventeenth centuries, owing in part to the dual nature of some occupations (specific comment being made on the difficulty of differentiating between the mariner-fisherman and the farmer-carter), has been recognised,[16] but there is also the matter of different activities that a man might have been involved in, either concurrently or at different times in his life.

In Lowestoft's case, there are six examples of what may be loosely termed dual occupations for the period 1560–1599, though only one of them shows a man involved in two different trades at the same time. For instance, James Philip was a

[13] P. Burke, 'The European Context', in *The Urban Setting*, p. 62. This book is volume 1 in the OU's *English Urban History, 1500–1700* (Milton Keynes, 1977–8). M. Reed, 'Ipswich in the Seventeenth Century' (unpub. PhD thesis, University of Leicester, 1973), p. 38.

[14] A. Dyer, *The City of Worcester in the Sixteenth Century* (Leicester, 1973), p. 136, and Hoskins, 'An Elizabethan Provincial Town: Leicester', in *Provincial England*, p. 95. L. A. Clarkson, *The Pre-Industrial Economy of England, 1500–1750* (London, 1971), p. 83, also notes that butchers were the most numerous urban tradesmen connected with supplying food.

[15] Leet court minutes of the 1580s and 1620s refer to nuisance caused by pigs wandering at large in the streets and on the common greens.

[16] S. M. Jack, *Trade and Industry in Tudor and Stuart England* (London, 1977), p. 27.

mariner in November 1561, when one of his children was baptised, but he was a roper at the time of his death in December 1588.[17] Derick Harman is called a shoemaker in a baptism entry of February 1562, but his will of 9 May 1575 clearly shows that he was a merchant of sorts, as much involved in fish–curing as he was in making and retailing footwear. In August 1572 Andrew Taylor is referred to in the will of his master, Robert Freeman (a singing-man), as 'my late servant and shipwright' – a case perhaps of a skilled man working in another capacity because of particular circumstances. Wyllyam Wright is classed as a husbandman in his marriage registration of September 1584, but he is termed a labourer in the burial entry of one of his children in August 1588. Either his circumstances had changed or differing views were held as to the scale of his farming activities. William Meeke was more substantial. He is called a butcher in a leet court entry of 1584, but the preamble of his will (June 1602) refers to him as a yeoman. The document shows that he owned property in the town, including *The Cock* inn, and that he was keeping livestock – the latter interest being entirely compatible with his involvement in the meat trade.

Only Hugh Bond, described as both baker and brewer in his burial entry of July 1592, can be shown to have followed two occupations concurrently (the common agent linking both trades would presumably have been yeast). Three of the earlier examples (the mariner-roper, the servant-shipwright and the husbandman-labourer) indicate not dual occupation in the sense of a man pursuing two callings concurrently, but probably show people changing their employment according to circumstances – personal or otherwise. Two more (the shoemaker-merchant and the butcher-yeoman) demonstrate the mixed nature of the local economy for those involved in trade or business – a feature to be discussed later. Attention will now be given to the occupations collected for the period 1601–1650, which do not differ greatly in number and type from those listed above, but which show in the number of people engaged in certain activities a considerable change in the fortunes of the town.

The sum total of occupational and social references for the period covered in Table 18 came to 560 – a number which finished at 471, once the required adjustments had been made. The most noticeable feature of this period is a decline in the sea-going population and a dramatic increase in the number of people involved in agriculture. No fewer than fifty-seven husbandmen are recorded, as well as twenty-one yeomen. There are risks in classifying the latter term as an agricultural one, because it was sometimes used of artisans and tradesmen in the lower to middling ranks of society (especially in urban environments).[18] However, in Lowestoft, 90% of all the references to yeomen throughout the whole period of study describe men who had a connection with agriculture.

The dramatic rise in the number of people working the land was due in some

---

[17] He may well have come ashore and found employment because of advancing years. The practice was common among Lowestoft fishermen even during the twentieth century.

[18] Reed, 'Ipswich', p. 44.

Table 18. *Occupations, 1601–1650*

Category	Occupations and the number of people involved	Total	% of the whole
Maritime (at sea)	Boatman (1) Fisherman (10) Sailor (54)	65	13.8
Maritime (on land)	Boatwright (1) Cooper (11) Hoop-maker (1) Shipwright (6) Ship's carpenter (2)	21	4.5
Agriculture	Husbandman (57) Neatherd (1) Ploughwright (1) Yeoman (21)	80	17.0
Retail & Distribution	Draper (3) Grocer (2) Merchant (10)	15	3.2
Food & Drink production	Baker (10) Brewer (13) Butcher (8) Miller (12)	43	9.1
Leather Trades	Cobbler (3) Cordwainer (9) Currier (3) Glover (5) Knacker (1) Shoemaker (9) Tanner (6) Tawer (3)	39	8.3
Clothing	Hatter (2) Tailor (24)	26	5.5
Textiles	Linen weaver (2) Shearman (1) Weaver (18)	21	4.5
Building	Carpenter (8) Glazier (1) House carpenter (1) Housewright (1) Joiner (2) Mason (9) Reeder (1) Sawyer (1) Thatcher (6)	30	6.4
Metalwork	Blacksmith (13) Smith (5) Tinker (3)	21	4.5
Professional & Services	Alehouse keeper (15) Barber (2) Innkeeper (5) Minister (5) Preacher (1) Schoolmaster (3) Scrivener (4) Surgeon (1) Victualler (1)	37	7.8
Miscellaneous	Chimneysweep (1) Fiddler (1) Flag-graver (1) Firr-maker (1) Gunner (1) Hair-weaver (1) Pedlar (3) Wheelwright (1)	10	2.1
		408	
Gentry	Gentleman (24)	24	5.1
Labourer	Labourer (32)	32	6.8
Servant	Maidservant (2) Servant (5: 3 male, 2 female)	7	1.5
15 categories	65 occupations	**471**	

measure to the decline of the fishing industry, which underwent a period of difficulty during the first half of the seventeenth century.[19] It is no coincidence that the number of seafarers shows a marked fall from the total recorded for 1561–1600 (about 32%), and it is possible that some men changed their way of earning a living from maritime pursuits to tilling the soil. There was ample opportunity for growing crops on a small scale in the parish, and the dividing line between farming and fishing in coastal areas often tended to be blurred, with people moving from one to the other as need dictated.[20] The increase in the number of husbandmen from six to fifty-seven, and of yeomen from one to twenty-one, cannot be wholly accounted for by the fall in the numbers of seafarers from ninety-six to sixty-five, but it does illustrate an overall trend – something which is also detectable in the higher number

[19] The town must also have had a demographic problem at this time, because it lost over 400 of its inhabitants in the two plague outbreaks of 1603 and 1635.

[20] B. M. Short, 'The South-East: Kent, Surrey and Sussex', in *Agrarian History*, v, i (Cambridge, 1984) 307.

of men involved in metalwork (farm implements requiring more iron-based fabrication than either fishing vessels or gear) and in brewing. Continuing the theme of the decline of fishing (which will be fully dealt with in Chapter 8), it is also noticeable that the number of merchants recorded fell from twenty-two to ten, and the number with maritime interests dropped from seventeen to six.

There is no definite way of accounting for the very obvious decrease in the number of servants employed, though the feature was probably partly due to the fact that there were fewer merchants and substantial mariners to give such people employment. Another clue to their apparent decline during this period may perhaps lie in the attitude of the ministers and parish clerks of the first half of the seventeenth century when it came to acknowledging such people in the registration process, because there is only one reference to be found in the registers, as opposed to forty-six for the previous period. Or perhaps servants began to become more itinerant in their movements, spending less time with one particular employer in a given place and therefore having less opportunity to make an impact on parish registers.[21] There are no such problems of interpretation with the occupation of tailor, which remained predominant in the Clothing category, though that of butcher dropped from twenty-seven in number to eight in the Food & Drink section, giving way in order of importance to baker, brewer and miller. Again, this decline in numbers may have partly resulted from the retraction in the fishing industry, in that fewer boats required to be provisioned for sea voyages.

Apart from certain differences caused by maritime troubles, the overall trade structure remained much the same as it had been in the previous period. A comparison of both tables shows a diversity of pursuits, with a number of the groupings probably serving the needs of a wider area than the town itself. The categories of Retail & Distribution, Food & Drink, Leather Trades, Clothing and Textiles (and even Metalworking) must have catered for the requirements of the rural hinterland as well as for those of the town itself. The weekly Wednesday market would have been the focal point for commercial activity, the time when trading was at its busiest, but it is likely that people from the surrounding parishes were also drawn into the town at other times, as need dictated and opportunity offered.

A small minority of occupations in Table 18 may appear to have some ambiguity or obscurity about them. The ship's carpenters, for instance, may not have been permanent crew members in the normally accepted sense of the term, but worked on shore as shipwrights.[22] Similarly, there may have been linen weavers among the eighteen textile workers classified as 'weavers', because Lowestoft had no strong tradition of manufacturing woollen cloth. On the other hand, hemp was grown both in the town itself and in the surrounding area, and it is possible that the increased number of weavers

[21] Kussmaul, *Servants*, p. 51. Most servants (76%), from the seventeenth to the nineteenth centuries, are said to have worked only their contractual year with an employer before moving on to a new one.

[22] One of them, John Herne, drowned after falling overboard from a local herring boat in November 1610. The discovery of his body, and that of a Scotsman drowned in the same incident, is recorded in the Kirkley and Pakefield water leet of 27 December 1610. Herne had 5s 6d in his purse when he was washed ashore. See SRO(L), 194/B1/20, p. 163.

recorded (especially if linen was being made) was the result of fishing families turning to another trade. Fishermen often had spinning wheels with which to produce their own twine for making nets and lines, so it is conceivable that some of them might have switched to producing textiles.[23] The hoop-maker is unequivocal. He would have earned his living by making the ash-wood bands which reinforced casks and barrels.

A particular aspect of local topography is revealed in two of the occupations listed: while 'reeder' is synonymous for 'thatcher', it may also imply that the man actually harvested the material as well as worked with it. Reed beds were abundant around the edges of 'The Fresh Water', or Lake Lothing, and this locality is also where the flag-graver made his living. He was a digger of peat, to be used as fuel, and the extent of both Lake Lothing itself and the nearby broad at Oulton had, over the years, been considerably increased by the digging of peat from around the edges. Rather more esoteric is the gunner (an occupation which also features in Table 17), who was employed by the Crown to supervise the batteries which had been set up in 1539 to strengthen local coastal defences. The solitary wheelwright was placed in the Miscellaneous section because his skills would have been required for the manufacture and repair of carts used in both agriculture and transportation. And the hair weaver is to be found there because the fabric he produced would not have been a textile intended for clothing, being used instead for making sieves and for covering heating-vents in the floors of malt-houses.[24]

The appearance of fifteen alehouse keepers in the Professional & Services category is an interesting development, since their presence in the statistics is the result of their being indicted at the annual Leet Court for selling beer by unlawful measure on their premises (short measure, of course!). This occurred for just a few years either side of 1620, when there was either a particular problem in town or the authorities of the time were more rigorous in dealing with a perennial state of affairs.[25] Of the fifteen offenders, nine had other, identifiable interests: two were bakers, two butchers, one was a labourer, two were husbandman and two yeomen. This may mean that lesser places of refreshment (lesser, that is, than the town's recognised inns) were run as subsidiary interests to the owners' main lines of business. If this were the case, the practice would match the situation detected elsewhere during the first half of the seventeenth century.[26] What is not known about these alehouse keepers is whether or not they were brewing on the premises – but it is likely that some of them were. The two bakers would have used yeast as part of their stock in trade, while the husbandmen and yeomen may well have produced malt from the barley which they grew on their holdings.

---

[23] For a detailed account of the East Anglian linen manufacture generally, see N. Evans, *The East Anglian Linen Industry* (Aldershot and Brookfield, Vermont, 1985).

[24] P. Mathias, *The Brewing Industry in England, 1700–1820* (Cambridge, 1959), p. 411. The vents were covered with hair-cloth in order to decrease floor temperature and produce lighter-coloured malt.

[25] SRO(L), 194/A10/5.

[26] Hipkin, 'Rye', p. 215. In the Sussex town, 'tippling houses' were usually run as a secondary interest.

Apart from the nine alehouse keepers who can be identified as belonging to other employment groups, there are a further ten examples of dual occupations (in the broadest sense of the term) between 1600 and 1650 – though only one of them shows a man working in substantially different spheres at the same time. This was William Sewter, whose burial entry in August 1629 refers to him as a tanner, but whose will preamble of the same month calls him a husbandman. Another man, named John Browne, is listed in the registers as both baker and brewer (a combination which occurred once in the previous period), but as there is a five-year gap between the two references he may not have practised both trades concurrently. William Meeke, butcher and yeoman-farmer, appeared in the previous listings; but while he was certainly involved in both activities at the same time, there is obviously quite a close connection between raising livestock and slaughtering it for retail.

The business interests of John Knights show much more of a contrast. He is referred to as an inn-holder in the preamble of his will (July 1631), but the document gives no evidence of such employment. What it shows is that he owned a domestic messuage in Southwold, which incorporated both salt-houses and fish-curing premises. Diversity is also revealed in the will and probate inventory of William Harrison (June and September 1603, respectively). He is described as a merchant both in the will and in his burial entry, but the inventory shows clearly that he was carrying on a retail trade mainly in drapery, with groceries thrown in for good measure. Simon Fifield was another man of mixed interests. As with Derick Harman, previously, he is referred to as both shoemaker and merchant. The former title is found in his burial entry of December 1631, but his will (November 1630) classes him as the latter and shows that he owned fishing boats and curing-houses.

Two other people who may have followed varied activities, or who had changed occupations at some stage, are Richard Davye and Francis Linsy. The former is described as a labourer in his wife's burial entry in April 1602, but he is termed husbandman thirty-three years later, in January 1635, when he himself was laid to rest. The latter is called an innkeeper in a Half-hundred Court minute of October 1605, but by the time he died in November 1613 he was a husbandman.[27] Wyllyam Burges, who died in June 1601, was both a tanner and a tawer – trades connected with leather, albeit of a differing nature – while John Browne (not the man mentioned two paragraphs above) earned his keep from digging peat and bundling faggot-wood.[28] His wife's burial entry in February 1605 places him in the former occupation (he was the flag-graver referred to earlier), but a Half-hundred Court minute of October 1608 describes him as a 'firrmaker'.[29] He was obviously a labourer of some kind who supplied local people

---

[27] SRO(L), 194/C1/1, p. 312. He was fined 4d for not sufficiently maintaining the road surface outside his house. He may well have combined keeping an alehouse with farming activity.

[28] Tanning turned cowhides into heavy-duty leather, used mainly for footwear, saddlery and harness; tawing converted different kinds of animal skins (e.g. from horses, sheep, pigs, deer and even dogs) into lighter leather for making gloves, belts, soft jerkins etc.

[29] He was fined 4d for depositing muck in Lowestoft High Street. The first element of 'firrmaker' is almost certainly a variant of *furze*, as gorse was cut and bundled for firing bread ovens.

with fuel from the marshy parts of the parish and from the gorse and thorns which grew on the heathland areas.

For the period 1651–1700, the occupational and social designations collected added up to a total of 480 – a figure which converted to 427 once the necessary omissions had been made. There was a considerable fall in the number of parish register references as little occupational detail was recorded during the 1680s and 90s, a shortcoming due to the clerk of the time not continuing the tradition established by so many of his predecessors. However, this did not affect the weighting of individual categories because the lack of information was spread across the whole range of the town's male population. Table 19 presents the data and, as was the case with the previous one, it shows marked changes in the town's circumstances.

The most striking feature is the great increase in the number of seafarers compared with the previous fifty-year period and the marked decline in the number of men involved in agriculture. This was partly the result of fifty fishermen being named in the parish tithe accounts and forty-one seamen being similarly identified in a late seventeenth-century woollen burials register.[30] But there are economic factors to be considered, too. The fishing industry underwent a marked recovery during the second half of the seventeenth century, and the town's maritime life was aided further by being freed from the domination of the head-port, Great Yarmouth, during the post-Restoration period. Success in diminishing the adverse influence of a large and powerful neighbour culminated in 1679, when Lowestoft was granted port status, with specified rights of export and import.[31] The steady revival of the town's maritime prosperity thereafter proceeded to manifest itself in as marked a fashion as the period of decline had done earlier: men returned to seafaring in appreciable numbers, some of them no doubt leaving the land to do so – thereby abandoning the way of life which had provided an alternative means of making a living in adverse circumstances.

The mercantile side of Lowestoft's maritime existence also proceeded to flourish during the second half of the seventeenth century, and the increased prosperity can be seen in the recovery and rise in the number of people involved in retailing and distribution compared with the previous fifty-year period. The number of merchants rose noticeably and, of the twenty-seven recorded, sixteen had specific and identifiable maritime interests. The presence of customs officers in the town (the waiters and searchers listed) bears testimony to the importance of seaborne trade, but the general upturn in fortunes was not reflected by a consequent increase in the number of shipwrights and coopers plying their respective trades.

Within the general expansion of maritime activity, a greater variety of sea-based

---

[30] NRO PD 589/3. The Woollen Burials Act of 1678 required that everyone be buried in a woollen shroud, to boost the native textile industry. Records were kept, and anyone wishing to be buried in a linen shroud had to pay a £5 exemption. The wealthier people in Lowestoft (as noted elsewhere) were buried in linen and had the fine paid by relatives or executors, using this as a means of social differentiation.

[31] W. A. Shaw (ed.), *Calendar of Treasury Books*, v, ii (London, 1911), 1219.

Table 19. *Occupations, 1651–1700*

Category	Occupations and the number of people involved	Total	% of the whole
Maritime (at sea)	Boatman (1) Ferryman (1) Fisherman (66) Mariner (48) Pilot (1) Royal Navy (5) Seaman (72)	194	45.4
Maritime (on land)	Blockmaker (1) Boatwright (4) Cooper (5) Lighthouse keeper (1) Roper (2) Sailmaker (1) Ship's carpenter (1) Waiter & searcher (3)	18	4.2
Agriculture	Farmer (1) Husbandman (8) Park keeper (1) Shepherd (1) Yeoman (10)	21	4.9
Retail & Distribution	Draper (1) Grocer (4) Merchant (27) Woolen draper (1)	33	7.7
Food & Drink production	Baker (1) Brewer (7) Butcher (3) Maltster (1) Miller (7) Oatmeal maker (1)	20	4.7
Leather Trades	Cordwainer (4) Corviser (2) Currier (1) Glover (1) Shoemaker (1) Tanner (6)	15	3.5
Clothing	Tailor (9)	9	2.1
Textiles	Linen weaver (1) Weaver (2)	3	0.7
Building	Bricklayer (2) Carpenter (3) Dauber (1) Glazier (4) House carpenter (1) Joiner (3) Mason (5) Painter (1) Plumber (1) Sawyer (5) Thatcher (1)	27	6.3
Metalwork	Blacksmith (6) Smith (1) Tinker (2)	9	2.1
Professional & Services	Apothecary (1) Doctor (2)) Innkeeper (9) Minister (3) Registrar (2) Schoolmaster (2) Scrivener (3) Tapster (1)	23	5.4
Miscellaneous	Carter (1) Chimneysweep (1)	2	0.5
		374	
Gentry	Esquire (1) Gentleman (17)	18	4.2
Labourer	Labourer (10)	10	2.3
Servant	Maidservant (1) Servant (24: 8 male, 16 female)	25	5.8
15 categories	68 occupations	**427**	

occupations appeared. The boatman and ferryman would have brought goods to land in small craft, offloading cargoes from the larger vessels that lay at anchor offshore, while the pilot (a Trinity House appointment) would have navigated safe passage through the shoals for the increasing number of trading vessels. Shore-based occupations were not as numerous as in the previous period (largely owing to a fall in the number of coopers recorded), but there was greater variety. A blockmaker and sailmaker appear for the first time, while the presence of a lighthouse keeper was the result of Trinity House erecting a stone-built lighthouse on the north cliff in 1676.

The maltster who appears may represent an expansion in output, because the malting of barley had always been previously carried out by certain of the merchants or by the brewers themselves. Generally speaking, the production of food and drink seems to have declined overall, as does the manufacture of clothing, textiles and leather – a development possibly indicating that the town was becoming less of a provider of goods and services for the surrounding area and more of a specialist maritime community. Labourers had also declined in numbers, which suggests a less wide-ranging economy, while servants had increased – perhaps suggesting that greater wealth now existed to employ more of them. Finally, while building trades experienced a drop in overall numbers of carpenters, masons and thatchers, they also saw an increase in the number of glaziers, while a bricklayer, a painter and a plumber are recorded for the first time.[32] So is a plasterer (dauber). The impression formed is of a shift from traditional timber-framed and thatched houses to ones built of brick and with tiled roofs, a trend that was in keeping with developments of the time.

As far as dual occupations are concerned, there are only three examples detectable in the period and two of them of them seem to be genuine examples of men involved in two trades at the same time. Christopher Swift was both fishermen and weaver. His will of May 1670 gives him the former title; his burial entry in December the same year refers to him by the latter. There is no other direct evidence of his involvement with textiles, but he probably combined linen-weaving with his maritime activities – by-employment that was not unknown along the East Coast.[33] Then there was Thomas Pacy, who is termed a brewer in the will of Henry Ward of Stepney, in June 1677, but who also styled himself a yeoman and certainly had land in the parish that he worked. Finally, Mathew Ottmer is referred to as a fisherman in the will of fellow-mariner Robert Sowell, in May 1666, but his own will of March 1673 states that he was a maltster. Presumably, he had come ashore at some point and changed occupations.

Altogether, 774 references were collected for the last fifty-year period – a number which was reduced to 592 after previously outlined adjustments had been made. As in the previous period, seafarers are seen to dominate the reckoning, with the parish tithe accounts contributing the names of large numbers of fishermen and the registers doing the same for mariners. An interesting feature to emerge from the documentation this time, however, is less of an overlap between the two occupations. About 70% of the fishermen recorded were not classified elsewhere as mariners and about 60% of the mariners were similarly not identified as fishermen. This suggests that fishing and maritime trade had become more separated in nature, with less dual use of vessels and more specific shipbuilding for the task required. Further evidence of the upturn in maritime fortunes may be seen in the fact that eighteen of the twenty-two merchants listed had an interest in seaborne activity, while the increased presence of customs officers reflects growth in the amount of inward and outward trade.

Against this background of maritime expansion, clothing and textiles had diminished even further in importance from the previous period – to the point where they really had very little significance in the town's pattern of employment.

---

[32] The term 'bricklayer' is misleading, because the two men concerned (John Patteridge and Thomas Walsby) manufactured bricks. They probably possessed building skills too, but were not simply bricklayers in today's sense of the word. The plumber would have been mainly employed in making lead channelling for window-glazing.

[33] Evans, *Linen Industry*, p. 65. In particular, the writer draws attention to the production of woollen stockings in East Anglian fishing communities. Also, see J. Thirsk, 'The Farming Regions of England', in *Agrarian History*, iv, 46.

Table 20. *Occupations, 1701–1750*

Category	Occupations and the number of people involved	Total	% of the whole
Maritime (at sea)	Fisherman (150) Keelman (1) Mariner (100) Pilot (4) Royal Navy (4) Sailor (6) Seaman (4)	269	45.4
Maritime (on land)	Blockmaker (1) Boatwright (2) Cooper (9) Customs officer (4) Excise gager (4) Lighthouse keeper (1) Sailmaker (2) Shipwright (1) Waiter & searcher (4)	28	4.7
Agriculture	Farmer (2) Gardener (3) Husbandman (14) Yeoman (13)	32	5.4
Retail & Distribution	Draper (1) Grocer (4) Haberdasher (1) Merchant (22)	28	4.7
Food & Drink production	Baker (5) Brewer (5) Butcher (3) Maltster (3) Miller (5) Millwright (1)	22	3.7
Leather Trades	Collar maker (1) Cordwainer (19) Glover (2) Knacker (1) Shoemaker (5) Tanner (1) Tawner (5)	34	5.7
Clothing	Knitter (1) Tailor (5)	6	1.0
Textiles	Woolwomber (1)	1	0.2
Building	Bricklayer (4) Brickman (2) Brickstriker (3) Carpenter (6) Glazier (4) Floor mender (1) House carpenter (2) Joiner (4) Mason (7) Sawyer (1)	34	5.7
Metalwork	Blacksmith (6) Locksmith (1) Smith (1) Tinker (1)	9	1.5
Professional & Services	Apothecary (1) Arrerer (1) Attorney (1) Barber (2) Civil Law reader (1) Doctor (1) Innkeeper (12) Midwife (3) Minister (3) Nurse (1) School dame (1) Schoolmaster (4) Scrivener (1) Surgeon (2) Town Clerk (1) Victualler (1)	36	6.1
Miscellaneous	Carter (9) Chimneysweep (1) Fiddler (1) Warrener (1) Wheelwright (1)	13	2.2
		512	
Gentry	Esquire (1) Gentleman (10)	11	1.8
Labourer	Labourer (41)	41	6.9
Servant	Maidservant (6) Servant (22: 15 male, 7 female)	28	4.7
15 categories	80 occupations	**592**	

Food and drink production remained at about the previous level, though the presence of a millwright in Table 20 is interesting because it suggests a sufficiency of work in Lowestoft (the town had at least two to three windmills operating at this time) and the surrounding area for a man to make his living from construction and maintenance. An increase in farming activity also seems to have been taking place during the first half of the eighteenth century, in the sense that more people seem to have become involved in agriculture than was the case in the previous fifty-year period. And this, added to the buoyancy of maritime enterprise, with greater quantities of goods having to be moved, is almost certainly the reason for the marked increase in the number of both carters and labourers (with the latter proliferating especially after 1730).

Another obvious increase in commercial enterprise can be seen in the shoemaking trade, with the number of craftsmen involved going up from seven to twenty-four. This was undoubtedly partly due to the increase in Lowestoft's population at the time, as noted in the previous chapter, but there must also have been a demand for work boots in certain different spheres of employment – especially the leather sea-boots worn by mariners and fishermen.[34] A less dramatic increase in the building trades is also detectable, with the addition of brickstrikers to the category suggesting that production of bricks was on the increase in order to meet the demand either for new houses or for re-styled facades.[35]

The last change worthy of comment is the increase in the variety of what may be termed professional people living in the town, together with greater numbers of people involved in the provision of certain services. This is noticeable in the sphere of education and particularly in that of medical provision (especially if the two barbers are included). The midwives and the nurse, whose activities were recognised in their registration details, were certainly not of the 'neighbourhood crone' variety of practitioner. They were women from substantial families, who were performing necessary relieving work during their respective widowhoods and may also have done this while their husbands were alive.

When it comes to dual occupations, there are thirteen recorded examples to be found, three of whom were former mariners who had given up a sea-going career at some stage and become merchants (John Brame, Benjamin Ibrook and Thomas Manning). In a completely different sphere, John Evans is found. There are thirty-seven surviving wills from between 1686 and 1705 that were drawn up by him; he kept the overseers' accounts in an exemplary hand during the late seventeenth and early eighteenth centuries; and he also ran a writing-school in the town. He seems, therefore, to have been a scrivener of some kind, but his burial entry in January 1706 calls him 'Town Clerk', which suggests that municipal business was a notable part of his activities. His literacy was obviously the common factor in his interests.

In the lower ranks of society Joseph Sterry is to be found. The preamble to his will in October 1717 gives him the title of yeoman, but his burial record in February 1723 reduces him to mere gardener. The size and value of his estate suggests that the parish register gives the correct assessment of his status and that Sterry was being grandified either by himself or the person responsible for drawing up the will.[36] When William Shank made his will in December 1710, he was sixty-six years of age and a mariner of some kind. When he died in May 1723, he was a carter. There was no retirement in those days, so he had come ashore at some stage – presumably when the rigours of life at sea became too much to bear. Richard Ward was land-

---

[34] It is possible that the first recorded presence of a knitter in town, at this time, was partly due to maritime industries, in that the person concerned may have been producing socks to be worn in sea-boots.

[35] Brickstrikers made bricks from the excavated loam. The *strike* was a piece of wood used to scrape surplus material from the top of the mould, prior to the brick being removed for drying and firing.

[36] M. Spufford, *Contrasting Communities* (Cambridge, 1974), p. 37, has an interesting comment to make regarding occupational definitions in wills in rural Cambridgeshire: 'A man's description of himself as a 'yeoman' may be suspect and include an element of wishful thinking; his neighbours, when they draw up his inventory, are unlikely to make the same mistake.' No inventory for Sterry has survived, but the parish clerk probably reveals the truth of his situation.

based. His burial entry in July 1728 terms him a labourer, but his will of April 1724 refers to him as a woolcomber and his inventory of March 1729 shows that he (or perhaps his wife) was also running a haberdashery and novelty goods business. Besides the inevitable ribbons, buttons, needles, pins and thimbles, spectacles are also mentioned, along with horn books, crystal balls and nutcrackers. He may also have been weaving hair-cloth, because three bushels of hair were itemised among the contents of the garret. Simon Ling is referred to as a knacker in both the preamble of his will (June 1722) and in his burial entry in the parish registers (July 1724), whereas an apprenticeship record of 1702 calls him a collarmaker.[37] There is no contradiction inherent in the two titles: he obviously made harness and tack.

The five examples of men who had more than one occupation at the same time also show interesting variety. John Colby was listed as both apothecary and merchant in his burial entry of September 1719, though his inventory (drawn up in December of that year) shows no evidence of the former occupation. That is not to say that he did not practise it, and the presence of a fishing-boat, various nets and curing premises among the items listed in the document suggests that he was yet another merchant with mixed interests. Also to be found in the upper levels of local society is John Peach. The tithe accounts show him to have been one of the more substantial farmers in the parish, but his burial entry of December 1749 designates him as a brewer – a combination of activities noted with Thomas Pacy in the previous fifty-year period. John Day was one of the more important innkeepers in the town, and his burial registration of April 1748 records this occupation. But it also reveals that he functioned as a barber, thereby providing a range of services in his hostelry.

William Bull, at seventy years of age, was another innkeeper with more than one string to his bow. His establishment was of a lesser nature than Day's and he also carried on a carting business at the same time, if his burial entry of January 1739 is to be believed. William Salter was a carrier, too, according to the burial register information (December 1729), whereas his inventory of January 1730 suggests that he was also a small farmer. Various entries in the tithe accounts confirm that the latter designation is accurate and that he worked small plots of land in and around the town and kept a few cows. Farming and carting often went hand in hand, so it should come as no surprise to find a combination of these activities.

Changes in emphasis

The most notable feature of the whole occupational structure is the overall dominance of maritime activity (see Table 21), especially after the town was granted port status in 1679. The middle of the seventeenth century seems to have been a watershed, marking the point at which fishing and seaborne trade began to assume increasing importance and the production of food, textiles, clothing and metalware started to decline. It is not suggested that the success of one sphere had an adverse effect on certain types of

---

[37] SRO(L), 01/13/1/3, p. 9. The volume in question is one which contains settlement details as well.

Table 21. *Occupations, 1561–1750*

Category	Occupations and the number of people involved	Total	% of the whole
Maritime (at sea)	Boatman (2) Ferryman (1) Fisherman (227) Keelman (1) Mariner (191) Pilot (5) Royal Navy (9) Sailor (112) Seaman (76)	624	31.1
Maritime (on land)	Blockmaker (2) Boatwright (2) Boatwright (5) Cooper (39) Customs officer (4) Excise gager (4) Hook-maker (1) Hoop-maker (2) Lighthouse keeper (2) Roper (5) Sailmaker (3) Ship's carpenter (3) Shipwright (19) Waiter & searcher (7)	98	4.9
Agriculture	Farmer (3) Gardener (3) Husbandman (85) Neatherd (4) Park keeper (1) Ploughwright (1) Shepherd (2) Yeoman (45)	144	7.2
Retail & Distribution	Draper (10) Fishmonger (1) Goldsmith (1) Grocer (10) Haberdasher (1) Merchant (81) Merchant tailor (1) Woolen draper (1)	106	5.3
Food & Drink production	Baker (24) Brewer (30) Butcher (41) Maltster (4) Miller (34) Oatmeal maker (1) Millwright (1)	136	6.8
Leather Trades	Cobbler (4) Collar-maker (1) Cordwainer (37) Corviser (2) Currier (6) Glover (11) Knacker (4) Shoemaker (20) Tanner (16) Tawner (9)	110	5.5
Clothing	Hatter (3) Knitter (1) Tailor (74)	78	3.9
Textiles	Dyer (1) Liner weaver (3) Shearman (1) Weaver (29) Woolwomber (1)	35	1.7
Building	Bricklayer (6) Brickman (2) Brickstriker (3) Carpenter (25) Dauber (1) Floor mender (1) Glazier (10) House carpenter (4) Housewright (1) Joiner (13) Mason (32) Painter (1) Plimber (1) Reeder (1) Sawyer (9) Thatcher (9)	119	5.9
Metalwork	Blacksmith (28) Locksmith (1) Pewterer (1) Smith (17) Tinker (8)	55	2.7
Professional & Services	Alehouse keeper (15) Apothecary (2) Arrerer (1) Attorney (1) Barber (8) Civil Law reader (1) Doctor (3) Innkeeper (29) Midwife (3) Minister (18) Nurse (2) Preacher (1) Proctor (2) Registrar (2) School dame (1) Schoolmaster (10) Scrivener (9) Surgeon (4) Tapster (1) Town Clerk (1) Victualler (3)	117	5.8
Miscellaneous	Carter (14) Chimneysweep (4) Fiddler (2) Flag-graver (1) Firr-maker (1) Fletcher (1) Gunner (2) Hair-weaver (1) Ostler (1) Pedlar (3) Singing man (1) Warrener (1) Wheelwright (2)	34	1.7
		1656	
Gentry	Esquire (2) Gentleman (63)	65	3.2
Labourer	Labourer (119)	119	5.9
Servant	Maidservant (15) Servant (150: 105 male, 45 female)	165	8.2
15 categories	125 occupations	**2005**	

manufacturing, because it might be argued that increased maritime prosperity should have served to stimulate a growth in the production of food and drink – if only to provision the increased number of vessels in operation.[38] What it probably reveals is that Lowestoft, after about the middle of the seventeenth century, began to develop increasing maritime specialisation and functioned less as a provider of goods and services for the neighbourhood.[39] The demise of the local textile industry is particularly noticeable, and it may have been partly the result of events which occurred some distance from the town. The city of Norwich experienced an economic boom during the seventeenth century, especially in the woollen textiles trade (the so-called 'new draperies'),[40] and it is possible that some of Lowestoft's craftsmen were drawn to the city. It was, after all, situated less than thirty miles away.

Another factor to be considered with regard to the manufacture of clothing and also to food and drink production is that the decline may not have been as marked as the figures suggest. Scrutiny of a whole range of records suggests that, instead of there being considerable numbers of tailors, bakers, brewers and butchers operating on their own, the businesses became concentrated in the hands of a relatively small number of men, who acted as employers of suitably skilled operatives. Little probate material for bakers has survived, but the wills and inventories which exist for brewers show that, by the end of the seventeenth century and the beginning of the eighteenth, some of them were very substantial men indeed.[41] And the main butchers in the town, the Mewse family, were also comfortably off. Tailors are a little more problematical to assess. The five late sixteenth- and early seventeenth-century wills which are extant do not suggest great wealth, but four of the men in question owned the houses in which they lived and three of them were able to make modest monetary bequests to their children. Two late seventeenth-century wills show that one man owned his house, but not the other – and while both of them left money to their children, the sums are not specified.

Given the emphasis on its maritime activities, it is not perhaps surprising that, in terms of the basic structure of occupational groupings, Lowestoft does not conform to accepted patterns of urban identification. It has been said that about 75% of the workforce in pre-industrial towns was employed in textiles, clothing, leather crafts, metalworking, building and food and drink production.[42] During none of the four individual sub-periods reviewed in this chapter did these particular occupations

---

[38] Ale and beer production did not diminish in volume in Lowestoft, but the number of people involved in brewing did. During the first half of the eighteenth century particularly, the industry became concentrated in the hands of a few powerful and wealthy operators. Nationally, the number of brewers is said to have risen by 50% at this time. See D. C. Coleman, *The Economy of England, 1450–1750* (Oxford, 1977), p. 120.

[39] This aspect of a small town's function is noted in Jack, *Tudor and Stuart Towns*, p. 66.

[40] J. T. Evans, *Seventeenth Century Norwich* (Oxford, 1979), pp. 16 and 19.

[41] Coe Arnold and John Durrant, for instance, were considerable property holders in the town, owning real estate that was well in excess of their manufacturing needs and that was of different types.

[42] Clarkson, *Pre-Industrial Economy*, p. 80. Coleman, *Economy of England*, p. 72, gives much the same kind of breakdown, relating to Coventry, Northampton, Norwich and Leicester during the 1520s.

constitute more than 38% (and this at a time of maritime depression), and taken over the whole spread of 190 years they stand at just over 26%. Another view is that, in large and medium-sized towns, food and drink production, the making of clothing and footwear, the building trades, the manufacture of household necessaries and retailing and distribution collectively involved about 60–70% of all the people employed.[43] Lowestoft went no higher than 37% in any of the four sub-periods investigated, while for the whole time-span the proportion was just under 30%. Nor does the town fit in with the opinion expressed that, during the sixteenth and seventeenth centuries, the victualling, clothing and building trades employed anything between 23% and 40% of the available labour in urban centres.[44] It went no higher than about 22% in the later sixteenth century to as low as 13% by the end of the seventeenth. There is, however, evidence of the growth, seen nationally, in the production and consumption of household and luxury goods from about 1550 onwards.[45] Glovers, hatters, drapers and grocers all suggest a retail trade in consumer items.

In spite of comparatively low numbers of men involved in what are supposedly classic urban trades, Lowestoft still had a respectable number of craftsmen among its working population. Using all the sources available, the proportion was one man in four between 1561 and 1600, one in three between 1601 and 1650, and one in six between 1651 and 1700 and between 1701 and 1750. Again, the maritime factor can be seen as influential: the highest ratio of craftsmen is to be found in the first half of the seventeenth century, when fishing and overseas trade were in decline, and lowest in the two sub-periods when enterprises connected with the sea were flourishing. This close association with the maritime environment probably identifies Lowestoft as a specialist town of a kind which has been previously recognised.[46] One thing is certain. A lot more work needs to be done on such communities before wide-ranging claims concerning urban typicality can be made.

Dual occupation or mixed economy?

In attempting to make a pertinent comment on the variable nature of occupation in Lowestoft between 1561 and 1750, it is important to define terms. Genuine dual occupation can only really be taken to mean the carrying-on of two different trades concurrently, not the following of different lines of work at different times in an individual lifespan. The evidence which exists for either of these situations is, in any

---

[43] Clay, *Economic Expansion*, i, 195. Leicester, Norwich, Exeter and York are used as examples at varying points during the sixteenth and seventeenth centuries.

[44] N. Goose, 'English Pre-Industrial Urban Economies', *UHY* 9 (1982), 24, cites the former percentages relating to work carried out on Colchester and Reading. Hoskins, 'Provincial Towns', in *Provincial England*, p. 80, concluded that 35%–40% of the workforce would have been similarly involved 'in any provincial town with the rudiments of an urban character'.

[45] C. Muldrew, *The Economy of Obligation* (London and New York, 1998), pp. 18–21.

[46] Patten, *English Towns*, p. 173. The writer claims that what specialised towns there were generally included shipbuilding and fishing among their occupations.

case, slender. Figures produced for the four sub-periods reviewed in the previous section show that there were only forty-one definite instances of a man being formally recorded by one means or another as having two different occupations in his lifetime (the combination of mariner and fisherman excepted, because of the overlap between maritime pursuits) – which is a mere 2% of the overall number of the 2,005 people documented.

Of those forty-one, only seventeen can conclusively be proved to have carried on two occupations at the same time – and nine of them were alehouse keepers who featured in the leet court minutes around about 1620. It may well have been the case that alehouse-keeping was a secondary occupation in Lowestoft across much, if not all, of the period under review, but one that manifested itself clearly only at this one particular time. If the alehouse keepers are removed from the reckoning, then only these eight men remain as examples of positive, documented, concurrent, dual occupation: Hugh Bond, baker and brewer (ob. 1592), William Sewter, husbandman and tanner (ob. 1629), Christopher Swift, fishermen and weaver (ob. 1670), Thomas Pacy, yeoman and brewer (ob. 1680), John Colby, apothecary and merchant (ob. 1719), William Bull, innkeeper and carter (ob. 1739), John Day, innkeeper and barber (ob. 1748) and John Peach, yeoman and brewer (ob. 1749).

It is possible, of course, that there was more of the practice than the various sources suggest, but in the absence of firm evidence the figures have to be taken as they stand. There is, in any case, a matter of interpretation to be considered when dealing with dual (or multiple) occupation. Taking some typical Lowestoft employment situations, for instance, it is pertinent to ask the following questions. Was the labourer who had an involvement in both agricultural and building trades a man of the land or a construction worker? Or was he simply someone who could turn his hand to more than one skill as time and necessity dictated? Was the fisherman who hired and cultivated a quarter-acre yard in some part of town a seafarer or small farmer? Or did his agricultural activities simply act as a supplement to the living made on the waves? Was the husbandman who used his horse and cart to provide conveyance for hire a farmer or a carrier? Or was he merely using constituents of his primary calling to earn extra money as opportunity offered? And was the grocer or merchant who had an involvement in fishing, fish-curing and brewing skilled in all of these trades, or just a man who had diverse business interests?

In the end, it all comes down to the interpretation of what 'dual occupation' or 'multiple occupation' really means – and that may differ from commentator to commentator. What Lowestoft shows, especially in the surviving probate material, is evidence of a mixed economy at all levels of society, not just among the merchants and trading classes.[47] The middle of the seventeenth century saw arguments from

---

[47] Among the writers who have remarked on the economic versatility of the two latter groups are Vanessa Parker and Alan Metters (King's Lynn) and Alan Dyer (Worcester). See Parker, *King's Lynn*, p. 43; G. A. Metters, 'The Rulers and Merchants of King's Lynn in the Early Seventeenth Century' (unpub PhD thesis, University of East Anglia, 1982), p. 302; and Dyer, *Worcester*, pp. 86–7. There are also references to urban economic diversification among industrial producers in Clay, *Economic Expansion*, ii, 100.

contemporary pamphleteers in favour of the diversification of trade nationally, so that England no longer relied so heavily on the export of cloth and draperies and would find greater economic strength in a larger range of goods for foreign consumption.[48] Perhaps such writers saw the versatility and strength of local economies and felt able to predict the success of such diversity if it were developed on a far larger scale and applied to the matter of national overseas trade.

It may well be that the terms 'dual occupation' and 'multiple occupation' should not be used too readily, because they perhaps suggest specific skills and training in more than one trade (which may not have been the case) and an equal amount of time and attention devoted to each (which may not have been the situation). Perhaps it is more a matter of ascertaining a man's primary occupation and then looking for what else he may have been involved in as subsidiary interests.[49] In Lowestoft, in the lower echelons of society, these latter pursuits probably served to act as a supplement to the income earned from primary occupations – which introduces an element of subsistence into the situation. In the more elevated levels, it was probably more a case of how to use accumulated wealth to the best advantage. In fact, the impression gained from the most substantial merchants and retailers is that their activities were not in any way skills-based on a personal level, but were the result of investment in a range of interests calculated to bring a reasonable return on the capital committed and to spread the risk inherent in having too much money tied up in only one area. Such people thus become identifiable with those businessmen of today who have diverse interests and who may well have entre- preneurial flair in developing new fields, but who nevertheless remain classified by the single title of 'businessmen'.

What does need to be acknowledged in the case of Lowestoft (and perhaps in other cases) is that a proportion of the adult male population was probably involved in farming as some kind of supplement to whatever primary occupations were followed.[50] The only systematic and assessable information as to such practice is to be found in the parish tithe accounts. During the first three decades of the eighteenth century, about ninety men were involved in growing crops or keeping animals on varying scales (not all them necessarily at the same time); of these, some twenty or so were primarily farmers and the other seventy were drawn from a wide cross section of local society. Thus, considering that there were at least 350 families (consisting of parents and children) in the town at this time who are identifiable by the family reconstitution process, plus sixty-five older couples, the proportion of heads of household involved in farming is not large: 22% if all ninety men are considered, 17% if the seventy non-specialists are the ones assessed, and only 5% if

---

[48] C. Wilson, *England's Apprenticeship, 1603–1763* (London, 1965), p. 60; B. E. Supple, *Commercial Crisis and Change in England, 1600–1642* (Cambridge, 1970), p. 223.

[49] See J. F. Pound, 'The Validity of the Freemen's Lists: Some Norwich Evidence', *EHR* 2nd Series 34 (1981), 54 and 59. The writer makes an interesting point about use of this particular source, judging the lists to be a valuable guide to men's primary occupations, but lacking the capacity to indicate what other interests they may have had at some stage during their respective life-spans.

[50] Jack, *Tudor and Stuart Towns*, p. 66. This characteristic is said to be typical of small market towns.

the specialist farmers are those chosen for analysis. Such a comparatively low level of agricultural activity per capita must have at least partly resulted from so much of the male population going to sea for lengthy periods of the year.[51]

In conclusion, no matter what semantic stance is taken by historians on the interpretation of 'dual occupation' or 'multiple occupation', it is probably best to regard the pre-industrial economy in small towns as being of mixed or diverse nature – at the same time, taking account of any specialism that may have existed, such as Lowestoft's maritime pursuits. People at all levels of society were involved in local production and manufacture (especially the merchants, the retailers and tradespeople, and the craftsmen), but with differing commitment in terms of labour, cash investment and financial reward. In Lowestoft the pattern among the labourers, lesser craftsmen and fishermen seems to have been for a man to work at his primary occupation and supplement his earnings from other activities as time and opportunity allowed. Among the more substantial craftsmen, and particularly among the retailers and merchants, it was largely a matter of a man using his money to develop a wider range of interests than the ones he began with. The overall impression gained from a study of the available sources (especially wills and inventories) is one of varied activity spread across the different occupation groups – but the level of interest was probably subordinate to each person's primary occupation. Genuine dual occupation, in the sense of two areas of work carried on concurrently and with an equal amount of time and effort devoted to each, seems to have been rare.

---

[51] About 200 men and boys were employed on fishing vessels, in addition to those working on trading craft, whose numbers cannot be calculated.

Housing, Population and Social Geography

Houses and families, 1618–1725

A summary of Lowestoft's expansion in terms of the number of houses built between 1618 and 1725 was given in Chapter 2.[1] Broadly speaking, eighty-three plots were developed and a total of 153 dwellings constructed, and added to these were a further twenty-nine dwellings which could not be traced in the manor court books, but which had been erected at some point between 1618 and 1725. The total of 182 was then reduced to 170, because of twelve houses which had been removed at various stages. This rise in the number of homes took place against a background of gradual population increase – from around 1,200 or more (it had been 1,500 until the plague epidemic of 1603) up to 1,850 – and it is fair to assume that the buildings were erected to meet the growing demand for living space.

A crude calculation, whereby the total number of new houses built is multiplied by an average household size of 4.75, gives a figure of just over 800 as the number of people who could have been accommodated – which might seem to suggest that the population increase was more than catered for. However, household sizes would have varied considerably and there must have been wide differences in the respective numbers of people occupying the dwellings available. The increasing survival rate of older people (both married and widowed) whose children had grown up would have resulted in a substantial minority of households being below the accepted average size.[2] And if such small *ménages* were established in their own individual dwellings, there would probably have been the need for house-sharing for at least some of the town's inhabitants.

If the 170 dwellings referred to above are added to the 211 houses listed in the 1618 manor roll, a total of 381 is arrived at in which to accommodate Lowestoft's population – to which a further fifteen or more dwellings created at some point by

---

[1] These two years, respectively, have an intact, surviving manor roll and a list of all copyhold premises in the town. These documents, together with the Rev. John Tanner's court baron extracts and the minute books themselves, enabled most of the housing development to be tracked.

[2] Such survival is an increasingly noticeable feature in the family reconstitution material during the late seventeenth and early eighteenth centuries.

Table 22. *Houses and families, 1618–1725*

Year	Number of houses	Number of families	Unmarried people and others
1618	211	270	Not known
1650	248 (+10)	252	Not known
1700	315 (+20)	367	Not known
1725	351 (+30)	458	Not known
1725	**c. 400 dwellings** (subdivisions included)	**458**	

subdivision need to be added, resulting in an overall total approaching 400. Again, applying the multiplier of 4.75 for an average household size to the number of dwellings produces a figure of around 1,900 – which is not a great deal more than the actual population total. However, the point arises again that certain households would have been well below this average number and account has to be taken of the effect this would have had on the available housing stock. The family reconstitution exercise is able to throw light on the matter because it allows an accurate assessment to be reached of the numbers of family units, large and small, living in the town at any one time.[3]

Table 22 presents an outline statement of the number of houses available in the town between 1618 and 1725, as well as the number of families known to have required accommodation. The twenty-nine houses that cannot be accounted for in the court baron material have been rounded up to thirty and split into three units of ten, with each being added cumulatively to the number of recordable dwellings in each of the three timespans assessed. What cannot be calculated is the number of unmarried adults (and even itinerants) requiring shelter – a factor that would have placed extra demand on the housing stock. Even a cursory perusal of the table shows that house-sharing of some kind must have been practised in Lowestoft during the century or more under review, with the least pressure for it detectable between 1618 and 1650 (probably as the result of the combined effect of the plague outbreaks of 1603 and 1635) and the greatest need existing by 1725.

Apart from being an important indicator of the number of copyhold houses in town, the list of such properties drawn up by the Rev. John Tanner in c. 1725 (see page 19) also provides evidence of some houses being subdivided into separate living quarters. This had probably been going on for a long time prior to the third decade of the eighteenth century, but it is not possible to trace any more than about five specific examples, in the court baron records, between 1618 and 1725. Thus, while there are signs of it occurring, it was probably never carried out on a large scale. In

---

[3] Family units are those consisting of parents and children, parents whose children had left home, and widows and widowers living alone. What cannot be inferred from reconstitution material is the number of unmarried people living in town, either on their own or in shared accommodation.

1725, John Tanner noted at least fifteen examples of subdivision, mainly in some of the larger houses on the east side of the High Street, with thirty or more dwellings thereby provided. This means that the 381 houses in Lowestoft at this time (copyhold and freehold) provided about 400 dwelling-spaces – a figure still well short of the number required to accommodate the number of families requiring roofs over their heads.

Surviving probate inventories of both the seventeenth and eighteenth centuries suggest that, in certain cases, people were living in part of a house rather than occupying the whole of it.[4] Unfortunately, there is no way of ascertaining whether this was the result of subdivision, whether the people in question had taken lodgings, or whether they had a 'suite' of rooms in the house of a relative. It has been said that about one family in twenty, during the pre-industrial era, was multi-generational (in other words, there were three generations living under the same roof),[5] but the proportion may have been higher than this in Lowestoft in view of the number of houses available for the number of households requiring accommodation.

It is unfortunate that firm totals cannot be calculated for unmarried people living alone and for those families which do not manifest themselves via entries in the parish registers. If this were possible, a more comprehensive idea of the total number of families and individuals in need of housing could be gained. Yet, even with accommodation being at a premium, as must have been the case for much of the seventeenth century, there were still times when houses stood empty. The manor roll of 1618 lists five such properties, while the Hearth Tax return of 1674 records six dwellings in town which had been unoccupied for a year.[6] The two figures represent 2.4% and 2.1% of the town's housing stock at each respective date, which conforms to a contemporary estimate of 2%–2.5% of all houses in England standing empty.[7]

A particularly interesting aspect of the 1674 Hearth Tax is that the return for Lowestoft, in its printed form, is seriously defective.[8] The number of houses in town is put at 222, which is only eleven more than the total given in the 1618 manor roll. In the light of what is known from the court baron material, it is impossible that there could only have been 222 houses (both assessable and exempt) in the town in 1674. A number in the region of 290–300 is much more likely. The impression of incomplete information is reinforced by the absence in the document of surnames which feature prominently in the parish register, whose bearers were certainly resident in the place and who should have been eligible to be assessed for taxable purposes. The Adams family, the Arnolds, the Buxtons, the Feltons, the Haweses, the Neales, the Pyes, the Spratts and several more are all conspicuous by their absence.

---

[4] There are two instances of such practice for 1601–1650, three for 1651–1700 and five for 1701–1730.

[5] P. Laslett, *The World We Have Lost Further Explored* (London, 1983), p. 92.

[6] S. H. A. Hervey (ed.), *Suffolk in 1674*, SGB, xi (Woodbridge, 1905), 198.

[7] D.V. Glass, 'Two Papers on Gregory King', in Glass and Eversley, *Population in History*, p. 185.

[8] This is a national problem. See C. Husbands, 'Regional Change in a Pre-Industrial Economy: Wealth and Population in England in the Sixteenth and Seventeenth Centuries', *JHG* 13, 4 (1987), 349.

Fifty years later, when John Tanner compiled his list of copyhold properties and owners, 146 of the 225 residential plots recorded had single houses standing on them, sixty-four had two or more dwellings occupying the ground space (whether joined to each other or detached cannot be determined), fourteen had undergone subdivision of a single house, and there was one example of a messuage which had experienced both subdivision and multiple building.[9] Altogether, this produced in excess of 320 homes. The subdivision of houses in urban areas, as a means of accommodating growing populations, is well-established.[10] In Lowestoft's case, it would appear that the housing needs generated by a population increase from about 1,500 people in 1650 to 1,850 or so by 1725 were largely met by the systematic infill of plots within the built-up area and, to a lesser extent, by the subdivision of existing houses.

In any case, a 23% increase in the number of inhabitants over a seventy-five-year period would have posed fewer problems than the population explosions which occurred in some pre-industrial cities.[11] There is no evidence in Lowestoft of labourers' cottages being built anywhere in the parish in order to provide housing for those in the lowest levels of society, and both the manor roll of 1610 and that of 1618 show clearly that the various out-of-town common grazing areas were free from encroachment of the kind observed in other communities.[12] The only one to be used for building was that on the western edge of town – and this development was, in any case, part of the manorially controlled relocation of the town described in Chapter 2.

Owner-occupancy of the housing stock

No listing of houses in the town of Lowestoft showing the residents of individual dwellings (as opposed to the owners) has so far come to light. However, it is still possible to work out a notional rate of owner-occupancy. The impression given in most of the surviving wills, where a single house was bequeathed, is that it was the dwelling of the testator alone. Those people who owned more than one house often referred to tenants when disposing of dwellings other than the one in which they lived, which suggests that much of the rented accommodation in town was available in buildings that certain of the inhabitants owned over and above their immediate needs.

In reaching an estimate of the degree of owner-occupancy in town, certain

[9] The site is now occupied by Nos 43–44, High Street. Substantial timber-framing survives from a house of the second half of the sixteenth century and there are later features that are also of interest.

[10] Dyer, *Worcester*, p. 164.

[11] The population of York, for instance, doubled between 1548 and 1600. See D. M. Palliser, 'A Crisis in English Towns? The Case of York, 1460–1640', *NH* 14 (1978), 113. See also, D. M. Palliser, *Tudor York* (Oxford, 1979), pp. 112–13.

[12] Laslett, *World Further Explored*, p. 97.

adjustments had to be made. Inns were not considered as part of the calculation because of their function in meeting the needs of travellers rather than of inhabitants, and any houses that were subdivided (or appeared as if they may have been) were also ignored. After both of these omissions, the manor roll of 1618 lists 147 people as owning 186 houses, both copyhold and freehold. Twenty-four of them had two or more houses each – a total of sixty-three dwellings. If each of these figures is deducted from the overall reckoning, 123 people are seen to have had one house only belonging to them, in which it is presumed that they (and their families) lived as occupants. If it is presumed further that each of the twenty-four people who owned two houses or more lived in one of them as sole occupant, then 147 dwellings out of 186 had owner-occupation. However, about twenty of these houses were removed from the reckoning because they belonged to owners who seem to have had no connection with the town and may not have lived there. Even so, the revised total of 127 dwellings with owner-occupation is still 68% of the whole – a far higher proportion than that detected in other places.[13]

The Rev. John Tanner's listing of copyhold properties produces a total of about 323 homes, which constituted 85% of the town's housing stock. After inns and subdivided dwellings have been omitted, the figure is reduced to 301. Of this number, eighty-six are identifiable as the only property belonging to a particular individual and the other 215 were distributed among seventy-nine different people. By adopting the line of reasoning adopted in the previous paragraph, whereby the owners of one house only are regarded as its occupants, and whereby those people who possessed two houses or more are reckoned to have lived in one of them, 165 houses are found to have had owner-occupation – which is 55% of the number under consideration.

The fifty-eight houses which stood on the two areas of freehold land in town seem to have had a slightly higher rate of owner-occupation than this, though it cannot be quantified exactly because of the lack of documentation.[14] If the rate is taken as having been about 60%, and a further thirty-five houses are added to the 165 copyhold ones, a total of 200 residences which were owner-occupied is arrived at. This is still about 55% of the whole, after inns and subdivided houses have been omitted. The reduction in the proportion of owner-occupiers by 1725 was probably partly the result of an increase in population which took place during the later decades of the seventeenth century, whereby many of the people migrating into town were in the lower ranks of society and could not afford to buy houses of their own. In addition to this was the fact that established residents, who could afford to do so, began to acquire property as an investment and rent it out to people requiring accommodation.[15]

---

[13] Reed, 'Ipswich', pp. 50–1. Using a church rate of 1637 and a tax record for the year 1689, the writer found that owner-occupancy rate in eight parishes was c. 20% and 25% respectively.

[14] Transactions concerning freehold properties did not require entry in court baron minutes as the transfers were completely without encumbrance.

[15] P. Clark, 'English Country Towns, 1500–1800', in Clark, *Country Towns*, p. 6. Urban property is identified as an attractive investment from the mid sixteenth century onwards because of the number of migrants arriving in towns. R. Grassby, *The Business Community of Seventeenth-Century England* (Cambridge, 1995), pp. 373–8, cites an annual rate of return of 6%–8% on the investment made.

Social geography

In seeking to establish whether or not there was any recognisable social aspect to the residential pattern in Lowestoft, it is necessary to establish which people were living in different parts of the town. This can be done with a good degree of accuracy for the years 1618 and 1725, because of documentation previously cited.[16] The process of identification can be further enriched with social and occupational details drawn from other sources and collated with the family reconstitution data. In order to achieve the maximum effect of showing the distribution throughout the various occupational and social groupings, women property-owners (mainly widows) have been placed in their husbands' or fathers' categories, where known, with their presence in the tables which follow acknowledged by having their numbers placed in brackets beside the overall group total. In both the High Street as a whole, and in the side-lane area to the west, their possession of real estate increased during the century in question: from 19.6% to 24% of owners in the former case and from 10.4% to 25% in the latter.

The manor roll of 1618 states that there were sixty-seven houses above the cliff, on the east side of the High Street, and it also gives the names of the owners.[17] Apart from ten cases of people owning more than one residence, it is probably correct to assume that most of the individual properties were occupied either wholly or in part by the people to whom they belonged. As Table 23 shows, the social mix was quite a wide one, in the sense that most of the town's occupational and social groups were represented. However, the emphasis in both ownership and occupation lay very much with the better-off levels of society (especially merchants and craftsmen), while the poorer sections had scant representation. A similar situation prevailed in 1725, even though the number of houses had increased to 110, providing 132 homes in all (subdivision having been carried out on some properties). Merchants remained prominent, while craftsmen were less conspicuous, and retailers/tradesmen had increased their presence.[18] So, too, had members of the seafaring fraternity, benefiting from increased prosperity deriving from maritime trade after the town had gained port status in 1679.[19] One caveat which has to be made is that the pattern of ownership in 1725 may be less indicative of social zoning than that of 1618, because with increased numbers of people owning more than one house the question arises as to whom the properties were rented. No answer to this has manifested itself.

---

[16] The manor roll of the former year and the vicar's copyhold listing carried out during the latter.

[17] There were also four houses south of the High Street area, on much lower ground. These have not entered the reckoning.

[18] The growth in the number of retailers/tradesmen in the most favoured part of town was probably due to a national trend: an increase in the number of shops from the late seventeenth century onwards. See D. Davis, *A History of Shopping* (London, 1966), p. 147.

[19] If the significance of surnames is any indicator, a majority of the people in the 'Unknown' category, both in 1618 and 1725, also belonged to families in the wealthier levels of society.

Table 23. *House ownership and occupancy (east side of the High Street)* [20]

Occupational/ social groupings	Number of dwellings (1618)	Number of owners (1618)	Number of dwellings (1725)	Number of owners (1725)
Gentlemen	9	5	2	2
Merchants	16	11(2)	42	21(6)
Retailers/tradesmen	4	4	25	10(2)
Yeomen	2	1	3	1
Craftsmen	11	10(3)	5	4(1)
Mariners	8	6(3)	24	19(6)
Fishermen	0	0	12	7(2)
Husbandmen	1	1	0	0
Labourers	1	1	0	0
Others	0	0	2	1
Unknown	15	13(2)	17	13(5)
	67	52(10)	132	78(22)

The west side of the High Street cannot be examined in such detail because of the two freehold areas at either end not appearing in John Tanner's listing, but there are still a substantial number of copyhold dwellings to be considered.[21] The manor roll of 1618 records twenty-four houses, and this had increased in number to forty-one by 1725, thereby providing a total of forty-three homes. As may be seen in Table 24, the emphasis in both ownership and occupation of property rested once again with wealthier members of society. Merchants, retailers/tradesmen, craftsmen and seafarers are all represented, and an increase in the number of people with maritime interests between 1618 and 1725 also conforms to the pattern observed in the previous paragraph.

With the High Street having been assessed, the remaining part of town to be considered is the side-street area to the west of the main thoroughfare.[22] The dwellings in this part of town were smaller for the most part and stood on less generously sized plots – a feature due in some measure to the fact that the messuages had never been as large as those fronting the High Street and also to the fact that progressive infill in this part of town had resulted in many of them becoming smaller

[20] The 'Others' category's presence in 1725 was the result of a local clergyman, the Rev. Gregory Clarke, of Blundeston, owning two properties. He lived in neither of them.

[21] In the 1618 manor roll, ownership of the freehold messuages was as follows. Northern end (fourteen houses): three gentlemen, one merchant, one scrivener, one yeoman, two craftsmen, five unknown and the lord of the manor. Southern end (twenty-one houses): one merchant, one yeoman's widow (three dwellings), five craftsmen (including a blacksmith's widow with two dwellings), one mariner, one husbandman, seven unknown (one with two dwellings), and the Town of Lowestoft (almshouses). Thus, it can be seen that the northern end tended to have wealthier owners than the area to the south.

[22] The seventeen houses situated outside the built-up area, in the parish at large, do not form part of the analysis.

Table 24. *House ownership and occupancy (west side of the High Street)*

Occupational/ social groupings	Number of dwellings (1618)	Number of owners (1618)	Number of dwellings (1725)	Number of owners (1725)
Gentlemen	2	1(1)	1	1
Merchants	5	4(1)	8	5(1)
Retailers/tradesmen	3	3(1)	2	2
Yeomen	3	2(1)	4	1
Craftsmen	4	3	8	5
Mariners	2	2	11	6(3)
Fishermen	0	0	2	2(1)
Husbandmen	0	0	1	1
Labourers	0	0	0	0
Others	0	0	0	0
Unknown	5	5	6	4(2)
	24	20(4)	43	27(7)

and smaller. The 1618 manor roll shows fifty-four houses in this particular area, while John Tanner's listing gives 157 dwellings, providing a total of 161 homes. In broad terms, the ownership of the properties in 1618 was probably largely synonymous with the occupancy – except in the case of the three gentlemen specified and the twenty-five people in the 'Unknown' category (fifteen of these do not appear in the family reconstitution material and may therefore have lived outside the town).

As Table 25 shows, however, ownership and occupancy were not so closely connected in 1725. Merchants, tradesmen, craftsmen and seafarers had all purchased property over and above their own immediate needs and were renting it to other people. The opportunity to do this probably resulted from an increase in wealth in the community at large, which was itself the result of an upturn in maritime trade.[23] The same pattern is detectable in the 'Unknown' category, where sixteen of the nineteen owners can be found in the family reconstitution material and are seen to have belonged to the retailing, manufacturing and seafaring fraternities, though without specific occupations recorded for them in any documentary sources.[24]

The opportunity to ascertain well-differentiated residential zoning in Lowestoft is limited by the town's size, both in terms of topography and the number of people living there. It was simply not big enough (sixty acres in area and with a population of 1,500 to 2,000 people) to allow the kind of scrutiny and analysis applied, for

---

[23] The granting of port status to Lowestoft in 1679 not only boosted economic opportunity, it also acknowledged an existing state of affairs in which maritime trade was already on the increase.

[24] For the purposes of analysis here, innkeepers have been included in the 'Retailers/tradesmen' category, together with shopkeepers and people involved in food and drink provision.

Table 25. *House ownership and occupancy (side-street area)* [25]

Occupational/ social groupings	Number of dwellings (1618)	Number of owners (1618)	Number of dwellings (1725)	Number of owners (1725)
Gentlemen	7	3	4	1(1)
Merchants	1	1(1)	14	5(1)
Retailers/tradesmen	6	5(1)	14	9(3)
Yeomen	3	3	3	1
Craftsmen	7	7	26	15(4)
Mariners	1	1	23	13(3)
Fishermen	0	0	28	14(2)
Husbandmen	0	0	2	2
Labourers	1	1	1	1
Others	2	2	15	4
Unknown	26	25(3)	31	19(7)
	54	**48(5)**	**161**	**84(21)**

instance, to Newcastle.[26] Lowestoft had no wards within its built-up area, and was only about 1,000 yards long by 370 yards wide at its broadest point. The one comparison which can be made with larger communities of maritime status is that the merchants tended to live where their economic interests and purposes were best served.[27] That was on the High Street, on either the east side or the west – the former being the better siting because of proximity to the fish-curing premises and net-stores at the bottom of the cliff. However, the zoning became progressively looser throughout the seventeenth century, with townspeople other than merchants also living along the main roadway.

The presence of retailers, tradesmen and craftsmen is detectable, too, though the last-named were not as numerous on the eastern side of the street in 1725 as they had been in 1618 (the increase in the number of merchants and tradesmen probably reflects increased retail capacity and function). In contrast to this, the presence of mariners and fishermen had increased considerably – the result, as previously pointed out, of wealth deriving from increased maritime activity. In fact, it is noticeable how the ownership of more than one house had become a feature of the

[25] The 'Others' category consists largely of charitable accommodation. In 1618, a clergyman of unknown origins owned one dwelling and there was also a parish almshouse which accommodated three people. In 1725, a carter owned a house in this part of town, the vicar of the parish had one (which he rented out), the churchwardens had responsibility for eight almshouses on two different sites, and a merchant administered a block of four privately endowed almshouses.

[26] See J. Langton, 'Residential Patterns in Pre-Industrial Cities: Some Case Studies from Seventeenth Century Britain', *TIBG* 65 (July 1975), 1–27. The analysis is based on a hearth tax return of 1665.

[27] *Ibid.*, 21, and Parker, *King's Lynn*, p. 40. The river in King's Lynn was the equivalent of the beach at Lowestoft, providing means of entry and despatch for all kinds of merchandise.

better-off sections of society generally by 1725. People were investing money in property to rent out to those who could not afford to purchase homes – a factor which makes it harder to establish a social geography for the town in the earlier decades of the eighteenth century than for the same part of the seventeenth, when the pattern of ownership was more a matter of one house per person. Having said that, it is true in general terms that Lowestoft's merchants, retailers, tradesmen and its better-off craftsmen and seafarers tended to live on the High Street, while the lesser artisans, mariners and fishermen occupied the side-streets.

Such, then, is the social geography which is identifiable. Because the information available for the town only gives ownership of houses, and not occupancy, the question of where the poorest members of the community lived must remain conjectural. A number of them probably dwelt in rented accommodation in the side-streets and others perhaps in the buildings which had been subdivided. As mentioned earlier, John Tanner's listing refers to fifteen examples of subdivision, and most of the conversions were to be found among the larger houses on the east side of the High Street. No evidence has been found of low-grade shelter being built for the least fortunate and the impression given by the documents used for topographical reconstruction is that Lowestoft's houses, even when small, were well constructed – corroboration perhaps of the comment made by a leading servant of the crown, which is cited at the beginning of the next chapter.

– 6 –

House Design and Interior Arrangements

Construction details

In May 1545, the Duke of Norfolk was carrying out a review of coastal defences between Great Yarmouth and Orford because of a perceived invasion threat from France. Having commented on the landing capacity of both anchorage and beach at Lowestoft, as well as on the positioning of the three small batteries, he made the following remark concerning the place itself: 'The town is as pretty a town as I know any few on the sea coasts, and as thrifty and honest people in the same, and right well builded.'[1] It is the final part of this statement which will form the starting-point of this chapter.

There are two houses still standing on the High Street in Lowestoft, at opposite ends, which were there when the Duke of Norfolk made his visit (Plates 9 and 10). Both of them are of high-quality construction, with framing that is impressive both in terms of the size of timber used and in its decorative nature.[2] If they were typical of the standard of architecture at the time, then the town was indeed 'well builded'. Most of the timber-framed houses surviving from Tudor times (either largely intact or radically altered) date from the second half of the sixteenth century and from the first part of the seventeenth. Altogether, there are seventeen of them on the High Street, mainly on the eastern side, and most of them have long functioned as shops rather than private houses – and nearly all of them have later, eighteenth- or nineteenth-century, façades.[3]

The size of timber used for beams and wall-posts in the best of the existing buildings is impressive, often being up to twelve inches square, with joists of six to eight inches' width embellishing the ceilings. Some of the axial beams and cross-beams are decorated with scrolling vine-leaf and bunch-of-grape motifs, or with tear-drop quatrefoils – and the joists sometimes have similar decoration or are deeply fluted. An authority on East

---

[1] Gairdner and Brodie, *LPFD, Henry VIII*, xx, i (London, 1905), 717.

[2] The houses in question are Nos 36 and 102–104. The jettied front of the former dates from c. 1490–1500 and there is a high-quality extension or rebuilding to the rear, constructed a generation or so later. The latter, dating from c. 1520–30, has long been subdivided into three shops, but its former integrity and quality of construction are plain to see.

[3] Nos 27, 30, 31, 35, 36, 43–44, 75–77, 78–79, 80, 81–83, 102–104 and 148–149 all have complete timber frames or substantial remaining sections. Nos 45, 46, 55, 68 and 150 have vestiges of this construction, either within the main building or in earlier cross-wings.

Plate 9. *No. 36, High Street: the oldest house in Lowestoft, dating from c. 1500. The quality of its timber-framing is of the highest level – especially that in the jettied first-floor room overhanging the street. The nineteenth-century shop front is a particularly good one.*

Plate 10. *Nos 102–104, High Street: a former merchant's residence dating from c. 1530 (shown here as it appeared over thirty years ago). Its jettied upper section is still visible and there was no division of the original roof-trussing when the building was subdivided into three shop-units. The position of the stack identifies the house as belonging to the cross-passage/lobby-entry type.*

Anglian timber-framed buildings once remarked that the quality of construction observed in Lowestoft was superior to much of what he had recorded in Norwich, in the sense that the city's houses were sometimes built to look good at first sight without always having the quality of timber and construction methods to match – whereas what he had seen in Lowestoft was first-class, both in terms of the size and standard of oak used and in the artistry of the decoration.[4]

Other evidence regarding the quality of houses on the High Street may be seen below ground level. Reference was made earlier, in Chapter 1, to the cellar beneath No. 160, and there is another mediaeval vault on the opposite side of the road, a little further to the south, built largely in brick and dating from the fifteenth century.[5] It is not as lofty as the earlier

---

[4] The authority in question was the late Alan Carter, of the University of East Anglia. He based his comments on a scrutiny of Nos 27, 36, 43–44 and 102–104, High Street. These buildings, along with Nos 30 and 31, offer the best examples of the carpenter's art.

[5] This is to be found beneath Nos 41–42 (site of what was once *The Swan* inn).

one, but the groined ceiling is impressive nevertheless. Other buildings in the area also have cellars, but while being of similar dimensions they have largely been reconstructed at some stage – mainly in the nineteenth century. Obviously, cellars were once a feature of many merchants' houses and inns standing on the High Street and, on the evidence of the two early ones which have survived, no short cuts were taken with either materials or construction techniques. Surviving probate inventories contain only six references to cellars, but four of these relate to houses which stood on the east side of the High Street.[6]

The principle adopted for building Lowestoft's larger houses (and probably the smaller ones, too) was half-timbering, whereby ground-floor walls were constructed of rubble and brick and the upper storey was timber-framed, with the plate resting on the masonry and with stud-work walls infilled with either brickwork or wattle and daub. This type of construction became increasingly common in southern and eastern England from the late mediaeval period onwards, owing partly to shortages of suitable oak for sumptuous full-framing of the kind which became ever more fashionable as the fifteenth century advanced.[7] A more economical use of timber, whereby it served constructional needs rather than made a visible declaration about the status of the householder, placed less strain on the available resources and in no way diminished the capacity for rich interior decoration.[8]

Lowestoft had between twenty and twenty-five acres of woodland in the parish at the time of the 1618 manor roll (only 1.5% of the total area), most of which seems to have been managed. It is not possible to estimate accurately the amount of timber this area would have produced for house-building, but it would have made a contribution, as would trees left standing in the hedgerows.[9] However, these sources would not have been sufficient on their own and, with the additional need for good oak caused by shipbuilding, timber must have been brought in from outside sources – the estates at Somerleyton, Mutford and Sotterley being likely contributors.[10]

---

[6] Caution has to be exercised regarding use of the word 'cellar', because it may not refer to a room below ground-level. In Norwich, it was sometimes used of a ground-floor storage space within a house or even outside in the yard. See U. Priestly and P. J. Corfield, 'Rooms and Room Use in Norwich Housing, 1580–1730', *JSPMA* 16 (1982), 119. The other contributor to this article was the late Helen Sutermeister, whose preliminary work formed its basis.

[7] Opinion has long varied as to the significance of half-timbering and to the matter of timber shortages. R. J. Brown, *English Farmhouses* (London, 1982), p. 148, says that close-studding persisted into the seventeenth century, when the need to economise brought changes.

[8] O. Rackham, *The History of the Countryside* (London, 1986), p. 86, draws attention to the surface appearance of lavishly exposed timber thus: 'a wealth of exposed beams looked picturesque and expressed prestige; it was not necessary to hold up the structure'.

[9] H. Beevor, 'Norfolk Woodlands, from the Evidence of Contemporary Chronicles', *TNNNS* II (Norwich, 1924), 488–508, gives a range of five to forty trees per acre during the sixteenth century. The total of forty, recorded at Barningham, is said to be exceptional. Totals of twelve, eight and five (Pulham St Mary, Tunstead and Acle/Dereham respectively) are adjudged to have been more typical. O. Rackham, *Trees and Woodland in the British Landscape* (London, 1976), p. 84, refers to the use of non-woodland trees in building.

[10] Rackham, *Countryside*, p. 87, cites a large, fully framed, fifteenth-century Suffolk farmhouse as containing 330 trees of varying sizes. In *Woodlands* (London, 2006), p. 292, he gives a figure of 200–250 trees for a medium-sized hall house of c. 1400.

Plate 11. *A late eighteenth-century view of the High Street. Richard Powles' study of 1784 takes liberties with the perspective, expanding it to left and right. The focal point is Lion (later Crown) Score and the inn sign visible on the left is that advertising* The Queen's Head.

The framing of Lowestoft's oldest houses is not visible externally today. Nor, in all likelihood, was it ever meant to be. The fashion throughout much of Suffolk and south Norfolk was for the exterior of timber-framed houses to be plastered over – unless faced with good-quality bricks or dressed flint.[11] There is an excellent pen and wash drawing of Lowestoft High Street in 1784, by a local artist, which shows a number of the pre-Georgian houses visible with plastered exteriors (Plate 11).[12] All the roofs, regardless of period, are tiled, though it is not possible to identify whether plain-tiles or pantiles were used. The latter type is the more likely, as it became an increasingly popular cladding from the middle of the seventeenth century onwards and can still be seen on many High Street roofs today.[13]

Contrary to popular belief, importation of pantiles into England (prior to manufacture in the country) was a specialist trade, not the result of their being used as ballast in ships.[14] Originally, the roofs on the sixteenth- and seventeenth-century houses in Lowestoft would have been thatched, a fact which is discernible even now on those buildings which have a substantial distance (usually, at least twelve to fifteen inches) between the top edge of their gables and the roof-covering itself – this space having at one time been occupied by thatch. The conversion to roof-tiles in Lowestoft was probably aided by a fire which devastated the middle part of town on 10 March 1645, having started in fish-curing premises on the northern Denes and moving southwards.[15] Eighteen dwellings and twenty-one fish-houses were either damaged or destroyed,

[11] E. Sandon, *Suffolk Houses* (Woodbridge, 1977), p. 84, gives a good description of the method, as well as its historical length of use.

[12] I. Gillingwater, 'Drawings Illustrative of the History of Lowestoft, Mutford and Lothingland' (1807) (SRO(L), 193/2/1). This collection of illustrations accompanies a three-volume manuscript account of the area, written by Edmund Gillingwater's older brother. The picture in question here shows a view of the High Street, with expanded perspective, looking down what is now Crown Score.

[13] R. W. Brunskill, *Illustrated Handbook of Vernacular Architecture* (London, 1970), p. 88. A. Clifton Taylor, *The Pattern of English Building* (London, 1962), p. 263, cites an example of early pantile production, in the granting of a patent by Charles I, in 1636, for the manufacture of 'Flanders tyles'.

[14] R. Lucas, 'Dutch Pantiles in the County of Norfolk: Architecture and International Trade in the Seventeenth and Eighteenth Centuries', *JSPMA* 32 (1998), 87. The writer notes, on p. 76, that the importation of pantiles began to increase after the third decade of the seventeenth century.

[15] D. Butcher and I. Bunn, *Lowestoft Burning* (Lowestoft, 2003), p. 5. This HWC publication looks at the damage caused by the fire and relates it to the environment of today.

together with goods and fittings, and total damage was estimated at £10,297 2s 4d.[16] The right-hand side of the view of the High Street referred to in the previous paragraph shows the part of town mainly affected; among the features detectable is the re-styling of older houses in a classically influenced idiom.[17]

The replacement of thatch by tiles did not usually necessitate radically altering the trussing of the timbers underneath. Inspection of seven surviving early roofs has revealed that all are of butt-purlin type, sometimes with added strength given by collars and wind-braces.[18] Again, as with the framing in the rooms below, timber of good quality and size was used, and sound carpentering techniques are evident in the construction. Plentiful roof-space is a further feature, with at least one of the houses having staggered double purlins to accommodate the insertion of original dormers (which have since disappeared), while another of the buildings has ashlaring along the whole of its attic's length on both sides, and on the evidence of a surviving inventory of 1684 was used as servants' quarters and storage-area.[19]

With the emphasis directed so far towards timber and carpentry, some attention needs to be given to the other main building material: brick. Until a new style in architecture (to be discussed later) began to manifest itself in the later seventeenth century, placing emphasis on bricks as a feature in their own right, much of the brickwork in Lowestoft's houses may well have been rendered over. The sizes of brick used generally conform to the dimensions usual for the sixteenth and seventeenth centuries, being in the range of nine inches long by four to four and a half inches wide, by two to two and a half inches thick.[20] In Lowestoft, a very attractive bonding was formed by alternating bricks laid as headers with two, three or even four flint cobbles – patterning which can still be seen in a few surviving stretches of boundary walls along certain of the scores.

Two surviving older houses have squared and dressed flint covering their façades (Plates 12 and 13) – an expensive cladding, which was meant to impress people at the time of its construction and still has the ability to make an impact today.[21] Another has

---

[16] NRO, PD 589/112, p. 70. The Lowestoft Town Book has a full account of the damage, together with the names of those affected. E. Gillingwater, pp. 61–2, reproduces the information in tabulated form.

[17] Four houses have shaped gables of the mid seventeenth century, with later façades added. Two others, in the left-hand half of the picture, have quoining around the first-floor windows, and there are further signs of upgrading carried out on other dwellings. Such improvement was a national feature. See Borsay, 'Early Modern Urban Landscapes', in Waller, *English Urban Landscape*, p. 102.

[18] The houses in question are Nos 27, 35, 36, 43–44, 80, 102–104 and 148–149, High Street. The attic space of No. 36 is mainly covered in, allowing minimal inspection of the timbers. The trussing is probably of either crown-post or queen-post type.

[19] No. 35, High Street, is the house which once had dormers in its roof, No. 80 that with the servants' garret. The latter belonged to the Wilde family, leading merchants in the town, and the inventory cited is that of James Wilde, who died in February 1684.

[20] N. Lloyd, *A History of English Brickwork* (London, 1925), pp. 98–100. The writer gives a series of brick sizes, with measurements taken from a wide selection of substantial houses. Dimensions do vary slightly, but all conform to the basic 9 x 4½ x 2 inch model. J. A. Wight, *Brick Building in England* (London, 1972), pp. 28 and 43, refers to this particular size as 'an informal standardisation' of the year 1571.

[21] Nos 27 and 80, High Street: the so-called 'North Flint House' and 'South Flint House'.

Plate 12. *No. 27, High Street. The flint façade's effect has been marred by the application of white, weather-proof, masonry paint. The building dates from c. 1550 and is currently functioning as a public house. Its principle downstairs room has richly carved beams and joists in the ceiling. Stack positioning again reflects cross-passage/lobby-entry construction.*

vertical studwork on its upper elevation, with herringbone brickwork between – a feature that may well have been intended to be seen originally, but which has for many years been hidden behind render.[22] All three of these houses are of high quality, but may not be typical in their exterior embellishment.

Given that most of its surviving timber-framed houses date either from the second half of the sixteenth century or the beginning of the seventeenth, Lowestoft may be seen as being part of the so-called 'Great Rebuilding', which took place over much of lowland England from 1570 to 1640.[23] A price of £6 per bay to build a house in Leicester during the sixteenth century has been cited, though without comment on the

[22] Nos 102–104, High Street. The decorative brickwork was exposed several years ago, when the plaster was removed from No. 103 prior to its being re-rendered and sealed.

[23] This was identified in Hoskins, 'The Rebuilding of Rural England, 1570–1640', in *Provinicial England*, pp. 131–48. The chapter in question was originally published as an article in *P&P* IV (November, 1953), 44–59.

Plate 13. *No. 80, High Street. This building's squared flint cladding is enhanced by stone quoining around the windows and doorway. There is a date lozenge above the door, bearing details of the year the house was built (1586) and the Christian name initials of its occupants, William and Mary Wilde.*

standard of construction that such a sum purchased.[24] By the middle of the seventeenth century, the cost of rebuilding a demolished farmhouse in Essex was in the region of £40, a figure that corresponds well with the price of a residence of similar size in Lowestoft.[25]

By an agreement made on 15 March 1678, Benjamin Whipp (thatcher) borrowed £45 from Ann Swift (widow of a fishermen) on the understanding that he would put

[24] Hoskins, 'Rebuilding', 143.

[25] *Ibid.*, 143. Hoskins is quoting here from F. W. Steer, *Farm and Cottage Inventories of Mid-Essex, 1635–1749* (Chelmsford, 1950), p. 11.

into operation, on or before 24 June, the building of a house on the site of a dwelling which had recently been pulled down on the freehold land at the High Street's northern end (now occupied by No. 167).[26] No interest was to be charged on the loan, but Ann Swift was to have her place of residence in the northern end of the house during the term of her natural life. Her suite consisted of a parlour and a buttery, with a chamber above, a garret over the chamber and a place to store coal. She was also allowed the use of a well in the yard. No details are given concerning the number of rooms in Benjamin Whipp's section of the house, but it must have been at least as large as that of his financier. The thatcher had no trouble repaying the loan within the stipulated six-year period and he sold the property for £50 to John Daynes (beer brewer) on 25 May 1687.

Plan-forms and types of dwelling

The terminology used in describing Ann Swift's quarters suggests a building of traditional nature. Inspection of the ten most unaltered High Street houses confirms that they were all of the inside-cross-passage/lobby-entry type, of three to four bays' length and one cell depth.[27] As such, they belong to the hall-parlour-kitchen and buttery family, with chambers above the ground-floor rooms, and with either end-stacks or off-centre stacks to provide heating and cooking facilities – and sometimes, in the case of the biggest houses, with both types of hearth location. The fieldwork carried out is confirmed by a scrutiny of surviving inventories dating from the sixteenth and seventeenth centuries, in which seventeen out of a total of thirty-one suitable documents indicate the type of house described above.[28] Other inventories seem to suggest two-bay, and even one-bay, versions of the cross-passage/lobby-entry model, but no surviving examples have as yet been identified.[29]

The buildings which remain above ground today usually stand facing the street, but two of them are placed end-on to it – the positioning probably being the result of the size of the plot.[30] Each of these houses now has buildings adjoining on either side, but

---

[26] WDC deed packet no. 86.

[27] The houses in question are Nos 27, 29–30, 31–32, 43–44, 75–76, 77–79, 80, 81–83, 102–104 and 148–149, High Street. Some of them stand full-fronted onto the roadway, others gable-end. The three- to four-bay type of house under discussion is referred to (in relation to Lincolnshire and the Trent Valley) in M. W. Barley, 'English Farmhouses and Cottages, 1550–1725', *EHR* 2nd series VII (1955), 297.

[28] The thirty-one documents are ones which definitely show a complete house, not part of a dwelling. In this chapter, individual source references for probate documents will not be given – a practice adopted earlier for Chapter 4.

[29] Both simple and more complex versions of this basic house-type are recognisable as the kinds of dwelling described in C. J. M. Moxon, 'Ashby-de-la-Zouche: A Social and Economic Study of a Market Town, 1570–1720' (unpub. PhD thesis, University of Oxford, 1971), pp. 180–1.

[30] Both types of siting have been observed, during the seventeenth century, in bigger towns than Lowestoft. See Reed, 'Ipswich', p. 165 and D. Portman, *Exeter Houses, 1400–1700* (Exeter, 1966), pp. 24–6. In each of these communities, houses fronting the street tended to be located in back-street areas where land was more plentiful. The two surviving houses in Lowestoft which stand end-on to the roadway are Nos 36 and 43–44, High Street.

the side-passage which once gave access to it is still discernible. So is the internal arrangement of rooms. Probate inventories, in cases where they relate to a complete house, give a good idea of the number of rooms in existence at the time that the individual documents were drawn up and, while this does vary (especially where internal partitioning had obviously been carried out), broad classifications can be made for certain of the occupation groups in town.[31] Merchants and the more substantial tradespeople seem to have had as many as twelve to fifteen rooms on occasions (including annexes and outhouses), but the usual number was in the range of six to ten. Craftsmen appear to have had from three to six on average, along with husbandmen,[32] while mariners and fishermen had between three and eight depending on their degree of wealth and their status at sea.

One feature concerning room layout and use in the pre-industrial houses of Lowestoft is the presence of attics in the larger buildings, and in some of the smaller ones. Contrary to what has been observed elsewhere, it was not unusual for dwellings to have a third, usable storey in the roof-space before the end of the sixteenth century – and, by the early years of the eighteenth, it had become common.[33] The obvious presence of attics or garrets in houses on the High Street is shown in the panoramic view cited earlier in this chapter and there are frequent references to them in probate inventories. Out of eighty-five documents which are suitable for analysis, covering the period 1561–1730, thirty-eight make reference to garrets.[34] The term *vance roof* (or *vaunce roof*) is used from time to time during the sixteenth and seventeenth centuries, but it disappears from the records after 1700 and the word *garret* is the only one encountered.[35] Between 1700 and 1730, twenty-three of the thirty-six appropriate documents studied relate to houses which had garrets. This is a proportion of 64% – one which is in excess of that ascertained in Norwich.[36]

---

[31] The analysis of the number of rooms present in houses is based on a study of 100 surviving probate inventories: fifteen for the period 1561–1600, twenty-one for 1601–1650, eighteen for 1651–1700 and forty-six for 1701–1730. Of this 100, sixty-six relate to a complete building.

[32] Hoskins, 'Rebuilding', in *Provincial England*, p. 145, shows 'typical farmers' of the mid seventeenth century owning houses with this number of rooms.

[33] Spufford, *Contrasting Communities*, p. 74, and Hoskins, 'Leicester', in *Provincial England*, p. 103, both comment on the comparative scarcity of attics. The former cites evidence drawn from probate inventories relating to villages in Cambridgeshire, while the latter makes a more generalised comment on the town of Leicester using early nineteenth-century drawings as the source.

[34] Fifteen of the 100 surviving inventories contain no mention of rooms, which means that the deceased people were probably living in lodgings. There are also four wills which do not have accompanying inventories, but which refer to garrets.

[35] It has been said that the term *vance roof* was confined to East Anglia. See M. Reed, *The Ipswich Probate Inventories, 1583–1631*, SRS, XXII (Ipswich, 1981), 5.

[36] A. Carter *et al.*, *The Norwich Survey*, Sheet A7.1b (c. 1980). Much of this data was used as the basis of an article on housing in the city between 1580 and 1730. See Priestley and Corfield, 93–123. There are forty-six surviving Lowestoft inventories for the period 1700–1730, fifteen of which cannot be used for assessing rooms and room-use. Four have no references to rooms, five record part of a house only, two refer to the same house and four mention rooms only (contents are not itemised).

The use of roof-space in Lowestoft houses may well have been the result of limited plot-size (especially after the infill process referred to in Chapterss. Even the large plots on the east side of the High Street were restricted in building potential, partly by the frontage already having been taken up by those houses which stood lengthways to the road (a majority) and partly by the terracing of the cliff preventing substantial rearward development. In King's Lynn, there was a relative scarcity of attics among merchants' houses sited along the river bank, because plentiful land to the rear allowed cross-wings to be built.[37] The Lowestoft merchants living along the edge of the cliff had plots as long as any in King's Lynn (if not longer); what they did not have was ground which was all on one level. Their houses could not be extended in the usual L-shape to any great degree, because of the instability caused by building too close to the edge of the uppermost terrace and because the yard space at the back of the house was needed for storage and other domestic uses – and, in some cases, for activities connected with the occupant's trade or occupation.

Much has been said, thus far, about the traditional hall-parlour-kitchen type of house and its smaller variants. The surviving Lowestoft probate inventories also seem to suggest that a different model of dwelling was being built from the late seventeenth century onwards. There is one indication of it in a document of 1691 and eleven more from between 1700 and 1730. Using the terminology of the time, it may conveniently be described as a parlour-and-kitchen type, with service-rooms such as pantries and wash-houses annexed on the ground floor to the rear of the two main rooms, both of which had chambers above.[38] The shape was far less elongated than the older type referred to above, having only one bay – and, in being of two rooms' depth (instead of one), it has been referred to as the 'double pile' (or cell) variety.[39] It is possible that this new design of house was not free-standing, but constructed as one of a pair, each integral with the other.

An original example of the new form has not yet been positively identified, but certain features of its construction were radical departures from the practice of the past. Firstly, there was less need for timber-framing, because internal load-bearing walls made greater use of masonry and brickwork to take the strain. Secondly, the positioning of chimney-stacks tended to move to end-walls, which did away with the classic off-centre location – and this, in turn, influenced the positioning of stairs, which were no longer made to rely on the stack as main means of support. Finally, the exterior elevations made use of brick as a material in its own right, not something which merely served as the medium to support a plaster surface.[40] The increase in brick-making capacity in Lowestoft in the period 1700–1730 was a feature noted in Chapter 4 and the particular change in architectural style described here was probably a contributing factor.

Another aspect of probate inventory material is the marked presence of wash-houses for the laundering of clothes and household linen after 1700. There are only two

---

[37] Parker, *King's Lynn*, p. 40.

[38] A necessary caveat is that changes in word-usage may have to be considered, whereby rooms previously termed 'halls' became 'parlours', in order for the householder to keep abreast of fashion.

[39] Brunskill, *VernacularArchitecture*, pp. 104–5.

[40] Borsay, 'Early Modern Urban Landscapes', in Waller, *Urban Landscapes*, p. 102, notes the increasing use of brickwork from the late seventeenth century onwards.

references to these before the eighteenth century (in 1682 and 1693) and both facilities are noted in connection with older-style houses, one of which is still standing.[41] However, the number recorded between 1700 and 1730 is eighteen – out of a total number of thirty-six documents which refer to complete houses.[42] This represents 50% of the whole – a proportion which is the same as that detected in the city of Norwich.[43] The distribution is well spread across the occupation groups, if with an emphasis towards the wealthier end of the town's population: four merchants, a brewer, a grocer, a victualler, four mariners, a butcher, two fishermen, a carpenter, a carter, a husbandman and a labourer. With regard to the type of dwelling having a wash-house as part of its facilities, a majority seem to have been of the double pile variety, but also detectable are those of the older, traditional, form. In most cases (if not all), it appears that the room in question was independent of the main structure.

This need not be surprising since, with usable space being an important consideration in houses of all kinds, one means of creating it was by the construction of ancillary buildings to the rear of the main one. These may have been either annexed to it or free-standing, but the utility afforded was the same. Another type of extra domestic area detectable in the inventories was the back-house – a classic lean-to addition well known throughout the whole of East Anglia. This one-storey addition butted up to the rear wall of the house and provided space for the storage of all kinds of domestic artefacts associated mainly with the kitchen, as well as for washing and brewing activities.

Another building which stood free of the main house, somewhere to the rear, was the privy. Probate documents indicate that houses had them, though the references are few in number (four only in the 132 wills which have survived for the period 1700–1730, and none earlier). Not surprisingly, none of the surviving inventories mentions privies because there would have been no contents worth appraising! Three of the wills cited – those of Coe Arnold (brewer), John French Snr (fisherman) and Thomas Utting (grocer) – refer to privies because each testator was dividing real estate among his children and the facility was to be shared by them once the messuage had been split up. Two other references to the building occur in manor court minutes of the late seventeenth century. At the leet of 1680, Jabez Aldred and John Marshall were each fined 6d for depositing sewage from their latrines in Swan Score, while at a court baron of March 1690, John Hayle (grocer) purchased a small piece of land from his next-door neighbour, Matthew Fisher, for the purpose of building a 'necessary house' to the rear of his own residence.[44] Hayle lived on the east side of the High Street, at the top of Lion Score (the site today of Nos 51 and 51a) in what John Tanner was to describe in his listing of 1725 as 'one house divided into several tenements', but which had once been an inn called *The Lion*.[45]

---

[41] Nos 81–83, High Street.

[42] There are forty-six surviving inventories altogether, but four of them make no reference to rooms of any kind, another five obviously show the deceased person living in part of a dwelling and two record the same house (being documents which relate to a husband and wife).

[43] Carter, *Norwich Survey*, Sheet A7.1b.

[44] SRO(L) 194/A10/12 and 13.

[45] The word 'several' is not to be taken in the way we use it today. In the earlier decades of the eighteenth century it meant 'separate'.

Inns

The configuration of roads and the importance of land transport have always been major influences on the development of towns and their inns. Large yards were necessary for stabling horses, and for standing carts and carriages; buildings were required for storing hay and other forage; and provision had to be made for watering the animals. Adequate accommodation was also needed for those people making overnight stops or staying in a place for longer. Comment has been made on 'the remarkable expansion of innkeeping' between the reigns of Elizabeth I and George III, especially in towns situated on the principal English roads.[46] Lowestoft was not in this category, but it was an important enough place with regard to local routes and its maritime activities helped to draw in outsiders.

The manor roll of 1618 shows that the town had eleven inns, three of which were situated on the east side of the High Street, seven on the west and one in the side-street area, in West (or Back) Lane.[47] By the time that John Tanner compiled his list of copyhold properties in the town, the number of inns in the built-up area stood at nine: six on the customary land, with a further three on the freehold area north of Swan Lane. Two of the hostelries were situated on the east side of the High Street, five on the west, one in Swan Lane and one in West Lane. In addition to the premises which appear in both documents, there were others which appeared and disappeared between 1618 and 1725, as well as one or two which stood in outlying parts of the parish. None of these establishments was the kind of small, semi-domestic beerhouse referred to in Chapter 4, whose proprietors were fined at the annual leet for serving short measure.[48]

It is evident from the surviving references that a majority of Lowestoft's inns were transient in terms of their hospitable function. Only six establishments remained in business throughout the century or more between 1618 and 1725, and they were the largest and most successful in the town. This raises the question of whether they survived because they were large and successful, or whether they became large and successful because they had survived. There is no ready answer, but one significant factor may have been access. Four of the five High Street hostelries had curtilages with side-lanes or scores running alongside (*New White Horse/Queen's Head, Crown, Bell* and *Swan*); the remaining one stood on a large plot and was free of other buildings abutting it (*Dolphin*); and the last one of all stood on a corner-site in the side-street area (*Old White Horse*). Thus, all of them offered easy access for horses and carriages, whereas many of the others had street frontage only.[49]

---

[46] A. Everitt, 'The English Urban Inn, 1560–1760', in Everitt, *Perspectives*, pp. 94–5.

[47] The High Street's west side was better suited for the large yards needed because it was not terraced.

[48] According to a survey of inns carried out in 1686, Lowestoft's hostelries had stabling for 138 horses and enough beds to sleep 184 people. For some reason, the town is included in figures relating to Norfolk. See TNA: PRO WO 30/48.

[49] Everitt, 'English Urban Inn', in Everitt, *Perspectives*, p. 98, draws attention to the importance of inns having long yards in which to locate ancillary buildings. The writer cites Stony Stratford, in Buckinghamshire, with its back-lanes running parallel to the High Street on either side, as being ideally suited to this requirement. Lowestoft's street-pattern of side-lanes and scores was also able to provide elongated plots suitable for inn development.

In any case, in a town the size of Lowestoft, there must have been a limit to the number of inns which could be viable financially. And it looks rather as if some of the establishments which came and went couldn't make enough money to continue for long in the trade. Market places have been identified as one of the commonest sites for inns, though they became less suitable during the seventeenth and eighteenth centuries owing to the congestion caused by the growth of the coaching and carrying trades.[50] None of Lowestoft's major inns, during the period under review, stood adjacent to the original market place, and the proximity of seven or eight establishments to the later, overspill area (see page 25) was purely fortuitous: they were already there before the market-space was created.

At least one eminent observer has left his impression of a Lowestoft inn recorded for posterity. Thomas Baskerville visited the town in 1677 and this is what he had to say: 'Lostaft is seated on a pleasant hill, overlooking the sea, pretty well built, having in it many large houses to dry herrings. Here is no castle for defence, but we saw a fair church, tower, and steeple, at the entrance of the town, and one church more in the town. Here we dined, and had fish incomparably well dressed, with excellent good claret and beer, but the sign of the house and the name of our landlord and land-lady who dressed the fish I have forgotten.'[51] It is likely that the inn referred to was *The Swan* and the people mentioned John Wythe and his wife, Katherine, who kept the premises for many years and were notable hosts.[52]

With the town serving as the centre for its own locality, it is possible that some of the larger, more important inns functioned as meeting places for polite society – especially from the late seventeenth and early eighteenth centuries onwards. The social activity that took place in towns has been noted as being of benefit to the victualling trade nationally, while other observers have identified the increasing use of inns for all kinds of commercial dealings – a trend that had begun during the sixteenth and seventeenth centuries and developed increasingly during the eighteenth.[53] No positive documentary evidence has come to light so far (for the timespan covered in this book) of the more substantial Lowestoft inns performing such economic and social functions, but it is likely that they did. In 1760, *The Queen's Head* opened an assembly room and the impression derived from this is that it was the culmination of many years of sociable activity associated with the premises.

The premier inns were certainly the venues for various kinds of public business. The annual leet court was held in an inn and the court baron sessions may also have been, though there is no way of ascertaining whether such activity remained in one establishment only or was rotated. During the immediate post-Restoration period, the town was heavily involved in litigation with Great Yarmouth concerning herring fishing

[50] *Ibid.*, pp. 97–8.

[51] HMC, 13 (London, 1892), 266–7. This publication is Vol. II of the Duke of Portland MSS.

[52] A portrait of Katherine Wythe was still hanging in *The Swan* in April 1711, when a new proprietor, Humphrey Overton, advertised his tenancy in *The Norwich Gazette*.

[53] Clark and Slack, *Crisis and Order*, p. 14, refers to increasing social activity, while Corfield, *Impact of Towns*, p. 18, and Everitt, 'English Urban Inn', in Everitt, *Perspectives*, pp. 104 ff., comment on the use of inns for business deals.

rights. James Wilde, Lowestoft's leading advocate in the cause, kept a full account of all expenses incurred and there are a number of entries which concern expenditure of various kinds incurred at *The Swan*.[54] Some of the Lowestoft innkeepers, whether owner-occupiers or tenants, were men of some standing in the local community, if one can rely upon the title of 'Mr' which is often accorded them during the late seventeenth and early eighteenth centuries, while the hostelries themselves sound suitably impressive in the various sale and lease advertisements which appear in copies of *The Norwich Gazette* of the time.[55] One has to allow perhaps for a little 'sales-talk' in the wording, even in an age less commercially intense than that of today, but even so there is no reason to believe that a number of Lowestoft inns were other than sound undertakings.

Shops

A perusal of the view of the High Street previously referred to in this chapter reveals what appear to be nine or ten retail premises, with pentices, or fenestrated bays (for the display of goods), added to the main building. Sixty years earlier, when John Tanner drew up his listing, only two shops are mentioned anywhere on the main roadway and a handful of others in the side-streets.[56] There must have been other retail premises in town at the time (including some, possibly, on either of the two freehold areas), so perhaps there was something in the approach of the compiler or in the terminology he used which escapes us today. Certainly, the increased presence of merchants and retailers/tradesmen as property owners on the east side of the High Street between 1618 and 1725, which is apparent in Table 25, would seem to suggest some kind of increase in retail function, and a number of the surviving probate inventories make reference to shops of various kinds – some of which sold goods directly to the public and others which were the workplaces of craftsmen.

No fewer than nine documents out of the fifteen available for the late sixteenth century (including an incomplete one) mention shops in one way or another; among these references it is possible to recognise a draper's enterprise combined with grocery sales and books, two shoemakers and some kind of general trader. For the period 1600–1650, five documents out of the fifteen which record rooms make reference to shops (six inventories have no references to rooms at all) and three of these were retail outlets: a shoemaker, a baker and a draper. Only a single woollen draper is revealed in the eighteen inventories extant for the second half of the seventeenth century, but this is largely due to the occupations of the people in question – three members of the

---

[54] These are reproduced in full in E. Gillingwater, pp. 221–39.

[55] Copies of this newspaper are to be found in the Colman and Rye Library collection, Norwich.

[56] The two shops in question belonged to Thomas Mighells (merchant) and stood either side of his house. All three buildings can be seen in Richard Powles's view of the High Street: the fourth, fifth and sixth ones to the right of Lion Score (the plots now occupied by Nos 54, 55 and 56–57, High Street). Retail shops with glazed windows were present in Ipswich from the beginning of the seventeenth century (see Reed, 'Ipswich', p. 63), and it is likely that Lowestoft had them from quite early on, too.

gentry, five mariners and fishermen and one retired admiral among them – rather than to a decline in the number of shops. The number increases again between 1700 and 1730, with nine references out of a total of thirty-six appropriate documents, and the premises included an apothecary's, a butcher's, a grocer's and one which sold a variety of goods.

All references to shops in the documents used suggest a room that was an integral part of a house.[57] So does the illustration of the High Street cited earlier. Five inventories refer to a 'shop chamber' (on the first floor of the dwelling), but the shop itself is not included in the appraisal of goods and may have been let to another occupant. There are also references to shop chambers, as well as to shops themselves, in a number of wills and all of this information, together with the data present in John Tanner's listing, is sufficient to suggest general growth in the number of shops ascertainable during the sixteenth and seventeenth centuries, as well as in the consumption of luxury goods.[58] However, there is no evidence available with which to assess contemporary attitudes to retailing and purchase (especially the alleged capacity for moral laxity on the part of female shoppers).[59] The term 'shop' itself was, in any case, a dual-purpose one, describing both a retail premises and one where a craftsman plied his trade – with examples also where the two functions were carried on simultaneously under the same roof.

Comment has been made on the scarcity of material nationally, before the 1780s, regarding the number of shops.[60] This is certainly true of Lowestoft, though the facts gathered from available probate material and from John Tanner's listing serve to give a limited picture of the commerce taking place between the late sixteenth and early eighteenth centuries. Further retail establishments in the town are implied by the presence of occupations such as glover, hatter and tailor, to say nothing of other bakers, butchers, cordwainers, drapers and grocers whose wills and inventories have not survived – but the absence of documentation means there is no conclusive proof of shops being run by these people. However, the remark made by at least one observer concerning the varied stock carried by most shops in the pre-industrial era (especially in small towns) is certainly borne out in the two most lengthy and detailed Lowestoft inventories of the late sixteenth and early seventeenth centuries.[61] The list of stock in the shops belonging to Margaret Couldham (January 1585) and William Harrison (September 1603) shows an interesting mixture of fabrics, haberdashery, groceries and books in the first case and of fabrics, haberdashery and groceries in the second. Well over 100 years later, the shop belonging to Richard Ward (March 1729) had haberdashery, novelty goods and books for sale.

---

[57] Parker, *King's Lynn*, p. 124. The same situation prevailed in the Norfolk town.

[58] Clay, *Economic Expansion*, i, 177–8; Corfield, *Impact of Towns*, p. 19; D. Davis, *A History of Shopping* (London, 1966), p. 147; Muldrew, *Economy of Obligation*, pp 18–26 and 52.

[59] L. L. Peck, *Consuming Splendor* (Cambridge, 2005), pp. 61–8.

[60] I. Mitchell, 'The Development of Urban Retailing, 1700–1815', in Clark, *Transformation of Towns*, p. 259.

[61] T. S. Willan, *The Inland Trade* (Manchester, 1976), p. 80.

Room use, interior décor and household contents

The statement made earlier of what the houses in pre-industrial Lowestoft were like in terms of plan-form and the number of rooms says little about the comforts with which the inhabitants sought to cheer their lives. Any attempt based on probate material to depict aspects of domestic life can only give a partial picture simply because wills were made by people who had something to bequeath and because inventories of goods reflect some degree of worldly wealth. The general assumption that only the more prosperous members of village communities made wills has been called into question.[62] But even though this impression is wrong (in towns, as well as villages), and people of lesser substance did formally declare their intentions concerning the disposal of property, the genuinely poor did not. Thus, with estimates of the proportion of poor people in urban populations during the seventeenth century reputedly lying somewhere between 25% and 50%, it can be seen that information concerning the interior arrangements and embellishment of houses will not incorporate the lifestyle of a substantial minority of town-dwellers.[63] Lowestoft had 45.5% exemptions in the defective 1674 Hearth Tax return and while the proportion should be lower than this (in view of the number of townspeople known to be missing from the printed form of the document), it still leaves a considerable number of residents who probably did not have the financial capacity to make wills.[64]

   The 507 wills covering the period 1560–1730 used for various purposes through-out the whole of this book represent a good cross section of the population above the poorer element.[65] Together with the 100 inventories which remain (fifty-two of which accompany a will), they give an interesting picture of the way that people decorated, furnished and appointed their houses.[66] One feature to emerge over the whole of the timespan is one which has been observed elsewhere: the way in which houses improved their amenity in terms of heating capacity and the use of window glass, curtains, soft furnishings and consumer products.[67] The influence of women in this improvement of living conditions is probably crucial (particularly in the wealthier

[62] M. Spufford, 'Peasant Inheritance Customs and Land Distribution in Cambridgeshire from the Sixteenth to the Eighteenth Century', in J. R. Goody *et al.* (eds), *Family and Inheritance: Rural Society in Western Europe, 1200–1800* (Cambridge, 1976), pp. 169–72.

[63] Clark and Slack, *Towns in Transition*, pp. 21, 113 and 121; Clark and Slack, *Crisis and Order*, p. 177; Patten, *English Towns*, p. 151. All three books cite this substantial degree of urban poverty.

[64] Moxon, p. 110, gives 23% as the proportion of exemptions in Ashby-de-la-Zouche.

[65] There is one surviving Lowestoft will made by a poor man. Thomas Youngman bears no such title in the document, but his burial entry in the parish register, in September 1579, classifies him so. He left a house and a yard, together with certain movable goods, and a cow. Thus, there would seem to be some question of interpretation here regarding the phrase 'poor man'.

[66] Inventories contain more information than wills, usually naming all the rooms in a house and listing the contents. Four surviving documents relate to a house which is still standing: Roger Hill, merchant (1588), Richard Mighells, merchant (1590), Elizabeth Pacy, merchant's widow (1682) and James Wilde, merchant (1684). The buildings are the present-day Nos 31–32, 27, 81–83 and 80 High Street.

[67] Borsay, 'Early Modern Urban Landscapes', in Waller, *English Urban Landscape*, p. 102.

levels of society), as they sought to express themselves in the purchase of goods that brought attractiveness and style to their home environments.[68]

Halls and parlours

Until the beginning of the eighteenth century, most of the houses in Lowestoft had a hall downstairs and, in the great majority of cases, it constituted the main living room in both large and small dwellings – sometimes with an element of prestige about it in the former, with good-quality furniture and decorative objects on view. The word had its origins in the mediaeval, open-plan house and it retained its use through the cross-passage and lobby-entry phases of architectural development right down to the emergence of the double-pile model in the late seventeenth/early eighteenth centuries. Nowhere in Lowestoft did the hall ever become just the main entry to a house and nothing more.[69] It was always important as a functional living space, serving various purposes, and in all but one case (out of forty-four dwellings which are recorded as having halls) it had a hearth. Cooking and eating often took place there, even into the eighteenth century, and sleeping was another regular use – though one which noticeably diminished after 1700.[70]

The parlour was common to both the more substantial cross-passage type of house and to the newer double-pile variety. It was a ground-floor room, usually with a fire-place (often sharing the stack with the hall in the older type of dwelling) and with varying roles to fulfil. One of them was to provide sleeping accommodation, a role that seems to have been important up to about the middle of the seventeenth century and which then diminished. This characteristic has been observed in Norwich, as has the fact that cooking seems never to have been an important use in the existence of a parlour (only three instances of this are detectable in thirty-four relevant Lowestoft inventories).[71] Progressively, throughout the seventeenth century, it is clear that the room became important as one in which to sit and, by the by the early years of the eighteenth, that was probably its primary function – again, a feature that is detectable in houses in Norwich.[72] The interpretation of the term 'sitting' offered here is one that has a social meaning attached to it. In other words, the inventories consulted had to suggest that there was some kind of communal aspect to the activity. A single chair listed in the contents of a parlour was not construed as 'sitting' in a social (or sociable!) sense. Two or three chairs, or more, were taken to imply that people sat down together for at least some of their available leisure time.

---

[68] L. Weatherill, 'A Possession of One's Own: Women and Consumer Behaviour in England, 1660–1740', *JBS* 25 (1986), 131–56. The writer draws back from terming the lives of married women 'a sub-culture', but she obviously believes that women sought to express themselves in a male-dominated world by the purchase of consumer goods which improved their homes.

[69] Priestly and Corfield, 105; F. E. Brown, 'Continuity and Change in the Urban house: Developments in Domestic Space Organisation in Seventeenth Century London', *CSSH* 28 (1986), 580.

[70] Reed, *Ipswich Inventories*, p. 5, makes reference to the use of halls for cooking – especially in houses without kitchens.

[71] Priestley and Corfield, 107–8. Brown, 'Urban House', 583, states that no cooking took place in London parlours during the seventeenth century.

[72] Priestley and Corfield, 108.

Kitchens and butteries

During the later sixteenth century, and throughout the seventeenth, it seems that kitchens were a room associated with the bigger houses in Lowestoft. The number of inventories consulted is not large, but twelve of the sixteen dwellings which are specified as having kitchens consisted of seven rooms or more. The first thirty years of the eighteenth century show the kitchen to have been a space of considerable importance, with twenty-two of the thirty-two buildings recorded as possessing one. At this time, it can be seen to have been present in both large and medium-sized cross-passage/lobby-entry dwellings and also in the newer double-pile type.

The dominant use of the room, throughout the whole period of study, was the preparation and cooking of food – and also the eating of it, from the late seventeenth century onwards.[73] It never seems to have served as a living or sleeping room, devoid of cooking facilities, as was the case in Norwich.[74] Only one example is to be found of a bed located in the kitchen (that of Richard Ward, labourer and woolcomber, in 1729), and the room was obviously the main downstairs space in a six-roomed dwelling, with cooking, eating and sitting taking place, and with the pantry being used for storage and the wash-house for brewing. Another obvious aspect of kitchen use, during the years after 1700, is its function as a sitting-room – probably because it was heated and because tables and chairs were present as a result of its being used for eating.

Ten of the sixteen houses recorded in sixteenth- and seventeenth-century inventories as having kitchens are also found to have had kitchen chambers above them – which suggests a room with load-bearing walls within the main fabric of the building. The other six, which do not have specific mention of a chamber above, may have had kitchens which were additional service rooms annexed to the rear of the main house. During the first thirty years of the eighteenth century, seventeen of the twenty-two houses with kitchens also had chambers above them – which, again, suggests a room fully integrated within the house.[75]

Butteries survived in the older type of house in Lowestoft well into the eighteenth century – unlike Norwich, where they had almost disappeared by the early 1700s.[76] They seem to have been situated next to either the hall or parlour, and they functioned largely as storage areas for domestic utensils of all kinds – especially those connected with the preparation and cooking of food.[77] There are only two examples of a buttery having a fireplace and being used for cooking (out of a total of thirty-two houses recorded) and they both occur in the later years of the sixteenth century. In the case of Thomas Eache (cordwainer, 1590), his house is seen to have had three butteries, so there

[73] Brown, 'Urban House', 585, gives the same uses(s) in London homes.

[74] Priestley and Corfield, 106.

[75] *Ibid.*, 107. The observation made here is that, in Norwich, the kitchen became less of a service room at the rear of a house and was more likely to have been fully incorporated within the main building.

[76] *Ibid.*, 110.

[77] The buttery was originally used, in the mediaeval period, for the storage of drink. The word derives from the Latin *botaria*, meaning a bottle or cask.

is obviously a matter of interpretation required here. The house inhabited by Richard Wells (merchant, 1587) is unequivocal, however, in having only one buttery, and it was undeniably the room where cooking was done. One interesting feature of the inventory is that the contents of the two downstairs living rooms give no indication of where the food was eaten, there being no mention of tables.

Of those houses which had butteries, only one late sixteenth-century dwelling is specified as having a chamber above it – that of William Rogers, goldsmith (1595) – whereas in Norwich the proportion was 25%.[78] However, most of the butteries which are not designated as having a chamber above were still probably incorporated within the main structure of the house. The inventories seem to suggest that they were adjacent to one of the larger downstairs spaces (hall, parlour or kitchen), so if there was a room above, it was likely to be called 'hall chamber', 'parlour chamber' or 'kitchen chamber' by association with the more important room on the ground floor.

Service rooms

There are only two examples of a scullery to be found in the Lowestoft probate inventories, dating from 1717 and 1730 respectively (Leake Bitson, merchant, and William Colman, fisherman). This is a low rate of adoption compared with Norwich, where the scullery has been identified as taking over some of the functions of the buttery and where it was quite common. Pantries, on the other hand, were a feature of some of the Lowestoft houses (the larger ones mainly) from the last quarter of the seventeenth century – though this may well have been the result of a change in the naming of rooms as much as any evolution taking place in the design of houses. Whatever its origins (either linguistically or architecturally), the pantry was invariably used to store household utensils. It also stored food as well, but few specific items other than cured herrings and dried cod are referred to in the inventories – perhaps because of the perishability and lack of long-term value of other commodities.

Both back-houses and wash-houses have been referred to earlier in this chapter, the former being very much a feature of larger houses during the late sixteenth and the seventeenth centuries, while the latter seem to have been mainly an eighteenth-century development. Both were used for storage of all kinds of domestic utensils and equipment, as well as for brewing. Interestingly, very few of the fifteen wash-houses recorded for the period 1700–1730 give any hint of their designated function on the evidence of contents, though it is possible that the tubs and coppers mentioned in connection with brewing might also have been used for the boiling of clothes and household linen. However, there is no indication that any of the wash-houses (or back-houses, for that matter) had fireplaces and flues, because none of them has fire-irons of any kind listed in connection with it – a feature that contrasts strongly with Norwich, where a high proportion of the wash-houses had heating.[79] Of course, it is possible that this lack of equipment is purely the result of chance or that it was kept somewhere else nearby and brought into the room as and when needed.

---

[78] Priestley and Corfield, 112.

[79] *Ibid.*, 113.

Low rooms

The term *low room*, as used in the Lowestoft probate inventories, indicates a ground-floor living space of some kind. It is met with particularly during the eighteenth century (there are also three instances of it between 1600 and 1649) when, in four out of the eight cases in which it occurs, it obviously refers to the main living area in the house. The other four references bring together the functions of sleeping, sitting and storage in different combinations, while the three earlier examples are just as varied, with one case where the room was even used as a study.[80] Other inventories, which are not complete or which itemise the goods of someone living in part of a house, also use the term. It seems almost as if it was applied in situations where the normal terminology of 'hall' and 'parlour' was not deemed appropriate. It has nothing to do with the foibles of a single person who was drawing up the documents, because the ones in question were written by a number of different people. A clue to the physical structure of low rooms is perhaps to be found in an architect's plan of what is now No. 79, High Street. The drawing was made during the mid/late 1960s and shows a cross-wing (since demolished) projecting eastwards into the yard. The ground-floor room is plainly shown to be partly below ground level – a feature that would certainly fit with the term 'low room' itself.[81]

Chambers

In Lowestoft, the word 'chamber' refers almost exclusively to a room on the first floor – a feature noted also in London during the seventeenth century.[82] The rooms above ground-floor level, while having sleeping as their primary function, were also utilised for the storage of household goods – especially items of linenware and other fabrics.[83] They were often heated in the larger houses from the 1580s onwards, with either the one above the hall or above the parlour being favoured – though, occasionally, both rooms had fireplaces.[84] Such an arrangement was not difficult to make with a chimney stack running through the room from the ground-storey level beneath. The presence of a chimneysweep in Lowestoft at this time – Wyllyam Garret (identified in his wife's burial entry of May 1580) – suggests that there were a sufficient number of flues in the better-quality houses to enable him to make at least a partial living from keeping them clean.

By the eighteenth century, a number of the medium-sized houses in town (three to six rooms) also boasted the comfort of a heated bedchamber, but the inhabitants were

---

[80] This relates to the house of John Gleason, the vicar (1610). Most houses associated with the term had three to six rooms, but there is a single case of one that had eleven (Robart Ward, merchant, 1604).

[81] I am indebted to Mr John French for showing me the drawing as part of a general discussion on Nos 77–79 and No. 80, High Street.

[82] Brown, 'Urban House', 586.

[83] Moxon, pp. 180–1, notes the feature in Ashby de la Zouche. So do R. W. Ambler and B. and L. Watkinson, *Farmers and Fishermen: The Probate Inventories of the Ancient Parish of Clee, South Humberside, 1536–1742* (Hull, 1987), p. 33.

[84] Reed, *Ipswich Inventories*, 5, gives the first reference to a heated bedchamber in 1606. Lowestoft had generous provision of fire-places (especially in the larger houses) from quite early on in the sixteenth century, perhaps because some of its merchant craft were involved in the coastal coal trade.

all people who were reasonably well off. Best endowed of all the houses, in terms of upstairs rooms with heating, were those of Elizabeth Pacy (merchant's widow) and James Wilde (merchant). Each of them had three of its chambers equipped with hearths by the years 1682 and 1684 respectively, making use of two stacks: an off-centre one and another on the end of the building. Both dwellings (which stood next to each other) have survived until the present day and are now known as Nos 80 and 81–83, High Street (Plates 13 and 14). As was the case in Norwich also, Lowestoft houses showed an increasing tendency for the first-floor rooms to be used for sitting.[85] This is particularly detectable from the second half of the seventeenth century onwards, and by the eighteenth the practice was well established. Out of the thirty-two houses for which inventories exist between 1700 and 1730, twenty-eight show at least one upstairs room being used for sitting.

Garrets

The third storey in Lowestoft houses has already been discussed as a feature of the plan-form and not much needs to be said about the rooms which occupied the roof-space – other than the fact that they were customarily used for sleeping and/or storage. No specific evidence of their being occupied by servants in the larger houses has come to light (in other words, there are no references to 'servants' attics' or the like), but that was probably one of their functions if the presence of trendle beds may be taken as an indicator. They may also have been useful for providing accommodation in families where three generations were living under one roof, or in cases where a house had been subdivided.

Closets

The first reference to a closet is to be found in 1674, in the inventory of Ann Hunt (gentleman's widow), and it shows that the facility was located in the hall chamber. Other townspeople's inventories show them to have been present in their houses during the last quarter of the seventeenth century and, as the eighteenth century progressed, they became more common. They were customarily used to store pewter and earthenware vessels of one kind or another, whether they were situated upstairs or down, and there are also references to napery, linen and clothes being kept within them, as well as various pieces of furniture and other household goods. There are sixteen references to them in all and, perhaps not surprisingly, they tended to be located in the houses of the wealthier members of society.

Interior décor and fittings

The most commonly mentioned items of interior decoration during the later part of the sixteenth century, in the houses of the merchants and the better-off tradespeople and craftsmen, are stained or painted canvas cloths. These served to decorate the walls on which they hung and they probably also served as draught-inhibitors.[86] They were

---

[85] Priestley and Corfield, 115.

[86] Reed, *Ipswich Inventories*, 5, draws the same conclusion regarding this secondary function.

present in bedchambers, as well as in halls and parlours, but no indication is given as to whether they had scenes depicted upon them or whether they were simply covered in patterns. None of the seventeenth-century documents makes reference to them, which may reflect their going out of fashion or could simply be the result of vagaries in the surviving records.[87]

A few of the merchants' inventories also refer to pictures of one kind or another. For instance, John Grudgfild had the following items in his hall when the assessors did their work in March 1590: a table of the Ten Commandments, set in a frame and with a silk curtain, three framed tables of arms, an escutcheon and a framed picture. William Rogers had a framed picture in his parlour (April 1595) and Richard Wells a table of the Ten Commandments, also with a curtain, in his hall (August 1587). Obviously, Old Testament authority meant something to two of these people and one of them may have had an interest in either heraldry or genealogy.

There are only four references to pictures in the seventeenth-century probate material. When the worldly goods of John Gleason, the vicar, were appraised in July 1610, among the objects itemised in the parlour were six small pictures and a map. Much later on, in December 1669, Riches Utber (retired admiral) had four pictures hanging in the hall and four in the parlour – one of the latter being a portrait of Charles II. In August 1682, Elizabeth Pacy (merchant's widow) had a total of thirteen pictures hanging in both hall and parlour, while the inventory of her next-door neighbour, James Wilde (merchant), which was compiled in March 1684, refers to nine: three each in the hall, parlour and hall chamber. It is to be regretted that the appraisers did not see fit to provide detail as to the subject matter.

By the eighteenth century, pictures of one kind or another were well established as a feature of internal decoration. Out of a total of forty-two appropriate inventories which have survived for the period 1700–1730 (there are forty-six documents altogether, but four make no mention of rooms), twelve refer to them – and while the hall and the parlour were the commonest rooms in which they were hung, they were also found in kitchens and bed-chambers. In one case (that of Michael Thurston, mariner), an exotic feeling is imparted in the reference to the two 'Indian pictures' which were present in his kitchen chamber and which had perhaps been acquired by him on voyages abroad.

A religious theme is touched upon in the will of Deborah Ashby (December 1727). She was the widow of a local merchant (Thomas Ashby), and among the numerous items she left to her maidservant, Frances Sherrington, were two small pictures depicting Joseph and his brothers and Christ's entry into Jerusalem. In addition to this pair, she also bequeathed to Elizabeth Landifield, the daughter of a cousin, three pictures which hung on or near the chimney-breast of her main living room: a still-life of fruit (seventeenth-century Dutch?), the Salutation of the Blessed Virgin Mary and the story of Esther.

Whether or not all the pictures referred to in the various documents were oil paintings cannot be determined. The only specific reference to prints is to be found in the inventory of Margaret Durrant (brewer's widow), in December 1716: three framed

---

[87] Portman, *Exeter Houses*, p. 44, categorically states that use of stained and painted cloths gradually ceased during the first half of the seventeenth century.

pictures and six prints are listed among the items present in the hall. The inventory of her husband, John, which had been drawn up the previous year, merely itemises 'divers pictures' in the same room. In some cases, the number of pictures present in a room tends to conjure up images of walls covered in High Victorian fashion. John Hovel (victualler) had ten in his parlour and Robert Baker (customs officer) had twelve in his. Even if they were not particularly large, they would certainly have made their presence felt in visual terms.

Only one surviving example of painting directly onto interior walls seems to have survived in Lowestoft, though it was common throughout the whole country from the late mediaeval period down to the middle of the seventeenth century.[88] This is to be found in the present-day Nos 43–44, High Street, a late sixteenth-century merchant's house, which stands gable-end onto the roadway and which was encased during the second half of the eighteenth century and given a new façade during the first half of the nineteenth. The plaster on the chimney-breast of the middle room on the first floor is embellished with a New Testament text, dating from the Jacobean period and surrounded by a semi-foliate border. The words are a variant of James 1.22–24: 'Be ye doers of the word, and not hearers only…' The earliest reference to this building in the manor court books occurs in March 1628, when Simon Fifield (merchant) bought it from the widow and son of John Thedam, citizen of London.

During the late sixteenth and early seventeenth centuries, there are a few examples of wainscot panelling inside a house featuring among the bequests made by a testator. Among the various items left by James Myhell (merchant) to his son Thomas in June 1584, in what is now No. 27, High Street (Plate 12), was all the *seelinge* in the house. Four years later, in August 1588, Roger Hill (merchant) left the *seelyng* in the parlour to his third son, Edmund – a legacy which is referred to in the accompanying inventory as 'joined seeling of oak' (the house in question being Nos 31–32, High Street). Then, in December 1610, Richard Berye (yeoman) left 'all the selinge' in one of his houses to a nephew, the latter to inherit this property after the death of the widow. Such legacies are not unknown in England at this time.[89] But as the seventeenth century progressed, and more and more people had panelling fitted in their houses, the woodwork became regarded as a permanent fixture and was no longer handed down in the same way.

The same is true of window glass, which was also treated at one time as a portable item because of its relatively high value.[90] There is only one instance in the surviving Lowestoft probate material of its being bequeathed, and it is to be found in the will of James Myhell. In the same clause that mentions the bequest of wainscot panelling to his son, there is also a reference to the handing down of 'all the glass in the windows'. The town had at least one glazier among its working population during the second half of the sixteenth century (Edward Jones, whose marriage was registered in November

---

[88] Portman, *Exeter Houses*, pp. 44–5. The practice was common in the city between 1550 and 1650.

[89] *Ibid.*, pp. 43–4.

[90] *Ibid.*, p. 48. Reference is made to the fact that glass in its lead mountings was easily transportable and was valued sufficiently to be included among movable goods until the early seventeenth century.

1597), and the growing popularity of window glass throughout the seventeenth century is perhaps best reflected by the fact that, during the last quarter, there were three glaziers plying their trade. And, in each half of the century, there was at least one plumber occupied in making the lead channelling into which the glass fitted.

It may well be that, as wooden shutters gave way to glazing in the windows of houses, curtains began to be used for the purpose of screening. There are five references to window curtains in the Lowestoft inventories and all of them are to be found relating to the houses of substantial people. It has been observed elsewhere that curtains were usually to be found in the dwellings of merchants and manufacturers (though not necessarily the wealthiest) and that their presence seems to have been a matter of personal taste rather than custom.[91] Roger Hill had window curtains hanging in his parlour (September 1588) and Margaret Couldham (merchant's widow) had them in the hall when the list of her worldly goods was made in January 1585. A century later, three more references to them occur in the contents of the parlours of Admiral Riches Utber (December 1669) and merchant James Wilde (March 1684), and in the hall, hall chamber and kitchen chamber of Elizabeth Pacy (August 1682).

A final item of domestic embellishment worthy of mention is the flower pot. A number of these are itemised in the late sixteenth- and early seventeenth-century inventories, but they do not appear in later documents. Whether this represents a change in fashion, or whether the vessels had become so common that they became incorporated in some such standard phrase as 'other old lumber' or 'other old things', is uncertain. Suffice it to say that their presence in houses was a feature that manifests itself between about 1580 and 1610. They were mainly to be found in the houses of the merchants, but not exclusively so. Margaret Rumpth (cordwainer's widow) had one in her hall (January 1593) and Ralfe Bache (blacksmith) had a couple in the hall chamber (December 1603). The hall was the room in which they were most commonly located and the material from which they were made was either pewter or *laten* (brass). No information exists, unfortunately, to show whether they were used to hold cut flowers or live plants.

Furniture

The late sixteenth- and early seventeenth-century wills and inventories are full of references to joined tables, framed tables, buffet stools, settles, forms, great chairs, backed chairs and benches. The terminology does not vary across the occupation groups, merely the quality of the pieces owned and their condition. It is noticeable in the more modest income groups that the word 'old' is used much more frequently to describe the various items of furniture in the different rooms. Such comfort as there was tended to be provided largely by cushions, made of silk or tapestry work, but the presence of such articles was concentrated in the wealthier sections of society. The same is true of carpets. These were used to cover tables, not lay on floors,[92] and their presence in houses is usually an indication of the status of the inhabitants.

---

[91] Portman, *Exeter Houses*, p. 39, fn. 3.

[92] Reed, *Ipswich Inventories*, 6. Such use of carpets is noted here.

As time went on, changes in taste and fashion occurred. Benches and forms diminished in number until, by the eighteenth century, they are hardly ever mentioned – and stools also decreased, though not to the same extent. Chairs became the main means of seating and developments in the materials of manufacture are to be seen. By the 1670s, it is evident that wealthier people were furnishing their halls and parlours with chairs upholstered in leather and the material continued to be used as the years went by, becoming available to a wider cross section of society – not to the point, however, of reaching the ranks of craftsmen or lesser tradespeople, in whose inventories leather-work chairs never feature. By the eighteenth century, cane was beginning to enjoy a vogue and chairs with seats (and backs) made from split and interwoven lengths of this occur from time to time in the inventories.[93] So do those with *segging bottoms*, the reference here being to a cheap substitute for cane made of sedge – a material that was widely available in Lowestoft from the edges of Lake Lothing and from the less well-drained areas of heath.

Bedsteads were a notable and expensive item of furniture (often the most valuable of all individual household goods) and had their own hierarchy. Best of all was the carved and panelled posted type, which only the wealthy people could afford to own, with its curtains and (until the fashion changed during the seventeenth century) its painted tester. A bedstead of this type, together with its bedding and coverlets, could be worth as much as £5 or £6 during the later sixteenth century. Next came the *livery* bedstead, a solid and well-built object but without the decorative quality of the grander sort. There was then a range of utilitarian models, some posted and some not, and some half-headed, which seem to have been worth about £1 5s 0d to £1 10s 0d, with the bedstead itself valued at anything between 6s 8d and 10s.

The bottom of the range was reached in the *trendle* or *truckle* bed. This was often used for children and servants and might conceivably have been stored during the daytime by being pushed underneath a larger bedstead in the same room. The value of this type was about 2s or 3s for the bedstead itself and perhaps up to £1 for the bedding, depending on quality. Bedsteads of all kinds were covered by a variety of mattresses, featherbeds (flock was sometimes used on the cheaper ones), bolsters, pillows, sheets and coverlets. The standard varied, according to the means of householders, but it was high in affluent homes, with bedlinen of excellent quality and with tapestry-work coverlets to provide a sumptuous finishing touch.

Storage inside the houses was provided by a variety of chests and cupboards, as well as by closets, from the late seventeenth century onwards. Chests usually contained linenware, clothing and valuables and were to be found mainly in chambers. Some of them were made from oak wainscot and from elm, but softwood grew in popularity from the late sixteenth century and there are frequent references to *spruce chests, fir chests* and *Danske chests*.[94] These became less frequently referred to as the seventeenth century progressed, until in the later years their presence in houses was no longer noted. Chests

[93] Peck, *Consuming Splendor*, p. 237, shows that the vogue for cane-work is detectable in aristocratic circles as far back as the 1650s. James Wilde (merchant) had two cane chairs in his parlour when the inventory of his possessions was compiled in March 1684.

[94] *Danske* is an archaic form of 'Danish', suggesting Scandinavian origins, but it and spruce might also refer to Northern Germany (specifically, Dantzig and Prussia).

are still mentioned from time to time, but with no details concerning the kind of wood from which they were made. The only type which is individually specified (especially after 1700) is the sea-chest, which was usually to be found in the chamber of a mariner's house. One possible reason for the decline in the number of household chests listed is the development of the chest-of-drawers as a specialist piece of domestic furniture, because this item begins to appear during the last quarter of the seventeenth century.

Free-standing cupboards of one kind or another were usually located in the main downstairs rooms. The *livery cupboard* is the one which tends to be individually named (it was customarily used for the storage of food), whereas the other ones which appear in the documents appear to be classified according to their size in such phrases as 'a great cupboard' or 'one small cupboard'. Those people who were sufficiently well off to be able to afford drinking glasses stored them in a box or cabinet called a *glass keep*. A number of these feature in inventories between the 1580s and the first decade of the eighteenth century, but they do not appear among the contents of houses below the level of the merchant fraternity and the better-off tradespeople, craftsmen and mariners. They were usually located in halls or parlours, but there are also occasional references to them in the contents of chambers.

By the early years of the eighteenth century, dressers begin to appear in kitchens and parlours to provide storage space for plates and other crockery and utensils, thereby endowing the houses in which they were found with a reference recognisable today. Specialist items of what may be termed 'culinary furniture' occur at either end of the period of study. During the late sixteenth and early seventeenth centuries, salt-boxes make their appearance among the various effects listed in halls, while 100 years or so later spice-boxes begin to feature among the objects recorded in both halls and kitchens.

One piece of furniture that was present in houses from the mid Elizabethan period right through to Georgian times is the mirror, or looking-glass. To begin with, only merchant families seem to have owned them and they were usually placed in halls or parlours.[95] Their exclusiveness in relation to the wealthier levels of society seems to have prevailed throughout the seventeenth century (James Wilde, merchant, had five in his house, in 1684: one each in the hall, parlour, kitchen, hall chamber and parlour chamber), but the first thirty years of the eighteenth show that they had become more widely available and were proliferating within individual houses. Out of the forty-six inventories which are extant for that period, twenty-seven have at least one looking-glass itemised among the household contents – and some of the documents show two or three per dwelling. Even Thomas Clarke (mariner), whose possessions were valued at only £11 4s 9d, had one among his goods and chattels. Halls, parlours and kitchens were the rooms most commonly associated with mirrors, but there are also examples of them being placed in chambers, too.

---

[95] One exception is Wyllyam Barrett (barber), who (not surprisingly) had one in his shop as well as in his hall.

Domestic equipment

The most common of the items chosen to feature in this sub-section is the warming pan, which was used to air bedlinen and to make the bed itself more inviting to get into during the colder months of the year. It appears in both wills and inventories from the 1580s onwards and, like the looking-glass, gradually became used by a wider cross section of the population as time went on. There seems to have been no special place where it was kept and its presence is referred to in various downstairs rooms and in chambers. The metal from which the object was made is only mentioned once: there was one made of laten (brass) in the kitchen of Ambrose King (merchant) when the inventory of his possessions was taken in November 1597.

There is more information regarding chamber pots. Pewter seems to have been the most common material of manufacture early on and, again, it seems to have been the larger and better-appointed houses which had them.[96] The rooms in which such receptacles are listed do not necessarily correspond with the places of use! They simply show where the vessels were stored.[97] From the middle of the seventeenth century onwards, the wealthier members of society in Lowestoft began to acquire imported ones from the Rhineland – made of good-quality blue and grey stoneware, generically known as Westerwald – and a number of their sherds have been found in archaeological work which has taken place to the rear of Nos 74, 75, 76, 77–79 and 80, High Street.[98]

Whatever material they were made from, the periodic disposal of chamber pots' contents is popularly supposed to have been a somewhat haphazard affair – a notion which would seem to be borne out by a leet court minute of 1706. David Cudden (husbandman) was fined 3d for throwing urine (*matulas*) out of the window of his house into Rant Score. He was probably disposing of the contents of a chamber pot and he may have been unfortunate enough to have done it (unless the action was deliberate!) at such time as the jurors were passing his house. The leet itself was held at an inn in the town on the first Saturday in Lent and the previous day was spent by members of its jury on a tour of inspection, with various arraignable offences being duly noted and complaints received.

Close-stools were the other means of accommodating the calls of nature within the house and such items of furniture have been variously noted in Norwich, King's Lynn and Exeter.[99] They also occur fairly regularly in the Lowestoft inventories, especially in the late seventeenth and early eighteenth centuries. Altogether, there are three references to them between 1585 and 1603, a further eight between 1656 and 1693 (two of which mention the pan, as well as the seat), and ten between 1700 and 1730. Again, they seem to have been associated with the wealthier members of the community, though their wider ownership during the first three decades of the eighteenth century meant that

---

[96] Priestley and Corfield, 116. The writers refer to pewter chamber pots often being listed in Norwich inventories.

[97] Portman, *Exeter Houses*, p. 51, makes reference to chamber pots being kept in kitchens and butteries. The Lowestoft inventories have examples of this practice, too.

[98] Durbidge, 'A Limited Excavation', 19–22, and 'Second Excavation', 32.

[99] Priestley and Corfield, 116; Parker, *King's Lynn*, p. 91; Portman, *Exeter Houses*, p. 51.

they were no longer exclusive to the merchant fraternity; a customs officer, a mariner, a cooper and a mason were all included among the owners. Close-stools always feature among the contents of chambers when listed, which is probably where they would have been used, and the earliest one of all in the Lowestoft documents is mentioned twice. It was one of the many possessions bequeathed by Allen Coldham (merchant) to his wife Margaret in November 1581 and he specifically refers to it as having a lock. Just over three years later, in January 1585, it was listed in the said Margaret's inventory among the contents of the shop chamber, with a value of 6s 8d placed on it.

The last piece of domestic equipment to be discussed is the coal-burning range, which seems to have been an introduction of the early eighteenth century as far as houses in Lowestoft are concerned. It is first mentioned in June 1706, in the will of Frances Canham, a widow, who bequeathed one to her grandson, Thomas Daines. This suggests that it was both removable and portable, which in turn implies an iron fabrication of some sort. There are five references to 'coal ranges' in the probate inventories, the first being that of John Hovel (victualler), who had one in his kitchen which was worth 10s with its accompanying implements (December 1710). Leake Bitson (merchant), who lived in the most northerly house on the east side of the High Street, had one in his kitchen and another in his parlour when the appraisal of his goods was made in February 1717. They were each valued at 12s. Robert Dixon (carpenter) also had one in his kitchen. His house stood on the south side of Blue Anchor Lane and his inventory of February 1723 gives a value of 13s for the range and its implements. Samuel Smithson (merchant), who lived at the western end of Bell Lane, died later in the same year and the assessors valued the range in his kitchen at 25s. Finally, in December 1730, the possessions of Samuel Baker (customs officer) were appraised. He had a range in both kitchen and parlour, the former being valued at £1 10s 0d and the latter at £1 1s 6d.

Clocks and watches

There are no references to mechanical time-pieces in the Lowestoft probate material earlier than December 1677.[100] The first one appears in the inventory of Richard Church (merchant), who had a case-clock worth £3 standing in his hall. Nearly five years later, in August 1682, the clock and case (also in the hall) belonging to his mother-in-law, Elizabeth Pacy, were valued at £2. In the same month and year, her next-door neighbour, James Wilde (merchant), bequeathed the clock in his hall to his oldest son, John, and in March 1684 this same clock was valued at £2 10s 0d in his inventory. Finally, in January 1693, the inventory of Simon Rivett (mariner) shows that he too had a clock standing in his hall. No case is referred to and the instrument's value cannot be ascertained because of damage to the document. There is only one probate record of the late seventeenth century which refers to a watch and that is the will of James Reeve (doctor), who bequeathed one to his wife in February 1679. It

---

[100] An hour-glass was listed among the possessions of Christopher Rant (gentleman) in February 1642 and another turned up sixty years later, in May 1701, in the effects of George Mayes (fisherman).

was obviously not in working order, because the testator described it as requiring repair by a Mr Manley of Beccles.

During the first thirty years of the eighteenth century, clocks appear in probate inventories in thirteen of the forty-six surviving documents (though two of them do relate to the same dwelling, being the lists of goods of a brewer and his widow) and watches in another four. Seven of the clocks were situated in halls, three in parlours and three in kitchens. Nine of the references are to clocks alone and another four to clocks and cases. Where individual values are able to be ascertained (sometimes the items were included with other household goods in a composite sum), the range is from £1 to £4 10s 0d, regardless of whether the clock had a case or not. The ownership of these clocks is as follows: three merchants, a brewer and his widow, a grocer, three mariners, a customs officer, an innkeeper, a mason and a farmer. The five watches recorded belonged to another customs officer (brother of the man who owned the clock), a merchant, a mariner, a cordwainer and a widow previously mentioned. The customs officer owned two watches, each with a chain, and that belonging to the cordwainer is described as being made of silver. Most valuable of all, however, was the one which belonged to Deborah Ashby (previously mentioned on page 112 in connection with her ownership of religious pictures) and which she bequeathed to her four-year-old nephew-by-marriage, Thomas Mighells, in December 1717: it was made of gold and set with diamonds.

Books

A total of forty inventories, out of the 100 available for study, reveal the ownership of books, and this 40% of the whole matches what has been found in part of rural Suffolk.[101] Both percentages are higher than the upper limit ascertained in a national study of literacy during the pre-industrial period and considerably in excess of what has been identified in Cambridgeshire.[102] There are far fewer references to books in the Lowestoft wills, with only fourteen documents out of 507 mentioning them. It is interesting to note, however, that twenty-one of the inventories which show the presence of books in a house have accompanying wills – and nowhere in the latter documents are books referred to. This was usually the result of individual testators handing over the bulk of their respective estates to one main beneficiary, without referring to the separate items that constituted them.

The books which are mentioned in wills are nearly always Bibles or religious works of some kind and they were valued sufficiently by their owners to be accorded the honour of individual bequest to relatives or friends.[103] Deborah Ashby, the widow noted earlier for her bequests of pictures with a religious theme, showed a similar propensity

---

[101] Evans, 'South Elmham', p. 250. In that part of High Suffolk, eighteen of the forty-six documents consulted showed the ownership of books.

[102] D. Cressy, *Literacy and the Social Order* (Cambridge, 1980), p. 48. Spufford, *Contrasting Communities*, p. 210.

[103] Among the religious titles encountered are the inevitable Foxe's *Book of Martyrs* and either Thomas Bilson's *The Perpetual Government of Christ His Church* or his *Effect of Certain Sermons Concerning the Full Redemption of Mankind by the Death and Blood of Jesus Christ*.

in her reading matter. She left her maidservant, Frances Sherrington, a Bible, five volumes of Mr Sibbs' works and *The History of the Saviour*; a cousin, Ashby Utting, was to receive two volumes of *Poole's Annotations*. It is to be hoped that each of them shared her apparent taste for didactic theological works! Richard Sibbs (1577–1635) was a Puritan divine who wrote books of sermons; Matthew Poole (1624–1679) was an Anglican minister of Presbyterian leanings who produced Biblical commentaries.

The forty inventories which record the presence of books in people's houses also show a slant towards the Christian religion, with thirteen references to Bibles. In seventeen cases, books (of whatever kind they were) were located in halls. Three of the documents make no reference to rooms of any kind, but the remaining twenty indicate the use of most other rooms in houses of the time as a location for books: they occurred in parlours (two), kitchens (five), butteries (one), studies (one), living rooms (one), shops (one) wash-houses (one), chambers (five) and lodging rooms (three). Occasionally, a specialist volume associated with the owner's occupation comes to light, such as the *wagginer* listed among the possessions of Admiral Riches Utber in December 1669,[104] but for the most part (with the exception of Bibles) no identification or titles are given.

This is to be regretted because there are collections of books which, if individually named (or even given generic classification), would provide an idea of people's reading tastes or areas of interest. John Gleason, the vicar, had £4 worth of books in his study (July 1610) and sixty years later (November 1671) John Collins, a young gentleman in his twenties, who had recently qualified in law at Emmanuel College, Cambridge, had eight folios, twelve quartos and ninety small books in his lodging chamber, worth a total amount of £11 5s 0d. A decade or so later, next-door neighbours Elizabeth Pacy and James Wilde, who have already been referred to a number of times in this chapter, had forty books (worth £3) and 'a library of books' (worth £5) in their respective halls, while in May 1691 Robert Knight (a gentleman from Kent who had married into the influential Mighells family) had books worth £10 in a chamber. The final collection of any note is that belonging to Michael Thurston (February 1714). He was the mariner noted earlier (page 112) as having exotic pictures in his kitchen chamber. Below them, in the kitchen itself, were twenty books worth 7s 6d.

Weapons and armour

Far from being the rarities that they were found to be in a study of villages in rural Cambridgeshire,[105] weapons of various kinds are mentioned a good deal in the Lowestoft probate material. Nor was their presence in houses anything to do with creating an impression on people entering a dwelling, as was the case with some of the grander Norwich residences during the second half of the seventeenth century.[106] Their existence was very much due to practical reasons. Coastal communities tended to be seen as the nation's first line of defence against foreign invasion, especially during the

---

[104] This was a book of navigational charts, the original one having been compiled by a Dutchman, Lucas Janssen Wagenaer, and first published in 1584.

[105] Spufford, *Contrasting Communities*, p. 74.

[106] Priestley and Corfield, 106.

Elizabethan period, when the threat from Spain was at its greatest. Then there was the need for seafarers to have the means of fending off attack from privateers, especially those from the Dunkirk area. Altogether, thirty-one of the Lowestoft inventories make reference to weapons of one kind or another, a proportion which again corresponds closely with what has been observed in that part of rural Suffolk mentioned four paragraphs above.[107] Of these thirty-one documents, eleven date from the last fifteen years of the sixteenth century and five from the early years of the seventeenth. By way of contrast, only four of the 507 wills have weapons referred to – a much lower proportion than that ascertained in the South Elmham area of rural Suffolk.[108]

The concentration of weaponry in the 1580s and 90s is not surprising, given the country's expectation of being invaded by Spain. A muster taken of Lowestoft in 1584 (the year in which the contingency plan for Lothingland, referred to on page 10, was drawn up) lists 240 men, not all suitable for military service and not all of whom had weapons.[109] In addition, there were four widows who were able to supply equipment, which had presumably belonged to their husbands. The weapons and pieces of armour listed are as follows: eighty-four bills, five pikes, two halberds, twenty-one calivers, seventeen bows, five swords, five daggers, twenty-six corselets and coats of plate, and thirty-six helmets and steel caps of various kinds. The calivers were largely owned by seafarers and merchants and the bills by landsmen, and there are four cases of weapons referred to in the muster turning up in probate inventories. Roger Hill's caliver and almayne rivet were listed among the contents of his hall (September 1588); Ambrose King's caliver was one of two itemised in the parlour chamber (November 1597) – but it must have been some years since he had been able to use either of them, as he was noted in the muster list as being blind; John Gaze, a cooper, had a bill and sallet in his hall (July 1590); and Margaret Couldham had her deceased husband's coat of plate stored in the shop chamber (January 1585).

The second half of the seventeenth century and the first three decades of the eighteenth show a continuation of the possession of arms by people involved in fishing or maritime trade, but further professional use (if it may be so termed) is evident in the ownership of swords and pistols by customs officers. Another feature concerning firearms is the use of sporting guns, which manifests itself from time to time across the whole timespan covered in this book. The earliest reference to a 'fowling piece' is to be found in the inventory of William Rogers (goldsmith), in April 1595. Henry Cobbe (innkeeper) had one in April 1618, while Admiral Riches Utber owned three of them (as well as three pairs of pistols, a rapier and a crossbow) in December 1669 – perhaps occupying some of his retirement hours in pursuit of wildfowl. The last time that sporting guns are referred to is in December 1677, when Richard Church (merchant) is seen to have been in possession of one.

There would have been ample opportunity to have used such firearms on the various areas of heathland in the parish and also around the margins of Lake Lothing.

---

[107] Evans, 'South Elmham', p. 288. Nearly one-third of the inventories record arms and armour.

[108] *Ibid.*, p. 288. Out of a total of 282 wills, thirteen mention weapons of one kind or another.

[109] Powell, 'Muster Roll', *PSIA*, xix, 65–70.

Presumably, the privilege would have been been enjoyed with the lord of the manor's permission and no cases of illegal shooting have been detected in the leet court minutes. The monetary value of firearms is hard to ascertain because they are never listed individually, but are bracketed together with other, similar guns or with associated equipment such as touch-boxes and flaskets. The nearest estimate that can be given for the earlier part of the seventeenth century is Henry Cobbe's fowling piece at 16s (though a yew bow-stave also formed part of the valuation), while that belonging to Richard Church was probably worth about £2, being itemised together with a musket in a valuation of £4. The usual rooms where weapons were kept were either the hall (sixteen examples) or the parlour (six examples), though chambers (five examples) also feature as places of storage.

Precious metal

Altogether, eighty-three of the 507 Lowestoft wills mention bequests of silverware and other valuables. At 16.3% of the whole, this is broadly comparable with the South Elmham area of Suffolk.[110] Specific items are not always referred to, but a standard phrase used, such as 'all my gold, silver, jewels and plate'. The inventories, however, show in detail the kind of precious objects which people had in their houses and they also draw attention to the way in which, by the first three decades of the eighteenth century, the possession of silver had spread across a broader cross section of society. Out of the 100 inventories available for study, no fewer than forty-nine record artefacts made from precious metal (mainly silver), which is twice the rate of ownership as that observed in South Elmham.[111] Presumably, the greater visible affluence in Lowestoft was the result of its being a community involved in fishing and maritime trade, as well as in agriculturally based pursuits, as opposed to one that was primarily concerned with agriculture alone.

Usually, household silver was located in halls and parlours and consisted mainly of items associated with the table. In the late sixteenth century, because of the number of their inventories which have survived, members of the merchant class are seen to have had goblets, cups, salts and spoons in their homes (some of the vessels being silver-gilt), as well as buttons made of silver. The latter are listed as if independent of garments, so perhaps they were awaiting use. There are also references to silver-rimmed mazers and stone cups and, occasionally, a touch of real personal luxury is noted in something like the reference to Roger Hill's gold comb and silver toothpick (September 1588).[112]

During the mid to late seventeenth century, a similar range of items is to be seen in the ownership of merchants, the more affluent tradespeople and members of the gentry. The one development in domestic silverware to be noted is the presence of tankards

---

[110] Evans, 'South Elmham', p. 289. The proportion of wills itemising bequest of precious metal is 14%.

[111] *Ibid.*, p. 289.

[112] Durbidge, 'A Limited Excavation', 22, discusses the finding of high-class stoneware sherds deriving from Cologne and Frechen ware mugs and tankards in the same area of the High Street previously referred to (Nos 74, 75, 76, 77–79 and 80).

(almost certainly with lids) among people's prized possessions, while in terms of the metal generally the word 'plate' starts to be used to describe a range of items. Riches Utber had 378 ounces of it in his house, as well as 'sundry rings and jewels', the total value of these assets being assessed at £114 10s 0d – by far the largest sum recorded in any of the inventories. Next in the overall hierarchy, though a long way behind, comes James Wilde. He had three tankards (one of which had been presented to him by the town for his efforts in opposing Great Yarmouth's attempts to control the local herring industry), a salt cellar, a porringer, a cup and nineteen spoons, all of which were valued at £35.

During the first thirty years of the eighteenth century, twenty-nine of the forty-six inventories reveal the ownership of silverware. The social range was wider than it had been previously, with craftsmen and fishermen joining the ranks of those who had items made of silver in their homes. The pieces themselves were broadly the same as they had been for the previous 100 years or more, consisting largely of cups, tankards, salts and spoons. Six references to plate are to be found, as a means of summarising the deceased's silverware, and the most valuable collection was that of Margaret Durrant (brewer's widow). Her pair of silver tankards, a salver, a cup, two salts and twelve silver spoons were estimated to be worth £25.

Most interesting of all, in social terms, is the reference to three silver tea spoons in February 1717, itemised among the possessions of Leake Bitson (merchant). And they are not the only ones recorded. Thomas Felton (cooper) had one among his various effects in July 1722, while Daniel Manning (cordwainer) had an unspecified number in his house and Samuel Baker, a customs officer, had six in his – both inventories being compiled in December 1730. Thus, a generation or so before the town's soft-paste porcelain factory went into production, people in Lowestoft were enjoying the vogue for drinking tea.[113]

Case studies

A small house (early eighteenth-century)

John Cousens (carter) lived with his wife Mary in a three-roomed house somewhere in the side-street area. Their son, Benjamin (aged twenty-four years) had left home, but their daughter, Mary (aged twenty years) was possibly still living there. When the inventory of Cousens's goods was made on 6 June 1711, his total estate was valued at £73 8s 9d. Out of this sum, £50 consisted of good debts and a further £16 17s 0d of his working equipment and horses. The household effects he owned therefore added up to £6 11s 9d, and £3 of this was accounted for by clothing kept in his bedchamber (a pair of green breeches, four coats, two waistcoats, a hat, a pair of shoes and a pair of stockings). The low room was the main living area and its contents consisted of fire cradle, iron trivet and frying pan, a smoothing iron and two metal heating plates, a

---

[113] The factory was established in c. 1757 (occupying former residential premises at the western end of Bell Lane) and closed down in about 1800. It was the third-longest-lived English soft-paste porcelain factory after Worcester and Derby. See E. Gillingwater, pp. 112–13 and S. Smith, *Lowestoft Porcelain in Norwich Castle Museum* (Norwich, 1975), pp. 1–23.

quantity of coal, two tables, two armchairs, three other chairs, a looking-glass, some earthenware crocks, two sieves, a posted bed with hangings and coverings, and one other, smaller, bed. The wash-house contained two pairs of tongs, two tubs, three keelers and a small boiler. Above these two ground-floor rooms was a bed-chamber, which accommodated one bed with its coverings, one livery cupboard, a trunk, a joined stool, one keeler, two swills, two other baskets and the clothes previously referred to. The single most expensive item of furniture in the house was the posted bed which, together with its coverings, was valued at 15s.

A medium-sized house (early seventeenth-century)

William Blanncher (cordwainer) lived with his wife, Elizabeth, in a house with five rooms, one of which was his workshop. They had six children altogether – a son aged eleven years and five daughters aged ten years, eight years, six years, four years and eighteen months respectively. If the number of beds in the house is anything to go by, all the children may still have been living at home, though the boy and two of the girls were to die the following summer in the epidemic of 1603.

Blanncher's worldly goods were appraised on 24 April 1602 and a value of £17 19s 9d was placed upon them – plus another £3 15s 9d in money owed to him. The shop's contents consisted of his tools, various pairs of shoes, items of leather clothing (mainly breeches and sleeves) and a certain quantity of unused leather. The value of all this came to £5 5s 0d, which means that the household effects were worth £12 14s 9d. The hall was the main living room, with a fireplace equipped with a range of associated implements (including two roasting irons) situated there. There were also various items of furniture present: a framed table, four small tables, one long form, two large joined stools and two small ones, two large chairs, six small chairs, four cushions, two coffers and one cupboard. This last-named item seems to have been the repository for various pewter plates and saucers, as well as porringers, salt cellars and candlesticks. Finally, there was also a posted bed in the room, complete with all its coverings. The kitchen was used primarily to store cooking and eating utensils. Skillets, brass pots and kettles, frying pans, latch pans, skimmers and basting ladles are all referred to. So are pewter dishes and saucers, wooden platters and dishes, earthenware vessels, porringers, salt cellars and basins. There was also a certain amount of brewing equipment in the place, as well as a currying pan (for treating hide) and a Bible.

Upstairs, above the hall, kitchen and shop, were two chambers. The principal one, above the hall, contained a posted bedstead with all its appurtenances and two truckle beds with their coverings. A Danske chest and a framed table stood in the room, a wooden candlestick was used to light it during the hours of darkness, and two drinking glasses were located there. It also served as storage place and among the items listed were a bushel and a half of wheat, two sides of bacon, two saddles (one of which was a pack-saddle), an empty barrel, four bow-staves and a bill. The chamber next door simply contained a bed and its fittings, a pole-axe and certain unspecified objects made of iron. The two most valuable items among all the household effects were the two big beds upstairs, which were appraised at £1 each. Next to them came a brass cauldron in the kitchen, estimated to be worth 13s 4d.

Plate 14. *Nos 81–83, High Street. The Pacy family home has long been divided into two shops, the left-hand one of which retains its nineteenth-century front. There is evidence to suggest that the whole building once had a jettied first floor. The dormers are nineteenth-century insertions.*

A large house (late seventeenth-century)

Samuel and Elizabeth Pacy (merchant and wife) lived in a mid/late sixteenth-century building on the east side of the High Street (Plate 14) and were the richest couple identified in Lowestoft throughout the whole period of study.[114] Pacy made his money from fishing, from the export of red herrings to Italy and from North Sea and Baltic trade – and his wife (a member of the Bardwell family) had brought him lands and rents in the south Norfolk parishes of Topcroft and Denton. He died in September 1680, his wife surviving him by about two years, and her inventory of 18 August 1682 is effectively his as well. At the time it was drawn up, it is likely that the middle one of their three daughters, Elizabeth Ward (a thirty-two-year-old widow), was living in the house, as well as two of their three sons: William (aged twenty years) and John (aged seventeen years).

---

[114] The house had been the family home for three generations. It has long been divided into two shops, but the basic room-plan of earlier times is still discernible.

According to the document, there were fourteen or fifteen rooms associated with the house, but this number could not have been accommodated within the building. The hall, parlour, kitchen and pantry can be ascertained, even today, together with the four chambers above, and the presence of both a cellar and a garret can be accepted. However, the three butteries and the wash-house must have been built on at the back of the house as annexes, with the possibility that one or two of them might even have been free-standing in the yard – unless, of course, there was a cross-wing on the house at one time, of which all external traces have disappeared.[115] From the total value of the inventory, which adds up to £2,849, the following sums have to be deducted in order to ascertain the value of the house's contents: £1,043 7s 6d in trading craft, fishing vessels, equipment and stock; £1,065 2s 2d in mortgages and bonds; £284 2s 10d in cash; and £282 13s 7d in good debts. This leaves a figure of £173 14s 8d as the value of all furniture, fittings, linenware and utensils.

The hall and the parlour were 'polite' rooms, for sitting in comfort. Both were heated and were furnished with leather chairs. The hall's main table was covered with a carpet (a smaller, round table is also referred to); there was a case-clock present in the room; six cushions were to be found there; the windows had curtains; firearms and swords were mounted on the walls; there were seven pictures hanging; and forty books were present to provide reading material. The parlour was even more refined, with its leather chairs, three Spanish tables (together with Turkish and Dornic carpets as coverings), drinking glasses in their own special cabinet, brass ornaments and a looking-glass, and landscapes on the walls. These pictures are especially interesting because, in the absence of an English school of landscape painters and given Samuel Pacy's trading links with The Netherlands, they might possibly have been works by Ruysdael, Hobbema and the like.

The kitchen had considerable seating capacity, with its eighteen stools and two chairs, which seems to suggest that substantial numbers of people sat down to eat there. There was a large, leafed table present in the room, which had a carpet to cover it, and also a smaller table as well. A total of thirty-four pieces of earthenware are itemised, as well as various fire-irons, jacks, spits and basting spoons, and thirty-six napkins and twenty-four towels were also kept there. The pantry was the chief storage place for the household pewter. There was so much of it that the individual pieces were not named, but the weight given instead (144 pounds). There were also thirty-six plates listed, but the material from which they were made is not specified. The three butteries are described as containing 'small goods', but apart from one press and three latch-pans nothing is individually named. The wash-house appears to have contained nothing associated with

---

[115] The discovery by Ivan Bunn of a blocked doorway, behind panelling in the eastern wall of the building, suggests that a cross-wing once existed. In Priestley and Corfield, 112, the difficulty of ascertaining whether sculleries were an integral part of a house or were free-standing is referred to. This problem may apply to other service rooms. There is evidence remaining of least one substantial building having been once situated in the yard of the Pacys' house: a brick gable-end dating from the seventeenth century, which now constitutes part of the northern boundary wall abutting onto Wilde's Score. On the visual evidence of the type of brickwork built up above the line of the gable, the conversion work was done during the late eighteenth/early nineteenth century.

washing, being largely the storage place for a variety of cooking utensils. The final space referred to on the ground floor was a writing closet. It stood somewhere at the back of the house and possibly served as an office of some kind, the contents being a quantity of paper and two old cases.

Upstairs, three of the four bedrooms were heated (hall, parlour and kitchen chambers), implying that the house was served by both off-centre and end stacks. The only one without such amenity was the pantry chamber, which contained one bed, one chest and a close-stool, and which had sheets, pillowcases and table-cloths stored within. The other three were more comfortably appointed, especially the hall chamber, which was the principal bedroom. Its two windows were curtained; it had a bed worth £10 (the most valuable item of furniture in the house); a small table and a nest of drawers featured among the pieces of furniture; it had six chairs upholstered with Turkish carpet material; and ten cushions added further to the general air of refinement.[116] A good deal of napery and linen was kept there, as was the family's gold and silver plate (worth £18 15s 0d). No chest or coffer is referred to in connection with the valuables, which means that they may have been on open display. There was also a closet in the room, which contained ten reams of paper and certain earthenware vessels. The parlour chamber, next door, was much more simply furnished. It contained bedding (a curtain, rug, valance and two pillows), but no bed, and it may have been used as some kind of upstairs sitting room because there was a table inside, with two chairs and two stools. The kitchen chamber had a bed inside it, worth £8, and its window had curtains. Six chairs and two stools stood within the room, and there were fire-irons for the hearth.

Above the bedchambers were two garrets, the north and the south ones (reflecting the alignment of the house, lengthways to the street). The terminology suggests that the roof-space was partitioned and that the southern room was heated, if the presence there of andirons is significant. It seems to have been the larger of the two spaces and contained two beds and bedsteads, two tables, six chairs, two stools, a standard (either a large wooden candlestick or a storage box), two trunks, a chest, a box and twenty-seven pairs of sheets – these last-named being worth £18. The northern room was more simply furnished, containing two beds, two settles and other, unnamed items, and may have functioned as servants' quarters.

The three examples cited here represent only a very small proportion of the surviving Lowestoft probate inventories studied (3%), but they do serve to give some sense of domestic arrangements in varying levels of society at different points within the overall timescale of the study. The Pacys' house is particularly interesting, serving perhaps to demonstrate the spread of luxury goods (from concentration in London society) into the provinces, which took place progressively throughout the seventeenth century.[117] And, in representing evidence of what has become known as 'conspicuous consumption', it (and others like it, such as the Wilde family residence next door) calls into question the

[116] Peck, *Consuming Splendor*, p. 237, shows the wife of Thomas Coke, a member of a leading Norfolk family of aristocrats and lawyers, requesting her husband in 1655 to purchase turkey-work chairs in London to match ones they already had.
[117] *Ibid.*, pp. 347–52.

attention paid to the eighteenth century as the great age of developing consumerism.[118] A good deal of study has been devoted in the last twenty years or so to increasing acquisition of consumer goods among the middling orders of society.[119] Lowestoft's wealthier inhabitants certainly had the means to indulge themselves in domestic comforts and the Pacys' dwelling may also reveal the influence of its female head in a number of internal arrangements. Women's predilection for looking-glasses, clocks and pictures was a feature of the time,[120] and it is likely that Elizabeth Pacy herself was more influential than her husband in the décor of their home. Given its maritime trading links with London and other English ports, as well as with European countries, the family was also well placed to be aware of developments in contemporary taste and fashion.

---

[118] S. Pennell, 'Consumption and Consumerism in Early Modern England', in *Historical Journal*, 42, 2 (1999), 549–64, challenges this focus – as do a number of other publications.

[119] L. Weatherill, *Consumer Behaviour and Material Culture in Britain* s (London, 1988; 2nd ed., 1996)

[120] Weatherill, 'Possession of One's Own', 131–56.

– 7 –

Wealth, Credit and Inheritance

Real estate

Houses and buildings

Both the manor roll of 1618 and the Rev. John Tanner's listing of 1725 show that there was no great concentration of ownership of residential and industrial property in town in the hands of any one person, or indeed in the hands of a small group of people. The dwelling-houses, inns, fish-curing premises, malt-houses, breweries, workshops and various yards were well spread across the merchant fraternity, the tradespeople, the craftsmen and the seafarers.

The manor roll shows that the 251 properties within the built-up area of the town and the southern extension of the High Street – 203 of which were houses and inns, the other forty-eight a combination of fish-houses, sundry industrial premises, barns, yards, pightles and hemplands – were owned by 178 people, twenty-seven of whom were women (15.2% of the whole), these latter largely being widows of men who had previously owned the particular properties. No fewer than 120 of the people feature in the family reconstitution material (67.4%), while at least another twenty-nine (16.3%) are known either to have had a connection with the town or to have lived in a nearby parish. In most cases, the ownership seems to have been in the form of sole possession of an individual property, but there are seven references to people who owned part of a house and a further four where a dwelling was held jointly by a husband and wife.

There are also examples of ownership of more than one property. Thirteen of the people listed held two houses each, a further ten held three, and three possessed no fewer than five. The occupation and status groups represented by the thirteen are as follows: gentlemen, merchants, yeomen, tradespeople (brewer, grocer) and craftsmen (blacksmith, hatter shoemaker and shipwright). The group of ten was almost identical in its make-up, though with the addition of seafarers, and the final group, of three, consisted of two gentlemen and a yeoman.[1] It is to be presumed that all of these people derived at least part of their income from property rents – especially those in the final grouping.

---

[1] The categorisation of the social and occupation groups includes widows of men known to have been of that status. Their presence as holders of real estate is indicated in the various tables reproduced.

One of the gentlemen, Christopher Rant, owned a block of land immediately south of the score which bore his family's name (and still does) and the houses in question stood on it, fronting the street.[2] The other, John Utber, not only had houses as part of his interests; he owned farmland in the parish as well.[3] The yeoman, Thomas Ward, seems to have retired from farming by the time that the manor roll was compiled and to have been more concerned with property ownership. Another gentleman featuring in the document, William Kettleborowe, definitely made money from property transactions. He is shown as possessing three houses (including *The Angel* inn) and, in the course of the next thirty years or so, he regularly bought and sold property in the town.

By the time that John Tanner drew up his list, the number of houses in the parish had grown to 381. However, he was dealing almost exclusively with copyhold property (the only exceptions were four houses on the east side of the High Street, which had become freehold at some stage). This means that, for the purposes of ascertaining definite ownership, the freehold houses to the west of the High Street, at either end, have to be ignored – their number being known, but not all of the owners. Tanner's list of the customary holdings in town gives a total of about 320 houses in the main built-up area and a further thirty-nine assorted fish-houses, malthouses, breweries, barns, slaughter-houses, stables and pieces of land independent of the residential plots.[4] These 359 individual properties were held by 186 different owners, 165 of whom (89%) are shown in the family reconstitution data to have been living in Lowestoft at the time the list was drawn up – which is a considerably higher proportion of resident property owners than had been the case 100 years earlier. In addition to these people, there were a further five men (most, if not all, of whom were non-resident) whose wives had local antecedents, either by birth or by marriage, and five men and a woman whose parentage was rooted in the town.

Thirty-four of the people who held real estate were widows (again, largely the relicts of the previous owners) and there were also thirteen single women and five married ones in the same situation.[5] This means that women having sole possession of a messuage constituted 28% of all property owners. In a further twenty cases, the husband held property in the right of his wife, while in another thirty-four instances the holding was owned jointly. There are a number of entries in the court baron minutes over the years which show transfer of real estate, whether by sale or bequest, being recorded in the name of the new owner and his wife. Sometimes both names are simply entered together; on other occasions, the man is admitted to the property in one entry, and this

---

[2] The plots are occupied today by Nos 70 and 71, 72 and 73, 74, 75 and 76 and 77–79, High Street.

[3] He was the grandson of Barnard Utber of Norwich, freeman of the city and cooper by trade. The claim to gentry status was based on the wealth which his family had acquired, not on breeding.

[4] Many of the dwellings, both in 1618 and 1725, had work premises incorporated in their messuages. And there were a number of other, similar buildings that were not part of residential plots.

[5] The married women all held their property under the terms of a father's will.

is then immediately followed by another one admitting him and his wife.[6] Such transactions were probably part of a marriage agreement.

Several examples of the ownership of more than one house are in evidence in both John Tanner's list and his accompanying court baron extracts. Sometimes the exact number is obscured by a reference to 'tenements' and nothing more, but in other instances a precise number of dwellings is given. By cross-checking with the information available in wills, the following distribution is arrived at: forty-three people with two houses each, twenty-four with three, nine with four, three with five, one with six and two with seven. The cross section of society owning the properties is similar to that of 1618, but without the presence of anyone of true gentry status and with an increase in the number of mariners and fishermen.

Thus, merchants, yeomen, tradespeople (brewer, butcher, draper, grocer and innkeeper), craftsmen (blacksmith, carpenter and shoemaker) and seafarers are all represented, but in greater numbers than previously. This development was probably due in part to the increase in population which had taken place from about 1680 onwards, but the rise in the number of seafarers who owned property (about ten in 1618 compared with forty or so in 1725) also resulted from Lowestoft's increased prosperity after being granted port status in 1679. As many as seventeen or eighteen mariners and fishermen were able to own more than one house during the second and third decades of the eighteenth century, all of them being masters of the vessels in which they sailed.

Another fact to emerge from analysis of the information given in the manor roll and in Tanner's list is that there was greater average ownership of property per capita in 1725 than there had been in 1618.[7] In the latter year, the 206 copyhold messuages in town had been in the hands of 138 people (1.49 per person), but a century later the 359 holdings belonged to 186 people (1.93 per person). Within this increased rate of possession, there was also a substantial increase in the number of women who held real estate. In 1618, there had been twenty-three women among the 138 owners of copyhold messuages in the town (16.7%), but by 1725 there were fifty-two out of 186 (28%).[8] The change in proportion may partly reflect changing social attitudes towards ownership of property by women. But it is also possible that, with more property being held by individuals, there was a greater amount of real estate for testators to dispose of among widows and daughters.

Agricultural land

The manor roll of 1618 shows that the thousand or so acres of farmland, of various kinds, was almost entirely held by freehold tenure (about 960 acres, in fact). This resulted from progressive selling-off from quite an early period and, with the transfer of freehold

---

[6] The latter practice has also been observed in the Cambridgeshire parish of Chippenham. See Spufford, *Contrasting Communities*, p. 89.

[7] With an annual return of 6%–8% on the investment, acquiring houses to rent was sound business.

[8] The female property owners in 1618 consisted of sixteen widows, three married women, one spinster and three of unknown status.

property not requiring entry in manorial records, the only chance offered to ascertain ownership of this valuable resource is the manor roll itself. Obviously, the pattern of ownership is only relevant for the time at which the document was compiled and it shows that there were fifty-eight different holders of the land: fifty-six private individuals (including the lord of the manor and three other local lords) and two corporate bodies.[9] The latter consisted of the trustees of the town's charitable lands and Magdalen College, Oxford, and these organisations also happened to hold the largest areas: 106 acres and 123 acres respectively.[10]

The demesne was sixty-eight acres in size (exclusive of the large areas of heath and common green) and most of the other substantial holdings belonged to local members of the gentry, who lived either in Lowestoft itself or in adjacent parishes. Gislam Wolhouse (sixty-eight acres), John Grenewood (forty-five acres), Francis Whayman (forty-three acres), John Utber (twenty-seven and a half acres), William Grenewood (eighteen acres) and William Canham (seventeen acres) were all townsmen. Robert Jettor (ninety-seven acres) and Thomas Jenkinson (fifty-three acres) lived in Flixton and Oulton respectively, and Francis Wrott (sixty-three acres) resided in Gunton.[11] None of these men seems to have been involved in working the land he held. Instead, it was presumably rented out to people who worked it for themselves or who may have sub-let it to other tenants. There were a further three gentlemen who also held land in the parish (Anthony Hobert from Oulton, Benedict Campe from Kessingland, and William Kettleborough, who was mentioned in the previous section), but their acreages were very small.[12] This pattern of ownership meant that 700 acres (70% of the whole) were controlled by nine members of the gentry, the town's charitable trustees and an Oxford college.

Next to the twelve gentlemen, the largest group of people to own land were widows. There were eight of them altogether, but their holdings were not large. Only two of them (Alice Clarke and Katherine Rowse) had acreages that reached double figures – ten and twelve respectively – and the rest were a good deal smaller. Of the eight, two were the widows of seafarers (Agnes Eastgate and Margaret Gooch) and another two the widows of merchants (Elizabeth Hill and the Katherine Rowse). All four of them, together with Alice Clarke, were resident in the parish. The remaining three were outsiders, one of whom (Katherine Church) lived in nearby Kirkley and another (Alice

---

[9] The three manors in question were those of Gunton (40+ acres), Oulton Hall (3 acres) and Somerleyton (2 acres).

[10] Magadalen College came into possession of the small, pre-Domesday manor of Akethorpe because William Waynflete (Bishop of Winchester and Chancellor of England) diverted certain bequests made by Sir John Fastolf (ob. 1459) towards founding a college for seven priests at Caister, in Norfolk. The revenues were used to maintain seven scholars at Waynflete's new college in Oxford. Waynflete obviously came to an arrangement with his co-executor, John Paston Snr, but it wasn't until 1479 that the college was confirmed in its ownership of the Fastolf bequest. See R. C. Fowler (ed.) *CPR, Edward IV to Richard III, 1476–85*, p. 143.

[11] He was lord of the manor there, which meant that his combined land-holding was in excess of 103 acres (sixty-three of his own and forty plus belonging to the manor).

[12] Hobert was lord of the manor of Oulton Hall. As well as a small parcel of half an acre to an acre of land (independent of the three acres belonging to his manor), he also held *The Dolphin* inn on Lowestoft High Street.

Welles) at Seething, in south Norfolk. It has not been possible to establish a place of residence for the last one, Alice Phillippes. Two other Lowestoft women also held small areas of land: Christian Fullwood (merchant's daughter) and Margaret Burgis, whose family members included blacksmiths and carpenters.

The remaining thirty holders of land were all men, only four of whom owned an acreage sufficient to reach double figures. William Cuddon and John Osborne had forty-five acres and twenty-nine acres respectively, while William Crowe and Thomas Drawer held fourteen and eleven. Included in the thirty were four merchants (Robert Allen, John Arnold, Thomas Drawer and Thomas Webb), three yeomen (Nathaniel Bentley, William Meek and Thomas Smyter), two seafarers (John Fowle and Abraham Peirson), a baker-and-brewer (John Browne), a carpenter (John Burgis), an innkeeper (John Candler), a tanner (Edward Browne) and the vicar (Robert Hawes). The last-named had one and three-quarter acres of glebe next to the parish church, which he farmed in a small way. Altogether, thirty-three of the fifty-six individual people who held land in the parish can be found in the family reconstitution material (60%), while a further thirteen (23%) either had a connection with the place or lived in an adjacent community. It is likely that most of the remaining ten also resided close at hand, but it has not been possible to identify their parishes of residence.

Property ownership inside and outside the parish

Out of 102 wills which are extant for the last four decades of the sixteenth century, sixty-four show testators who owned real estate of some kind. In the majority of cases, the property was held within the parish and was concentrated, predictably enough, in the hands of the wealthier members of the community. Exactly half of these people (twenty-five men and seven women) owned a single dwelling-house and appurtenances at the time that their wills were written. But among the merchants, the craftsmen and the seafarers (and also, to a lesser extent, among the tradespeople) there was also the acquisition of buildings and land beyond their immediate needs.

A certain amount of this property was owned in communities beyond the town. Altogether, thirty-eight different parishes are named, twenty-two of which were situated within a five-mile radius, while the other sixteen lay largely within a range of six to fifteen miles' distance. Only three places mentioned (Fundenhall, Long Stratton and Mattishall, in Norfolk) were situated more than twenty miles away. It is tempting to view this ownership of property outside the town, especially in the case of the merchants, as evidence of economic diversification of the kind found in King's Lynn during the early seventeenth century.[13] But there is another possible explanation of such a feature and it may apply to places other than Lowestoft. It is this: unless a man (or woman) can be proved to have been indigenous to a particular community by a family reconstitution exercise, he (or she) may not have been a native. If, when he (or she) died, property in a parish removed from the place of residence was left to heirs, that parish may have been the place of origin.

---

[13] Metters, 'Rulers and Merchants', pp. 321–4.

In the case of Lowestoft during the later part of the sixteenth century, two of the merchants who left real estate in communities outside the town definitely came from those places. Allen Coldham had his roots in Great Yarmouth (having been one of its four bailiffs in 1559), while John Cullier came from Southwold. A man referred to as Mr Cornelys Bryght also had his origins in Great Yarmouth (having served as bailiff in 1546, 1556 and 1564), while John Bootye (labourer) seems to have originated from the south Norfolk parish of Fundenhall, having no previously detectable family links with Lowestoft. The same is true of John Bristowe (yeoman), who has no antecedents in the family reconstitution data, which means that his likely place of origin was one of three nearby parishes (Kirkley, Pakefield and Gisleham) where he left property in his will.

The desirability of neighbourhood studies, as opposed to single community ones, has been argued for.[14] This would certainly be beneficial in terms of a family reconstitution exercise, but parish registers have to be of sufficiently high standard in terms of detail and unbroken sequence for the process to be possible. Then there is the matter of finding an individual (or individuals) with the time, skills and commitment necessary to do the work.[15] If it were able to be done, a clearer idea of people's origins would result from the project, together with a better understanding of why they owned property where they did. Even among the established sixteenth-century Lowestoft merchants, such as Thomas Annot and his son-in-law, William Frenche, while there may have been a certain degree of property acquisition as a means of widening business interests and making a safe investment, some of the lands and houses held in other parishes were probably the result of family connections there.

During the seventeenth century, 191 of the 273 testators whose wills have survived owned real estate of one kind or another. As was the case with the second half of the sixteenth century, most property was held within the parish and belonged to the more affluent sections of society. One noticeable difference was that yeomen and tradespeople featured more prominently than previously (twelve examples compared with one and sixteen examples compared with five). Merchants remained important, as might be expected, and both craftsmen and seafarers had increased their level of ownership. The trends observed have nothing to do with variability in the survival rate of the documents; they reflect a genuine increase in the amount of property acquired by the levels of society concerned. One-third of property-owning testators (fifty men and fifteen women) had a single dwelling-house to dispose of when they made their wills, which means that the other 126 were in possession of more real estate than was required to provide shelter and a workplace for an individual family.

The possibility, outlined a little earlier, that ownership of real estate in communities removed from Lowestoft may indicate a testator's place of origin is strengthened by

---

[14] C. Phythian Adams (ed.), *Societies, Culture and Kinship 1580–1850: Cultural Provinces and English Local History* (Leicester, 1993), chapters 9 and 17. The argument in favour of such an approach was further reflected in a review of this book: see P. Corfield, 'New Approaches for Old Towns?', *JUH* 23 (i) (November, 1996), 96–7.

[15] Close to Lowestoft itself, the parishes of Kirkley, Pakefield and Corton have registers which fall short of the criteria necessary for reconstitution. The Lowestoft exercise took 1,500 hours to complete.

evidence in the surviving seventeenth-century wills. Out of the 191 which refer to the bequest of land and/or buildings, thirty-four make reference to other parishes. The status of the people who made these particular wills is as follows: four gentlemen and a gentleman's widow, eight merchants, six yeomen, two fishermen, two tailors, two tanners, two widows, a boatwright, a brewer, a doctor, a grocer, a hatter, a mariner and a miller. Altogether, forty-three different places outside Lowestoft are mentioned, with eleven of them being found within a five-mile radius of the town, twenty-eight lying in other parts of Suffolk and in Norfolk, and four situated in Kent. Seven of the merchants were indigenous to the town (Robert Allen, John Arnold, Robert Ashbye, Samuel Pacy, John Wild, Josiah Wild and Wyllyam Wylde), and so was one of the gentlemen (Henry Coe), the brewer (John Durrant) and the mariner (Simon Rivett).[16] The boatwright (John Barker) and one of the tailors (James Smiter) had both been resident in the place for about thirty years and can therefore count as locals. So can the grocer (Robert Tooly), who had lived in town for nearly fifty years and had originated from Holt, in north Norfolk.

The other twenty-one people were of much shorter periods of residence and must, presumably, have originated from elsewhere because they have no antecedents in the family reconstitution material. There is little to be gained by looking at all of them individually – yet, as a group, they are indicative of what may be termed the demographic ebb and flow of the time. Two of the gentlemen, Robert Baily and John Collins, appear to have been temporarily based in town at the time of their respective deaths, while a third one, Robert Knight (who seems to have originated from Kent, if property owned there in the Whitstable–Canterbury area is anything to go by), married into the wealthy Mighells family.

Three of the yeomen (Richard Berye, William Meeke and Edward Sparrow) all farmed in the parish, but seem also to have had interests in other places. Berye left money to both the church and the poor in six local Suffolk parishes, and it is difficult therefore to pinpoint his place of origin, but Sparrow seems to have had a connection with the Lothingland parish of Belton because he made a bequest to the poor there. Two other yeomen, William Church and Richard Willsonne, appear to have lived in Lowestoft during the latter stages of their lives, but to have farmed in the adjoining parish of Kirkley. Church's son, Richard, married into the influential Pacy family and established himself as a merchant in the town. Finally, one of the four craftsmen who came into Lowestoft from outside, Robert Whick (tailor), referred in his will to a charity child brought up by his father in the south Norfolk parish of Brooke.[17]

The first thirty years of the eighteenth century show that ninety-nine of the 132 testators owned some kind of real estate. Yet again, most of the property held was situated in the parish and belonged to people in the upper echelons of the local community. The seafaring fraternity continued to occupy a prominent place in the property-owning levels of society, while the other interested groups of people also

---

[16] Coe was not a genuine member of the gentry, but belonged to a local merchant family and had elevated himself on the strength of accumulated wealth.

[17] Whick served as parish clerk from the beginning of 1606 until his death in July 1610.

remained much the same as previously. The decline in the proportion of testators owning a single dwelling-house continued, with just over a quarter of the documents (sixteen men and eleven women) showing the characteristic. Again, as in the previous century, it seems that people were using their wealth to purchase land and buildings (especially houses) over and above immediate needs. The attraction was presumably twofold: the possession of realisable assets which could also be used to yield a regular income from the rents.

Twenty-six of the testators who owned real estate had some of it located outside Lowestoft. This number included a mariner and his widow (Richard and Alice Browne), a yeoman and his widow (Robert and Olive Hullock) and a bricklayer and his widow (John and Margaret Chandler), so the true figure is really twenty-three. The various occupational and social groupings are as follows: five mariners and a mariner's wife, three merchants and a merchant's widow, two gentlemen, two surgeons, two yeomen, two brewers, a customs officer, a bricklayer, a sailmaker, a single man and a widow of unknown social background. Ten parishes within a five-mile radius of the town are referred to, as are seven communities further removed in Suffolk and ten in Norfolk. Nine of the properties located in the latter county (two in the central part and seven in the western fenlands) belonged to the customs officer, John Syer, who had presumably originated from either of the areas where his property lay.

Twelve of the men referred to in the preceding paragraph can all, to a greater or lesser extent, be considered local. The three merchants (Thomas Mighells, William Rising and Thomas Walsby), the two gentlemen (John Jex and James Wilde), one of the surgeons (Joseph Pake), one of the mariners (Simon Canham), the two brewers (John Daynes and John Durrant) and the bricklayer (John Chandler) all have antecedents in the family reconstitution material.[18] In addition to them, another of the mariners (William Goddle) had lived in Lowestoft for fifty years and the sailmaker (James Postle) had been resident for forty. The other seven men were much more recent arrivals in town, but their previous places of residence are known from information revealed in various parish documents. Richard Browne and Robert Capon (mariners) came from Pakefield; Abraham Hawker and Robert Hullock (yeomen) were from Carlton Colville; Thomas Peach (occupation unknown, but whose family members were involved in agriculture and brewing) came from either Oulton or Blundeston; Abraham Freeman (surgeon) had formerly lived in Great Yarmouth; and Nicholas Marriner (mariner) originated from Ipswich.[19]

As far as the six women are concerned, three of them (Alice Browne, Olive Hullock and merchant's widow Deborah Ashby) were natives of Lowestoft, while another one (Margaret Chandler) had lived in the town for forty years. Mary Ward, the widow of the man whose status is not known (but whose family included merchants), had been resident for over thirty years when she made her will in March

---

[18] Jex and Wilde were both members of local merchant families. Their gentrification was more the result of accumulated wealth and self-elevation than of genuine status.

[19] Freeman's will indicates that he had no property in Yarmouth, but owned a house in Beccles – so his origins may have been in that Suffolk town. Marriner owned a farm at Bredfield, about seven miles north-east of Ipswich, so his family roots could have been in that village.

1711, and she may have been from Thorington in Suffolk if the property she owned there offers any clue. Margaret Godlee, the wife of Peter Godlee or Goddle (mariner) seems to have come from the town of Leiston, in Suffolk, because she left her son Thomas a messuage there.[20]

Liquid and illiquid assets

It is probably fair to assume that the people who owned what appears, in some cases, to have been quite extensive real estate in Lowestoft and elsewhere derived satisfactory income from it – the other main use being to provide security for credit.[21] Equally, it is to be presumed that the various business activities undertaken brought a reasonable return on the capital invested, thereby allowing both a profit margin and the opportunity for growth.[22] No real sense of the success of economic activity, however, is derived without there being some references to cash in either wills or inventories. Quantities of real estate may appear impressive, especially where values are given, but the amount of money bequeathed by a testator says much about his or her standing in economic terms, however simple that criterion may be. What cannot be ascertained is the amount of cash which may have been disposed of before a will was made.

Tables 26, 27 and 28 present the details concerning cash bequests. No legacies conditional upon the sale of real estate have been included, nor any payments made to legatees by principal beneficiaries (the latter often having to produce the money from real estate they had been left). The only cash bequests recorded are those made without reference to any third party.[23] As might be expected, the largest sums bequeathed are to be found among merchants, though substantial amounts are also in evidence in other social and occupation groups. Any approximate sums given are the result of specific individual payments being left to an uncertain or an undeclared number of legatees (e.g. 'all my grandchildren'), while the presence of female testators as members of the various groupings is indicated, as previously, by a number in brackets or by the symbol (F). In all three tables, the Unknown category contains a majority of people who, on the evidence of family reconstitution, belonged to the various social and occupation groups – though without specific documentary references being recorded for them. Median sums of money are recorded where there are sufficient references to make the figure worth reproducing.

---

[20] The Goddles themselves had long been established in Kirkley and Pakefield as mariners and fishermen, but their earlier roots had been in Southwold.

[21] Muldrew, *Economy of Obligation*, p. 153.

[22] P. Deane and W. A. Cole, *British Economic Growth, 1688–1959* (Cambridge, 1962), p. 260, cites an annual capital-formation rate of between 3% and 6% at the end of the seventeenth century. An estimate by a contemporary commentator, Gregory King, was used to help make the calculations.

[23] Any deferred payments (such as those made to heirs at the age of eighteen or twenty-one years) may have been financed by the sale of assets by the executor(s) or by those responsible for organising the payments – but they have been included in the tables.

Table 26. *Cash bequests in wills, (1560–1599)*

Social/ occupational group	Total number	References to cash	Largest amount	Smallest amount	Median amount
Gentlemen	0	0			
Professional and services	5(1)	3	£30	£5 12s 0d	
Merchants	24(4)	21(3)	c. £1,000	£1	£82+
Retailers/tradesmen	10(1)	7(1)	£62+	11s 8d	£28+
Yeomen	1	1	£151	£1 10s 0d	
Craftsmen	18(1)	11	£58 6s 8d	6s 8d	£11
Seafarers	19(5)	10(3)	£48 5s 0d (F)		£5+
Husbandmen	4	1	£20		
Labourers	4(2)	3(1)	£9 6s 8d	6s 8d (F)	
Unknown	17(10)	13(10)	c. £42 (F)	3s 0d (F)	£7 15s 0d
	102(24)	**70(18)**			

Table 27. *Cash bequests in wills, (1600–1699)* [24]

Social/ occupational group	Total number	References to cash	Largest amount	Smallest amount	Median amount
Gentlemen	14(1)	7(1)	£100+	£35 15s 0d	£58 10s 0d
Professional and services	8(3)	8(3)	£240	£5 (F)	£23
Merchants	33(5)	22(3)	£2,387	£11	£137 10s 0d
Retailers/tradesmen	34(4)	22(5)	£463	£1	£35 10s 0d
Yeomen	21(2)	14(2)	£294 10s 0d	£2	£20
Craftsmen	63(15)	32(8)	£300	£1	£21 10s 0d
Seafarers	61(8)	29(4)	£285	10s 0d	£10
Husbandmen	12(3)	4(1)	£18 (F)	£1	
Labourers	1	0			
Unknown	26(20)	14(9)	£166 10s 0d (F)	5s 0d (F)	£16 10s 0d
	273(61)	**152(36)**			

The surviving probate inventories give far less information regarding possession of cash. Out of 100 documents, only twenty-eight refer to ready money as part of a deceased person's assets – and ten of those include in the sum recorded either debts owing or some kind of personal property, thereby obscuring the true figure. It may appear surprising that there were not a greater number of people holding cash in the house at the time they died. Merchants, retailers, tradesmen and craftsmen would presumably have needed a certain amount of coin with which to conduct their

---

[24] It is worth noting that the largest amount of money bequeathed by a craftsman in this table (£300) belonged to John Wells (cordwainer). His burial registration of 24 September 1706 describes him as 'a miserable miser'.

Table 28. *Cash bequests in wills, (1700–1730)*

Social/ occupational group	Total number	References to cash	Largest amount	Smallest amount	Median amount
Gentlemen	3	2	£863	£128	
Professional and services	4	3	£300	1s 0d	
Merchants	13(3)	9(3)	£300	£60 (F)	£17
Retailers/tradesmen	13(3)	6(1)	£80 10s 0d	£7 (F)	£16 7s 6d
Yeomen	8(2)	6(1)	£108 2s 0d	2s 6d	£25 15s 0d
Craftsmen	17(5)	6(1)	£35	£15	£16
Seafarers	56(19)	20(9)	£313	1s 0d (F)	£10
Husbandmen	2	0			
Labourers	2	1	£127		
Unknown	14(13)	6(5)	£12 12s 0d (F)	5s 0d	£1 11s 0d
	132(45)	**59(20)**			

businesses (by far the two largest amounts recorded, £268 16s 8d and £284 2s 10d, belonged to merchants), but possession of ready money does not seem to have been universal if the inventories are to be believed – evidence, most likely, of its general shortage in the sixteenth- and seventeenth-century economy.[25] Nowhere, in any of the inventories consulted, does the amount of cash held in the house exceed the value of cash bequests made.[26] Any shortfall in these would presumably have been made up by the sale of goods and chattels, by the calling-in of money owed, or by the transfer to beneficiaries of the bills, bonds and mortgages that a lot of people are seen to have held.[27]

Among the assets with positive value owned by people were various articles made from gold and silver (particularly the latter). It is difficult to regard possession of the various spoons, salt-cellars, goblets, etc. as a form of financial investment, simply because the values are not large enough. In only five cases noted in the inventories was a person's amount of plate worth more than £20 – though, interestingly enough, one of the five, Roger Hill (merchant), is seen to have pawned a parcel-gilt goblet for the sum of £8 and five silver spoons for the sum of £1 (September 1588). No other examples are to be found in the inventories of such valuables being used to raise cash, but it is something which may well have have been practised more widely. For the most part, people probably acquired their modest numbers of silver utensils for personal use, for adding a degree of elegance to their lives and perhaps for impressing others. By far the largest amount of plate is that listed in the inventory of Admiral Riches Utber (December 1669), which shows him as having 378 ounces worth £94 10s 0d.

[25] Muldrew, *Economy of Obligation*, pp. 99–100.

[26] There are fifty-two matching wills and inventories, but only twelve pairs refer to ready money.

[27] For the complexity of credit networks, see Muldrew, *Economy of Obligation*, Chapters 4 and 6.

Table 29. *Ownership of vessels and shares in shipping (1560–1730)*

Period	Social/ occupational group	Vessels only	Shares only	Vessels and shares	Total number of documents
1560–1599	Professional and services	1			6(1)
	Merchants	2	1	3	29(5)
	Craftsmen	3	1(1)		20(5)
	Seafarers	2	1(1)	2	20(2)
		8	**3(2)**	**5**	**75(13)**
1600–1699	Gentlemen		1		18(2)
	Merchants	8	3(1)	5(1)	41(7)
	Retailers/tradesmen	1		1	39(6)
	Yeomen		1		21(2)
	Craftsmen	1	2(1)		66(15)
	Seafarers	3(1)	6	1	68(9)
		13(1)	**13(2)**	**7(1)**	**253(41)**
1700–1730	Gentlemen		1		3
	Merchants	6	3(1)	1	19
	Retailers/tradesmen		3(2)	1	16(3)
	Craftsmen	1	1		22(5)
	Seafarers	6	5(1)	2	71(22)
		13	**13(4)**	**4**	**131(30)**

One definite form of investment practised by some of Lowestoft's inhabitants – who could afford to do so – was the purchase of shares in fishing vessels and trading craft.[28] The practice was not widespread, but it is noticeable as an aspect of people's financial activity in both wills and inventories, and it was not limited to merchants and mariners – though these were the dominant groups. There was also, of course, outright ownership of vessels of one kind or another. In either case, whether a person had sole possession of a craft or a part-interest in it, the asset could always have been sold to an interested party and thereby converted into cash. Table 29 presents the information available in probate material regarding the ownership of vessels and of shares held in them and, in showing its spread beyond the seafaring and merchant sections of local society, helps to foster further the idea of a mixed economy at work. Again, as in previous tables, women are bracketed as a sub-total in their respective social and occupational groups.

The third and last type of illiquid asset discernible in the Lowestoft probate documents is the various kinds of credit note for money which had been loaned. A good deal has been written about the provision of credit in pre-industrial England and there is ample evidence of its practice among the inhabitants of Lowestoft, providing funds for

[28] P. Clark, 'English Country Towns, 1500–1800', in Clark, *Country Towns*, p. 5, draws attention to the way in which some urban capital was used, in port communities, to acquire shares in shipping.

both members of the local community and for those living further removed. The origin of what may be termed 'the culture of credit' has been placed in the middle of the sixteenth century, as the result of increasing consumption of manufactured goods and the limited amounts of gold and silver in circulation.[29] There were varying attitudes in mediaeval England towards the charging of interest on loans, but the prevailing opinion was generally against the practice.[30] However, late in the reign of Henry VIII, the existing laws against usury were recognised as being ineffective and lenders of money were allowed to charge up to a maximum of 10% interest. The act sanctioning this was repealed in 1552 (the result perhaps of Queen Mary's catholic conscience), but in 1571 the charging of interest on loans up to a maximum of 10% was once more authorised by act of Parliament.[31] The rate gradually fell thereafter, but the return possible for people who had money to lend was not unattractive – even at a rate of 5% in the early eighteenth century.[32]

Only fifteen of the ninety-five Lowestoft probate inventories which are complete (15.8%) provide evidence of money-lending in the form of bonds and bills. This seems at first sight to be much lower than the incidence of this practice in the South Elmham parishes of High Suffolk (45.6%) and in rural communities in Norfolk and the East Midlands (40%).[33] However, another thirty of the Lowestoft documents refer to debts of one kind or another owing to the deceased which, if regarded as a sign that credit arrangements of some kind had been negotiated, would increase the proportion to 47.3%.[34] In some ways, an overall percentage can be somewhat misleading because of the varying survival rate of the documents and any possible difference in money-lending activity at different times. In order to get a more accurate idea of the provision of credit by Lowestoft people, on the evidence of their inventories, the total timescale is best divided into four separate sub-periods.

Out of the eleven complete inventories which remain for the late sixteenth century (there are fifteen documents in all, but four of them are incomplete or defective), eight show that some kind of credit had been extended (72.7%), while for 1600–1649 the number is nine documents out of a total of twenty which are intact (45%). If the two periods are taken together, the seventeen inventories represent 54.8% of the total number suitable for scrutiny – which is about 9% higher than the proportion for the area of rural Suffolk referred to in the previous paragraph, with a similar period of time

[29] Muldrew, *Economy of Obligation*, p. 3.

[30] The teachings of the Church were opposed to it, based upon a whole range of Biblical texts: Exodus 22. 25, Leviticus 25. 36, Nehemiah 5. 7 and 10, Psalms 15. 5, Proverbs 28. 8, Ezekiel 18. 8, 13 and 17, and 22. 12.

[31] J. W. Gough, *The Rise of the Entrepreneur* (London, 1969), p. 24; Clarkson, *Pre-Industrial Economy*, p. 151.

[32] Clarkson, *Pre-Industrial Economy*, p. 167. The relevant interest rates cited are as follows: 8% in 1625, 6% in 1651 and 5% in 1714.

[33] Evans, 'South Elmham', p. 276 (a total of twenty-one out of forty-six documents contain some reference to money on loan); B. A. Holderness, 'Credit in English Rural Society before the Nineteenth Century, with special reference to the period 1650–1720', *AHR* 24, ii (1976), 102.

[34] Holderness, 'Credit', p. 102, identifies two kinds of credit: money-lending and deferred payments for goods or services. Comment is made upon the impossibility of saying which was the more important.

covered.[35] Only eighteen Lowestoft inventories have survived for the second half of the seventeenth century, though all of them are complete, and seven make reference to money on loan in one form or another (39%). Between 1700 and 1730, twenty-one of the forty-six available documents (all of which are complete) give evidence of the practice (45.6%). If the years 1650–1730 are treated as one period, the twenty-eight cases of credit provision represent 43.8% of the whole, which does not differ greatly from the 40% relating to rural Norfolk and the East Midlands cited in the previous paragraph, which covered much the same timespan.

The wills form both an interesting complement and contrast to the inventories, with the 507 documents including eighty-eight (17.4%) that provide evidence of credit being made available in one form or another – whether by bill, bond or mortgage.[36] If, however, the overall timescale is broken down into the four separate sub-periods used in the previous paragraph, a different picture emerges. Out of the 102 wills surviving for 1560–1599, only eight (7.8%) make reference to any kind of credit provision. Yet the late sixteenth-century inventories show the highest incidence of credit being advanced in the whole period of study, a feature partly explained by the high survival rate of documents appertaining to merchants. Of the 129 wills extant for the period 1600–1649, a mere ten refer to loans of one kind or another (7.7%). This is also well below the level of activity suggested by the inventories, which are spread much more equitably across the different occupation groups.

During the second half of the seventeenth century, the situation regarding the will changes noticeably, with twenty-five documents out of 144 (17.4%) referring to bills and bonds and, increasingly, to mortgages. The upward trend continues with greater emphasis between 1700 and 1730, when forty-five wills out of a total of 132 (34.1%) show money being loaned by the testators. Again, mortgages are frequently mentioned. Presumably, the greater protection afforded to borrowers nationally after the middle of the seventeenth century must have encouraged people to mortgage real estate as a means of raising capital.[37] The need to do this in Lowestoft may have been partly created by the expansion of maritime activity after the town had been granted port status in 1679. The greater opportunities which then existed for the development of commerce might well have generated a demand for funding new enterprise.

The wills show a smaller proportion of people involved in credit provision than do the inventories because the testators do not usually make reference to any kind of debt other than money loaned by bill, bond or mortgage. The inventories, of course, also

---

[35] It is possible that the percentage is inflated by the high proportion of credit providers in the small body of documentation surviving for the late sixteenth century – which in turn results from the high survival rate of merchants' inventories.

[36] Holderness, 'Credit', p. 100, has this to say: 'Loans were classically of three kinds, not counting the pawn: the promissory note, or bill without specialty, generally a debt without security, usually in a small sum intended as a short-term loan; the bond; and the mortgage.'

[37] R. O'Day, *Economy and Community* (London, 1975), pp. 88 and 92; Wilson, *England's Apprenticeship*, p. 207. Both writers refer to the way in which mortgagors were able to retain possession of their property as long as the interest on the loan was paid. Up until about 1640, default had resulted in immediate foreclosure. The introduction of 'equity of redemption' gave the borrower much greater protection.

record money owing to the deceased for goods or services provided, in order to ascertain the total value of the estate. Thus, they constitute a more detailed and wide-ranging source than the wills. It has been claimed that the greatest part of credit extended during the early modern period was that given in everyday trading and retail, with an average period of loan reckoned at nearly nine months' duration.[38]

Altogether, there are fifty-two wills and accompanying inventories – although, with four of the latter being incomplete, the number is reduced to forty-eight. Of these forty-eight pairs of complementary documents, only four give evidence of the extension of credit by one means or another.[39] This says a great deal about the vagaries of the documents themselves, especially in the way that wills may be worded. A considerable amount of money out on loan, which is plainly ascertainable in an inventory, can be rendered invisible in a will by the bequest of assets in some stock phrase such as 'all my other estate whatsoever'. Thus, the particular legal phraseology used by different scribes becomes of considerable importance regarding the amount of information able to be elicited.

Provision of credit in the community

The importance of scriveners as community bankers in London during the second half of the seventeenth century has been duly noted, as has their role as providers of funds elsewhere.[40] Nor has the function of the goldsmith escaped attention.[41] Lowestoft, being a town of modest size, had few professional scriveners among its inhabitants (no more than six or seven have been identified between 1560 and 1730), and most of them had other occupations.[42] None of them, as far as can be ascertained, was involved in money-lending. Neither was the town's only goldsmith.[43]

The main lenders of money in town in terms of numbers, on the evidence of both wills and inventories, were tradesmen and craftsmen of one kind or another (25.8% of

---

[38] Muldrew, *Economy of Obligation*, pp. 124 and 174.

[39] The documents in question are those of Josiah Wilde, merchant (1656), Simon Rivett, mariner (1692), Margaret Utting, widow (1708) and Daniel Manning, cordwainer (1730).

[40] D. C. Coleman, 'London Scriveners and the Estate Market in the Later Seventeenth Century', *EHR* 2nd Series 4 (1951–2), 221–30; J. A. Chartres, *Internal Trade in England, 1500–1750* (London, 1977), p. 53; and Wilson, *England's Apprenticeship*, p. 155.

[41] P. Gregg, *Black Death to Industrial Revolution* (London, 1976), pp. 229–30; Wilson, *England's Apprenticeship*, p. 208.

[42] George Rugge, who lived in town during the 1590s and early 1600s, kept a shop at the top of Lion Score, on its southern side. Matthew Fullwood, also resident on the east side of the High Street, during the first half of the seventeenth century, was a merchant. Thomas Tye, who wrote a number of wills during the late seventeenth century, functioned as a schoolmaster. And John Evans, a citizen of the late seventeenth and early eighteenth centuries, ran a writing school and acted as a part-time town clerk.

[43] Wyllyam Rogers is referred to as a goldsmith in his burial registration of 17 April 1595, but his inventory shows no evidence of such activity. He was mainly involved in fishing and fish-curing and he may have had a taste for alcohol, his cellar containing quantities of muscady, sack, white wine and London beer. The volume of liquor does not appear sufficient to suggest a commercial enterprise, nor do the contents of the rooms in the house suggest a drinking establishment of some kind.

documents), mariners and fishermen (21.8%), merchants (18.8%) and widows (15.8%). The function of widows as providers of funds for other people has been variously expounded upon.[44] However, their importance in Lowestoft was perhaps not as important as has been noted in rural communities, the urban and maritime nature of the town creating a different social and economic structure and making it possible for a greater range of people to provide credit.[45] Having said that, they did increase their money-lending capacity across the whole of the period, having 19.7% of their number involved in the activity between 1700 and 1730.

Analysis of the documents shows periodic fluctuations in the importance of main lending groups. Mariners and fishermen, for instance, became influential during the second half of the seventeenth century and thereafter, reflecting the increase in maritime prosperity after the town became a port. An apparent lull in merchant activity between 1600 and 1650 is probably as much to do with inconsistencies in the documents as to the town's economic decline at the time.[46] And the decrease in the contribution of tradesmen and craftsmen during the second half of the seventeenth century is due to their not being particularly well represented in the documents, especially inventories.

The provision of credit during the late Tudor period has been referred to as 'bye-employment'.[47] In the sense that people involved in the activity were, in some cases, putting out surplus funds to work to their advantage, the term may not be inappropriate – but it probably fails to accommodate the reality behind the granting of trade credit. The latter practice was almost certainly much more a case of simple expediency in retaining the custom of clients who could not always pay cash for goods or services received and who might, in some cases, never be able to settle their debts. In a major study of 4,650 probate inventories relating to communities in Norfolk and the East Midlands for the period 1650–1720, it was found that, of the overall total value of the assets listed (£295,000), 13% consisted of trade credit and money on loan.[48] The Lowestoft sample of documents is much smaller and three of the ninety-five complete inventories have to be omitted from the reckoning because two of them have relevant information which cannot be read and the third shows so much money out on loan that it would distort the calculations if it were to be included.[49]

---

[44] Clarkson, *Pre-Industrial Economy*, p. 148; P. J. Corfield, 'A Provincial Capital in the Late Seventeenth Century: The Case of Norwich', in Clark and Slack, *Crisis and Order*, p. 294; B. A. Holderness, *Pre-Industrial England* (London, 1976), p. 214.

[45] Evans, 'South Elmham', p. 277, fig. 52, shows widows constituting 23.8% of the people who loaned money. Yeomen made up 38%, whereas in Lowestoft they formed only 6% – a striking contrast between a rural economy and an urban/maritime one.

[46] Metters, 'Rulers and Merchants', p. 318. Comment is made on merchants' involvement in various kinds of credit provision.

[47] R. H. Tawney (ed.), *A Discourse Upon Usury* (London, 1925 and 1962), pp. 19–21. The book's original author was Thomas Wilson and it was published in 1572.

[48] Holderness, 'Credit', p. 102.

[49] The two imperfect documents are those of Robert Knight, gentleman (May 1691) and Simon Rivett, mariner (January 1693). The one relating to Admiral Riches Utber shows £3,400 out on loan (the total value of the inventory being £4337 3s 0d). Utber had retired from naval service and returned to his home town, and it is likely that a substantial proportion of his wealth derived from prize-money.

The ninety-two documents thus remaining add up to a total value of £15,470 1s 4d, of which £2,948 0s 11d constituted credit of some kind (19.1%). This, of course, covers the period 1560–1730, but a division into two sub-periods can easily be arranged for comparison with other data. The earliest complete surviving Lowestoft inventory dates from 1585, and the thirty-one documents which are extant from that year until 1649 produce a total value of £2,750 15s 2d, of which £595 15s 8d took the form of credit (21.7%). Between 1650 and 1730, a total of sixty-one inventories produced a value of £12,719 6s 2d, of which £2,352 2s 1d was credit of some kind (18.5%). This is more than 5% above the figure cited for Norfolk and the East Midlands during the same period.

The range of the various individual sums of money loaned by Lowestoft people between 1585 and 1730 stretches from 10s to £1,347 15s 9d. The mean amount stands at £68 6s 4½d and the median at £17 10s 0d – the latter figure showing that overall weighting tended towards smaller sums rather than larger ones. If the period 1585–1649 is considered, individual loans ranged from 10s to £160 16s 6d, with a mean value of £34 9s 4½d and a median one of £7 6s 8d. This contrasts with part of rural High Suffolk, where the amount of money on loan for roughly the same period varied between £1 10s 0d and £229 10s 0d, with a mean value of £52 6s 8d and a median amount of £32 15s 0d.[50] In Lowestoft, between 1650 and 1730, the individual sums granted ranged from 10s to £1,347 15s 9d, with mean and median amounts of £92 5s 11d and £22 2s 7d respectively.

Apart from the merely statistical matter of the amount(s) of money on loan, the inventories are also able to reveal what this credit represented as a percentage of the assets belonging to certain social and occupational groups. And, more importantly, they can also show what it represented in terms of the proportion of personal wealth committed on the part of those people who actually made the loans. The four main money-lending groups, as identified earlier, were tradesmen and craftsmen; mariners and fishermen; merchants; and widows. Table 30 shows the percentage of assets committed to loans both for the occupation groups and also for their members who made funds available. A scrutiny of the second and fourth columns shows that two of the groups, mariners/fishermen and widows, had fewer of their overall group number making credit available than the other two categories, but that those who were involved committed substantial resources.[51]

Apart from the practice of lending money by bill or bond, or by extending trade credit, use of the mortgage secured by real estate was another important method of providing finance. According to the Rev. John Tanner's court baron extracts, 248 mortgages were arranged on the copyhold properties in town between 1611 and 1725.[52]

---

[50] Evans, 'South Elmham', p. 277, fig. 52.

[51] One feature of credit provision by Lowestoft people is the fact that some of the borrowers lived a considerable distance from the town. Among the places named are Norwich, Southwold and Ipswich. Sometimes, family ties are discernible; on other occasions, business interests were probably the link.

[52] SRO(L) 454/2. Taking up a mortgage was technically a surrender of property into the hands of the mortgagee and the transaction had to be recorded in the court baron minute books. Redemption and forfeiture were also duly noted.

Table 30. *Credit as a percentage of personal assets*

Period	Occupation group	Credit as a % of assets	Lenders	Credit as a % of assets	Comments
1585–1649	Tradesmen/craftsmen	28.5	Tradesmen/craftsmen	29.3	
	Mariners/fishermen		Mariners/fishermen		Too few inventories
	Merchants	17.2	Merchants	17.7	
	Widows		Widows		Too few inventories
1650–1730	Tradesmen/craftsmen	15.0	Tradesmen/craftsmen	18.6	
	Mariners/fishermen	8.3	Mariners/fishermen	21.2	
	Merchants	25.2	Merchants	37.5	
	Widows	14.3	Widows	40.4	
1585–1730	Tradesmen/craftsmen	17.9	Tradesmen/craftsmen	21.3	
	Mariners/fishermen	7.8	Mariners/fishermen	21.2	
	Merchants	23.7	Merchants	32.4	
	Widows	14.0	Widows	40.4	

There was a noticeable increase in such activity after 1650, which may partly reflect the national development of the mortgage market.[53] However, another factor to be considered (and one which has already been referred to a number of times) is the growth of Lowestoft's maritime prosperity towards the end of the seventeenth century, with increased business activity creating the need for some people to raise capital. Altogether, sixty-four mortgages were negotiated in the town between 1611 and 1649 – an average of 1.7 a year.[54] From 1650 to 1725, the number was 184 – an average of 2.4 per annum. And these transactions are solely connected with copyhold tenure. There is no way of ascertaining mortgages which were almost certainly arranged on freehold lands and tenements (such transactions not having to be entered in the court baron records), which means that practically all of the farmland and about 15–20% of the housing stock cannot be analysed.

As far as customary property is concerned, out of the 248 mortgages arranged between 1611 and 1725, 174 relate to dwelling-houses (70.2%), fifty-six to messuages that were both domestic and commercial (22.6%), seventeen to premises that were purely commercial (6.8%) and one to a piece of undeveloped land (0.4%).[55] In terms of numbers of individual properties, there were eighty-five dwelling-houses, twenty

---

[53] Chartres, *Internal Trade*, p. 53.

[54] The main sequence of manor court minute books begins in 1616, but there are a number of references to earlier transactions.

[55] Those premises which were both domestic and commercial consisted of inns and any houses which had some kind of industrial building on the plot (e.g. fish-house, brewery or tannery). Wholly commercial ones consisted almost entirely of fish-houses, with the inclusion of one windmill.

messuages of a mixed domestic and commercial nature, seven purely industrial buildings and the piece of undeveloped land. If dwelling-houses and mixed plots are added together to produce the number of residential plots which were mortgaged at one time or another, the figure comes to 105 – which represents 32.5% of the 323 houses recorded by John Tanner in his listing. The distribution of these houses was a fairly even one, with sixty being situated on the High Street and forty-five in the side-street area to the west. If each one of these figures is taken as a proportion of the total number of houses present in its own particular area (163 and 160 respectively), it can be seen that 36.8% of houses on the High Street and 28% in the side-street area were mortgaged at one time or another. The difference was probably caused by the heavier concentration of merchants and tradespeople in the High Street, with both groupings using their real estate, as occasion demanded, to raise capital.

The relative value of property in the two areas is shown in the amounts of money raised. As might be expected, the larger messuages in the High Street were mortgaged for greater sums of money than the ones in the side-streets. This not only reflects the difference in size and quality of the holdings; it also probably suggests the differing levels of need for cash on the part of the people who lived in each sector of the town: the merchant with his mixed business interests would have required greater sums of money than the fishermen with a part-share in a boat or a carpenter with his own small yard or workshop.[56] Not all mortgage transactions specify the amounts of cash involved, but the information which is available produces some interesting data.

A total of seventy-seven transactions on thirty-nine High Street properties produced the sum of 6,080 9s 0d, which is an average of about £79 per mortgage deal and £156 per premises. In the side-street area, forty-eight transactions on twenty-nine properties generated a total of £1,780 13s 10d, which is an average of about £37 per mortgage and £61 per premises. These latter figures are inflated by five deals which took place on two extensive messuages of a mixed residential and commercial nature (a brewery complex and a slaughter-house/butchery), which were not typical of the area. If they are removed from the calculations, the sum of £1,109 13s 10d produced by forty-three transactions on twenty-seven properties averages out at about £26 per mortgage and £41 per premises.

Foreclosures and forfeitures were not uncommon, and of the 248 transactions recorded no fewer than fifty-one (20.6%) resulted in the mortgagor losing his or her property – which is over twice the rate recorded in the South Elmham district of Suffolk, albeit for a different timespan.[57] The defaulters' holdings were fairly evenly distributed over the built-up area, with three commercial premises below the cliff at the northern end of town (six transactions), twenty-three messuages on the High Street (twenty-six transactions) and sixteen properties in the side-street area (nineteen

---

[56] The amount of money raised on a property should not be regarded as a valuation. It probably reflects the borrower's needs at the time the loan was made. Obviously, any messuage had a market value, beyond which the lender would have been reluctant to make an advance, but the varying sums raised on certain plots suggest that full market value was seldom reached in each transaction.

[57] Evans, 'South Elmham', p. 281. Of the seventy-eight mortgages recorded in the court rolls here, for the period 1550–1640, seven ended in foreclosure (9%).

Table 31. *Mortgagors and mortgagees in Lowestoft, 1611–1725*

Social/ occupation group	Mortgagors		Mortgagees	
	Townspeople	Outsiders	Townspeople	Outsiders
Gentlemen	3	5	5	16
Professional & services	0	1	4(1)	6
Merchants	17(2)	1	24(4)	9(1)
Retailers/tradesmen	24(3)	3	11(2)	3
Yeomen	5	5	3	11
Craftsmen	24(2)	2	18(1)	5
Seafarers	30(4)	1	23(6)	3
Husbandmen	3(1)	0	3	2
Labourers	0	0	0	0
Unknown	32(9)	14	15(7)	29(8)
	138(21)	**32**	**106(21)**	**84(9)**

transactions).[58] There was also an equitable spread across the occupation groups in the twenty-seven cases where forfeiters are able to be classified: three merchants and a merchant's widow, six tradesmen, eight craftsmen, seven mariners and a mariner's widow, and one gentleman.[59]

As Table 31 shows, men and women (bracketed again) who mortgaged property to raise cash and those who acted as lenders of money were drawn from the same social and occupation groups, with a predictable concentration in those levels which had the largest numbers of people both requiring funds and able to provide them. Only twenty-four examples can be found of men and women who were both borrowers and lenders, which is about 7% of the total number of people recorded as being involved in such negotiations. In the 248 mortgage deals referred to in these pages, there were 170 people involved as borrowers and 190 as lenders. In the former case (using evidence deriving from both the family reconstitution exercise and from manorial records), 81% were inhabitants of the town, while the other 19% outsiders who owned property there. In the latter case, 56% were townspeople and 44% were outsiders.

The places of origin of outsiders who raised money by mortgaging property held in Lowestoft, or who advanced funds to people requiring credit, are often referred to in the court baron records. The available evidence shows that the majority of places mentioned (70% relating to mortgagors and 87% to mortgagees) lay within a ten-mile radius of the

---

[58] The three premises at the northern end of town consisted of two lots of fish-houses and a tannery with adjacent dwelling-house. The High Street properties comprised eighteen houses, two inns and three fish-house complexes at the bottom of the cliff. Those in the side-street area consisted of fifteen houses (five of which were tenemented) and one inn.

[59] There are two cases of men who forfeited twice, on different properties: John Aldred (grocer), in 1683 and some time during the 1690s, on houses located on the west and east sides of the High Street; John Daynes (brewer), in 1687 and 1701, on houses situated on the south side of Blue Anchor Lane.

town. Thus, most of the financial transactions which took place may be regarded as confirmation of the fact that borrowing by mortgage tended to be localised. Out of the sixty-four people who lent money and whose place of residence is known, twenty-one lived in Great Yarmouth and nine in Beccles. Thus, the two nearest market towns to Lowestoft (especially the former) obviously had some degree of importance as sources of credit – and it is likely that Lowestoft acted in a similar capacity to both those places. The inference to be drawn from a scrutiny of the various mortgage arrangements which took place is that trading and business contacts were probably an important factor in forging the relationship between both parties. In a lesser number of instances (sixteen in all), family ties are also detectable. In all cases, with credit-worthiness having a moral and social connotation, as well as an obvious financial one, the factor of trust was of key importance in establishing and maintaining networks of loan provision.[60]

There is no evidence available to reveal the amount of interest charged, but it is possible to gain some idea of the various periods of loan. Over half of the 248 mortgage transactions recorded have a termination date. Eighty-two of these are the result of repayment of the debt, fifty-one the result of forfeiture. Repayment of money borrowed may well have been made before settlement was due, but forfeiture almost certainly indicates the end of the agreed period of borrowing. The shortest timespan discernible is one year and nine months, the longest twenty-eight years and two months, with a median period of six years and nine months. Termination by repayment was of lesser duration, with four months as the shortest identifiable period, twenty-one years as the longest, and three years and one month as the median. This may suggest that, wherever possible, people tried to repay what they had borrowed before settlement was due and that their need of funds was relatively short-term. In 129 cases, the amount borrowed is known. The smallest sum was only £2, the largest £385, and the median amount £44 16s 0d. Most of the loans negotiated (one hundred in all) were £100 and below, and half of those were £30 and under.

Unfortunately, it is not possible to infer what prompted people to mortgage their real estate. But study of the records demonstrates that, while certain properties were mortgaged only once, some messuages show a regular sequence of transactions. A selection of the latter can be cited for the purpose of example. The first concerns Isabella Monument, her husband Christopher (fisherman) and their two teenage children (also named Christopher and Isabella). They all lived in a small cottage at the northern end of the High Street, on the east side. The wife owned the dwelling herself, having been given it by her mother, Ann Stanford, after the decease of the latter's husband in July 1708. One month later, Isabella mortgaged the property for £8 8s 0d to Jonathan Belgrave (shoemaker) – a debt that was cleared in December. In October the following year, she re-mortgaged the property to Hannah Smithson (woollen draper's widow) for £12 12s 0d, and then for a further £16 16s 0d to James Postle (cordwainer) in December 1711. Both of these loans were repaid, but the dates were not recorded, and there is nothing to suggest a reason for the money being borrowed. It may have been to help her husband finance fishing ventures of some kind. Whatever the case, no further money was

[60] Muldrew, *Economy of Obligation*, pp. 152 and 172.

raised on the house and she lived in it until early in 1724, when she sold it to William Manthorpe (cordwainer) and his wife. By then, she had been a widow for eight years, her husband having been drowned at sea in the autumn herring season of 1716. She herself lived only three months after disposing of the property, dying in May 1724.[61]

Ann Harvey, widow of Thomas Harvey (draper) inherited her husband's dwelling-house and shop in April 1663, having been left it by the terms of his will made ten years earlier. The property, located on the eastern side of the High Street (the site of the present-day Nos 47 and 48), had been bequeathed to her for life and was then to pass to the oldest son, Thomas. Between October 1668 and January 1673 she took out four mortgages on the property, to a total value of £232 11s 6d, the mortgagee being Joshua Smithson (woollen draper). It is possible that she was continuing to run her husband's business and that Smithson had an interest in it. Whatever the case, all four mortgages were repaid (again, no dates are given) and she held the property until her death in November 1673. At this point, her youngest child, William (cooper), acceded to it – the oldest son, Thomas, having died some time before. Between January 1674 and January 1691, he mortgaged the property four times, to a total value of £201. Two of his mortgagees were Lowestoft men, Samuel Pacy (merchant) and John Stroud (mariner), and the other two were from out of town: Richard Townsend from Beccles (cordwainer) and John Phipps from Great Yarmouth (barber). All the money was repaid and he remained in possession of the property until his death in March 1724. The following year, his heirs disposed of it to John and Susan Slop, a mariner and his wife.

Simon Barnard (shipwright), who had moved from Lowestoft to Southwold during the 1640s, retained ownership of the large messuage on the east side of the High Street at its southern end, which had been in his family's possession for at least four generations (the site, and the plots on either side, are now occupied by a divisional police headquarters and magistrates' court). Between July 1660 and some time in 1669, he mortgaged the property six times, raising a total of £420. The loans were each repaid within a year or two, but the family's ownership of the messuage came to an end in April 1670, when Barnard sold it to a cousin, Simon Peterson (mariner). Four of the transactions (totalling £208) were negotiated with Mary Barrett, a spinster from Carlton Colville, the other two (totalling £212) with George England of Great Yarmouth (merchant). Barnard's connection with Lowestoft seems to have terminated with the sale of the property, and it is possible that he needed the money for new ventures in Southwold or elsewhere (he was sixty years old in 1670). He may have been the forbear of the Barnard family of Ipswich, and later of Harwich and Deptford, largest independent shipbuilders in England during the eighteenth century, but no positive link has yet been established.[62]

---

[61] Isabella Monument's cottage stood somewhere between the present-day Nos 4 and 27, High Street. This area sustained serious bomb damage during World War II and underwent clearance during the post-war period. It was not re-developed and is kept as open green.

[62] A. G. Jones, 'Shipbuilding in Ipswich, 1700–1750', *MM* 43 (1957), 298–304; J. Barnard, 'The Barnard Shipyards', *SR* New Series 8 (1987), 1–17; J. Barnard, *Building England's Wooden Walls* (Oswestry, 1997). The Barnards built East Indiamen and naval ships up to the third rate (frigates).

Early in 1682, William Wells (victualler) bought one of Lowestoft's premier inns, *The Crown*, from Roger Castle (gentleman) of Raveningham in Norfolk.[63] Wells's origins are not known, but in November 1676 he had married Deborah Leake, a merchant's widow and the daughter of James Wilde, one of the town's wealthiest and most influential men. Wells arranged a mortgage for £280 with his father-in-law upon purchasing the premises and the loan was repaid after six years (Wilde having died in February 1684), the redemption duly being recorded in the court books in February 1688. The following month Wells borrowed £242 from George Spilman of Great Yarmouth (merchant), and this time the loan was repaid within twelve years, its clearance being recorded in January 1700. At the very same time, he took up another mortgage, for £210, with another Yarmouth merchant, Thomas Cooper. The date of repayment is not recorded, but the debt must have been honoured because the property passed unencumbered, on Wells's decease, to his daughter Ann, wife of Gregory Clarke, rector of Blundeston. She was admitted to the property in September 1710 and had it made out in the joint names of her husband and herself.

It is likely that the £732 raised on *The Crown* was part of Wells's means of building up a considerable holding for himself in Lowestoft. He had begun his ventures by purchasing *The King's Head* (east side of the High Street, opposite *The Crown*) in September 1681 – an acquisition that was followed up, as seen, by *The Crown* itself, just a few months later. In September 1685 he bought a malt-house immediately south of Swan Score, to the rear of *The Swan* inn, thereby ensuring a supply of the raw material needed for brewing beer at both his inns – and no more than 100 yards from either of them. Finally, in September 1700, he acquired *The Cock*, a small hostelry at the southern extremity of the High Street, on its eastern side. None of these other properties was mortgaged at any stage and all four messuages passed to his daughter Ann when he died, his wife having predeceased him.

Henry Butcher (fisherman) and his wife, Mary, lived in a small house on the south side of Swan Lane, on the western side of the junction with West Lane (the plot now lies under Jubilee Way, the northern section of Lowestoft's inner relief road). The couple had inherited it in August 1664, having then been married for about ten years, from Mary's mother, Jane Webster. At varying times between the time of inheritance and their deaths in the 1680s the property was mortgaged no less than eight times, for a total value of £51 4s 10d. The first five transactions, worth £28 1s 4d, were arranged with John George (bricklayer); the last three, amounting to £23 3s 6d, were negotiated with Joshua Smithson (woollen draper), who was referred to four paragraphs above. All of the loans (except the last one) were repaid, though no dates are given, and there is no suggestion as to why such a regular sequence of small sums of money was required.[64] Given their irregularity, which even included pence in the reckoning, it is possible that Henry Butcher was using the house as security for financing fishing ventures and that the separate mortgages represented amounts of money needed to purchase nets and other items of gear. He died in September 1681,

---

[63] The Castle (or Kastell) family was long established in Raveningham, South Norfolk, and the surname is perpetuated in the parish today in the presence of 'Castell Farm'.

[64] The smallest was £2 12s 0d and the largest, £8 8s 6d.

but the date of his wife's decease is not recorded. Their son William acceded to the property under the terms of his sister Jane's will (October 1694) – but he was not able to pay off the final mortgage (for £6 16s 0d), thereby conceding the property to Joseph Smithson, the mortgagee's son, in March 1719.[65]

Inheritance patterns

Money

Lowestoft wills show that, in the majority of cases, money was distributed primarily among immediate members of the family: in other words, those closest in relationship to the testator. This feature is consistent throughout the various social and occupational groups, and in the event of a testator having no children the beneficiaries tended to be more distant members of the family on either the male or female sides, or both. Bequests to minors usually stipulated that they should receive their portions at the age of eighteen or twenty-one years, or when they married. There are few examples of legacies remaining unpaid and thus becoming the responsibility of a later generation of heirs – a situation which differs from that identified in part of rural Leicestershire during the sixteenth and seventeenth centuries.[66] It seems that Lowestoft testators who bequeathed sums of money had the capacity to ensure that they were paid at the appointed time by whoever was responsible for doing so.

Although money was kept largely within the immediate or wider family groups to which the testators belonged, bequests were also made to people and agencies outside. The various forms of charitable gifts will be considered in Chapters 10 and 11, but a number of other cash legacies were made to godchildren (who were not always members of the family), to friends and acquaintances, and to servants. The amounts were not usually large, but there are enough of them to contrast markedly with remarks made concerning will material in Earls Colne (Essex) and Kirkby Lonsdale (Westmoreland): in both of these communities bequests of money were rarely left to people other than kin.[67]

Out of 102 Lowestoft wills which are extant for the period 1560–1599, thirty-six reveal the bequest of money to people not related by blood to the testators (35.3%). For the seventeenth century, the number is thirty-two out of a total of 273 documents (11.7%), with an equal distribution in each half of the century. This decline in the number of cash legacies left to people outside the family group is even more marked in the years between 1700 and 1730. Out of 132 wills, only eleven make reference to money bequeathed to outsiders (8.3%). There was also a marked decrease in the number of charitable bequests after 1600. It seems almost as if people became, not necessarily less generous in their response to others, but less expansive in their view of the world around

[65] This last mortgage may have been the longest of all those arranged in Lowestoft during the seventeenth century, but without a starting-date no proof is available.
[66] C. Howell, 'Peasant Inheritance Customs in the Midlands, 1280–1700', in Goody, *Family and Inheritance*, p. 145. E. P. Thompson, 'The Grid of Inheritance', in *ibid.*, p. 346, makes much the same point.
[67] MacFarlane, *Reconstructing Historical Communities*, p. 142.

them. It is possible that there was also a practical side to the phenomenon, arising out of the social and demographic conditions of the time: the desirability of retaining strong kinship ties because of the need for relatives to perform all kinds of surrogate functions within the family group.[68]

Real estate

In broad terms, the *post-mortem* inheritance pattern in Lowestoft was a combination of primogeniture and partible inheritance (*pre-mortem* disposal of property only made up about 11% of direct transfer within the immediate family group). Thus, it constitutes what may be termed a 'halfway house' between the rural parishes of South Elmham, Suffolk, where the former system prevailed, and the urban environment of the city of Worcester, where normal practice was division of an estate as equally as possible among all the children.[69] This is not to suggest that Lowestoft, as a maritime town combining both rural and urban elements in its make-up, was bound to have an inheritance pattern which reflected both kinds of practice. More investigation needs to be carried out on systems of bequest before any notions of typicality can be arrived at. For instance, the Leicestershire market town of Ashby-de-la-Zouche adhered to primogeniture, whereas three particular rural parishes in Cambridgeshire adopted a combination of primogeniture and partible inheritance.[70]

It is the three latter communities (Chippenham, Orwell and Willingham) which offer the best comparison with Lowestoft. In each of them, testators with more than one son divided their holdings in such a way as to give those sons a share of the family lands.[71] It may not have been an equal share, but it was nevertheless part of the patrimonial estate. Over the course of time, this practice resulted in the holdings becoming progressively smaller, until they reached the point where some of them were no longer viable as agricultural units – a feature also observed in at least one Leicestershire community.[72] The practice of dividing family estates in Lowestoft did not have this effect because most people in the parish were not primarily involved in agriculture. Even if lands were bequeathed by the merchants and tradespeople, they were not the sole means of producing the family income. The urban and maritime nature of the parish meant that there were other spheres of activity which generated money. The diversity of the Lowestoft merchants and tradespeople allowed them, quite often, to split their various properties two, three and even four ways, thereby enabling beneficiaries to set up on their own in an established and viable enterprise.

---

[68] Stone, *Family, Sex and Marriage*, p. 130.

[69] Evans, 'South Elmham', pp. 100–2; Dyer, *Worcester*, p. 180.

[70] Moxon, p. 92; Spufford, *Contrasting Communities*, chapters 3, 4 and 5.

[71] *Ibid.*, pp. 87, 106 and 159.

[72] *Ibid.*, pp. 87 and 160. The point is made that the fenland parish of Willingham, with its richer soil, was better able to stand the fragmentation of family holdings than the chalkland parish of Chippenham and the clayland one of Orwell. Also see Howell, 'Inheritance Customs', in Goody, *Family and Inheritance*, p. 146. Comment is made here about how equal shares by bequest could lead rapidly to the minimum viable economic size of holding being reached – especially in areas where land was short.

Three examples of the practice may serve to demonstrate its operation. When Wyllyam Wylde (merchant) made his will in February 1612, he left his oldest son, John (aged forty years), all his tenements and lands in the neighbouring parish of Corton, a dwelling-house in Lowestoft that was rented out and a bruery dole on Drakes Heath. His two surviving younger sons, Daniel and Derick (aged twenty-two years and twenty-one years respectively), were also well treated. The former was bequeathed half his father's mackerel nets and herring nets, a house on the freehold land at the top of the High Street (the site of present-day No. 176) and its fish-curing premises – to be inherited after the death of the widow – and all goods, chattels and money not otherwise bequeathed. The latter was to receive all of his father's herring speets and salting vats and a good quantity of household furniture. He was also left a house on the High Street (situated on the plot now occupied by No. 2), which was rented out, and its appurtenances both above and below the cliff (the buildings below the cliff included fish-curing premises and net-stores). Thus were the three sons intended to make their way in life: one assisted by rents deriving from the lands he had been left, the other two with their fishing and fish-curing activities.[73]

Samuel Pacy (merchant) made his will in September 1680. Besides cash legacies of £600 to each of his three surviving sons, he also bequeathed them a considerable amount of property and goods.[74] The oldest son, Samuel (aged twenty years), was left all of his father's lands and tenements in Denton and Topcroft, south Norfolk, to be inherited after the death of his mother.[75] The next in line, William (aged eighteen years), was left the family dwelling-house on the High Street (now Nos 81–83) with all its fish-houses and outbuildings, while the youngest son, John (aged sixteen years), received a house belonging to his father in another part of town, together with its outbuildings and stables, plus a six-acre meadow opposite the market place and a barn and a yard in Blue Anchor Lane. Both of them were to inherit after the death of their mother. The provision made for the three sons by their respective inheritances enabled Samuel, the eldest, to set himself up as gentleman and the other two to carry on in branches of the maritime industries (fishing and fish-curing) that had brought their father so much of his wealth.[76]

Finally, John Durrant (brewer) made his will in December 1695. He left his oldest son, John (aged twenty-eight years), his home messuage on the High Street (what is now No. 84), with brewing facilities, malt-house and fish-curing premises. His two younger sons, Thomas and Henry (aged eighteen years and eleven years, respectively) he also

---

[73] John Wilde was already a well-established Lowestoft merchant, living at what is now No. 80, High Street. Within a few years of his younger brothers receiving their legacies, he had bought the messuage left to Derick (May 1615). Daniel Wilde, who had settled in Great Yarmouth and worked there as a cooper, had already sold his house and appurtenances to Francis Knights (merchant) in July 1613.

[74] There were also legacies for three, older, married daughters.

[75] This property had come to Samuel Pacy Snr as part of his wife's marriage settlement.

[76] It is possible that Samuel Pacy did not trust his oldest son to carry on the family business. The latter became Receiver-General for the County of Suffolk and died suddenly in 1708 at Epsom (while taking the waters), owing the government £18,628 13s 8d in taxes he had collected. William Pacy eventually left Lowestoft for Great Yarmouth, prospering in the rival town and becoming mayor there. See. G. Geis and I. Bunn, *A Tryal of Witches* (London and New York, 1997), p. 209.

treated generously. The former was bequeathed an inn called *The George* (the site of what is now No. 87, High Street), close to the messuage left to his older brother, two dwelling-houses that were rented out, and a shop and warehouses adjoining these houses. The latter received two complexes of dwelling-houses with associated farm buildings in the parishes of Carlton Colville and Kessingland. The intention of the bequests was much the same as in the two previous cases: to enable the young men to make an independent living and, hopefully, to prosper.

As well as the men who had real estate to bequeath, there were also a lesser number of women similarly placed. They, too, followed the same pattern as their male counterparts, thereby producing a combination of primogeniture and partible inheritance. In the absence of sons, both sexes bequeathed real estate to daughters, and there were also cases in which girls inherited property while there were brothers living.[77] The examples are few in number and the amount of property not large, but the cases do exist and must have resulted from particular affections and ties within the family units. There are also a number of instances where real estate was required by the testator to be sold by the executor(s) in order to settle debts, pay the various legacies which had been bequeathed and meet the cost of funeral expenses.

This particular feature is noticeable at either end of the range of people who owned property. The wealthy may have ordered the sale of a house or two to help finance the various commitments undertaken; the person who owned his or her own dwelling-house, and nothing more, may have been forced to cash in the main asset just to meet his or her obligations. Of the forty-two cases of the sale of real estate ordered by testators between 1560 and 1730, thirteen were solely to finance the upbringing of children, another thirteen were to jointly pay off debts and pay for children's upbringing, six were solely to honour debts, and three were to finance legacies. Six of the remaining seven show varying combinations of the causes listed, with provision also being made for family members such as grandchildren and nephews, and there is one isolated example requiring property to be sold and the money applied to charitable uses.

In order to show the disposal of land and buildings by Lowestoft testators as clearly as possible, the four sub-periods adopted previously in this chapter will be used in the tables which follow, together with overall figures for the whole timespan. There were 354 property-owning testators altogether and their bequests of real estate will be considered from two viewpoints: the initial pattern of inheritance, followed by the longer-term one. Of the 354, 282 were men (including eight unmarried ones) and seventy-two were women (sixty-two widows, seven wives and three spinsters). The focus will thus be largely on male testators, but with an important female minority also considered.

The initial pattern of bequest, if it may be so termed (in other words, the initial disposal of property before longer-term stipulations took place), may be seen in Table 32. It is based on those wills made by men who owned real estate in excess of a single house, who had a wife living at the time the document was drawn up and who, in most cases,

---

[77] J. R. Goody, 'Inheritance, Property and Women: Some Comparative Considerations', in Goody, *Family and Inheritance*, p. 10, states that roughly 20% of all families would have had daughters only. The introduction to this book says on p. 2 that among the departures from primogeniture in England and Western Europe was one where daughters sometimes received bequests of land.

Table 32. *Bequest of real estate: initial pattern (1560–1730)*

Period	No. of testators	Widow only	Details	Widow for life	Children (widow alive)	Other
1560–1599	40	13	3 cases of no children and 2 of no sons	16	10	1
1600–1649	62	11	4 cases of no children and 1 of no sons	36	14	1
1650–1699	71	8		48	11	4
1700–1730	51	12	2 cases of no children	32	7	0
1560–1730	**224**	**44**		**132**	**42**	**6**

had at least one child alive. It can be clearly seen that the great majority of bequests were to the widow for life, it being largely her responsibility to ensure the proper bringing-up of the children (i.e. those who were minors). Out of seventy-two cases where young children were left without a father, fifty-five of the testators placed the duty of care on their wives. Most of the Lowestoft testators seem to have had confidence in their spouses' integrity, even in the case of second marriages, and such phrases as 'my loving wife' and 'my good and true wife' suggest that many of the marriages were happy and affectionate ones.[78]

In the sense of the wife/widow being left some, if not all, of the property for life (or, in fewer cases, until the oldest son came of age), the provision resembles that found in Cambridgeshire – but there are fewer examples in Lowestoft of widows being granted house-room than in the parish of Orwell.[79] Only four instances of the practice are specifically referred to in the townspeople's wills: one between 1560 and 1599, two between 1600 and 1649, and one between 1650 and 1699. If an heir was made responsible for the care of his mother, it was not usually under the same roof – at least, not according to the strict wording of the will. What a man might have chosen to do of his own volition is another matter.[80]

The motivation to make a will because of necessary provision for young children was less compelling in Lowestoft than might have been the case in other communities. In the Cambridgeshire parish of Willingham, for instance, between 1575 and 1603, 75% of the male testators had to provide for two or more sons or for under-age children.[81] Between 1560 and 1599, Lowestoft had thirty-seven of its seventy-two married testators in this category (53%), while for the period 1600–1649 it was thirty-nine out of ninety-

---

[78] Such descriptions used to describe the widows are not the result of clichéd phraseology employed by professional scribes who drew up the wills. The Lowestoft documents were written by a wide range of local people, including testators themselves.

[79] Spufford, *Contrasting Communities*, pp. 89, 113–14 and 162.

[80] There is limited evidence in Lowestoft of widows residing in part of a house belonging to a son. Some of the inventories suggest it.

[81] M. Spufford, 'Peasant Inheritance Customs and Land Distribution in Cambridgeshire from the Sixteenth to the Eighteenth Centuries,' in Goody, *Family and Inheritance*, pp. 171–2.

one (43%). Between 1650 and 1699 there were fifty-two men out of ninety-eight in such circumstances (53%), and for 1700–1730 it was thirty-one out of seventy-nine (39%). Thus, for the whole span of time between 1560 and 1730 47% of male testators had either two or more sons, or under-age children, to provide for. And, whereas in the Cambridgeshire parish the poorer occupational groups produced most wills,[82] in Lowestoft it was the better-off members of local society who were largely responsible for their creation.

In the absence of a wife, and if the oldest son had already reached his majority, the responsibility for the welfare of younger children fell upon that oldest son. He was usually made responsible, too, for paying them their portions at the appointed time, but the Lowestoft testators do not seem to have made the legacies unrealistic in terms of what the estate was able to bear. The point has already been made that cash legacies did not remain unpaid years after they were due. Nor was the situation ever reached, as it was in the Gloucestershire village of Bledington, where the burden of paying legacies led to heirs taking up mortgages or borrowing money by other means to meet the commitments placed upon them.[83]

The longer-term pattern of the bequest of real estate is more complex to ascertain than the initial one, because it entails working out the identity of legatees who were to inherit after the death of the various testators' widows. It also necessitates concentrating on those families with more than one son living at the time a will was made and it means that only the wills of those testators (both male and female) with more than a single dwelling-house to dispose of can be used.[84] Of the 343 married, property-owing testators (including widowers and widows), 111 meet the criteria established in the previous sentence, which is 32% of the whole. The remaining two-thirds either had only one surviving son at the time a will was made, no sons at all,[85] or only a single dwelling-house to bequeath. Among the 111 testators whose wills can be used to work out the longer-term pattern of the bequest of real estate are sixteen women. Details relating to them are shown in brackets in Table 33. In all cases where primogeniture applied, whether relating to male or female testators, there was no abuse of the system such as that identified in certain rural communities, during the eighteenth century, whereby yeomen left their younger sons with a pittance in order that the oldest one might ape the lifestyle of the gentry.[86] Younger sons in Lowestoft were always well provided for.

Table 33 clearly shows the predominance of primogeniture and partible inheritance as the principal means by which real estate was bequeathed with long-term intentions

---

[82] Spufford, 'Peasant Inheritance', in Goody, *Family and Inheritance*, p. 172.

[83] M. K. Ashby, *The Changing English Village: A History of Bledington* (Kineton, 1974), pp. 162–4 and 194–5.

[84] This is because ownership of a single dwelling would have severely limited a testator's options regarding disposal. The constraints placed upon any course of action would not have allowed full, unrestricted choice to be made between primogeniture, partible inheritance and Borough English.

[85] Where there were no sons, daughters were usually made the heirs.

[86] J. Thirsk, 'The European Debate on Customs of Inheritance, 1500–1700', in Goody, *Family and Inheritance*, p. 191.

Table 33. *Bequest of real estate: longer-term pattern (1560–1730)*

Period	No. of testators	Primogeniture	Partible	Younger son	Youngest son
1560–1599	16(2)	8	7(2)	0	1
1600–1649	35(4)	16(1)	11(1)	3(1)	5(1)
1650–1699	36(3)	16(1)	14(1)	3(1)	3(1)
1700–1730	24(7)	8(3)	9	3(2)	4(2)
1560–1730	**111(16)**	**48(5)**	**41(4)**	**9(4)**	**13(4)**

in mind. However, possession of a single dwelling-house and nothing else gave those people making wills less choice in disposing of property than would have been the case had they owned more than one messuage. Therefore, both the initial pattern of bequest and that showing longer-term inheritance may be expected to show differences from the trends visible in Tables 32 and 33. The single largest type of bequest deriving from the sixty-nine documents analysed was to the widow for life (thirty-two examples), though not as predominantly as in Table 32. Property left to the widow for her sole use was next in popularity (nineteen examples), which again compares with Table 32, but bequests to children with the widow still living were considerably reduced (seven examples). Finally, there were seven instances of the stipulated sale of property and sharing-out of the money derived – a practice which does not appear earlier – and there were four other diverse means of disposal.

The longer-term pattern for the disposal of a single dwelling-house indicates that a clear majority of the twenty-seven men and nine women who owned only one residence and had two or more sons living at the time the will was made decided in favour of selling the property and dividing the money among the children (who, in some cases, included daughters). There are sixteen examples of this practice; next in popularity was the decision to follow the principle of primogeniture (eleven examples). Partible inheritance is detectable in a further five cases, while there is one instance of bequest to a younger son (made by a woman) and three examples of disposal to the youngest son of all.

Up until now, the emphasis has been on the bequest of real estate to male children – but, as was mentioned earlier, cases do exist where daughters inherited property while sons were alive. The practice is in evidence where both male and female testators are concerned and the number of people who disposed of property to female offspring is not inconsiderable. Of the 174 married men and women who owned more real estate than just a single dwelling-house and who had at least two living children when the will was made, one of whom was a son, no less than sixty (forty-five men and fifteen women) bequeathed at least some of the property to daughters – a proportion of 34.5%. Of the ninety-two married men and women who owned a dwelling-house only and who had at least two children alive when the will was made, one of whom was a son, nine (four men and five women) bequeathed that house to daughters – a proportion of 9.8%.

Female testators

The disposal of real estate during the pre-industrial period was predominantly a male affair, though in Lowestoft it is interesting to note that, for every four men bequeathing property to children, there was one woman doing so. With regard to female testators as a whole, irrespective of whether or not they had real estate to pass on, the Lowestoft probate material shows that women constituted a substantial minority of those people in the parish who made wills – especially during the first three decades of the eighteenth century. In most cases they were widows, but there were small numbers of married women and of spinsters. Table 34 shows the respective numbers of male and female testators over the total length of time chosen for analysis.

Among the features to emerge is a higher percentage of widows making wills than that ascertained in the Norwich archdeaconry and consistory courts between 1560 and 1686.[87] Much of the area covered by these jurisdictions would have been rural in nature and it is possible that Lowestoft, being of urban character, allowed wealth to be generated across a wider range of people – thus enabling a larger proportion of the population, including the female element, to make bequests. Another factor to be considered is that Lowestoft, as a town (albeit a small one), drew in widows from surrounding parishes to live in a more congenial environment, thereby increasing their number to a certain degree. About 40% of the Lowestoft widows were the relicts of either merchants or mariners, and it is known (especially in the case of the latter) that they had often assisted their husbands in the running of commercial enterprises – a factor that must have elevated their status in society and perhaps enhanced their ability to hold property. Finally, although the numbers were small, the first thirty years of the eighteenth century showed an increase in the will-making capacity of both married women and spinsters.

Table 34. *Lowestoft testators, male and female (1560–1730)*

Period	Total	Married men	Single men	Widows	Married women	Spinsters	Women as a % of the whole	Widows as a % of the whole
1560–1599	102	70	6	25	1	0	25.5	24.2
1600–1649	129	91	6	30	1	1	24.8	23.2
1650–1699	144	98	18	25	1	2	19.4	15.3
1700–1730	132	79	8	36	4	5	34.1	20.5
1560–1730	**507**	**338**	**38**	**116**	**7**	**8**	**25.8**	**22.9**

---

[87] Evans, *Linen Industry*, p. 5. The proportion of widows making wills was 17% during the second half of the sixteenth century and 13% throughout much of the seventeenth.

Categories of bequest

The bequests made by testators in Lowestoft break down into three main categories: real estate, cash payments and goods in kind. Throughout the whole timespan used for the analysis of wills, these types of legacy observed the same order of precedence, with cash gifts being most common, bequests of goods and chattels being next in order and those bestowing real estate coming third. However, although the basic order remained the same, there were changes in the ratios of the three categories, one to another, which can be clearly seen in Table 35. Bequests of real estate rose steadily throughout the whole period, with the most noticeable increase occurring during the seventeenth century. Cash legacies declined modestly in number from one end of the timespan to the other, while gifts in kind decreased during the second half of the seventeenth century and then underwent a minor recovery during the early eighteenth.

Table 35. *Types of bequest: Lowestoft wills (1560–1730)*

Period	Total no. of bequests	Real estate	% of the whole	Cash	% of the whole	Kind	% of the whole	No. of wills
1560–1599	1042	88	8.4	572	54.9	382	36.7	102
1600–1649	932	125	13.4	429	46.0	378	40.6	129
1650–1699	909	171	18.8	479	52.7	259	28.5	144
1700–1730	852	174	20.4	399	46.8	279	32.7	132
1560–1730	**3735**	**558**	**14.9**	**1879**	**50.3**	**298**	**34.6**	**507**

Comparisons may be made with a study of similar nature relating to a community located in the East Midlands – the parish of Knibworth Harcourt.[88] Here, the proportion of cash payments (at 48%) was 7% lower than in Lowestoft during the second half of the sixteenth century and (again at 48%) 2% more during the first forty years of the seventeenth. A decline (to 36%) followed between 1641 and 1680, but the last twenty years of the seventeenth century saw cash legacies increase to a level of 52% (a figure broadly in line with Lowestoft's). Lowestoft had an appreciably lower rate of the bequest of goods in kind than the Leicestershire settlement, which may reflect a difference between urban and rural communities whereby more of the wealth in the latter was tied up in stock and materials. In general terms, the individual value(s) of cash legacies in Lowestoft showed an increase during the seventeenth century, over and above what had been bequeathed during the sixteenth, and this matches the trend discernible in Knibworth Harcourt. However, there was no upward movement from 1680 to 1720, in contrast to the situation in the Leicestershire parish. If anything, the value of cash legacies in Lowestoft dropped back slightly after 1700 and testators did not make so many of them.

---

[88] Howell, 'Inheritance Customs', in Goody, *Family and Inheritance*, pp. 149–52.

− 8 −

Fishing and Maritime Trade

Introduction

Reference was made at the beginning of Chapter 1 to the geographical advantages of Lowestoft's position on the East Coast. A substantial number of its male inhabitants made a living from going to sea, while others remained on shore and earned money from processing catches of fish and handling other cargoes. A select minority of these latter even grew wealthy through maritime activity, because they were the people who owned the vessels which caught herrings and cod or which carried merchandise of different kinds. A considerable amount of research has been devoted to various aspects of English coastal and overseas trade in the pre-industrial era, but fishing has not fared so well. The balance was partly redressed by publication of a national fisheries history some years ago,[1] but the country still does not have a body of material to compare with Scotland, Holland or the Scandinavian nations. Much of the material in this chapter has been reproduced elsewhere, but no apology is made for its presence here because sea-based industries were probably the single most important factor in Lowestoft's development from the end of the thirteenth century onwards.[2]

Fishing and trading

The types of vessel used

There is comparatively little surviving pictorial or documentary information to enable accurate assessment of the structure and working practice of fishing craft in the sixteenth and seventeenth centuries. Details found in official records suggest that the vessels ranged from about ten or fifteen tons burden up to seventy or eighty tons, with some of the larger Iceland barks reaching as much as 120 tons.[3] These capacities would probably have

---

[1] D. Starkey et al. (eds), England's Sea Fisheries (London, 2000).

[2] See D. Butcher, The Ocean's Gift (Norwich, 1995) and 'The Herring Fisheries in the Early Modern Period: Lowestoft as Microcosm', in Starkey et al., Sea Fisheries, pp. 54–63.

[3] TNA: PRO, SP 12/38/8/II; Gairdner and Brodie, LPFD, Henry VIII, xix, i, 76. At this time, a boat's tonnage referred to the dead weight or quantity of cargo (reckoned as the number of casks, or tuns, which could be carried). It had nothing to do with the modern calculation for a vessel's capacity (net tonnage), by which one ton is the equivalent of one hundred cubic feet of enclosed storage space below decks (usually minus non-earning spaces, such as the engine-room and crew's quarters).

Plate 15. *Late sixteenth-century fishing and trading vessels: these computer-enhanced images are vignettes added to embellish the map of c. 1580. The details revealed of hull, masting, sail-plan and rigging are sufficient to give a good impression of certain craft in use at the time.*

meant overall lengths ranging from twenty or twenty-five feet up to sixty or seventy. Most of the vessels would have been decked, probably with a raised foredeck and poop, and they would have had two or three masts. These latter would have been square-rigged and extra sails could have been set on bowsprits and outriggers, as required. Vessels of this type appear on a late sixteenth-century map of the Lothingland coastline (Plate 15) and they may be taken as typical of the time.[4]

The map also has two vignettes of a smaller, inshore vessel, which would probably have been in the range of twelve to sixteen feet in length. It has a single mast amidships and is shown carrying a furled lugsail. Further pictorial information is to be had from the map drawn to accompany the Lothingland defence survey of 1584 referred to in Chapter 1.[5] This shows two three-masters of the kind referred to above lying at anchor off Lowestoft, as well as three smaller *crayers*. Two of these latter are double-masted (one of the craft is very small), while the third one has a single mast. Plying between the five vessels and the shore are three ferry boats, which offloaded fish and general cargo and which conveyed supplies and merchandise to visiting ships. All of them are shown as being crewed by four oarsmen.

[4] BL, Add. Mss. 56070; SRO(L), 368. The latter is a copy of the original map. For further information concerning it, see H. Cobbe, 'Four Manuscript Maps Recently Acquired by the British Museum', *JSA* 4, viii (October, 1973), 647–9.

[5] TNA: PRO, MPF 283.

One problem which arises when discussing vessels of 400 years ago is their dual–purpose nature. Although both Henrician and Elizabethan surveys refer specifically to merchant ships, craft up to 100 or 120 tons would also have been used on fishing voyages. This has been observed in the port of Rye and also nearer to home, in Aldeburgh.[6] In the latter town, chamberlains' accounts of the late sixteenth century show that six vessels were involved in both fishing and the coastal salt-carrying trade, eleven in fishing and coastal coal voyages, and three other craft in all three activities. Lowestoft would probably have been no different from these other two communities – but, up until now, nothing in documentation of the time relating directly to the town has been found to confirm dual use.[7] Nor do customs records seem to have survived from the time that port status was granted (1679) right through to the nineteenth century. Dual use was certainly a feature of smaller inshore craft, however, and these combined fishing with ferrying goods to and from the shoreline.[8] It is worth noting that any vessel is only useful to its owner when it is working; laying it up simply removes earning capacity and causes the planks to spring.

As far as larger craft are concerned, dual use would have not made much difference to storage facilities below decks. The hold compartments (*pannells*) were easily re-arranged to suit the cargo and the main task would have been one of cleaning the spaces after either fishing or coal-carrying. However, the organisation of deck-space would have been of major importance in herring or mackerel fishing. Whether the nets were hauled for'ad or amidships, there was one vital requirement: adequate room for the removal of fish from the meshes and for stowing the gear. The usual way of providing necessary working space, and getting rid of the obstruction caused by stays and shrouds, was to drop the foremast back into a cruck or support of some kind and leave it there for as long as the boat was hanging to its nets or the work of hauling was in progress. There were no such problems with line-fishing for cod or ling, because the hauling of lines and the handling of the fish required far less deck-area.

As the seventeenth century progressed, it seems that the distinction between fishing craft and trading vessels became more clearly defined. Certainly, in Lowestoft's case, by the time that the surviving tithe accounts book began to record farming and fishing in the parish in the year 1698, the larger, deep-sea fishing vessels (or *great boats*, as they were known) seem to have been distinct from the traders which were operating out of port.[9] Each type could have been converted to other uses if need arose, but the design and

---

[6] Hipkin, 'Rye', pp. 109 and 111; M. Allen, 'The Development of the Borough of Aldeburgh, 1547–1660' (unpub. MA dissertation, University of Wales, 1982), pp. 52–3.

[7] It is possible that the Great Yarmouth port books, in the PRO, might provide evidence of the practice. The names of a number of Lowestoft craft and the masters are known, so if their activities were recorded in the ledgers of the head-port (as they were supposed to be) dual or single use could be established. However, it was the constant complaint of Yarmouth bailiffs that Lowestoft vessel-owners constantly ignored official procedures and established an illegal autonomy.

[8] Lowestoft had no harbour until the year 1831. Prior to that, fishing craft and trading vessels had to lie offshore and transfer their cargoes to smaller boats, whose crews then rowed the goods ashore.

[9] NRO, PD 589/80. The Lowestoft tithe accounts run in an unbroken sequence from 1698 to 1787.

construction had diverged, leading to distinct differences in appearance. The fishing vessels had become lower in the water than the traders and they carried large lugsails on their three masts, as opposed to smaller sails set on yards. Plates 4 and 8 show both types of craft more effectively than words can describe, with the latter also depicting two great boats under construction on the shoreline – these being instantly recognisable by the grooved crossbar on the stern, in which the mast rested while fishing was in progress.

Little is known about the cost of building such vessels. Details found in probate inventories refer to craft already in use, without reference to age or condition. In any case, it is not until 1656 that the first valuation is recorded, when a fishing vessel belonging to Josiah Wilde (merchant) was appraised at £55, without its gear. Twenty-six years later, Elizabeth Pacy (merchant's widow) had two fishing craft, called the *Herring* and the *Mackerel*, worth £100 each with nets and other equipment, while a third one, the *Susan* (named after the oldest daughter) was valued at £45 exclusive of gear. Elizabeth's next-door neighbour, James Wilde (merchant), owned five fishing boats when he died in February 1684. They were called the *Envoy*, the *Mermaid*, the *James*, the *Swallow* and the *Amity*, and they were valued at £200, £140, £100, £100 and £50 respectively. In 1699, the two vessels belonging to Joseph Barker (merchant) were reckoned to be worth a total of £300, inclusive of fishing gear, while a year later three craft owned by William Rising (merchant) had a combined value of £500 placed upon them – again, inclusive of gear. The *Mayflower*, which belonged to Samuel Munds (merchant), must have been smaller than all of these others because it was only worth £25, exclusive of gear, in the year 1711.

Six years later the great boat (and that is the description of it in the inventory) owned by Leake Bitson (merchant) was appraised at £87 3s 0d, while in 1719 and 1723 John Colby (merchant and apothecary) and Thomas Utting (grocer) had a vessel each, assessed at £100 and £60 respectively. All three valuations did not include the vessels' gear. During the same period as that covered by the nine inventories cited, ferry boats and small inshore craft ranged in value from £1 to £6, depending on age and on how many oars and other pieces of equipment were included in the valuations.

Finance and organisation

Leaving the question of dual use aside, it is possible to ascertain the pattern of ownership of Lowestoft vessels from both wills and probate inventories, but the most detailed information is to be found in the parish tithe accounts. Between 1698 and 1725, fifty-three individuals are seen to have either owned fishing craft outright or to have shared ownership with other people.[10] Seven of the former were boat masters and the rest largely merchants – along with a grocer, a victualler and a yeoman, whose presence maintained the local tradition of a mixed economy. Details available in the probate records suggest that, up until the middle of the seventeenth century, more people of craftsman status were involved in fishing than was the case later on. No definite reason

---

[10] This particular length of time was chosen because it was sufficiently long to give the detail required, without becoming unwieldy in terms of the effort required to collect and collate the information.

can be given for this, but it may be a sign that part of the town's economy was beginning to change and develop from its previous diversity into something more specialised.[11]

Fishing seasons tended to be unpredictable in their yield (this was especially the case after 1700) and it may be that the industry needed a stricter financial regime in order to be successful. There was also a tendency for the larger boats to become bigger and more expensive to build as time went on, and this possibly discouraged what may be described as a 'part-time' interest in fishing. Furthermore, it is likely that a number of people were forced out of fishing during the period of decline in the first half of the seventeenth century and never returned to it.

As far as smaller, inshore craft are concerned, evidence in both probate material and the tithe accounts suggest that these were owned and worked primarily by the fishermen themselves. The latter records are particularly compelling, showing that of the eighty-five owners recorded between 1709 and 1725 (the former year being the first one in which the vessels were recorded for tithe purposes) only fifteen were merchants and the other seventy fishermen. The *small boats*, as they were known, were much less expensive to finance, carrying a crew of only two or three men (as opposed to ten or eleven) and working far fewer nets. Their operators constituted, for the most part, a body of men which was largely independent of the merchants where the fishing operation itself was concerned, but who relied upon their more influential neighbours to buy catches for processing and retail.

As Table 36 clearly shows, control of the fishing industry was dominated by the merchant and seafaring levels of society if evidence provided by wills and inventories is to be believed. The information available in both types of document has been amalgamated to produce a single statement regarding which kinds of people owned boats, fishing gear and curing materials, and in which combination. Most important of all in the industry were those able to be classified in all three categories. As in previous tables, the presence of women is indicated by a number in brackets in the relevant social and occupational groups. It is to be observed that they do not feature in the final period analysed – perhaps because the industry had become more specialist in nature than previously and less spread across the whole community.

The proportion of those people in society who had an interest in the fishing industry and for whom wills and inventories have survived remained fairly constant throughout the whole period investigated. It was 16.2% for 1560–1599, 15.1% for 1600–1699 and 15.2% for 1700–1730.[12] Financial control of the industry evidently lay largely in the hands of merchants and wealthier members of the seafaring fraternity, for it was these people to whom a majority of the larger vessels belonged. This capitalist élite, if it may be so termed, either owned fishing vessels outright on an individual basis or had shared interests in craft. The latter system is most noticeable up to about the middle of the

---

[11] Diversity, in the sense that many people, who had an interest in fishing, were also involved in other areas of economic activity.

[12] Probate documents for the first half of the seventeenth century show only 10.2% of people involved in fishing activity, which reflects the period of economic depression that occurred at this time. The second half has 20% – a proportion partly due to recovery and partly the result of the maritime success deriving from Lowestoft being granted port status in 1679.

Table 36. *Financial interest in fishing: probate material (1560–1730)*

Period	Social/ occupational grouping	Boat only	Gear only	Curing only	Boat & Gear	Gear & Curing	Boat, Gear & Curing
1560–1599	Professional & services						1
	Merchants		1(1)	2(1)	1		5
	Craftsmen						4(1)
	Seafarers		2(2)	1	1(1)		1
			3(3)	**3(1)**	**2(1)**		**11(1)**
1600–1699	Merchants	1		2	3(2)	4(1)	11
	Retail & distribution						1
	Craftsmen	2(1)		1		1	1
	Seafarers		12(1)	1	4	1	3(2)
		3(1)	**12(1)**	**4**	**7(2)**	**6(1)**	**16(2)**
1700–1730	Merchants			2	2		7
	Retail & distribution			1			1
	Craftsmen						1
	Seafarers		6		4		1
			6	**3**	**6**		**10**

seventeenth century, but single ownership increased thereafter – especially during the first three decades of the eighteenth.

In principle, the basic idea behind financing fishing voyages was to invest capital in the purchase of vessels or shares in vessels, to contribute a certain amount of the gear used (this varied, according to individual agreement) and to provide the victuals. At the end of the season, when all catches had been sold, it was hoped that the amount raised would exceed the expenses (equipment, provisions, repairs and wages), thereby producing a profit. This was then distributed according to the amount of money which individual people had committed, with the largest investors receiving the largest pay-outs. In the event of a poor season, there was often no profit to draw. This factor was no doubt one of the reasons why the merchants tended to specialise in curing fish as well as financing the catching of it: losses incurred during periods of poor yield could be partly offset by the money made from selling processed herrings and cod at premium prices. The other advantage was the amount of overall control exercised by having an interest in both fishing and curing, because the price that catches fetched was less liable to fluctuation when both branches of the industry lay in the same hands.

If the information revealed in Table 36 is matched with the number of wills and inventories studied (507 and 100, respectively), it is seen that 33% of merchants identified between 1560 and 1599 had a direct interest in the ownership of both fishing boats and gear and in fish-curing. For 1600–1699 the proportion was 34%, and for 1700–1730, 64%.[13] If those merchants whose interests embraced two of the three elements of the

---

[13] The percentage was lower for the first half of the seventeenth century and higher for the second, for exactly the same reasons as those outlined in the note immediately preceding.

industry are added to the people involved in all three, the proportions for the three periods rise to 40%, 47% and 82% respectively. The figures suggest a tightly knit élite which had considerable influence in the conduct of both fishing and curing. The ties formed by mutual business interests were further strengthened by about 30% of the merchants being related to each other by marriage.

Kinship was an even stronger factor among the maritime classes, with about 40% of seafarers having marriage connections. As Table 36 indicates, their interest lay primarily in the possession of boats and gear, rather than in the processing of catches, but there was an influential minority which had an involvement in all three facets of the industry. It was customary for crew members on board fishing vessels to contribute a certain number of nets or lines (depending on the nature of the voyage) towards the overall amount of gear carried, the idea being to spread the investment over as many people as possible and provide the justification for paying fishermen by a share system.[14] Given a degree of good fortune and sound business sense, it was possible for enterprising fishermen to rise in the world: in three generations during the seventeenth century, one branch of the Pacy family progressed from seafarer status to become the wealthiest merchants in Lowestoft.

In the absence of any references to net-makers in the occupational data, manufacture of fishing nets and lines, a labour-intensive and specialist task, seems to have been carried out by the fishermen and their families (including children).[15] But there is also the possibility that equipment was brought in from outside sources, even though none has as yet been found. Routine repair would have been carried out on board ship while a voyage was in progress and crew members would also have been involved in maintenance work between fishing seasons. In addition to this, casual labour would have been available at times of peak activity (chiefly, the autumn herring season) to ensure that the equipment was kept at a serviceable level. The battle against wear and tear was never-ending – a vital task in ensuring that the gear worked effectively and that expenditure on new equipment was not undertaken lightly.

Probate inventories dating from between 1590 and 1730 give a range of values for fishing nets. Those for herring, depending on their depth, ranged from 3s to 12s each; mackerel nets were worth between 1s and 13s 4d (the former must have been a very poor specimen); and sprat nets worked out at about 2s 6d to 3s 6d. All this gear had been used and was of varying age and condition. The only prices available for what was obviously new gear occur in 1682 and 1719, when valuations of £1 per net were given. The constant exposure of fishing gear to salt water caused the fibres of the twine to rot and regular treatment was needed to counter this. Both nets and lines were steeped in a tanning solution before and after voyages – a process much the same as that which helped to convert animal hides into leather. Some of the equipment may well have been

---

[14] For herring voyages, ordinary crew members usually supplied one dole of nets each (a dole consisting of two individual nets), with masters and mates making a larger contribution. The same applied to line-fishing for cod and ling, where ordinary crew members usually provided one set of hand-lines and masters and mates a greater number.

[15] M. Gray, *The Fishing Industries of Scotland, 1790–1914* (Oxford, 1978), pp. 48–50, has information concerning family labour north of the border during the early nineteenth century.

treated in oak or ash bark solution in either of the town's leather tanneries, but a number of leading merchants had tan-houses of their own inside their yards. Because of the material used, the process of treating nets and lines was also known as *barking* – a term which remained in use well into the twentieth century, long after oak and ash bark had ceased to be used.

Apart from the financing of fishing voyages, the other matter of major economic importance in the industry was the organisation behind the handling and processing of catches. Dried and salted cod was primarily intended for local markets, travelling perhaps no further than Norwich[16] – but the cured red herrings were a different matter, being conveyed in considerable quantities to the Italian port of Leghorn as well as to other, less distant, places. Some idea of the scale of the curing operation in Lowestoft during the second half of the seventeenth century is given in the record kept by James Wilde (merchant) of expenses incurred in contesting Great Yarmouth's claim to domination of the East Coast herring industry during the immediate post-Restoration period. Wilde co-ordinated Lowestoft's response to its neighbour's monopolistic manoeuvring and the detailed accounts he compiled of money and materials disbursed were luckily given permanent form in Edmund Gillingwater's late eighteenth-century history of the town.[17]

Altogether, a total of £869 9s 3d was spent on fighting Great Yarmouth in the House of Lords, £581 13s 3d of which was raised by a levy collected from people who were curing red herrings and from others who were involved in the manufacture of casks (coopers and brewers, largely). A toll of 2s per last was the charge made on herring curers for the year 1660, followed by one of 5s per last for 1661, 1662 and 1663, with a late final imposition of 2s in 1674. Just over 450 lasts of red herrings were cured in 1661 by sixteen merchants, a total which had risen to 668 lasts in 1663, with seventeen men involved. By 1674, production had increased to 700 lasts and there were twenty-one merchants involved. At ten barrels to the last and with each barrel containing 1,000 fish, the quantities produced were considerable.[18] Most of the curing-sheds, or fish-houses as they were called, stood at the base of the cliff in Lowestoft, below the dwelling-houses of the people who owned them – a topographical feature previously commented on.

The proximity of their living quarters to the fish-houses would have enabled Lowestoft merchants to exercise strict quality control over their product, which enjoyed a good reputation far and wide. Each merchant probably employed one skilled man, who supervised a team of servants and casual workers. The task of curing was seasonal in nature and occupied the period September to December. Once it was over, fish-house personnel would have switched to other employment, either with the same master or with another. The manufacture of containers required for packing and transporting the

---

[16] Some of it may have found its way to Sturbridge Fair, the great market held annually near Cambridge (24 August to 29 September). Huge quantities of cured fish were traded there annually.

[17] E. Gillingwater, pp. 221–44.

[18] The fishermen counted out a last as 100 long hundreds of herrings (a literal count, by hand), at 120 fish to the long hundred, thus making the measure a total of 12,000 fish. At 1,000 fish to the barrel, this meant a total of twelve barrels. The merchants regarded the last as 10,000 cured fish, or ten barrels. This meant that for every five lasts of fresh herrings purchased, there were six lasts of cured fish to sell.

red herrings would have been an important undertaking. The 700 lasts of red herrings cured in 1674 would have required a total of 7,000 barrels – which helps to explain why coopering was one of the most important land-based maritime trades in terms of the number of people employed. Large numbers of casks would also have been needed for transhipment of dried and salted cod, as well as for other goods, both dry and liquid.[19]

It would appear that, during the sixteenth century, London fish merchants exercised some degree of influence in the exporting of Lowestoft red herrings, but their presence does not seem to have been a feature of the trade after about 1600.[20] A fishmonger from the capital called Gabriel Puckle actually owned a house in the town, which he bequeathed in July 1593 to a child who had still to be born. No positive evidence of his trading activities has come to light, but he must have been involved in the local fish trade to have been a resident. There is more information regarding John Archer (fishmonger), who is revealed in a manor court entry of December 1584 as dealing in red herrings.[21] He was the man identified as the largest shipper of red herrings out of Great Yarmouth in the year 1580–1.[22] It is very likely that he was trading in fish in both Great Yarmouth and Lowestoft, in which case his shipments from the former place may well have included herrings cured in the latter. Alternatively, he may have changed his operating base from one town to the other.

The Italian port of Leghorn (Livorno), to which the product was sent, became the great centre for English goods transported to the Mediterranean during the later part of the sixteenth century. Red herrings were regarded as a particular delicacy in Italy.[23] That meant Lowestoft was ideally placed to participate in an expanding trade. Traffic from Great Yarmouth to Leghorn increased noticeably during the 1580s and 90s, with red herrings as a main commodity, and London merchants were noted as shipping Lowestoft fish as well as those cured in Yarmouth.[24] According to one observer, the Leghorn trade was first developed in Great Yarmouth during the 1570s and 80s, which would tie in with the Duke of Tuscany's promotion of the place as an entrepôt.[25] If references to *Leghorn barrels* in various Lowestoft probate inventories are significant, it remained a port of reception well into the eighteenth century.

Given the lack of references to London merchants after about 1600, it seems possible that their interest in the direct handling of Lowestoft red herrings came to an end

---

[19] During the early years of the twentieth century, an experienced cooper was capable of making about seventy barrels a week: see D. Butcher, *Following the Fishing* (Newton Abbot, 1987), p. 15. Rates of manufacture may not have differed greatly two centuries or more previously. Therefore, it would have taken ten men about ten weeks to have made the casks required for the 1674 herring season.

[20] This may have been partly due to the decline in the town's maritime fortunes, which occurred during the first half of the seventeenth century.

[21] SRO(L) 194/A10/4, p. 104. The transaction recorded is Archer's purchase of *The Swan* inn.

[22] N. J. Williams, *The Maritime Trade of the East Anglian Ports, 1550–1590* (Oxford, 1988), p. 149.

[23] Davis, *English Shipping*, p. 245.

[24] Williams, *Maritime Trade*, pp. 128–9.

[25] A. R. Michell, 'The Port and Town of Great Yarmouth and its Economic and Social Relationships with its Neighbours on Both Sides of the Sea, 1550–1714' (unpub. PhD thesis, University of Cambridge, 1978), p. 101.

comparatively early on during the seventeenth century. The evidence thereafter suggests that local merchants were arranging their own transhipments. It made economic sense to do this, especially if local vessels were used for carriage. Both wills and probate inventories of the second half of the seventeenth century and the first thirty years of the eighteenth show considerably more men and women with investment in merchant shipping than had been the case before 1650. Any kind of maritime venture entailed a good deal of risk and one way of spreading this was to have more than one person involved in ownership of a vessel. The shares were usually organised in halves, quarters, eighths, sixteenths, thirty-seconds and sixty-fourths,[26] and a person's holding was arranged according to how much of an interest he or she was prepared to purchase. It is likely that the larger a vessel was, the larger the number of people having shares in it would be.

Table 37 shows that the people involved in owning merchant ships, or shares in such craft, belonged to the same levels of local society as those who had an interest in fishing boats. In some cases, certain merchants and mariners had direct involvement with both types of vessel. Thus it was that trading craft were controlled by the same élite as that which directed the fishing industry. There was a mutuality of interest in such an arrangement, because not only were cargoes of cured fish exported on merchant vessels, but necessary supplies of marine stores and salt brought in from abroad. However, there is some suggestion that the shares held by Lowestoft people in trading craft may not have been held exclusively in vessels belonging to the town. There is at least one reference, in a will of March 1702 (that of Nicholas Utting, grocer), to a share held in a Yarmouth *pink*. Thus, it is interesting to note that, in spite of the civic posturing by one town against the other with regard to trading privileges, at least some of the inhabitants were prepared to work together in commercial undertakings. More than a century earlier, in the 1570s, two former Yarmouth officials had even moved into Lowestoft to live there: Allen Coldham (bailiff in 1559), to operate a retail enterprise; Cornelius Bright (bailiff in 1546, 1556 and 1564), to spend what may best be described as his retirement.

The number of seafarers who, increasingly throughout the second half of the seventeenth century and into the eighteenth, either owned or partly owned the vessels which they commanded, was relatively small when taken as a proportion of all the men who made their living on the oceans (probably no more than about 3% or 4%). However, a hint of what the promotion to master could mean for a mariner, in terms of earning capacity and subsequent social elevation (regardless of any financial interest in the vessel), has been pertinently commented on elsewhere.[27]

Samuel Munds is a good example of such advancement. He was the son of James Munds (mariner) and in August 1682, at the age of thirty-nine, he was the master of a trading vessel called the *Black Lyon*, which was part-owned by Elizabeth Pacy (via her husband's will) and which was involved for at least some of the year in coastal coal traffic.

---

[26] Davis, *English Shipping*, p. 82. The writer describes a share-system in merchant vessels broadly comparable to Lowestoft's, but he does not mention half-shares or quarters.

[27] *Ibid.*, p. 84. The writer has this to say: 'The advance from chief mate to master of a ship effected for the individual concerned a transformation in status and a trebling of income, and opened the way to much greater prizes. It took the lucky individual into the middle class and offered him the possibility of saving for old age or of turning into a merchant'.

Table 37. *Financial interest in trading vessels: probate material (1560–1730)*[28]

Period	Social/occupational grouping	Sole ownership	Shares	Comments	Interest in two vessels or more
1560–1599	Merchants		3		3
			3		**3**
1600–1699	Gentlemen		1		
	Merchants		8(2)		6
	Retail/distribution		2		1
	Yeomen		1		
	Seafarers	1	5	1 man in all 3 categories	3
		1	**17(2)**		**10**
1700–1730	Gentlemen		1		
	Merchants	2	3(1)		4
	Retail/distribution		4(2)		1
	Craftsmen		1		
	Seafarers	3	5(1)	2 men in each category	
		5	**14(4)**		**5**

When he died, in April 1710, Munds had by then become a merchant himself and his inventory shows that his worldly goods were worth a total of £258 8s 3d. He lived in a house on the east side of the High Street at its northernmost end,[29] and his interests in farming, brewing, fishing and fish-curing were sufficiently diverse to necessitate nine appraisers being required to value his property. The one boat which he owned, the *Mayflower*, was a fishing vessel. It would not be true to say that he was a typical figure in Lowestoft maritime circles, but he was certainly one of a handful of men of his time who were influential in both fishing and trading and who had learned the business thoroughly from the inside and at a lower level than the one where they finished up.

Fishing seasons and catching methods

The cod voyages

The spring and early summer sailing to Faeroe and Iceland from east coast ports may have begun as early as the beginning of the fifteenth century and was a well-established feature by the start of the sixteenth. Lowestoft's involvement is proven, but it is not possible to say how many vessels were regularly involved and over what sequence of years they were sent. There is a record of seven craft returning from Iceland in 1533, all

---

[28] During the first half of the seventeenth century only one person (John Wilde, merchant) was detected as having an interest in a trading vessel.

[29] What should be No. 1, High Street – except that no house has stood on the site for many years.

of them between fifty-two- and seventy-two-tons burden, with a levy per boat payable to the Crown of either £4 or £6.[30] The number of East Anglian vessels engaged in the northern fishery that year was seventy-eight craft[31] – a number which is said to have fallen to forty-three by 1550.[32] By 1593, the number had risen to 111, but no Lowestoft vessels appear in the list.[33] Nor does the town feature in Tobias Gentleman's assessment of the Iceland fleet in 1614.[34]

This is not surprising since, as already noted, some vessels were also probably used for trading voyages. Alternatively, craft may have been engaged in other fishing activities. Thus, it would have been possible for a survey of vessels engaged in a fishery to have been carried out at a time when a port may not have had any boats involved. The fluctuations in the number of Lowestoft craft working in Icelandic waters between the 1530s and 1560s seems, on the slender evidence available, to have been considerable. The seven vessels which returned from the voyage in 1533 were referred to in the paragraph above. On 31 January 1566 an inquiry was held in town into the valuation of the vicarage, because the minister's income had declined as a result of the decrease in the value of fishing tithes. The number of boats sailing north that year was said to be only one, whereas twenty years previously there had been thirteen or fourteen *doggers* involved in the Iceland fishery.[35]

It is unfortunate that no figures are available for Lowestoft's Iceland fleet during practically the whole of the seventeenth century, since it has been claimed that the number of East Anglian boats committed to this voyage reached its peak in the 1630s, with about 200 craft involved – a total which had declined to seventy vessels a matter of forty years later.[36] The town obviously had some kind of connection with the fishery during the early years of the seventeenth century, because two probate inventories give evidence of it. Thomas Myghell (merchant), who died in February 1602, had fifty

---

[30] TNA: PRO, SP 1/80 f65v. The levy referred to was known as *composition fish* or *prise fish*. The charge was introduced during the reign of Henry VIII and remained in place until the end of the sixteenth century. Each boat returning from Iceland was taxed at a rate of the sale-price of 120 ling or 240 cod, which reflects the relative commercial value(s) of the two species.

[31] Gairdner and Brodie, *LPFD, Henry VIII*, vi (London, 1882), 548, no. 1380. The East Anglian fleet is listed as follows: King's Lynn (10), Wells and Blakeney (17), Great Yarmouth (14), Lowestoft (7), Dunwich (22), Orford (1), Orwell Haven (7).

[32] Williams, *Maritime Trade*, p. 96.

[33] *Ibid.*, p. 96. The figures given here are as follows: King's Lynn (55), Wells (13), Blakeney (5), Great Yarmouth (6), Southwold (16), Walberswick (2), Dunwich (2), Sizewell (2), Aldeburgh (4), Orford (2), Harwich (4).

[34] T. Gentleman, 'England's Way to Win Wealth', *Harleian Miscellany*, iii (London, 1744), 385–6. Altogether, 110 vessels are listed that year: King's Lynn (20), Wells and Blakeney (20), Great Yarmouth (20), Southwold, Walberswick and Dunwich (50).

[35] NRO, PD 589/92, pp. 72–9. The source in question is the memorandum book of the Rev. John Arrow, rector of Lowestoft 1760–89. The evidence concerning the minister's income was given by three well-established Lowestoft merchants: Richard Mighells, Anthony Jettor and John Grudgefield.

[36] A. R. Michell, 'The Fishing Industry in Early Modern Europe', in E. E. Rich and C. H. Wilson (eds), *The Cambridge Economic History of Europe*, 5 vols (Cambridge, 1977), v, 164. Great Yarmouth is said to have supplied half the fleet.

Iceland cod stored in his yard, while Thomas Grudgfild (merchant) had 1,800 in his salt-house, worth a total of £27. This works out at a value of 3½d per fish, but whether that represents wholesale or retail price is not known. Grudgfild also had a one-third share in an Iceland *bark*, which was away from home, fishing northern waters at the time he died (May 1603), and the value of his part-interest was estimated to be £17 19s 2d. The vessel was undoubtedly the boat called *Richard*, and he bequeathed his interest in it to his second son, James. If the craft did not return safely from Iceland, then James Grudgfild was to have £20 paid to him by his older brother, Thomas, out of the estate which the latter had been left.

Edmund Gillingwater makes reference (though without citing evidence) to the flourishing state of the Northern Fishery in the middle of the seventeenth century and talks of how, at one time, the Lowestoft fleet would return home not only with catches of cod and ling, but with woollen stockings, blankets and caps acquired by trading with the inhabitants of Iceland, Faeroe and the Shetland Isles.[37] Such goods are perhaps further evidence of the mixed economy of the time (they certainly show a willingness on the part of people involved in fishing to deal in other items) and their carriage home may be compared with the way in which vessels from the Norfolk port of King's Lynn brought back, from Iceland, quantities of hard-wearing wadmal cloth in addition to their catches of fish.[38]

It is possible that Lowestoft never had many boats committed to the Northern Fishery after about the middle of the sixteenth century (in spite of Gillingwater's reference to its later, healthy state) – although the trade did continue on a limited scale until the middle of the eighteenth. In its latter stages, the voyage was very limited indeed. Any vessels making the journey to Iceland were included for tithe purposes with the various other craft engaged upon the North Sea spring voyage, and the accounts book shows only one boat involved in 1699 (owned and commanded by a man called Richard Browne). There was then a gap of ten years before a single vessel again sailed to the far north in 1710 and 1711 – this time commanded by James Pacy and belonging to a relative, Samuel Church (merchant).

Fifteen years later, a man called Gabriel Middleton, who was both owner and master of his boat, went to Iceland for six consecutive years (1726–31), before being joined in 1730 and 1731 by vessels belonging to William Balls and John Jex (merchants). The former of these two also sent a craft on the voyage in 1732, 1734, 1736, 1737 and 1743 – the last year being the final occasion recorded in the tithe accounts of an Iceland fishing venture being undertaken. Edmund Gillingwater says that the last Lowestoft voyage to Iceland took place in 1748, when a Mr Copping sent a boat northwards, but there is no trace of this enterprise in the tithe records.

When working Iceland and Faeroe, both owner and the master would have tried to ensure that a vessel left for the fishing grounds as soon as it was safe and convenient to do so. The voyage usually began in March or April and lasted until July/August, when the vessel returned to port in order to re-equip itself for the important autumn herring

[37] E. Gillingwater, p. 110.
[38] Metters, 'Rulers and Merchants', p. 156.

season. If good catches were made early on, it was possible for a boat to sail for its home base, discharge its fish and return once more to northern waters (or to switch to the spring mackerel fishery).[39] Because of the time involved in getting to Iceland or Faeroe, the Lowestoft boats had, well before the end of the seventeenth century, begun to operate three North Sea voyages closer to home: in the late winter and early spring, in the late spring and early summer, and in the autumn.[40] They probably went no further north than Shetland on the first venture and concentrated their efforts on the Dogger Bank thereafter.[41] Cod, hake and ling would have been the species sought on the voyage to Shetland and the more northerly areas, cod and other demersal species on the grounds nearer home.

The vessels involved in what may be loosely termed the cod fishery would have carried a crew of at least ten to twelve or fourteen men (depending on size) and used an identical method of catching and processing the fish. The gear mainly employed was the *great-line*, of which there is a good description given in a book published in the late seventeenth century.[42] A heavy hempen line, some ninety fathoms in length (540 feet) and weighted at its far end, was paid out by hand over the side of the boat. Attached to the line, a little above the weight, was a cross-shaped piece of iron, and tied to the ends of this were four shorter, less substantial lines with baited hooks *snudded* to them.

This device was operated by individual fishermen, but another, longer, type of line had weights or small anchors fixed at periodic intervals along its length, with hooks individually snudded onto the line and set apart at intervals of three to six feet. This was paid out over the side of a small boat known as a *skave* (which was carried on board the main vessel specifically for the task) and allowed to lie on the seabed for a period of time, before it was hauled by crew members.[43] It was often referred to as *line-laying* and was a form of fishing practised in relatively shallow waters, its effectiveness drawing complaints from the Icelanders regarding depletion of their inshore fish stocks. The initial bait used in both cases consisted of fish which had been caught in a net carried specifically for the purpose.[44] Large specimens would have been cut up into pieces, smaller ones impaled whole upon the hooks. When the lines were hauled, some of the crew members

---

[39] The second sailing might not have been as far as Iceland or Faeroe. There was a tendency for vessels to work off the Shetland Isles or the Scottish coasts.

[40] In favourable conditions, the journey to and from Iceland could take as little time as a week. In adverse weather, it could take up to a month. See E. Jones, 'England's Icelandic Fishery in the Early Modern Period', in Starkey *et al.*, *Sea Fisheries*, p. 108.

[41] The Dogger Bank had been fished from the middle of the fourteenth century onwards (and possibly earlier). See W. R. Childs, 'Fishing and Fisheries in the Middle Ages: The Eastern Fisheries', in Starkey *et al.*, *Sea Fisheries*, p. 22.

[42] J. Collins, *Salt and Fishery, a Discourse Thereof* (London, 1682), pp. 106–7.

[43] This method of fishing necessitated vessels having larger crews because of the use of skaves. The *Jaymes* of Dunwich, which sailed for Iceland in December 1545, carried a crew of thirty men altogether, whose number included two skave masters, a soldier, a gunner, a carpenter and a cooper. See Jones, 'Icelandic Fishery', in Starkey *et al.*, *Sea Fisheries*, p. 109. The crew list reproduced here was originally part of an article by E. R. Cooper in *MM* 25 (1939); he also mentions it in his book, *Memories of Bygone Dunwich*, 2nd edition (Southwold, 1948), p. 19.

[44] The bait-net employed was probably some kind of seine or trawl which was dragged along the sea bed, or just above it, to catch any species available.

disengaged the fish which had been caught and re-baited the lines, while others gutted and packed the catch. Once a line-fishing voyage had started, the lines themselves would have provided much of the bait used – in the form of small fish and species which were not processed for the journey home. The crew would also have eaten a certain amount of the fish caught.

There was a strict procedure to be followed to ensure that fish selected for processing stayed in the best possible condition until the return home. The catches were gutted, decapitated, split open and boned, salted thoroughly in a trough or tub, and then packed 'sardine-fashion' in special compartments down in the hold. As each layer of fish was put down, more salt was sprinkled on to act as a preservative.[45] Medium-sized and larger fish were the ones processed; smaller specimens and unwanted species were either used for bait or eaten by the crews. All livers were placed in casks and left for two days, and the oil which floated to the top was skimmed off, strained and barrelled. The livers were then sealed in their casks for transportation home, because there was still oil to be had from them.

As soon as a vessel reached Lowestoft, whether returning from Iceland or from fishing grounds nearer at hand, it anchored in the offshore shallows and the salted fish, livers and liver oil were taken ashore in ferry boats. The cod (and ling) were then washed and partially dried, before being re-processed. There were three main methods of doing this: one was to dry out the fish completely, sometimes after compacting the flesh by beating it with wooden paddles, thereby producing a type of *stockfish*; another was to allow them to desiccate more gently and become what were known as *haberdines*; and the third was to re-salt the catch and pack it into barrels.[46] The drying process was carried out in a *barf-house*, which was an open-sided shed containing racks or shelves for fish to be laid on. Once re-processing was complete, the fish was ready for sale, either locally or further afield. During the first half of the seventeenth century, stockfish (the coarsest variety) retailed at 3d a pair, haberdines at 1s 2d, re-salted Iceland fish at 1s 5d and North Sea ones at 1s 10d.[47]

Good use was made of the livers which had been saved from the initial oil-producing process on board ship. They were themselves processed further for the extraction of yet more *train-oil*, which was used to provide fuel for lamps and to dress leather.[48] In

---

[45] It has been estimated that about two pounds of salt per fish was required, which means that considerable quantities must have been carried on board ship. See Jones, 'Icelandic Fishery', in Starkey *et al.*, *Sea Fisheries*, p. 109.

[46] Some stockfish was purchased from the Icelanders and Faroese themselves, who had dried it on shore without the addition of salt. The name derives from the Dutch word *stok*, meaning 'a pole', because the Icelanders dried the cod in the open air by tying the fish in pairs to vertical posts. Haberdine is a variant of the Dutch *abberdaen*, which in turn derives from *laberdaen*, a word for the Basque district of Labourd, where salted cod from Newfoundland had been a staple product for generations. Shipments of salted Icelandic or Faroese cod from Lowestoft to Southampton during the 1430s are recorded in the latter port's records: see C. M. Woolgar, 'Take This Penance Now, and Afterwards the Fare will Improve: Seafood and Late Mediaeval Diet', in Starkey *et al.*, *Sea Fisheries*, p. 41.

[47] Michell, 'Yarmouth', pp. 112–13.

[48] The term *train-oil* had its origins in either the Low German *trân* or the Middle Dutch *traen*, both of which mean 'oil'.

Lowestoft, the livers were rendered down in iron coppers which stood out on the Denes, north of the present-day Birds Eye factory. Edmund Gillingwater says that the trench in which they stood was visible at the time he was writing his book (c. 1790).[49] It is still just about discernible today.

A manor roll of 1610 (which is neither as detailed nor as well presented as that of 1618) notes that a man called Simon Fyfyld (merchant and shoemaker) held land 'sup le Denes ad faciend sum [sic] lez blubbers' – the last word in this strange mixture of Latin, French and English being one commonly used for cod livers.[50] Another reference to the manufacture of oil is to be found in the accounts of the administration of the estate of Thomas Mighells (merchant), who died in September 1636.[51] Among the many items sold by his executors was a quantity of oil and old barrels left at the coppers. Two local merchants, Francis Knights and Thomas Fullwood, bought the goods for £10. There is also reference in the accounts to a payment of 2s made to Erasmus Utber (gentleman) for measuring the quantity of oil. Extraction of oil from cod livers continued well into the eighteenth century and, in October 1720, Joseph Smithson (merchant) left his oldest son, Samuel, blubber pans and other utensils located on the Denes.

The herring voyages

The focal point of fishing activity in Lowestoft was the autumn herring voyage, which lasted from mid/late September until the middle of November. There were lesser fisheries for the species in early spring and at midsummer, but the presence of the shoals was unpredictable and the quality of the fish inferior to those caught in the autumn. The October and November herrings particularly were in prime condition, full of milt and roe and with a low fat content, rendering them less perishable than the ones caught in the summer, both locally and elsewhere.[52] The catching and processing of the fish was one of the cornerstones of the prosperity of both Lowestoft and Great Yarmouth (to say nothing of numerous other English and Scottish communities) and herrings remained of considerable economic importance in both towns right up to the decline of the North Sea fishery during the 1950s and 60s. For over 300 years, from the 1350s through to the 1660s, Yarmouth used its considerable influence as a large port and major supplier of ships to the Crown (whenever required) to dominate Lowestoft and other coastal

---

[49] E. Gillingwater, p. 110.

[50] SRO(L), 194/A10/72, p. 2 . Fyfyld (more commonly rendered as Fifield) lived in the house which is now Nos 43–44, High Street. The *faciend sum* of the document is, of course, an error for *faciendum*.

[51] NRO, PD 589/80. The document is bound into the front of the parish tithe book, placed there by the Rev. John Tanner, who married into a branch of the Mighells family and used the accounts to prove the incumbent's entitlement to a mortuary fee of 11s for burials inside the church. Such a payment to Robert Hawes, vicar at the time of Mighells' death, is listed among the various disbursements made.

[52] The fat content of North Sea herrings can be as high as 25% of body-mass during the period May–July, when the species' feeding is at its height, and it drops to below 5% during the winter. By October, the East Anglian stock of herring was hardly feeding at all and was in prime condition, ready to spawn. See W. C. Hodgson, *The Herring and its Fishery* (London, 1957), p. 110.

settlements.[53] But the Suffolk community refused to be overawed and managed to develop its own economic independence.

Herrings were caught in drift nets, known universally as *flews*. The meshes were made from hemp or linen twine, hence the frequent references to them as *lints*, and each individual mesh was about an inch square. The nets were probably made by the fishermen themselves, and by members of the family, and the *twining wheel* sometimes encountered in fishermen's inventories was a device used to spin the material required. Lowestoft did not grow sufficient hemp to produce anything like enough twine and, in any case, the type of plant it did grow was more suited to linen manufacture. However, supplies of suitable material would have been brought in from outside sources – especially from the Baltic countries, with *Riga hemp* being especially favoured. The nets themselves were twenty yards long and of variable depth according to the depth of water fished. The *six scores*, *nine scores* and *twelve scores* which are referred to in wills and inventories of the sixteenth and seventeenth centuries reveal their dimensions simply because the size of drift nets was always calculated in scores of meshes depth. The *nine scores* seem to have been those most commonly used and they would have been about fifteen feet deep.

Each individual net consisted of four separate knitted sections laced together, the topmost and lowest of which – known, respectively, as the *hoddy* and the *deepyne* or *deepen* – were of thicker twine than the other two because of the greater strain imposed on the extremities (Plate 16). The four sections of mesh were marled onto a framework of hemp cord in order to give each net its form. Two of the nets, joined side to side, constituted one *dole* – a different use of the word from that applying to an individual share of the profits of a fishing voyage, but one which is commonly encountered in probate material.

In order to be able to function effectively, the various individual nets (or doles, as the case might be) had to be fixed along the top to a double cord with large, flat corks tied in at periodic intervals along its length. This gave the nets extra buoyancy in the water. Just before they were cast over the side of the boat, they were secured to a large hemp master-rope, known as the *warp*, and they hung suspended from this below the surface of the water. The warp itself was held up by small wooden casks, known as *buoy barrels* or *bowls*, fixed at regular intervals along its length. According to one late eighteenth-century source, the Lowestoft boats shot about a mile of nets, and this matches details found in the tithe accounts.[54] References there show that Lowestoft vessels usually worked fifty doles – in other words, 100 single nets. At an individual length per net of twenty yards, this would have meant an overall length of 2,000 yards for the whole series.

[53] For the late Tudor phase of the Yarmouth–Lowestoft rivalry, see D. M. Dean, 'Parliament, Privy Council and Local Politics in Elizabethan England: The Yarmouth-Lowestoft Fishing Dispute', *Albion* 22, i (Spring 1990), 39–64. For the post-Restoration stage, see E. Gillingwater, pp. 170–216.

[54] I. Gillingwater, 'A History of Lowestoft and Lothingland', 3 vols (c. 1800), iii, 175. Isaac Gillingwater was the older brother of Edmund. His unpublished manuscript is superior to his sibling's work and the latter probably drew upon it. Isaac Gillingwater lived in Lowestoft all his life (he was a barber/wig-maker); Edmund had been non-resident for a number of years when he published his own book.

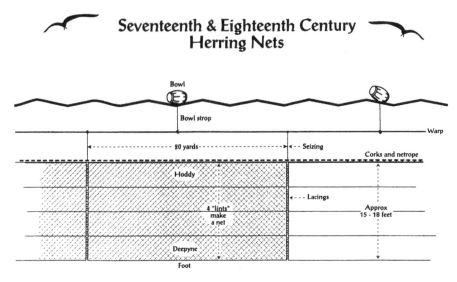

Seventeenth & Eighteenth Century Herring Nets

NOTE: the length of both the bowl strop and seizing could be (and was) adjusted, according to how near the surface the nets were required to be.

J.A.W.Bunn
1995

Plate 16. *Seventeenth- and eighteenth-century herring nets: this type of gear remained in use well into the nineteenth century, before giving way to loom-spun cotton meshes. No added weight was needed at the bottom of the nets to hold them down in the water, because the thickness of the twine (especially once saturated) was sufficient to do this on its own.*

The best analogy that can be given of a *fleet* of drift nets in the water (although simplistic) is that it resembled a continuous wall of netting stretching out ahead of the boat to which it was attached.

The nets were usually cast at about sunset, when the herrings rose from the seabed to swim in the upper levels. There, they became enmeshed by the gills and remained trapped until the nets were hauled. A vessel usually drifted along, hanging to its nets, for the duration of a tide (six hours), but the nets nearest the bow were periodically inspected by pulling in the warp to see if there were enough fish already caught to make hauling worthwhile. This might take two tides, or more, but once the master decided that the time was right, the nets were hauled. As they came in over the side of the boat, they were detached from the warp and the herrings shaken from the meshes (Plate 17). The warp was coiled neatly below decks ready to be used again, the nets were stowed on deck, and the herrings conveyed by chutes down into the hold. Once there, they were given a light salting, ready for the return to port.[55] The work was hard and dangerous, with everything done by hand, and many hours were spent before the last net was safely on board.

Lowestoft fishing masters liked to make a viable catch in a single night, but the usual period of time was two or three nights, or even more. For most of the season, the boats

---

[55] I. Gillingwater, iii, 176. There is a good description of the working practice on board a herring boat of the late eighteenth century. The procedures would not have differed greatly from those of previous centuries.

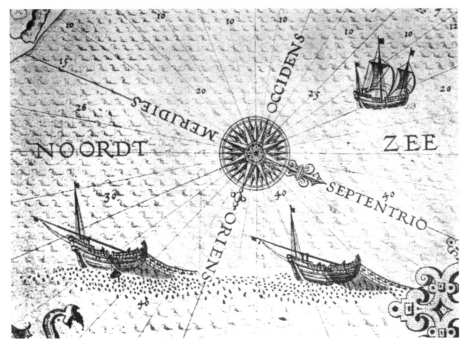

Plate 17. *Early/mid seventeenth-century Dutch busses: this detail from a contemporary chart of the German coastal area of the North Sea shows drift nets being hauled. The wooden casks used as floats are clearly visible; so is the mast resting on its support while hauling was in progress.*

were working within thirty to thirty-five miles of the town, so the distances to and from the fishing grounds were not great. At the end of the eight-week season, the vessels were got ready to resume line-fishing in the early months of the following year (at an earlier period, some of them probably converted to coastal trading). The voyage was not as profitable as lining for cod and ling in northern waters, but, being conducted in waters much closer to home, it was less risky. And it was not so expensive to finance because of the smaller outlay on victuals. Figures for the years 1748–89 show an average seasonal catch of 665 lasts of herring for a fleet averaging thirty-five vessels, which works out at almost nineteen lasts per boat. The average sale price per last over the same period was just over £13, with an overall price range per season ranging from £7 15s 0d to £20 10s 0d, according to whether catches were scarce or plentiful.[56]

From the late seventeenth century onwards, herring fishing was mainly carried out by craft of some thirty to fifty tons' burden (known as *great boats*) crewed by ten or eleven men, but there were also smaller vessels involved. The latter were somewhere between about twelve and sixteen feet long, with a single mast amidships, and they operated off the beach with a crew of two or three (perhaps even three or four) men. They do not appear in the tithe accounts until 1709, although they were in existence before that time. Their fifteenth- and sixteenth-century name was *fartill* or *fortill* boats and their autumn

[56] E. Gillingwater, pp. 445–80.

season was referred to as *fartillfare* or *fortillfare*.[57] After this enterprise was over, some of them fished for sprats in December and January while others went line-laying in local inshore waters for demersal species such as cod and whiting (and perhaps also for rays). When not in use for fishing, the vessels operated as ferry boats, conveying cargoes to and from the shoreline.

The question of why such craft suddenly appear in the tithe accounts, ten years after the surviving set of records begins, is one that cannot be answered conclusively. It may be that they had a different way of paying the vicar up till 1708, because that particular year (perhaps significantly) was the one in which John Tanner began his fifty-year incumbency. Whatever the reason, it can be seen from the records that their contribution to the minister's income could, on occasions, match that of the great boats. They carried far fewer nets and caught less fish – but, in operating close to land with much smaller crews, their expenses were a great deal lower. The procedure for tithe payment revealed in the accounts is that the small boats paid the vicar an agreed sum of 3s per vessel or gave him whatever sum half of one share of the end-of-season profits came to.

It is clear from the tithe book that some great boat masters owned small boats themselves and sometimes worked them during the autumn herring season, after having completed the earlier North Sea lining voyages and summer mackerel fishing.[58] The references to *shotten herrings* which were caught by the small boats show that there was, during the early part of the eighteenth century, a race of inshore herring locally which spawned in the late summer/early autumn.[59] Herrings that had spawned were past their best (until they had recovered and fattened once more), and they were therefore not worth as much as ones containing milt or roe. However, they were still curable and therefore commanded a price at market. The tithe accounts book shows that the number of small boats in operation did not rise as the number of great boats diminished, nor decline as the latter increased. Their level of activity was probably determined by the amount of inshore herring available from year to year.

The processing of herrings (apart from the initial light salting on board ship) was carried out ashore. Before bloaters and kippers were developed as types of cure during the nineteenth century, there were two main methods of preserving the species. The first was developed in southern Sweden towards the end of the thirteenth century.[60] It involved removing the gills and gut, after a neat incision with a knife had been made in the throat of the fish, and then packing the cleaned herrings into barrels, in layers or tiers, with a sprinkling of salt on each layer. Herring treated in this way were known as

---

[57] See M. Bailey, *The Bailiffs' Minute Book of Dunwich, 1404–1430*, SRS, XXXIV (Woodbridge, 1992), 89 and 120. The word *fartill* probably derives from *fardel*, a diminutive form of the Old French *farde*, meaning 'a bundle' or 'a burden' – a reference, perhaps, to such vessels also being used to ferry cargo to and from the shoreline.

[58] Any larger vessel which had its master go *small-boating* would have been put under the command of another skipper (possibly, the mate).

[59] No herrings that had spawned were caught during the autumn seasons of the twentieth century. Nor has the writer seen written or printed evidence of such a phenomenon occurring during the nineteenth.

[60] R. W. Unger, 'The Netherlands Herring fishery in the Late Middle Ages: The False Legend of Willem Beukels of Biervliet', *Viator* 9 (1978), 335–56.

white herrings or *pickled herrings* and they were of considerable importance in the European economy. Great Yarmouth produced large quantities of them, though of inferior quality to Dutch ones, but Lowestoft never went in for curing them on a significant scale.

Its own particular speciality was the *red herring* – a fish that was left ungutted, dry-salted or brined for two or three days, and then smoked over slow-burning fires. One commentator of the first half of the seventeenth century claimed that red herrings were only cured in Great Yarmouth, but even as he was writing (in the 1630s) Lowestoft's own manufacture of the product had been in operation from at least the first quarter of the fifteenth.[61] There are frequent references to fish-houses in wills and inventories of the sixteenth and seventeenth centuries, and the diagrammatic view of the town previously referred to (Plate 7) clearly shows these buildings at the base of the cliff. Furthermore, the Lowestoft product was considered superior to that of Great Yarmouth, where red herrings tended to be made from inferior fish and pickles from better-quality ones.[62] In Lowestoft, although shotten herrings were cured into reds (to fill a gap at a lean time of year, during the early spring), most of the product was made from fish in prime condition. The fish-houses themselves were built variously of timber, brick, flint and tile, but there is no specific information concerning size.[63] The curing process relied upon the impregnating effect of smoke on the salted fish, which were hung suspended over slow fires burning on the fish-house floors. It had nothing at all to do with heat.

There is a good contemporary description of the cure of red herrings in the late sixteenth century to be found in a court baron minute of December 1584.[64] As part of the agreement whereby he sold the *Swan Inn* messuage on Lowestoft High Street to John Archer (see above, page 169), George Phifeld (merchant) was to supply the purchaser with a certain quantity of red herrings. There were to be twenty lasts of them (i.e. 200 barrels): 'full red herrings, good able and marchant, of one night's taking, to be roared in vats with sufficient salt before they be two nights old, dried with ashen billets of the best usual manner and order of making of herrings for Leghorn beyond the sea, with a bright and clear colour, and without gorge to be packed in such good and dry cask as usually is transported to Leghorn aforesaid.'[65]

Two hundred years after Phifeld and Archer had made their arrangements, another

[61] M. Oppenheim (ed.), *The Naval Tracts of Sir William Monson*, NRS, v (London, 1914), 269. Shipments of Lowestoft red herrings feature in the Southampton port books for the 1420s and 30s. See Woolgar, 'Take This Penance Now', in Starkey *et al.*, *Sea Fisheries*, p. 41.

[62] R. Tittler, 'The English Fishing Industry in the Sixteenth Century: The Case of Great Yarmouth', *Albion* 9, i (1977), 50.

[63] Butcher, *Following the Fishing*, pp. 55 and 58, gives information regarding the dimensions of Lowestoft fish-houses during the nineteenth and twentieth centuries.

[64] SRO(L), 194/A10/4, p. 104.

[65] This account shows that the herrings were of finest quality. First, they had to be *full* – that is, containing milt or roe. Next, they had to have been caught in a single night and conveyed immediately to port. They had to have been salted in vats (rather than in heaps on the floor) for no more than twenty-four hours, before being hung in the fish-house. Finally, they were to be packed *without gorge*, which means that they had to placed carefully in the barrels – not crammed in just anyhow.

account of the process is encountered in Edmund Gillingwater's history of Lowestoft.[66] The cure was longer and harder than the earlier one, and there is more detail given regarding it. The fish were deposited in heaps on the ground, given a generous sprinkling of salt, then allowed to stand for two days.[67] At the end of this time, they were washed and drained, before being threaded through mouth and gill onto wooden rods about four feet in length. These *speets* (a variant of 'spits') were then lodged on wooden racks fixed to the sides of the fish-house. Once all the rods of herring were in place, slow fires of oak or ash billet-wood were lit on the floor and kept smouldering for anything up to a month. However, the smoking process (or *drying*, as it was often called) was not continuous and the fires were extinguished every other day and the grease of the herrings allowed to exude. At the end of the period of cure, they were packed into casks of thirty-two gallons' capacity (each containing 1,000 fish), ready for sale. Many of them were exported to Mediterranean countries, but they were also popular in England as breakfast fare.[68]

Two commodities of key importance in the curing of red herrings were salt and wood (the former was significant, too, in the processing of cod and ling). Grey salt, Bay salt and white salt are all regularly referred to in Lowestoft probate inventories, with considerable quantities sometimes held in store.[69] There needed to be. No figures exist for the amount of salt used to produce red herrings, but estimates varying from half an ounce to an ounce and a half per fish have been arrived at for *pickles*, which means (if the mid-point of one ounce is adopted) that a last of these would have required about a third of a ton for the curing process. If the salt needed for herrings is added to that used in curing cod and ling, it can be seen that many tons of the commodity were used each year.

Large quantities of oak and ash wood were also required, their function being twofold: to provide *clapboards* (barrel staves) for the coopering trade and to furnish *billets* for the smoking process. Ash was the species favoured for both uses, because it was less dense than oak (thereby leading to lighter casks) and burned less acridly.[70] However, there was not enough of it grown to meet the need, and oak was the commoner of the two species used. So great was the demand for casks that oak staves were brought in from

[66] E. Gillingwater, pp. 95–6. The process described was much the same as the one used right into the twentieth century.

[67] What Gillingwater does not say is that the herrings would have been periodically moved and re-heaped with wooden shovels, so as to distribute the salt thoroughly. This particular part of the process was known as *roaring* or *rousing*.

[68] P. Pullar, *Consuming Passions* (London, 1971), p. 133.

[69] White salt was of better quality than grey and was the type commonly used in curing fish. Bay salt was also of reasonable quality, having originally been imported from the Bay of Bourgneuf, to the south-west of Nantes. By the late sixteenth century, the term had tended to become generic for any salt produced in coastal areas abutting onto the Bay of Biscay. This often required refining (by boiling it in sea water), in order to get rid of impurities.

[70] Oppenheim, *Monson's Tracts*, 267. Reference is made to the preferable nature of ash – something also commented on in J. Thirsk, 'The Farming Regions of England', in *Agrarian History*, iv, 47, and in A. Simpson, *The Wealth of the Gentry* (Cambridge, 1961), p. 203. Both writers mention the use of ash in making barrels for the herring industry, the latter citing extensive areas of woodland on the Mettingham College estate in the Waveney Valley area, some fifteen miles or so from Lowestoft.

the Sussex weald and from German ports along the Baltic coastline.[71] Some idea of the passage of such materials can be derived from local admiralty court and water leet records of the second half of the sixteenth century, in which clapboards feature regularly as items of salvage washed ashore.[72]

The lengths of timber used for barrels, both from local and outside sources, would have necessitated the cutting and shaping of high-grade material. But the billet-wood could have been produced from all kinds of small trees and odd-shaped branches, either as split sections or as whole pieces.[73] The Beccles–Bungay area, which lay within a ten- to fifteen-mile radius of Lowestoft, has been identified as a major producer of billet-wood for Great Yarmouth, and it is possible that Lowestoft itself also drew upon this source.[74] As noted in the early pages of Chapter 6, the town had comparatively little managed woodland, but parts of the Hundred of Mutford and Lothingland were well endowed with coppices, plantations and parkland, and so were the neighbouring hundreds of Blything and Wangford.[75] It is a tribute to the efficiency of woodland management of the time that both Lowestoft and Great Yarmouth were kept supplied with the amount of billets required.

The mackerel voyage

Apart from lining for cod and other demersal species and the autumn herring season, there was one other main voyage in which the larger Lowestoft fishing vessels were involved: the mackerel catching, which took place in late spring. The working method was essentially the same as for herrings, another pelagic species, except that the nets had a slightly larger mesh, not nearly so many of them were cast and the fish were not salted down on board the boat. Because of their perishable nature, mackerel had to be landed as soon as possible after capture and a boat would stay out a second night only in the event of a very small catch. The fish were landed directly onto the beach, each boat's catch being heaped up separately from those of other vessels, and the fish were sold either by pre-arranged contract or by public auction.[76] The market for mackerel was a

---

[71] Williams, *Maritime Trade*, p. 172; J. Gee, *The Trade and Navigation of Great Britain* (London, 1729), p. 54. The former writer makes reference to the importation into Great Yarmouth of oak staves from the Sussex ports, while the latter considered Germany to be the chief European source.

[72] SRO(L) 194/B1/11 to 19b.

[73] D. Burwash, *English Merchant Shipping, 1460–1540* (Toronto, 1947; republished Newton Abbot, 1969), p. 119, fn. 55. The writer, citing a source of James II's reign, gives the billet's dimensions as forty inches length by seven and a half inches circumference (just under two and a half inches diameter). Poles or rods of this size would have been grown in coppices. It is likely that fish-houses used all kinds of wood, of varying length and thickness, as fuel – and the term *billet*, therefore, may have had a looser meaning than the official one.

[74] Michell, 'Yarmouth', p. 308. This district included the Mettingham College estate referred to in note 70.

[75] Rackham, *Countryside*, pp. 129, 267 and 357, refers to three important timber and wood-producing parishes to the south of Lowestoft (Sotterley, Mutford and Wrentham). But there were others, too (notably, Reydon) – and to the north-west of the town lay the Somerleyton estate, which had considerable areas of woodland.

[76] E. Gillingwater, p. 108–9.

local one, with the towns of Suffolk and Norfolk at not too great a distance from Lowestoft being the ones served – especially Norwich, with its important fish market on Fridays. By the end of the eighteenth century, fast-sailing cutters were running the catches down to London.[77]

The number of mackerel taken by any one boat was never as great as the number of herrings caught. A haul of between 1,000 and 2,000 fish would have been considered a good one. Writing towards the end of the eighteenth century, Edmund Gillingwater says that the vessels sailed 'into the north-east' at the beginning of the season, which means that they were probably working the Winterton Ridge or Smith's Knoll area.[78] Mackerel were known to be present in both places, though the latter was to win its fame ultimately (during the first half of the twentieth century) as the world's premier herring ground.[79] As the season progressed and the mackerel shoals migrated, the boats gradually moved southwards, nearer to Lowestoft – an identical sailing pattern to that which prevailed on the autumn herring voyage. The fishery lasted about six weeks, from the middle of May to the end of June, and it provided an alternative fishery to the second North Sea lining venture. It was never a great money-maker, but it did serve to keep vessels and men employed.

The freshwater fishery

The large expanse of water on the parish's southern boundary (Map 3) provided a freshwater fishery.[80] Theoretically, the resource must have been available to local people throughout the whole period covered by this book, but nearly all references derive from the late sixteenth century – and only because of infringement of manorial rules concerning its use. No specific reason can be given for this, but it may be that the lake and its fish came under less strict manorial control during the seventeenth and eighteenth centuries and that fewer people concerned themselves with the catching and eating of such species (pike, perch, eels, bream, etc.) as time went on.

The earliest, indirect reference to such a fishery occurs in May 1575, in the will of Richard Dericke (shoemaker and merchant), who left his freshwater boat to his son-in-law, William Wilde. Wilde (a merchant himself) was one of six people fined at the half-hundred tourn of 23 April 1589 for fishing in the lake with an illegal *kethe*.[81] This device was a wicker eel pot of some kind, but whether it was illegal in itself or because

---

[77] E. Gillingwater, p. 109.

[78] *Ibid.*, p. 100.

[79] Hodgson, *Herring*, p. 149; D. Butcher, *The Driftermen* (Reading, 1979), pp. 72–3.

[80] It was always referred to as 'The Great Water' or 'The Fresh Water' during the sixteenth and seventeenth centuries, later becoming known as 'Lake Lothing'. A shingle bank separated it from the sea – a barrier breached periodically by high tides, with salt water inundation affecting not only the lake, but the adjoining broad at Oulton and much of the surrounding marshland. One such flooding occurred in the winter of 1609–10. See D. Pickering (ed.), *Statutes at Large*, vii (London, 1763), 248–9.

[81] SRO(L) 192/4, p. 34.

it was woven too closely is not revealed. The other five people presented were John Wilde (William Wilde's eighteen-year-old son), Symon Page (weaver), who was married to one of Wilde's nieces, John Mayhew (mariner and merchant), Thomas Warde (yeoman) and Abraham Turnpenye (cordwainer). Whether the indictment is indicative of a one-off fishing trip carried out among friends and acquaintances or whether it reflects regular activity is not known, but the boat used may well have been the one bequeathed to William Wilde by his father-in-law.

Two other presentments in the local manor courts are to be found in the Lowestoft leet of 1582.[82] The first of these resulted in six men each being fined 6d for operating a *wheelinge* and thereby destroying fish. Again, some kind of eel pot was the object of concern. None of the six features in the family reconstitution material, so they may have lived in other nearby parishes. Their particular offence may have been a breach of local manorial custom, but it was also a contravention of a statute of 1559 which sought to prevent the excessive destruction of young fish.[83] By its terms, it was illegal to catch and kill, with any kind of net or trap, in any freshwater area or estuarine reach, the spawn, fry or brood of eels, salmon, pike and other species.

The second of the indictments concerned six men who were definitely from Lowestoft. John Lobbys, John Warde (barber), William Wilde (again!), William Barrett (barber), John Drawer and William Welles (merchant) were each fined 3d for illegal fishing in the lord's part of the water, near Mutford Bridge.[84] Barrett's inventory shows that he owned a freshwater boat and quite a large amount of specialist freshwater fishing gear, so it possible that all six men constituted a single party, using the boat perhaps on a regular basis. On the other hand, Wilde owned a freshwater craft himself, so it is equally possible that this particular presentment resulted from two boats being involved in the misdemeanour.

The last reference to fishing in connection with 'The Fresh Water' is to be found in June 1663, when town father James Wilde (merchant), grandson of the offending William, recorded expenses incurred in fishing near Mutford Bridge in the January of that year (Plate 18). His object was to catch enough coarse fish to provide a meal for the duly appointed gentlemen who had arrived in town to supervise the setting-up of a post on the Denes at Gunton, marking the southern limit of Great Yarmouth's maritime jurisdiction.[85] This might seem to suggest that the fishery served to provide a source of fresh food, by way of variety and change from the heavily cured saltwater species which the town produced so much of both for its own consumption and for export elsewhere.

---

[82] SRO(L), 194/A10/4, p. 13.

[83] Pickering, *Statutes at Large*, vi (London, 1763), 145–8.

[84] Mutford Bridge was the earth bank which separated the Fresh Water (or Lake Lothing) from the broad at Oulton and also carried the road from Lowestoft to Beccles. Thomas Baskerville gives a good description of it in notes made during a tour of England in 1677–8. He refers to it as 'a dam of earth between 10 and 20 yards broad, secured on the right hand seaward with piles of wood to break the fury of the waves…' See HMC, 13, 266–7.

[85] E. Gillingwater, p. 237.

Plate 18. *A late eighteenth-century view of Mutford Bridge. This structure carried the Lowestoft–Beccles road over the meeting point of Lake Lothing and the broad at Oulton, replacing an earth embankment. Richard Powles' study of 1787 shows the tower of Kirkley church in the distance, while in the foreground a keel (forerunner of the wherry) is shown under sail. Under the bridge itself, an angler's boat can be seen.*

Maritime trade and the granting of port status

Formal recognition of Lowestoft's status as a trading port might never have been given in 1679 had the town not managed to free itself from Great Yarmouth's claim to control all traffic in local waters – especially that connected with the herring trade. A number of passing references to this long-running dispute have already been made, and a summative comment now needs to follow. Much of the 300-year-old wrangle is too intricate to rehearse here, but certain aspects of it will serve to demonstrate Lowestoft's way of dealing with what was widely perceived in the town to be unnecessary and unreasonable interference from an over-mighty neighbour.

The trouble began in 1357, when Great Yarmouth exercised sufficient influence on both Crown and Parliament to have the Statute of Herrings passed in its favour.[86] Its leading citizens were worried about problems caused by silting-up of the harbour mouth and by the growing emergence of Lowestoft as a maritime rival. The main provision of the act, in practical terms, was to give Yarmouth complete control of the local trade in herrings during the period of its great autumn fair (29 September to 11 November) within a seven-league distance of its town quay.[87] However, the extent of the *leuk* or *leuca*

[86] It was the most important port on the east coast of England and a major supplier of ships to the Crown in times of foreign conflict.

[87] Seventeen years earlier, in 1340, the town had been allowed to adopt as its badge the three lions of England crossed with three herrings – a coat of arms which it still proudly bears. This was in recognition of the number of vessels it had contributed to the royal fleet at the Battle of Sluys.

was not defined (perhaps deliberately) and three centuries of dispute followed as to the actual length, with Yarmouth arguing for two (or even three) miles and Lowestoft resolutely maintaining that the distance was one – the latter placing it just beyond the Yarmouth's sphere of jurisdiction.

The issue dominated relationships between the two towns for over two centuries, until some attempt at a resolution was attempted late in the reign of Elizabeth I. In 1597, the *leuk* or *leuca* was fixed by act of parliament at one mile only and a post ordered to be set up on the shoreline to mark the southern limit of Great Yarmouth's area of control – an action which was duly carried out.[88] However, the Yarmouth authorities refused to accept the judgement and continued to press their case for another sixty years or more. Eventually, in February 1662, the judgement of 1597 was confirmed by the House of Lords and the order given for the erection of a new post – something which did not take place for about another year because of the spoiling tactics of Great Yarmouth and its supporters. Eventually, however, in January 1663, a standard oak from the parish of Sotterley (some eight or nine miles to the south-west of Lowestoft), duly burned at one end to harden it, was set up on the Denes at Gunton, a mile or so north of the town.[89] Replacement markers stood on the same spot right into the early years of the twentieth century, the last one of all (made of pitch-pine) being used by the village of Corton's rocket crew to anchor their breeches buoy equipment when practising rescue routines.

Apart from the long-running dispute over the herring trade, there was another bone of contention between Great Yarmouth and Lowestoft – one in which the Norfolk town had a certain degree of legality on its side. As head-port for its sector of the East Anglian shoreline, Yarmouth exercised control over lesser coastal stations, especially those in the bottom echelon. These were officially designated as *creeks*. They had no resident customs officers of their own and they were supposed to have all their traffic pass through the head-port or, at least, be entered in its records.[90] This must have been regarded as inconvenient by the Lowestoft merchants and seafarers, if not totally unreasonable, and thus the law was routinely flouted – with as much trade as possible being conducted in and out of the town's own haven.

Outward cargoes of red herrings have already been mentioned. Another notable

---

[88] For the political manoeuvrings behind the herring dispute, particularly the way that parliamentary lobbying was carried out with the assistance of local webs of gentry acquaintanceship, see Dean, 'Parliament, Privy Council and Local Politics', 39–64. Because the generic term 'Kirkley Roads' was so frequently used to define the local inshore waters off Lowestoft (particularly to the south of the town), the idea has arisen that the village of Kirkley was once an important fishing station. There is no evidence of this and, in fact, the shingle bar which blocked the seaward end would have prevented vessels sailing to and from the theoretical anchorage on the southern shore of Lake Lothing.

[89] E. Gillingwater, p. 236. The Great Yarmouth civic heads made one last attempt to assert their supposed privileges in 1729, but the leading Lowestoft merchants raised a contingency fund of £445 to oppose the legality of this claim, and it was not proceeded with. See E. Gillingwater, pp. 216–19.

[90] The level above *creeks* consisted of *members*, which had their own customs officers and kept their own records, thereby enjoying greater autonomy.

coastal trade was that in coal from Newcastle-upon-Tyne, which was already well established by the early sixteenth century.[91] However, it was not any irregularity in this particular traffic which seems to have concerned the authorities in Yarmouth. They were much more interested in the illegal import and export of grain, malt and other commodities, with both Lowestoft craft and foreign ships involved in the traffic.[92] It was this kind of irregularity which led the Great Yarmouth head customs official to declare that Lowestoft was 'a town of great smuggling' and which led to incidents of the kind involving George Whelplay (haberdasher, of London), a paid informer in the service of the Crown.[93] On 17 December 1539, Whelplay seized victuals that were being illegally exported from Lowestoft and he acted again on 3 March 1540, when a quantity of brass, lead, worsted cloth and victuals was confiscated. Eighteen months or so later, on 1 November 1541, a meeting of the Privy Council at Hampton Court heard John Lissle of Lowestoft testify that Thomas Bocking and others had illegally exported grain from the town.[94] Incidents like these probably occurred regularly, and it can only have been Great Yarmouth's determination to subordinate its neighbour which prevented Lowestoft from gaining some kind of recognition as a port and having its own customs officials.[95]

It has been said that the officials in Great Yarmouth were of the opinion that most of Lowestoft's trade went unrecorded.[96] However, some idea of the goods which were entering and leaving the latter's waters can be derived from regulations governing its establishment as a port in 1679. Coal, salt, timber, marine stores, pantiles, corn, butter, cheese and fish are all referred to – the third and fourth of them both connected with a flourishing Baltic trade which had been going on for generations. From 1640 onwards, the Customer at Great Yarmouth had sent a *waiter* over to Lowestoft to see that nothing was loaded or landed there.[97] The success of this must have been very limited, because on 11 November 1677 the Customs Commissioners requested that the Treasury pay a salary of £10 per annum to an able officer based in Lowestoft.[98] Lord

---

[91] See C. M. Fraser (ed.), *The Accounts of the Chamberlains of Newcastle-upon-Tyne, 1508–11* (Newcastle, 1987). This traffic was not exclusively for Lowestoft, but for the distribution of coal to other places, including London. The availability of coal in the town, however, may have been one reason why its houses were so well endowed with fire-places and chimneys by the middle of the sixteenth century.

[92] J. S. Brewer (ed.), *LPFD, Henry VIII*, iv, i (London, 1872), 1783, no. 4016; Gairdner and Brodie, *LPFD, Henry VIII*, xiv, i, 124, no. 319. During the middle of the fourteenth century, the illegal export of wool and woollen cloth had been the main issue to concern the authorities. See R. F. Isaacson (ed.), *CPR, Edward III (1340–3)* pp. 206 and 220; *(1343–5)* pp. 27, 75 and 180; and *(1345–8)* p. 276.

[93] Michell, 'Yarmouth', p. 325, records the particular description of Lowestoft cited here. For the account of Whelplay's activities, see G. R. Elton, *Star Chamber Stories* (London, 1958), p. 86. Thomas Cromwell authorised him to watch for illegal exports at various ports on the east and south coasts.

[94] Gairdner and Brodie, *LPFD, Henry VIII*, xvi, 605, no. 1310.

[95] In spite of the public rivalry between the two towns, a number of the leading citizens in each community were able to sink their civic differences and co-operate in matters of business.

[96] Michell, 'Yarmouth', p. 320.

[97] TNA: PRO, SP 28/171. Michell, 'Yarmouth', p. 320, makes reference to this document.

[98] W. A. Shaw (ed.), *CTB, v, i* (London, 1911), 784.

Treasurer Danby acceded to the request five days later, but stipulated that the payment was not to be made to the current officer.

Within a year, the townspeople of Lowestoft petitioned the Treasury for the privilege of being granted port status, claiming that the duties imposed on their goods at Great Yarmouth were a great burden on trade – as was the transporting of merchandise overland to and from the head-port.[99] It was stated that the landing of *gruff goods* (namely, salt, timber, deal boards, pitch, tar, resin, iron, hemp, rope, cordage and pantiles) there, and the subsequent conveyance to Lowestoft, took away 25% of the profit, with salt being particularly affected by the journey and susceptible to considerable loss. Moreover, it was pointed out that the town had sixty vessels at the time, which was a greater number than either Southwold or Aldeburgh – both of which places had a customs officer to receive entries and grant *cockets*. The number of vessels cited was almost certainly an inflated one and probably included craft from Kirkley, Pakefield and Kessingland.[100] And, in a sense, this was a legitimate tactic to adopt, because the one haven and its inshore *roads* served those other communities.

Whatever the truth of the matter, the petition was successful and on 31 January 1679 Lord Treasurer Danby accepted the Customs Commissioners' recommendation that Lowestoft be allowed to import *gruff goods* and export butter, cheese and fish.[101] The salt was probably brought in from the Bay of Biscay coastline, or possibly from Newcastle-upon-Tyne; the timber and marine stores came from the Baltic ports; and the pantiles would have been shipped across the North Sea from Holland. Entries of such merchandise were to be made first at Great Yarmouth and an officer sent over to Lowestoft, whenever necessary, to supervise proceedings there. It was the opinion of Mr Dunstar, a general customs surveyor, and also that of the Great Yarmouth officers, that acts of fraud might well take place if Lowestoft had its own resident customs officer. Fraudulent practices of one kind or another had only been brought under control in the head-port with the greatest difficulty.[102]

Just over three months later, on 13 May 1679, Treasurer Danby wrote to the Customs Commissioners, informing them that the citizens of Lowestoft were now requesting the right to export and import both coal and grain in addition to the privileges already granted.[103] The formal decision was not long in coming and on 24 May it was decreed that the town be allowed to export grain but not import it, and to import coal but not export it. Entry of all merchandise was to be at Great Yarmouth and the Lowestoft traders were to pay the daily allowance of any customs officer sent over from the head-port.[104] Six months later, on 22 November 1679, Thomas Glover was recommended for the post of *waiter and searcher* at Lowestoft (he actually became resident in the town),

---

[99] Shaw, *CTB*, v, ii, 1218.

[100] A vessel count of 1670 put the number of fishing boats in Lowestoft at twenty-five: see E. Gillingwater, p. 92. Michell, 'Yarmouth', p. 321, estimates its fleet to have had ten merchant craft and twenty-five to thirty fishing vessels.

[101] Shaw, *CTB*, v, ii (London, 1911), 1219.

[102] *Ibid.*, 1219.

[103] *Ibid.*, 1266.

[104] Shaw, *CTB*, vi (London, 1913), 65.

while on 16 October 1680 William Weddle, a *tidesman* at Great Yarmouth, was appointed as his assistant because of the great increase in shipping which had taken place.[105] Lowestoft, it would seem, was benefiting from its new-found maritime status.

Fleet size and employment

Given the fact that, during the sixteenth and seventeenth centuries, some Lowestoft craft were almost certainly used for both fishing and trading, it is not always possible to give precise numbers of vessels involved in each enterprise. Nor can a regular and detailed sequence of the number of boats operating out of the town be worked out. However, there is sufficient data available in both national and local sources to allow a broad view to be formed. In 1526 there were said to be twenty ships and 200 men engaged in the fishing industry[106] – totals which would seem to be accurate, as the larger craft did carry crews of about ten men. Not all the hands necessarily lived in Lowestoft, of course, but the number employed serves to indicate the importance of fishing in the local economy, as the population at this time was probably somewhere in the region of 1,200 to 1,300 people.

The number of ships cited above does not take account of the number of small boats working directly off the beach. The Tudor authorities were only interested in shipping for its potential use in wartime and thus mainly collected information about craft of fifteen to twenty tons' burden and more. The first of the official lists to give information about the size of the Lowestoft merchant fleet in the sixteenth century was the result of a military survey.[107] In 1544 the Council was thinking of sending an expedition to Scotland and was investigating the number of craft to be requisitioned. Lowestoft's fleet was put at fifteen (third in size in East Anglia after Great Yarmouth and Dunwich), but it may have included boats from Kirkley and Pakefield, the parishes immediately to the south. The town was credited with having three vessels of 120 tons' burden, one of 100 tons, three of eighty tons, five of sixty tons and three of fifty tons. This number of craft would have provided employment for about 100 men, if the crewing levels for the late seventeenth and early eighteenth centuries were applicable 150 years earlier. A proportion of the hands would have been involved in fishing voyages at certain times of the year and some of the vessels probably converted to fishing as well.

Twenty-one years later, in 1565, the number of trading craft had gone down to five, though it may be significant that neighbouring Pakefield had three ships listed in its own right.[108] By 1572 the number had risen again, to sixteen, according to a survey carried out by Thomas Colshill, the Surveyor of Customs in London.[109] There was one boat between fifty and 100 tons, seven between twenty and fifty tons, and eight below twenty

[105] Shaw, *CTB*, vi, 267 and 710.
[106] W. Page (ed.), *VCH Suffolk*, 2 vols (London, 1907), ii, 293.
[107] Gairdner and Brodie, *LPFD, Henry VIII*, xix, i (London, 1903), 76.
[108] Williams, *Maritime Trade*, p. 218.
[109] Page, *VCH Suffolk*, ii, 216.

tons. The information suggests a considerable reduction overall in the size and carrying capacity of the vessels, but no ready explanation for this offers itself. With sixteen trading craft, Lowestoft occupied sixth place out of nine Suffolk ports. It was behind Ipswich, Aldeburgh, Dunwich, Orford and Gorleston. Ten years later, in 1582, the number of boats had declined once more – this time to seven. The fluctuations are interesting because they seem to reflect changing fortunes in the sphere of maritime trade, but there is no other statistical information available to confirm or deny the impression.

It is impossible to be precise about the number of people involved in maritime trades in Lowestoft during the second half of the sixteenth century. However, on the information derived from the various lists of vessels above, it is likely that between 200 and 300 men and youths were employed at sea on the larger craft during those periods when the fishing industry and maritime trade were prospering. In addition to these hands, there would also have been a not inconsiderable number of men working on the smaller, inshore boats and on those craft ferrying catches and cargoes to land – to say nothing of the men involved in processing fish and servicing both ships and gear. In times of difficulty and depression, a large proportion of these people would either have had to seek alternative employment locally or move on to another area.

One such period of decline seems to have occurred during the earlier part of the seventeenth century, when the fishing industry suffered a reversal in fortunes – a situation exacerbated by severe loss of life in the plague outbreak of 1603. There is no means of ascertaining whether this retraction applied to trading also, but if there was less fish available for export it must have had some effect. Herring catching and processing were particularly affected, and the general reduction in activity can be seen both in the reduced number of people connected with maritime pursuits and the increased number of those involved in agriculture – a feature noted in Chapter 4. Not only do the parish registers reflect this change; the probate material shows fewer people owning fishing boats, items of gear and curing materials and equipment. What is not known, unfortunately, is the number of larger vessels still engaged in the fishery during the first half of the seventeenth century. Nor is there any information to show how many deep-sea fishermen still carried on their trade at a reduced level by working small boats off the beach. Large-scale commercial enterprise might have been undergoing a period of difficulty, but fishing for local and regional needs may well have remained largely unaffected. Moreover, there would still have been a market both at home and abroad for red herrings – a type of cure not much practised by the Dutch merchants who controlled so much of the international fish trade.[110]

It was, in fact, the Dutch who were primarily responsible for the decline in English fishing effort in the North Sea during the first half of the seventeenth century, and Lowestoft was not the only port affected.[111] The scale of the Dutch herring enterprise

[110] Even as late as 1680, someone who styled himself 'Philanglus' (literally, 'lover of England'), in a tract entitled *Britannia Languens; or, A Discourse of Trade*, was praising the efficiency of the Dutch and urging his own nation to bestir itself in the cause of maritime activity. See J. R. McCulloch, *Early English Tracts on Commerce* (Cambridge, 1952), pp. 29–31.

[111] Michell, 'Yarmouth', pp. 66 and 68, notes how the North Sea herring fishery underwent a general decline, especially after 1607.

was massive, perhaps the earliest example anywhere in the world of factory fishing, and the standard of its pickled herrings was superior to anything of similar nature in Europe. This is not the place to discuss the operation, which has been variously described elsewhere, but it was the subject of comment at the time and at least two observers made recommendations to the government (in open pamphlets) whereby it might be possible for English vessels to compete.[112] However, it was not until after 1670, when the English civil wars had ended and three naval conflicts with the Dutch had largely run their course, that the native North Sea herring fishery experienced a recovery.

Something of this can be seen at local level in figures relating to the number of larger fishing vessels working out of Lowestoft in 1670. A petition from local merchants was presented to Parliament that year, requesting exemption from the payment of duty on the beer (2s 6d per barrel) consumed on board craft which fished for herrings.[113] The number of vessels in operation was said to be twenty-five and it is likely that these boats were included in the sixty said to be working out of the town when the Lowestoft merchants petitioned for the granting of port status in 1678. In general terms, there had obviously been a recovery from the period of depression earlier in the century – a recovery that was sufficiently strong to encourage Lowestoft people to seek escape from the control of the head-port, Great Yarmouth.

The fact of this revival is confirmed by evidence available in the tithe accounts. In the years 1698 and 1699, thirty-five and thirty-seven *great boats* respectively took part in the autumn herring voyage – although the number dropped back during the first three decades of the eighteenth century to somewhere between twelve and twenty-seven craft in regular use. During this same thirty-year period, 168 individual fishing-boat masters, all of whom were resident in town, are named in the tithe book entries. The reasons for the fluctuation in the number of herring boats are not altogether clear, but it may have been partly due to adverse weather conditions and erratic shoal movements, as well as to the increase in maritime trade perhaps 'siphoning off' craft which had once been employed in fishing.[114] Another feature which is apparent in the tithe accounts is the length of service which individual boat masters put in with their employers. Some of them served only two or three years before moving on; others stayed for anything between five and eight years; and a small number performed genuinely long service, such as the twenty-five years put in by John French Snr for Benjamin Ibrook (merchant).

---

[112] Gentleman, *England's Way to Win Wealth*; E. S., *Britaine's Busse* (London, 1615). The name Edward Stephens, of Lowestoft, has been put forward as author of the latter work, but no one of that name features in any of the town's documentation. For comments concerning the Dutch *Groote Vischerij*, see J. T. Jenkins, *The Herring and the Herring Fisheries* (London, 1927), pp. 70–7; C. Wilson, *Profit and Power* (London, 1957), p. 33; Butcher, *Ocean's Gift*, pp. 75–6; and R. Robinson, 'The Common North Atlantic Pool', in Starkey *et al.*, *Sea Fisheries*, pp. 13–14.

[113] E. Gillingwater, pp. 88–92. It was claimed by local merchants at the time, in typical fashion, that the industry was in a desperate state. Among suggestions made to improve things was that all people able to afford it should buy small quantities of herring at an agreed rate and that two fish-days a week should be observed in the town.

[114] Any fishing boats converting to trading voyages (especially overseas ones) would probably have required modification, their lugsail rig being less effective than the square rig used on merchantmen.

Some idea of the overall number of men employed on Lowestoft fishing craft during the earlier part of the eighteenth century may also be derived from the tithe accounts. Between 1709 and 1725 (the former year being the first one in which the small, longshore boats were recorded), an average of thirteen small craft took part in the autumn and winter fisheries. This would have meant somewhere between about thirty and forty men being involved – perhaps even as many as fifty or sixty. Over the same period, there was an average of seventeen or so great boats working annually, employing a total number of 170 crew members or more. Thus, well in excess of 200 men and youths would have found employment on fishing vessels of one kind or another, exclusive of other hands engaged in the various shore-based industries.

The main imponderable is the number of men serving on merchant craft. Even though trading vessels and fishing boats had become more clearly differentiated from the end of the seventeenth century onwards, there was probably still a certain degree of interchange between the two types of craft and it is likely that fishermen joined traders as crew members when it was opportune to do so. A number of the men identified as 'fishing masters' in the tithe book are also referred to as 'mariners' in other sources.[115] All that can be safely concluded is that the fishing industry was a major employer, creating work for a large number of people at sea and for a substantial one on shore. It is possible that, during the late seventeenth and earlier part of the eighteenth century, the proportion of the town's male population involved in fishing at peak times was anything up to about 60%–65% – and, if it were possible to produce firm figures for men serving on board trading vessels, the percentage of people involved in maritime pursuits would rise.

Crew earnings and methods of payment

There is nothing in the Lowestoft records before 1750 that states directly how much the men engaged in fishing earned. Crew members were paid a share of the boat's profits at the end of the voyage, on top of a sum agreed at the start of the fishing. The profits were the money remaining after various expenses (covenants, gear, provisions and repairs) had been met. If no profit had been made, then the men had no share to take up – though they had received their keep on board while the voyage was in progress and the sum agreed at the start of the venture was guaranteed. This payment was known as the *covenant* and it was disbursed in varying amounts, according to rank and seniority on board. The money was meant to provide a bare, subsistence wage for ordinary crew members and probably amounted to no more than 4d a day. Masters and mates fared better, with respective payments of around 2s and 1s 6d. Most of the earnings cited below probably need to have the amount agreed by covenant added to them. In the absence of any covenant agreement, the value of the individual share was considerably higher.

---

[115] It is evident that terms *fisherman*, *mariner*, *sailor* and *seaman* tend to be synonymous with each other to a certain degree, especially during the Elizabethan period. Thereafter, they became more differentiated – though still with a certain amount of overlap, perhaps reflecting the way that seafarers worked on both fishing and trading craft.

Cod-lining boats each had thirty to thirty-five shares attached to them, which means that any profits were divided by the total number of shares in order to fix the value of the individual share, or *dole*, as it was more commonly known.[116] It is likely that the Lowestoft fishermen and merchants used much the same share-system as that adopted in Great Yarmouth, whereby crew members were apportioned a share or a share and a quarter each, according to their rank and seniority, and the master of the vessel was allotted a share and a half.[117] The fishermen may also have been allowed an agreed proportion of the catch as part of their payment, but they would have been expected to contribute a certain amount of the gear used on the voyage.[118] With a crew of ten, the shares taken up by the fishermen would have added up to between eleven and thirteen, leaving the rest to be taken by the boat's owner(s).[119]

It is possible to work out from the Lowestoft tithe accounts how much the men earned on North Sea lining voyages undertaken during the late seventeenth and early eighteenth centuries. The vicar was entitled to one half-share (known commonly as *Christ's half-dole*) of the profits of each vessel engaged in the various fishing voyages, and the money due is carefully recorded. The range is from nothing, when boats made no profit, up to £3 18s 4½d for a vessel engaged in the Michaelmas voyage of 1709. This means that the full share, or dole, on that occasion was £7 16s 9d – an exceptionally good pay-off, which would have earned crewmen nearly £1 a week (plus a weekly covenant payment of 2s), if the voyage was of an average eight weeks' duration.

Usually, the value of the dole was much lower, being in the range of 10s to £3. The former sum would have meant a weekly payment of 1s 3d for ordinary crew members on an eight-week voyage and the latter would have produced 7s 6d (both being augmented by the weekly 2s covenant payment).[120] In terms of profitability, a ten-shilling dole indicates net profit of £15 to £17 10s 0d per boat (the difference resulting from the variation in the number of shares outlined two paragraphs above), a £3 dole net gain of £90 to £105. A perusal of the Lowestoft tithe accounts suggests that the yield of the springtime lining voyage generally declined as time went by, while the Michaelmas one became more productive – though without ever involving a large number of craft, because of the demands of the autumn herring season.

Also observable in the tithe accounts is the difference in the number of vessels fishing for cod and other demersal species (on the spring voyage particularly) before 1700 compared with the size of the fleet in the years following. Twenty to thirty craft were involved at the very end of the seventeenth century, a maximum number of eleven or twelve in the early 1700s, and only two or three thereafter. Unfortunately, no figures are

---

[116] The word had as its origin the Old English *dāl*, meaning 'a share'.

[117] Tittler, 'English Fishing Industry', pp. 43–4.

[118] *Ibid.*, p. 44. The Yarmouth fishermen's entitlement was one barrel of cod per crew member.

[119] The crew's entitlement may have been higher than the figures cited if individual members had contributed a lot of fishing gear to the voyage. One set of lines was the standard contribution for ordinary crew members.

[120] A local quarter sessions wage-fixing of 1682 shows than an agricultural labourer would have earned 3s a week, with food provided, and a building craftsman in the region of 4s 6d. See I. Gillingwater, 'Lowestoft and Lothingland' ii, 1413–16 (SRO(L), 193/1/2).

available earlier than 1698, which makes it difficult to form an opinion about the cause of such noticeable reduction. It looks as if the end of the seventeenth century was a period of buoyancy for the spring and midsummer lining voyages, and the decline thereafter is unlikely to have resulted from a diminution in stocks of fish. However, it may have resulted partly from boatowners changing their sphere of interest from fishing to maritime trade, as Lowestoft's status as a port began to cause a change of emphasis in commercial maritime activity.

The shares in herring fishing were apportioned differently from the system used in lining. A herring boat usually had seventy-five to eighty-five shares or *doles*, depending on the particular arrangements made, but the individual share's value was again worked out in the manner adopted for line-fishing: any money remaining at the end of a voyage, after all expenses had been met, was divided by the total number of shares. After about 1730, some of the Lowestoft merchants and boatowners began to pay the fishermen either a weekly wage or an agreed price for every last of herrings caught (12,000 fish). This was because the autumn season had become unpredictable in yield and the men preferred not to be hostages to the vagaries of Nature. In fact, wage-payment is recorded as early as 1708 in the tithe accounts, with certain of the crews even at that time preferring to have the security of a fixed sum of money per week rather than taking their chance on a share-out at the end of a voyage.

There is one fortuitous surviving set of accounts for a single fishing master's herring voyage in 1688, inserted into the leaves of the tithe book. Clearly, the figures are not necessarily typical because arrangements may have differed from vessel to vessel. On the other hand, the document serves to illustrate how the share or dole system worked. Samuel Hetch's craft caught herrings worth £62 15s 6¼d. Its expenses (fishing-gear, provisions, repairs and covenant payments) came to £41 13s 7½d, which left a profit on the season of £21 1s 11¼d. The vessel had seventy-four shares allotted, which meant that the value of the individual dole came to 5s 6d. There were twelve crew members in this case (eleven men and a boy) and the shares were distributed in the following way: thirty-seven and a half to the vessel's owner, nine and a half to the master, seven and a half to the mate, two and three-quarters and two respectively to two of the men, one and three-quarters to six others, one and a quarter to another, one to the boy, half to the vicar as his tithe payment, and one and a half to general purposes (the owner would probably have taken this as well).

This apportionment added up to £20 7s 0d, which left 14s 11¼d to carry over to the next voyage or be taken by the boatowner. The number of shares held by the master and the mate show that they had contributed a lot of gear to the venture, but the settling was hardly a good one.[121] The master received £2 19s 6d for his two month's work (just under 7s 6d per week), although a further 12s a week covenant has to be taken into consideration. The crew members on one and three-quarter shares only received 9s 7½d, which is a little over 1s 2d a week. A labourer at this time would have earned a weekly wage of about 3s and a skilled craftsman about 4s to 5s (both with food provided), so

---

[121] Nets and other gear referred to in various fishermen's and mariners' wills and inventories probably represent the equipment contributed to a craft as their part of the venture.

the comparisons made are not especially favourable to fishing, even after the weekly covenant payments of 2s have been added to the crewmen's remuneration.

As far as the great boats are concerned in the earlier part of the eighteenth century, it is possible to work out the value of shares relating to the autumn herring fishery from the tithe accounts and arrive at an estimate of what the men earned. The value of the half-dole paid to the vicar ranged from nothing at all, when the boats made no profit, to £1 5s 0d. The average half-dole payment for the period 1698–1725 was 14s, which means that the average full share worked out at £1 8s 0d – an end-of-voyage profit of £105 to £119 (bearing in mind the range of shares per boat, from seventy-five to eighty-five). Most crewmen would have been on one and a half to one and three-quarters shares, which means that they would have earned, on average, between £2 2s 0d and £2 9s 0d for the eight-week voyage, plus the additional weekly payment of 2s agreed by covenant. Some seasons paid better than others, of course, but average earnings show that herring fishing was not notably lucrative for ordinary crew members, yielding about the same remuneration as that of rough masons and carpenters. Fishing boat masters and mates earned a good deal more than crewmen (at least three or four times as much in the case of the former, and two or three times for the latter), but they were expected to contribute much more gear.

The level of profitability for herring fishing in Great Yarmouth during the first half of the seventeenth century has been calculated at 8.8% in a good year.[122] No comment can be made for Lowestoft as a whole because of insufficient information, but Samuel Hetch's 1688 accounts show a net profit of about 20% for the owner in that particular year – though the calculation does not take account of depreciation in vessel and gear. From the crewmen's point of view, the autumn voyage could provide a reasonable living, though it was not so good on craft which fell below average earnings levels. Nothing is known about the system of payment employed on the small boats for their inshore fishery, but the suggestion inherent in the tithe accounts is that during a good season, given the smaller number of crew members and the lower running costs, earnings were probably better than those made on the larger vessels.

In general terms, the autumn herring voyage offered a better prospect of making a living than the summer mackerel fishing. The tithe accounts relating to the latter show that, between 1698 and 1725, the value of the half-dole payment to the vicar ranged from nothing at all to £1. The latter sum indicates an exceptional earning, however, because the average per boat worked out at only 6s 4d. This means that the average value of the full share was 12s 8d (end-of-voyage profit of £47 10s 0d to £53 16s 0d). A boat engaged in the mackerel fishery was allotted the same number of shares as for the herring voyage (seventy-five to eighty-five) and had the same number of crew (ten). Thus, an ordinary hand working for either one and a half or one and three-quarters shares would have had average earnings of 19s to £1 2s 3d for his six weeks' labour – weekly remuneration of 3s 2d to 3s 8d, additional to the 2s covenant. All rates of reward cited are, of course, average ones. Lower ones, especially when accompanied by the

---

[122] Michell, 'Yarmouth', p. 121. Though it does not say so, the figure presumably refers to the net return on the money invested, not the gross one.

unpredictability of employment, help to explain why fishermen with under-age children were sometimes in receipt of poor relief and why there are seventeen fishermen recorded among the 101 exemptions in the Hearth Tax return of 1674.

An extra source of income on the herring and mackerel voyages was derived from working a handline over the side of the boat while it was hanging to its nets and drifting along on the tide. Any demersal species caught in this way (mainly cod, haddock, whiting and rays) were the fishermen's to keep or sell. There is an interesting reference to the use of handlines in a Great Yarmouth apprentice indenture of March 1573, whereby Robert Catlyn of Bacton was to have half the profit of his line during herring and mackerel voyages throughout the whole ten years of his apprenticeship.[123] Lowestoft fishermen were still working handlines on the summer herring voyage to the Shetland Isles in the 1930s.[124]

Table 38. *Lowestoft fleet sizes: tithe book details (1698–1725)*

Voyage	Total	Max. no. in any year	Min. no. in any year	Median	Average	Comments
Spring lining	187	30; 1698	1; 1717	5	8.1	
Midsummer lining*	88	24; 1698	0; 1706	2	3.8	
Michaelmas lining	66	6; 1710	0; 1700	3	2.9	
Autumn herring (a)	509	37; 1699	5; 1707	16	22.1	Great boats
Autumn herring (b)	223	28; 1712	1; 1711	11	13.1	Small boats
Summer mackerel	334	23; 1699	7; 1708	14	14.5	

*Note that there were also no boats involved in midsummer lining in the following years: 1708–12, 1719 & 1725.

Table 38 presents statistics relating to the numbers of vessels involved in the different fishing voyages between 1698 and 1725, and it can be seen that they varied considerably. One reason for this, apart from possible fluctuations in shoal activity (of which there is no firm evidence), may lie in the dual use of vessels for both fishing and trading. It seems that trading voyages were more attractive to the seafarer. Life was no less risky and demanding, but the earnings were more predictable and regular. At the end of the seventeenth century, ordinary seamen were able to make 6s or more per week, mates were paid 25s to £1, and masters drew up to £1 10s 0d.[125] Payment of this nature may help to explain the increasing acquisition of dwelling-houses in Lowestoft by the seafaring community, both for living in and renting, during the first thirty years of the eighteenth century. But the increase in fortunes was not limited solely to trading vessel personnel. Some of the more successful fishing boat masters and mates were also able to invest in real estate.

[123] P. Rutledge (ed.), *Great Yarmouth Apprentice Indentures, 1553–1665*, NNGS, xi (Norwich, 1979), 17.

[124] D. Butcher, *Living from the Sea* (Reading, 1982), p. 91.

[125] Davis, *English Shipping*, pp. 135–8.

Conclusion

The most basic and obvious way of demonstrating the increased importance of maritime pursuits after Lowestoft had gained port status is to show the proportion of occupations recorded for seafarers as a percentage of occupations as a whole. The ninety years from 1561 to 1650 produce 161 occupations at sea out of a total of 986 recorded occupations in all (16.3%). The hundred years from 1651 to 1750 produce 463 out of out of a total of 1019 (45.4%).[126] Once the town had been given specified rights of import and export, it was able to develop an even more wholly committed maritime economy than it had previously had. More people in the wealthier levels of local society began to acquire trading vessels, or shares in them, and the older-style mixed economy (while it did not die out completely) was less pronounced than it had been previously. The town's population grew as well, from around 1,500 in 1650 to just short of 2,000 in 1750. This rise in the number of inhabitants, though not spectacular, is sufficient (25%) to suggest that something was perhaps occurring in Lowestoft to serve as the incentive for people to move there.

Another aspect of sea-borne trade in and out of Lowestoft after port status had been granted may be seen in the decrease in the amount of traffic handled by Great Yarmouth. At least one observer has commented on this, though without attributing any particular cause, and has also pointed out that it affected the outward movement of goods even more than the inward one.[127] Further evidence of Lowestoft's maritime expansion is to be found in the presence of Trinity House pilots – men who were recruited from among local mariners in order to use their knowledge of inshore sandbanks for the benefit of those less familiar with the danger. And it was almost certainly no accident that Trinity House also chose to build a new lighthouse on the top of the north cliff, just out of town, in the year 1676. Admittedly, this was some three years before the town was elevated to port status, but there was obviously the need for such a facility. An increase in the amount of trade in and out of Lowestoft, as well as up and down the coast, was probably instrumental in prompting the Elder Brethren to act as they did.

The town's first pair of candle-burning lights had been set up somewhere on the beach in 1609, two years after the provision of a similar amenity at Caister, to the north of Great Yarmouth.[128] The particular stimulus to provide lights on the beach at Lowestoft was the fact that the Stanford Channel had become dangerous to negotiate and the lack of markers of any kind had caused loss of life and goods.[129] With two leading lights

---

[126] Some allowance has to be made, however, for the sheer number of fishermen named in the tithe accounts, which does tend to inflate the figure. If these 168 are removed from the reckoning, a proportion of 30% of the whole is arrived at as the seafaring element in the occupational structure for the period 1651–1750.

[127] T. S. Willan, *The English Coasting Trade* (Manchester, 1967), p. 131. The book was originally published in 1938.

[128] G. G. Harris (ed.), *Trinity House Transactions, 1609–1635*, LRS, xix (London, 1983), 74.

[129] Evidence of the danger posed by both the Holm Sand and Barnard Sand can be found in the minute books of the Kirkley/Pakefield admiralty court or water leet. There are many references to items of salvage and wreck involving both fishing craft and trading vessels. See SRO(L), 194/B1/11 and 194/B1/15 to 23.

Plate 19. *A late eighteenth-century view of the High Lighthouse. Richard Powles' scene of 1784 shows trading vessels both anchored and under way in the roads, with the revenue cutter* Argus *also visible on the right-hand side. The group of buildings in the middle shows that encroachment onto The Denes had begun. The church tower on the extreme left is that at Corton.*

positioned correctly on the shore (either of which could be moved as need dictated), it would then become possible for vessels to line up the pair of markers and sail through the sandbanks into safe anchorage.

By 1628, one of the lights was in danger of being washed away and the decision was taken to build a new structure as an 'upper light'.[130] This stood immediately north of Swan Score, to the rear of what is now Nos 38–40, High Street. After Trinity House had acquired the land from the lord of the manor, had organised a supply of materials with which to build it and had recruited a gang of workmen, the conduct of construction was left in the hands of John Wilde (merchant). The light remained in operation until 1676, when a new, isolated, cliff-top site about a quarter of a mile to the north-north-west was chosen as being more suitable – perhaps because of fire-risk to adjacent properties from the earlier marker (Plate 19). After the old light had been dismantled, the redundant plot was conveyed to William Frary (blacksmith), against whose property it abutted. The new coal-burning light on the north cliff was built under the aegis of Samuel Pepys, as Master of Trinity House, and it performed long service before being superseded in 1873 by the building seen today. Thomas Baskerville, on his visit to the town, only a year or so after the construction of the new upper light, recorded seeing it in action, as well as its smaller, candle-burning companion on the beach.[131]

Safety measures of the kind described above showed awareness of the dangers posed by offshore sandbanks, but a more potent reminder of the perils of life at sea may be found elsewhere. Out of ninety-one seafarers who made wills which have survived, forty have no burial recorded in the parish registers – a fact that probably implies death occurring away from home by one means or another. There are also references in the Lowestoft burial entries to 'a stranger washed ashore', a simple statement that serves to

[130] Harris, *Trinity House*, 95.
[131] HMC, 13, 266.

illustrate the risks of life on the high seas and the anonymity of drowning in a place removed from one's own home area. The local manorial records abound with details of the retrieval of pieces of wreck on the beaches to the north and south of Lowestoft, but it is only occasionally that the human drama inherent in such events manages to convey itself.[132] Two examples will serve to illustrate the point.

On 27 December 1610, the Kirkley/Pakefield water leet recorded two references to a mishap involving a boat belonging to Nicholas Pacy of Lowestoft (mariner). The first records the finding of 'a parcel of nets' belonging to him. The second is worded as follows: 'Item we present two men which came ashore at Pakefield the one had in his purse vs. vid. which men came out of Nicol Pacy's boat and carried away by one Fisher's son of Lowestoft in his carte, and what the other man had they know not'.[133] The two events are almost certainly connected. In an entry of 3 November 1610, the Lowestoft parish registers record the burial of John Hurne (ship's carpenter) and James, a Scotsman (probably his Christian name). Both men are stated to have drowned in local inshore waters. The inquest into the finding of their bodies therefore took place eight weeks after they had been interred.

On 25 January 1669, the wreck of a trading vessel carrying groceries was enquired into.[134] Its cargo was a valuable one and worth considerable amounts of money to the salvors. Among the items retrieved, apparently without too much salt-water damage, were chests of oranges and lemons, barrels and cases of tobacco, casks of oil and soap, quantities of claret and brandy, and various items of furniture and clothing. Regardless of where the craft was bound, the high-quality grocery items may well have been the kinds of commodity available to the wealthier levels of Lowestoft society. It is the items of apparel, of course, which provide the touch of sadness. They were made of good-quality woollen cloth and linen and were all initialled W.I., M.I. or A.I. They obviously belonged to a family travelling on the vessel – passengers perhaps, or maybe the master's own immediate relatives. Whoever they were, their bodies were probably never recovered and their only memorial was to have certain of their personal effects recorded as wreck of the sea.

---

[132] Comparatively few cases of salvage and wreck were dealt with in the Lowestoft manor court itself. Owing to the position of the inshore channels and to the local tidal flow, most of the wreck was washed ashore at either Gunton or Corton (to the north of the town) or at Kirkley and Pakefield (to the south). Half the value of anything salvaged went to the finder, the other half to the lord of the half-hundred in whose jurisdiction the discovery was made.

[133] SRO(L), 194/B1/20, p. 163. Nicholas Pacy's fishing nets may well have been identified from his initials being either incised or burnt into the corks fixed along the head-line.

[134] SRO(L), 194/B1/23. The volume is not paginated.

– 9 –

Agriculture and Allied Industries

Land use in the parish at large

It is unarguable that maritime influences were the major factor in shaping Lowestoft during the late mediaeval and early modern periods. Yet agriculture was also an important element in the development of the town, creating employment for a number of the inhabitants (and limited wealth for a few) and leading to a number of associated trades and occupations. It also acted as a safety net for the community, something that was always there as part of the economic structure – something that could, in periods of adversity, provide subsistence until better times returned.

The manor roll of 1618 gives a detailed breakdown of land ownership in the parish and also of land use: whether the soil was growing crops or pasturing livestock, or whether it consisted of bruery or woodland (Map 3). Only the six main common greens (Denes, North Common and Warren, Goose Green, Church Green, the unmanaged parts of Drake's Heath with Smithmarsh, and South End Common) are unaccounted for in the document because, although in the ownership of the lord, they were available to townspeople on a controlled basis mainly for the pasturing of livestock. Their absence from the reckoning removed about 415 acres from the overall area of the parish which, when added to the sixty acres occupied by the town and a further twenty taken up by roads and trackways, left 991 acres available for farming and other uses.[1] The total area shown in the manor roll as committed to cultivation, to pasture, to bruery and to woodland came to over 990 acres, so the two figures agree very closely. Annual rent payable to the lord on the whole of this portion of the manor was 2d per acre, regardless of use, which means that the total financial yield of lands beyond the confines of the town (once the sixty-eight acres of demesne have been removed from the calculations) came to just under £8 a year.[2]

As previously noted, most agricultural land was freehold and, at the time the roll was compiled, was held by a total of fifty-six individuals and two corporate bodies. The larger holdings, ranging in size from about thirty acres to 123 acres, were largely

---

[1] The official measured area of Lowestoft parish, according to nineteenth- and twentieth-century surveys, is 1,485 acres, three roods and thirty-one perches – in other words, almost 1,486 acres.

[2] The total annual value of the rental in Lowestoft was about £14: £7 19s 2d from the farmland, £4 14s 10½d from the copyhold houses in town, and perhaps £1 5s 0d or so from the freehold dwellings (the last sum is an estimate). By 1676, the value had risen to £18 4s 2½d. See SRO(L), 194/A10/122.

concentrated in the hands of the two corporate bodies (Magdalen College, Oxford, and the town trustees) and nine local gentlemen. None of them farmed the land themselves, but leased it to people who did – some of whom may, in turn, have sub-let portions to other men.[3] There were fewer consolidated holdings at the time compared with the period of the tithe apportionment (1842), when ten nucleated farmsteads can be seen, regularly spaced throughout the parish.[4] The various abuttalments given in the manor roll show that the only really recognisable ones were those which were held by William Cuddon, Francis Wrott (gentleman) and Magdalen College in the north-western part of the parish, and by Robert Jettor (gentleman) and Thomas Jenkinson (gentleman) in the south-western sector.[5]

Altogether, there were 944.125 acres of freehold land specified as having some kind of productive use – a figure that can be rounded up to about 960 acres because of six small fields which do not have their areas recorded. Added to this was a further thirty four and a half acres of copyhold land – which puts the total in excess of 990 acres, as outlined in the first paragraph of this chapter. The use of the acreage available for agriculture and other purposes may be seen in Table 39. The dominance of arable land is apparent, but the importance of various types of grazing is also noticeable. All terms reproduced in the 'Use' column were employed in the manor roll, with the exception of 'arable', which may be inferred from frequent references to enclosures (*clm terr*) and to unenclosed 'pieces of land' (*peciam terr*). It is safe to regard these as the areas under cultivation because there are other references to 'pasture enclosures' (*clm pastur*) and to 'pieces of bruery' (*pec bruer*). There are even a few examples of mixed use within the same plot, such as 'an enclosure of land and pasture' (*clm terr et pastur*) or 'a piece of land and bruery' (*peciam terr et bruer*), thereby making clear the distinction between what was cultivated and what was not.[6] What may appear surprising is that the amount of arable land, at something over 600 acres, was only 150 acres more than it had been at the time of the Domesday Survey – 530 years before. That extra ground, however, would have been brought into cultivation with some degree of difficulty. The Lowestoft soils were largely light and poor, and the location of the parish bleak, hence the presence of so much waste and bruery.

As far as the seven specific terms used to describe land use are concerned, garden, woodland and osier yard speak for themselves (the last-named providing material used for making baskets), but the other four require some explanation. All of them relate to the feeding of livestock. *Bruery* was heathland, but of a managed nature. It was marked out in strips, or fenced off into enclosures, and used for rough grazing. Any gorse growing on it would have been cut for fuel and any bracken mown either for fuel or animal bedding.[7] The term *meadow* means permanent grassland, as opposed to *pasture*,

---

[3] See Spufford, 'Peasant Inheritance', p. 156. Manorial surveys are said not to reveal sub-tenancy and therefore serve to conceal the presence of the really poor and the landless.

[4] NRO, TA 658.

[5] Wrott was lord of the manor at Gunton; Jettor and Jenkinson were large holders of land in Flixton and Oulton.

[6] The expression *clm* used in the document is an abbreviation of *clausum*.

[7] The tithe accounts show that gorse cut on bruery or common green was taxable at 3s per thousand bundles.

Table 39. *Land use and acreages in 1618*

Tenure	Acreage	Use	%	Comments
Freehold	589.625+	Arable	62.5	
	16.25	Meadow		
	123.375+	Pasture	17.7	Combined % for all three types of grassland
	27.5	Stintland		
	166.0+	Bruery	17.6	
	21.0+	Woodland	2.2	
	0.375	Osier yard	0.04	
	944.125+			
Copyhold	24.5	Arable or garden		
	10.0	Bruery		
	978.625+			Six small fields have to be added to make up a total area in excess of 990 acres.

which was sown and maintained as grass for a desired period. At the end of this time, the land might well have been returned to arable use or ploughed up and re-sown with grasses once more. Both meadow and pasture were used for the direct grazing of stock or the production of hay. They were probably used for both purposes if the hay crop was cut first and the animals turned out onto the aftermath. *Stintland* was definitely organised in this way. It was either permanent or ley grass, often set out in strips, which had the hay crop taken off and then the animals put onto it. If the stints were unenclosed, then the livestock would have had to be tethered.

By the year 1618, much of the farmland in the parish was already enclosed. This fact fits in with comments which have been made about Suffolk being regarded by sixteenth-century commentators as either completely or largely enclosed.[8] It also matches what has been said about the eastern part of Norfolk – an area that was geographically close to Lowestoft.[9] Just how long the process had been going on cannot be stated with certainty because manorial documentation for the manor during the late mediaeval period does not seem to have survived. However, a clue may lie in certain documents relating to the ancient manor of Akethorpe, which was situated within the parish and which belonged to Magdalen College, Oxford, from the 1460s onwards.[10] A

[8] Thirsk, 'Enclosing and Engrossing', in *Agrarian History*, iv, 203.

[9] H. L. Gray, *English Field Systems*, xxii (Harvard, 1915), p. 307. The writer cites the work of William Marshall, *The Rural Economy of Norfolk, comprising the Management of Landed Estates and the Present Practice of Husbandry in that County* (London, 1787). Marshall declared that the eastern part of Norfolk generally 'may be said to be very old-inclosed country'.

[10] Once it came into the possession of the college, it seems to have lost its manorial status and become simply an agricultural estate. By the time that the Lowestoft manor rolls of 1610 and 1618 were compiled, it had become subsumed into the manor of Lowestoft.

fourteenth-century rental, an account roll of 1438–9 and a terrier of the early sixteenth century all refer to enclosures of varying sizes.[11]

The overall process of enclosing land was probably of the piecemeal and partial types, rather than the result of a single concerted move on the part of all interested landowners.[12] Furthermore, with the parish as a whole being well-endowed with areas of waste to provide common greens, enclosure of the common fields would have been able to proceed without great inconvenience being caused to people through loss of grazing rights. The process must also have been assisted by weak manorial control, because Lowestoft did not have a resident lord. Demesne land had probably been sold off piecemeal over a long period since, by 1618, it was only sixty-eight acres in extent (forty-six arable, nineteen bruery and three grassland), located in different parts of the parish and rented out to various people.

Of the combined overall area specified in Table 39, 68% was enclosed. If the three main categories of land within the overall total (arable, grass and bruery) are analysed, it is found that 73% of the cultivated acreage was enclosed, as was 92% of the meadow, pasture and stintland, and 31% of the bruery. The very high percentage of grassland that was fenced should come as no surprise, given the need to keep stock confined. Nor is it remarkable that so much of the managed heathland should have remained unfenced, in view of its traditionally open nature. However, the fact that three-quarters of the arable land was enclosed by 1618 shows just how far the move away from open-field culture had progressed. Vestiges of the strips remained in one or two areas, on either north–south or east–west alignments (Map 3), but for the most part the old mediaeval landscape had gone.

Ironically, by a combination of chance and municipal planning, a sector of the former South-west Field has been preserved as a park and playing-field (Plate 20) and it is just about posssible to ascertain (or at least imagine) something of its former nature.[13] The two words that give the clue to which land was enclosed and which was not have already been identified and commented on. The use of *clausum* (abbreviated to *clm*) is self-explanatory, but *peciam* is worth remarking upon. In at least one part of rural Suffolk the word simply meant an area of land somewhere, but in another it has been classified as an unenclosed remnant of the open-field system.[14] The latter view was definitely the case in Lowestoft, and it is possible to see from various abuttalments given in the manor

---

[11] Magdalen College Archives, 151/19, 73/4 and FP 105.

[12] J. A. Yelling, *Common Field and Enclosure in England, 1450–1850* (London, 1977), p. 6. Piecemeal enclosure is said to exhibit three features: a) enclosure which is completed in more than one stage; b) enclosure which is the act of an individual or small group of people, rather than all the common field proprietors acting together; c) enclosure that was a disorderly process, involving only limited consolidation. Partial enclosure is the term used for any enclosure which was not fully implemented, and thus it refers to the scale of the operation – not the decision-making process which lay behind it.

[13] Normanston Park constitutes about 15%–20% of the former South-west Field, largest of the three common fields. It has a pronounced slope from north-west to south-east, which means that the strips would probably have run on a north-east to south-west alignment in order to avoid soil-creep.

[14] Evans, 'South Elmham', p. 67. D. Dymond, 'The Parish of Walsham-le-Willows: Two Elizabethan Surveys and Their Mediaeval Background', *PSIA* xxxiii, ii (Ipswich, 1974), 202–4.

Plate 20. *Normanston Park: the 1618 Manor Roll shows this part of the common field to have been devoted to arable farming, with vestiges of strips on a north-east/south-west alignment to counter the slope of the land south-eastwards.*

roll whether the strips were on a north–south or east–west alignment. The *piece* has even been called the basic unit of land tenure in East Anglia, the equivalent of the Midlands *selion*: a strip of land, half an acre in area.[15] Some of the Lowestoft pieces were half an acre in extent, but the majority were between one and three acres. It is possible, therefore, that these larger sizes were the result of the amalgamation of strips which had taken place over the years.

The respective sizes of both enclosures and pieces varied a good deal, as may be seen in Table 40 – though the overall tendency was towards smaller ones than became the norm for fields later on. By the time of the tithe apportionment in 1842, a considerable change in the agricultural landscape had taken place in Lowestoft. The manor roll of 1618 shows a parish with about three-quarters of its arable land enclosed, much of it in small fields (thirty-five of the seventy enclosures were smaller than the median size of three and a half acres). The tithe map shows one which is totally enclosed (apart from the Denes), and not just the farmland: over 200 acres of common green had also been either parcelled up or built over.[16]

Presumably, the latter process really got under way as the second half of the eighteenth century advanced, because there is no evidence in the tithe accounts that it had begun on any significant scale before the end of the period covered in this book. With a basic charge of 2s per acre made on major field crops, it is noticeable that the

---

[15] M. R. Postgate, 'Field Systems of East Anglia', in A. R. H. Baker and R. A. Butlin (eds), *Field Systems in the British Isles* (Cambridge, 1973), p. 287.

[16] The only open space which remained was the Denes area, between cliff-base and shoreline.

Table 40. *The size of enclosures and pieces (in acres)*

Use	Largest	Smallest	Mean	Median	Comments
Enclosures					
Arable	20.0	0.25	4.86	3.5	
Meadow	8.0	2.0			Only 2 enclosures in all
Pasture	12.0	0.75	4.1	4.0	
Stintland	6.0	1.0	2.82	2.0	
Bruery	20.0	10.0			Only 3 enclosures in all
Pieces					
Arable	12.0	0.125	1.56	1.0	
Meadow	1.0				Only one piece in all
Pasture	1.0	0.25			Only 2 pieces in all
Stintland	2.0	0.5	1.29	1.25	
Bruery	14.0	0.5	2.75	2.0	

sums of money paid on certain, named fields (e.g. Paradise, Ringbell, Fir Pightle, Long Close and Gravel Pit) suggest sizes much the same as 100 years before, when the manor roll was compiled. If further consolidation had taken place in the meantime, it is not detectable. However, by the time that the tithe map of 1842 came to be drawn, all the little enclosures and strips of over 200 years before had been amalgamated into the classic, rectangular configuration of fields anything between three and twelve acres in area – the pattern which has become regarded as the quintessential English landscape.

Arable crops

Grain
The potential value of tithe accounts books as a source of information regarding agricultural practice was the subject of an essay nearly thirty years ago.[17] The surviving Lowestoft tithe records begin to record details of agriculture in the parish in the year 1698, but there is no reference to the growing of corn until 1749 – the year in which the Rev. John Tanner began to draw the rectorial tithes. No acreages or quantities are revealed, but it is noticeable that grain tithes increased the incumbent's annual income by about £70, from an average of £25–£35 derived from small tithes alone (these latter being paid on all field crops other than corn). Lowestoft was a light-land parish, which would have made it more suitable for the growing of barley, oats and rye than of wheat, but there is limited evidence to show that all four varieties were produced, with barley being the most important.

[17] N. Evans, 'Tithe Books as a Source for the Local Historian', *LH* 14, i (February 1980), 24–7.

Only five inventories for husbandmen or farmers have survived and, as two of the documents were drawn up in April, there are no references to grain in them.[18] Two others, however – those of Thomas Clarke (September 1619) and Thomas Gardner (December 1720) – do show certain quantities of corn held in store. The former itemises unspecified amounts of wheat, barley and peas worth £2 10s 0d, while the latter records fifteen coombs of oats, five coombs of barley, three bushels of wheat and two coombs of rye, worth a total of £7 10s 0d.[19] The only other reference to corn-growing which appears in the probate inventories is to be found in July 1610, when it is revealed that the vicar, John Gleason, had half an acre of standing barley on his glebe land, worth 13s. In addition to this material, the will of Rychard Youngeman (husbandman), in February 1570, records a bequest made to his wife of two coombs of wheat, three coombs of rye and five coombs of meslin (this last-named item being a mixture of rye and wheat, used for milling into flour).

In the absence of much firm evidence, it is difficult to project the acreage devoted to grain, but the tithe accounts hold a clue, at least as far as the middle of the eighteenth century is concerned. Corn was rated at 2s an acre for tithe payment, just like turnips, the other main field crop. As was pointed out above, John Tanner's annual income went up by £70 in 1749 and subsequent years, once the corn-tithes began to be paid to him – which means that 700 acres in the parish were growing corn at that particular time – though whether or not this represents an increase in area from the beginning of his incumbency, forty years before, is not known. It was certainly an increase in production from the time of the 1618 manor roll, when the total arable area added up to just over 600 acres. In fact, if the average acreages for turnips and clover are added to the 700 producing grain, a total of 800 is arrived at. This means that, between 1618 and 1750, 200 acres more had been brought into cultivation.[20] Leaving the total available area aside, it is likely, throughout the whole period covered in this book, that the bulk of the arable land in the parish (perhaps as much as 85%) was devoted to corn production. And, given the amount of malting and brewing which took place, much of it was undoubtedly barley.

Turnips

It is clear from the tithe accounts that turnips were an important field crop in Lowestoft by the end of the seventeenth century and the beginning of the eighteenth, with

---

[18] This is because there would have been no corn in store at this time of year. The seed corn would have been sown in either autumn or early spring; the surplus remaining for sale would have gone to the miller and the maltster.

[19] There were four bushels to the coomb by customary dry measure of the time. A coomb of barley weighed sixteen stones (two hundredweights).

[20] Given the fact that the Denes remained untouched (apart from use as open-air wharf and rough grazing area, they were unsuitable for cultivation), that Goose Green was too small and too near the town to be much good for growing crops, and that Church Green was left alone, arable conversion must have occurred on areas of bruery and waste adjacent to the three former common fields. Thus, the North and the South End commons, Smithmarsh, Drakes Heath and Skamacre Heath were the areas of reclamation – in addition to the extra acres gained from ploughing up pastureland.

anything between fifty and seventy acres grown annually. This suggests that the roots were well established by that time, though the absence of any earlier information makes it impossible to place a date upon their introduction. The cultivation of turnips (and carrots) has been detected in the Waveney Valley as early as 1630, and comment has also been made on the importance of innovations regarding roots crops made by Dutch immigrants in Norwich during the 1570s.[21] In view of the number of Dutch Protestants who were resident in Lowestoft between 1571 and 1574, it is just possible that turnips made their first appearance in the parish at that particular time. The neighbouring county of Norfolk had turnips grown over most of its land area by the 1660s and more than 50% of its farmers were involved in producing the crop by the second decade of the eighteenth century.[22] Problems encountered in extricating the root from clay soil meant that the large-scale introduction of turnips into High Suffolk did not occur until about 1670 or thereafter, with rotational use not really taking off until the eighteenth century.[23] It was a problem that would not have bothered the tillers of the soil in Lowestoft!

The largest area of turnips during the first three decades of the eighteenth century was recorded in 1712, when 151 acres were grown, but the usual area after c.1710 was somewhere between fifty and one hundred acres. The quantity produced by individual farmers depended on the size of their respective enterprises and ranged from two to twenty-five acres. No definite statements are made anywhere regarding the use of the roots, but much of the crop was probably grown for consumption by cattle, with a lesser proportion going to feed sheep and with some perhaps even eaten by the townspeople. References made to the hoeing of turnips would seem to suggest that they were grown for roots rather than foliage, but in poor years some of the crop was consumed by direct grazing and a lesser amount of tithe charged.[24] The liability of turnips for tithe payment does not seem to have been the cause of dispute, as noted elsewhere – at least, not during the years covered by the accounts.[25] Any grazing which took place on the foliage of poorly developed or immature plants would have been useful in building up the organic content of the light local soils.

Within an average annual area of seventy-five acres of turnips being grown, the

---

[21] J. Thirsk, 'The Farming Regions of England', in *Agrarian History*, iv, 47; M. Thick, 'Market Gardening in England and Wales', in *Agrarian History*, v, ii (Cambridge, 1985), 505.

[22] B. M. S. Campbell and M. Overton, 'A New Perspective on Mediaeval and Early Modern Agriculture: Six Centuries of Norfolk Farming, c. 1250 to c. 1850', *P&P* 141 (November, 1993), 60.

[23] J. Theobald, 'Agricultural Productivity in Woodland High Suffolk, 1600–1850', *AHR* 50, I (2002), 11. M. Overton, 'The Diffusion of Agricultural Innovations in Early Modern England: Turnips and Clover in Norfolk and Suffolk, 1580–1740', *TIBG* new series 10, 2 (1985), 208, says that turnip culture began in earnest in East Anglia during the 1670s.

[24] The hoeing of turnips shows that the plants were being spaced so as to allow full development. There would have been no need for such singling if the crop was being grown for its leaves.

[25] E. Evans, 'Tithes', in *Agrarian History*, v, ii, 400. The writer makes reference to the way that new crops, such as fodder crops and artificial grasses, often provoked strife concerning the payment of tithe. He cites the example of George Fakes of Bury St Edmunds, who was presented in the Sudbury Archdeaconry court in 1693 for the non-payment of tithe levied upon turnips at the rate of 2s per acre.

field spaces themselves ranged from three acres to ten. Sometimes this represented a single field; in other cases turnips were grown with other crops in a bigger field. There were also areas both smaller and larger than the ones cited, the former including quarter-acre plots in and around the town itself. Such restricted spaces were almost certainly producing the roots for human consumption. Lowestoft does not feature as a turnip-growing parish in at least one major study of East Anglian agriculture covering a period from the late sixteenth century to the early eighteenth, but this is because the data is based entirely on probate inventories.[26] Only three farmers' inventories have survived for the period in which turnips were produced as a field crop and none of them shows cultivation of the root. However, the tithe accounts indicate clearly that one of the men, Robert Lilley, was producing turnips in the earlier part of the eighteenth century – in addition to a number of other people. It all goes to demonstrate the dangers of working from a single source when compiling historical information – a point made in Chapter 4 with regard to collecting occupational data from will registers alone.

Other roots, peas and beans

Apart from turnips, the only other root crops which are referred to in the tithe accounts are carrots and parsnips. As is the case with turnips, there is no way of ascertaining how long they had been cultivated in Lowestoft but they appear to have been well established before 1700 – which perhaps fits the local pattern.[27] They were grown only in small quantities, a fact which suggests use for human consumption rather than for feeding livestock, and the areas of cultivation ranged from one eighth of an acre to three-quarters of an acre in size. The favourite location was the base of the cliff, where the various fish-houses and net-stores stood, and where the light, sandy soil was ideal for their culture. They were tithable at a rate of 7s to 8s an acre.

Neither peas nor beans were prominent crops in the agricultural cycle, which may reflect a regional characteristic. It has been suggested that these legumes were relatively unimportant in north-east Suffolk during the period 1550–1640 and the characteristic may have held good for the following 100 years.[28] Both crops were the subject of small-scale culture in Lowestoft, just like carrots and parsnips, with areas once more between one eighth and three-quarters of an acre put under cultivation. Again, people's yards were the most common location (especially below the cliff) and the limited scale of the operation suggests that the crops were grown with human consumption in mind. The tithe payable on them was 4s per acre.

---

[26] M. Overton, 'Agricultural Change in Norfolk and Suffolk, 1580–1740' (unpub. PhD thesis, University of Cambridge, 1980), pp. 148–51.

[27] E. Kerridge, 'Turnip Husbandry in High Suffolk', in W. E. Minchinton (ed.), *Essays in Agrarian History*, 2 vols (Newton Abbot, 1968), i, 143, mentions the growing of parsnips and carrots in the parish of Bradwell (Half-hundred of Lothingland) as early as 1620. J. Thirsk, 'Farming Techniques', in *Agrarian History*, iv, 175, refers to carrot production along the Suffolk coastal fringe, with various uses being found for them: human consumption, feeding cows and poultry, and fattening bullocks.

[28] Evans, 'South Elmham', p. 79.

Forage crops

Clover and hay

The appearance of clover in the tithe accounts for 1698 and 1699 would seem to suggest that its culture was an established part of agricultural practice in Lowestoft before the end of the seventeenth century. It was obviously a fairly important crop for livestock, but the annual area sown during the first three decades of the eighteenth century did fluctuate between seven and eighty acres – with the larger amounts being grown from 1721 onwards.[29] Observations concerning the Norwich area at this time have identified clover as being well established in the parish of Thorpe St Andrew, where its function seems to have been as a catch-crop amidst cereals and pulses.[30] This was not the case in Lowestoft where, on the evidence of particular field names mentioned in connection with certain crops from year to year, clover can be seen as part of a rotational system with turnips, grass and grain.[31] The size of the individual areas grown was largely in the range of two to ten acres (occasionally, larger parcels are recorded), and the spaces sown were either fields in their own right or areas within fields.

The crop was mown and stored or fed directly to livestock in the fields. In the former case, the animals were turned out onto the aftermath; in the latter, the left-overs were raked up and put away to provide fodder during the winter. Clover was grown as a one-year, two-year or three-year crop, with mowing or feeding and raking carried out according to its quality. The best clover was always mown and stored; poor crops underwent direct grazing. As was the case with turnips, clover was grown in all parts of the parish and it was tithable at 2s 6d per acre. The variety sown was probably *broad red*, the commonest type available, but whether or not it was imported seed cannot be ascertained. Nor can the date of its introduction into the parish.

In addition to clover, there is also evidence to suggest that both vetches and trefoils were grown as part of the ley rotation. The former are mentioned only once as a crop in their own right in the tithe accounts, and that is in 1720 when John Jex (merchant) was charged 16s on four acres of vetches 'cut for horsemeat'. It was their particular use as equine fodder which made them eligible for the payment of tithe, but they may at other times have been sown in with other 'grasses' and counted as part of the rotational pasture. The same is true of trefoils. There are no direct references to the crop in the accounts, but the name of at least one field in the parish, Nonesuch Pightle, suggests that they were grown ('nonesuch' being an alternative name for them).

---

[29] Clover had the capacity to produce as much as one and a half to two tons per acre on good land. See A. Young, *A General View of the Agriculture of the County of Suffolk* (Newton Abbot, 1968 – first published in London, 1797), p. 103. Campbell and Overton, p. 59, says that no more than 15% of large farms in Norfolk grew the crop between 1660 and 1739, but that by the 1830s it constituted 25% of the total acreage under cultivation.

[30] B. Holderness, 'East Anglia and the Fens', in *Agrarian History*, v, i, 226. J. Thirsk, 'Farming Techniques' in *Agrarian History*, iv, 180, dates the introduction of clover into Norfolk to the first three decades of the seventeenth century.

[31] This is earlier than has been detected in High Suffolk, where clover did not form part of a rotational system until the middle of the eighteenth century. See Theobald, 'Agricultural Productivity', 11–12.

The tithe accounts show that the annual area devoted to hay during the first quarter of the eighteenth century varied between two acres and nineteen acres, with an average of seven and a half. Its relatively limited production probably means that it was only used for feeding horses.[32] The crop was usually mown and stored, with various livestock (horses, cattle and sheep) turned out onto the aftermath. When sown as grass seed, it seems to have been grown in rotation with turnips, clover and cereals, while the other means of producing it was to mow permanent meadowland (a small quantity was also derived from ley grass being raked over after livestock had grazed on it). Hay was rated at 2s per acre for tithe purposes and the usual size of the spaces producing it was between two and four acres. It was grown in various parts of the parish, but with a tendency for it to be concentrated in enclosures on the western perimeter of the town.

Meadowland and pasture

There is no clear distinction made in the tithe book between the two different types of grassland, with each being classed as 'pasture' and assessed at 1s per acre. However, the impression given by various references to specific, named meadows in different parts of the parish is that the area of permanent grassland had increased from the time of the 1618 manor roll and that the amount of sown pasture had noticeably decreased (most of it probably converted to arable use). During the first three decades of the eighteenth century the area of permanent or semi-permanent grassland (i.e. meadow) used to provide grazing for livestock was established at about sixty-five acres, and it was largely located on the southern and western edges of the town. If its main purpose was to provide direct grazing, the tithe payment was 1s per acre; but if a hay crop was the prime objective, then a charge of 2s was made. At other times, if it could be shown that the grassland was worn out and needed a period of recovery, no tithe was levied. Sown pasture was a different thing altogether from long-term grassland and was part of the arable rotation. It was to be found in all parts of the parish and the annual area of such cultivation averaged about twenty-eight acres.

Minor arable crops

Hemp was grown on a very limited scale in town, in specific yards and enclosures which varied from a quarter of an acre to one acre in size. The annual area under cultivation ranged from a quarter of an acre to two and a half acres, with an average of about one and a half. The crop was tithable at 4s per acre and only about two or three people were involved in growing it regularly. Two of the inns in town, the *Globe* and the *Black Boy* (formerly the *King's Arms*), which had large yards to the rear, had hemplands situated within their curtilages. The plant had obviously been grown within the built-up area

---

[32] In terms of yield, hay was reckoned to produce at least one ton per acre, with one and half to two tons on low meadows and improved uplands. See Young, *General View of Suffolk*, p. 162.

over quite a long period, because the 1618 manor roll mentions three other hemplands which were no longer in use by the beginning of the eighteenth century. Two of them had been located on the western perimeter of the town, near Goose Green, and the third was situated on the freehold land at the High Street's northern end.[33] At no point in Lowestoft's early modern history did the amount of hemp grown in the parish supply more than a fraction of what was needed for twine or rope, or for linen-weaving, and supplies must have been brought in from other local sources, as well as from further afield.[34]

There are only two references to the growing of hops in the tithe accounts, made in the years 1699 and 1700. It is possible that both refer to the same hopyard, because the men in question owned inns on opposite sides of Swan Lane. Anthony Barlow (innkeeper) ran the *King's Head*, on the southern side of the road, while Samuel Munds (merchant and brewer) had the *Three Mariners*, on the northern side. No clue is given as to the specific location of the plot, nor to its size, but Munds paid 2s tithe on it in 1700. Again, as was the case with hemp, most of the hops used in the town's breweries must have been brought in from outside.

The final crop that manifests itself is weld, from which a yellow dye was extracted and which needed warm, dry soil for successful cultivation. It was grown in small plots below the cliff at the northern end of town in 1716 and 1717. The man who produced it, Charles Boyce (yeoman), paid tithe of 3s on the crop. Six years later, in 1722 and 1723, he grew larger quantities in a field called Bacon's Close (again, at the northern end of town) and he paid the vicar £1 and 10s respectively. The yield in 1722 was five cartloads, valued at £10, but the following year was a very dry one and the plants did not do as well. Boyce, who farmed largely in the adjoining parish of Gunton, seems either to have experimented with weld on almost marginal land or to have used it as a catch-crop. The plant can still be found growing wild in one or two locations near the cliffs at Gunton.

Animal husbandry

Cattle

The amount of grassland of one kind or another revealed in the 1618 manor roll (about 170 acres), when compared with that discernible in the tithe accounts (about sixty-five acres of permanent pasture, or meadow, and an annual average of twenty-eight acres of the sown variety) may appear to suggest that fewer cattle were being kept in the parish by 1700 than had been the case 100 years before. Such a notion, however, does not take

---

[33] The practice of growing hemp in the area where the latter plot had been located continued well into the nineteenth century and is perpetuated in a street name, 'The Hemplands'. The number of houses there was much reduced in the late 1970s by the construction of the Lowestoft inner relief road.

[34] Given the light, dry soil conditions in Lowestoft, the type of hemp grown would have been more suited to linen production than for making twine or rope. The Waveney Valley was a notable hemp-producing area and at least some of the town's raw material would have originated from there.

account of the improved feeding capacity provided by the cultivation of turnips and clover during the seventeenth century – innovations which would have allowed increased numbers of animals to be kept.

Altogether, only thirty-five of the 507 surviving wills make reference to cattle, and a mere nine of these were made either by husbandmen or yeomen. The rest are documents appertaining to quite a wide cross section of the population of craftsman status and above, with merchants, brewers, tanners, shipwrights and tailors all being represented.[35] A similar variety is to be found in the inventories, where, out of thirteen documents which mention cattle of one kind or another, only four are the lists of goods belonging to husbandmen or yeomen. The other nine relate to two merchants, a goldsmith, a brewer and his widow, a mariner, a mason, a tailor and a carter.

Given the fact that beast-keeping by such people does not seem to have been a primary interest, it becomes difficult to ascertain the true extent of cattle-rearing as part of a specialist farming enterprise. The possession of a single cow, in evidence in some of the probate material, probably means that the owner had the animal to produce milk (and dairy products) for the household. However, there are also examples of people with no obvious connection with farming who had considerably more stock – a fact which almost certainly reflects the mixed nature of the local economy. William Barnard (shipwright) had nine cattle to bequeath in 1580 (whether for milk or meat is not stated), while four years later the will of James Myhell (merchant) reveals ownership of seven cows – which would seem to suggest a capacity for substantial milk production. When Stephen Phillipp (schoolmaster) died in December 1605, he left his oldest son, John, all his cattle – though, as in the case of William Barnard, the type of animal is not divulged. The will of Robert Hawes (vicar) is more specific: he left the beef cattle in his possession to his wife, Alice, in August 1639. The four examples cited serve to illustrate the diversity of people's interests, a feature of the local economy explored in Chapter 4.

As far as recognised farmers are concerned, there is a little information in probate material to show that cattle-rearing was carried on for the production of both meat and milk, but there is no firm indication as to how many men were involved at any one time and no mention of the number of animals they were keeping. Nor do the tithe accounts afford much data, apart from the last two years of the short incumbency of the Rev. James Smith (1702–1708), who had his parish clerk, John Blaque, draw up a list of the people in the parish who owned cows. This was to enable the tithe of *lactage* (payment made on milk and dairy products) due to the minister to be collected – a levy which Smith's successor, John Tanner, did not proceed with when he became vicar. It is easy to understand why: when reading the remarks appended by Blaque to the numbers of cows owned by each person, it can be seen that there was considerable resistance towards paying the charge.

In 1707, thirty parishioners are listed as having a minimum of sixty-nine animals (one man has nothing entered against his name), while the following year twenty-nine are

---

[35] Twenty-six of the wills date from before 1650. This is partly due to the varying survival rate of the documents, but the bias also reflects the local economy becoming less mixed in nature as maritime specialism grew stronger.

seen to have had eighty-six. Altogether, nineteen men and four women are named in each of the two years, with a further thirteen people who appear in one year or the other (seven in 1707 and six in 1708).[36] No one is shown as having a large number of cows, and there are only two examples of people who had ten or more – a number placed at the lower end of commercial herds in the claylands of East Anglia.[37] Of the thirty-six people named, eight were primarily concerned with farming as their way of making a living. The rest were composed of merchants, brewers, innkeepers, butchers, mariners and fishermen, cordwainers, carpenters, blacksmiths, carters and labourers.

The response of the owners of cattle to the vicar's attempts to collect his entitlement varied a great deal. Some of them agreed to pay what was due, while others said that they would call on him and discuss the matter. Then there were those who either said that they had only just acquired the stock (and were therefore trying to postpone payment) or that they had no animals at all. One of the men, Robert Press (fisherman), reminded the clergyman that the latter owed him for a horse journey, while another, Abraham Hawker (husbandman), said that he would pay the tithe due on field crops but would not part with anything for lactage. Finally, there was the response of Thomas Salter (mariner and Nonconformist), who had one animal only. He refused payment and challenged James Smith in the following manner: 'Do your worst or what you will!'

With butchery being a notable service trade in town (especially up to about the middle of the seventeenth century), cattle reared for slaughter must have been of some significance in the farming economy – though there is no means of arriving at the number of beasts kept. And even after a decline in the number of individual butchers from 1650 onwards, meat production for local needs and for the provisioning of sea-going vessels was still important. The Mewse family (who operated a substantial butchery business for at least five generations) remained influential and a number of the yeomen and more substantial husbandmen slaughtered livestock themselves. If, at any time, the supply of bullocks was not sufficient from within the parish itself, stock could have been brought in from the hinterland; but with turnips and clover obviously well established as field crops before the end of the seventeenth century, there is a good chance that at least some of the fodder produced was used to stall-feed bullocks during the winter (the manure produced thereby being used to fertilise arable land).[38] There were at least three or four slaughterhouses in operation at any one time throughout the seventeenth century and the first half of the eighteenth and this, together with the fact that the town had two tanneries producing leather, suggests that substantial numbers of cattle were being killed for meat.

---

[36] The four women were all widows, one of them having been married to a husbandman. Of the seven people mentioned only in 1707, two were widows – of a merchant and a yeoman, respectively. Of the six referred to only in 1708, one was a woman – the wife or daughter of a butcher.

[37] Holderness, 'East Anglia and the Fens' in *Agrarian History*, v, i, 232, says that the size of commercial milking herds in wood-pasture areas ranged from eight cows to twenty, with a median number of eleven to twelve.

[38] *Ibid.*, 235. It is said that winter stall-feeding of bullocks became increasingly important after 1670.

Pigs and sheep

In view of ordinances passed in the leet court in 1585 and 1620 regarding the nuisance caused by pigs, it may seem surprising that there is only one reference to them in the surviving will material (Bartholomew Howard, yeoman, bequeathed one to his wife in May 1608). They were obviously kept on quite a large scale and they were not without monetary value, as some of the inventories show, but they do not seem to have been considered worthy of constituting individual bequests.[39] This may have been due to their comparatively humble nature, for they were very much creatures of the back yard and people kept them for producing bacon and ham for the house.

They do not seem to have been very important where full-time farming was concerned and, in the first thirty or so years covered by the tithe accounts, only four men are shown to have surrendered the proverbial 'tithe pig' to the vicar. Payment had obviously been commuted to a cash payment at some stage, and 2s per animal was the going rate. The two farmers who feature most prominently are William Utting and John Peach (both described as yeomen, though the latter was also a brewer), who seem to have kept the animals on a modest scale as part of their respective enterprises, each paying his dues on about three or four animals annually. It may seem strange that the inventory of Robert Lilley (April 1711), who farmed at Smithmarsh, shows his having six pigs, yet there is no reference to him in the tithe accounts. The omission may have been due to his having been resident in the parish for only about one year prior to his decease.[40] As far as the population as a whole is concerned, there does not seem to have been any attempt by the incumbent to levy tithe on all pigs kept in the parish, in the same way that James Smith tried to do with milk cattle.

Sheep seem to have been of minor importance in Lowestoft, being referred to only twice in the whole of the probate material. Thomas Dameron (merchant) left his wife, Isabell, all his sheep in November 1574, though no idea is given as to the number of animals he had, while Edward Sparrow (yeoman) left each of his godsons a ewe and each of his god-daughters a lamb in August 1609. It is likely that these particular animals were kept on Sparrow's land in the parish of Somerleyton, because the only property he owned in Lowestoft consisted of a dwelling-house and an inn called *The Spreadeagle*. In addition to the scarcity of references to sheep in probate documents (the surviving inventories do not mention them at all), there is also scant mention of them in the manor court minutes, either as causers of nuisance or because their owners were running too many of them on the common greens.

The tithe accounts, too, contain few references. William Utting, the yeoman mentioned two paragraphs above, paid 3s on thirteen lambs in 1722, but that is the only

---

[39] The value for a mature hog ranged from about 8s during the early seventeenth century to £2 by the second decade of the eighteenth.

[40] There is also the case of Samuel Munds (merchant), a life-long resident of the parish, whose inventory of March 1711 shows him to have owned pigs to the value of £7. Farming was part of his enterprise, yet he does not seem to have paid any tithe on pigs. The same is true of John Durrant (brewer), whose inventory was drawn up in November 1715. There must have been various local arrangements whereby some of the payments due to the vicar were both negotiable and convertible.

time such payment is recorded. The only person who apparently kept sheep on any scale during the eighteenth century did not even live in Lowestoft. William Woodthorpe (yeoman) had his residence in the adjoining parish of Gunton, but he was tithed on the number of sheep which he pastured on the Lowestoft dole-lands. These were located in the north-western sector of the parish and abutted onto the boundary with Gunton. In 1723 and 1725 he paid the sum of 2s 6d, while in 1724 he settled his debt by giving the Rev. John Tanner a fat pig. It may appear surprising that a parish on the Suffolk coastal strip (which was largely a sheep-corn farming area) did not have sheep-rearing on any scale, but that is the situation which prevailed. Both sheep and pigs, however, were slaughtered commercially for meat and evidence of their remains (and of cattle, too) have been found on land to the south of Rant Score – a location where the Mewse family operated one of their butchery enterprises.[41]

Horses

While oxen were almost certainly used as draught animals during mediaeval times, horses were the main means of pulling ploughs, wagons and carts in Lowestoft during the early modern period. The main animal employed was the sorrel horse, reddish brown in colour and lineal ancestor of the eponymous Suffolk Punch.[42] There are a number of references to horses in both wills and inventories (including sorrels), from which it is possible to infer their use in agriculture, in other trades and occupations, and also for riding. It is noticeable that, once yeomen and husbandman (and carters) have been allowed for, the possession of horses was concentrated in the wealthier levels of local society, especially among merchants and brewers. A number of animals of varying breed and size were used as personal mounts for local journeys and those made further afield, others being used to draw the light, two-wheeled carriages belonging to a handful of the most privileged families. They were probably fed on hay, clover and vetches, dross grain and bran, and there was ample grazing meadow available for them on the southern and western edges of town.

Poultry

There are no references in the will material to fowls of any kind, and only four in the inventories. In June 1591, Thomas Eache (cordwainer) had 'certain poultry' worth 1s 8d in his yard, while, in May 1606, Laurence Rooke (labourer) had two geese, a gander, ten goslings and a hen in his. The thirteen geese were valued at 6s 8d and the hen at 6d. In July 1610, John Gleason (the vicar) had a cockerel, six hens and three geese on his premises, but the fowls belonging to John Neale (husbandman) in April 1611 are simply described once again as 'certain poultry'. In neither of the latter two cases is it possible to arrive at a value for the birds, because they were included with other types of livestock for the purposes of assessment.

---

[41] They owned premises at what is now Nos 70–71, High Street. See Durbidge, 'A Limited Excavation', 32.

[42] The Punch first emerged as a breed in its own right from a stallion belonging to Thomas Crisp of Ufford, which was foaled in the year 1768. See G. E. Evans, *The Horse in the Furrow* (London, 1960), p. 158. Evans, 'South Elmham', p. 83, correctly identifies the sorrel horse as the Punch's ancestor.

There was probably considerably more poultry-keeping in the parish than probate documents suggest. Low value has been suggested as a possible cause for the lack of references in inventories generally, and this may have been a factor.[43] However, another consideration, in the case of Lowestoft, is the small number of farmers' inventories which have survived (five). Obviously, the name Goose Green for the piece of common immediately next to the town on its western edge acknowledges the fact that geese were turned out to graze there, and it is interesting to note that an ordinance passed at the leet court of 1582 sought to prevent the townspeople from pasturing the birds on any other of the common greens.[44]

Among what may be termed the minority items recorded in the tithe accounts are two lists of people assessed for the payment of tithe on geese.[45] The first one is dated 9ptember 1713 and has twenty names recorded. Both lists are in the handwriting of the parish clerk of the time, John Blaque, with additional comments appended by the vicar, John Tanner. A majority of the people were husbandmen, but a number of mariners and fishermen are detectable and one of them, Abraham Page, owned the largest flock recorded: forty-eight birds. It seems to have been the custom to give the vicar one goose for every twenty kept or to pay him 9d or 10d by way of commutation. In another part of the accounts, three of the more important farmers in the parish at the time, Robert Lilley (1711–12), John Peach (1710–1722) and William Utting (1714–1725), were also paying tithe on geese, while Lilley had to settle up for the number of ducks he was keeping, as well as for the eggs which they produced.[46]

The nature of farming in the parish

The type of agriculture practised in Lowestoft during the early modern era was of mixed variety, as was the case with most other communities in lowland England. And it was not only mixed in combining crops and livestock; it was also mixed in the sense that many of the people who farmed the land had other interests. It is unfortunate that the two key documents which reveal so much about conduct of agriculture in the parish stand in

[43] Evans, 'South Elmham', p. 84.

[44] SRO(L), 194/A10/4, p. 14.

[45] The ledger is primarily concerned with payments due on crops and fishing catches, but other items appear periodically. There may have been another book for less important tithable products, which has not survived, with certain of these lesser objects being entered from time to time in the main accounts. Such practice was probably the result of chance or whim, but it is fortunate that it occurred – otherwise, a valuable (if limited) insight into certain aspects of the parish's agriculture would have been lost

[46] He farmed briefly at Smithmarsh, an out-of-town holding, which lay in the south-western corner of the former South Field to the north of Lake Lothing (the farmhouse and yard being situated at the present-day junction of Rotterdam Road and Norwich Road). A good deal of this area was semi-marshland and ideally suited to the keeping of geese and ducks. An earlier name for Smithmarsh was 'Seethmarsh' and, given the boggy nature of the ground through its proximity to Lake Lothing, the first element almost certainly referred originally to water (either at the edge of the lake itself or concentrated in pools) which was frequently agitated by the effect of the wind.

isolation from each other. The manor roll of 1618 gives a full account of who held the land and what the field system was like, but does not reveal who was doing the farming; the tithe accounts of 1698–1787 show who the farmers were and what crops they were growing, but do not divulge who owned the land and what the field pattern had developed into. In spite of this, it is possible to bridge the eighty-year gap and establish certain characteristics regarding agricultural practice.

For instance, if a comparison is made between the fifty-six private individuals named as holders of land in the manor roll and the various yeomen and husbandmen identifiable during the first half of the seventeenth century, there is very little overlap at all. This presumably means that, in most cases, the landowners rented out to the people who farmed. The era in which the manor roll was compiled happened to be the one which saw the largest number of husbandmen ever recorded in the parish registers – a development resulting from men switching employment from sea to land at a time when fishing was in decline. In addition to the people identified as yeomen or husbandmen, there were also substantial numbers of merchants, tradespeople, seafarers and craftsmen having some kind of interest in farming. The impression gained at this time is that much of the agriculture was comparatively small in scale, with a wide variety of people involved. This is not to say that it was inefficient. It was more a case of the sum of little parts constituting a not inconsiderable whole. Most merchants who made money in Lowestoft during the early modern period did it by combining agricultural and maritime interests.

Eighty or ninety years after the manor roll was drawn up, the tithe accounts show the degree of diversity in the number and type of people involved in agriculture. As a generalisation, the first quarter of the eighteenth century had about sixteen or seventeen substantial farmers in the parish, about ten of whom were yeomen or husbandmen, the other six or seven merchants or brewers. The tier below them consisted of about the same number of middling men, the great majority of whom were either merchants, brewers, innkeepers or carters. Next came twenty or so small farmers, including seven or eight husbandmen, with the rest being largely composed of merchants, innkeepers and seafarers. And finally, at the bottom of this hierarchy, were seven or eight very small men: largely husbandmen, but with an innkeeper and a seafarer or two included. These sixty or more people were not all operating at the same time, but they were the ones who carried out farming over the twenty-five-year period assessed. There was, in addition to them, a further body of men (about thirty or so in all) from all the various occupation groups, including labourers, who farmed at occasional intervals by hiring a yard or piece of ground somewhere and growing a crop of hay or turnips on it. The practice has an air of opportunism about it: the chance for both affluent and poor alike to make some money.

The number of men involved in agriculture as a primary occupation was about twenty, which (as was pointed out in Chapter 4) constituted about 5% of family heads of the time – a proportion which increases to 14% if all sixty or so agriculturalists are considered and to 22% if the thirty occasional operators are added to the list. The tithe accounts make no reference to people who owned the land, just those who worked it – though, in a number of cases, they were almost certainly one and the same. On the evidence of wills of the time much of the parish's farmland seems to have been concentrated in the hands of merchants, brewers, yeomen and seafarers. Those people who hired land at this time usually paid £1 an acre per annum for arable use and 10s for meadow or pasture.[47] The usual term (nominally, at least) was seven years, but the period often fell short of this – especially among the less wealthy lessees. Lands for hire show a considerable and rapid turnover, with people often moving from one field or yard to another at annual or two-yearly intervals.

Essential differences in the nature of the 1618 manor roll and the parish tithe accounts are as important with regard to rental values as they are with regard to land use. The former document reveals that the various holders of land paid an annual lord's rent of 2d per acre, but does not divulge how much they leased it for; the latter discloses the rental charges levied by the people who owned the land, but does show how much they paid annually to the lord of the manor. On the evidence of a rental of 1675–6, lord's rent on the farmland must have increased by about 50% to 3d per acre at that stage – a development that was contrary to the trend observed throughout much of England, where freehold rents were fixed and not able to be increased.[48] It is possible to reach this conclusion because the overall value of the rental had increased by £4 4s 0d from that of 1618, and it is known from John Tanner's copyhold listing of 1725 that customary rents had not increased from the level of 100 years earlier. Therefore, the increase must have come from freehold land in the parish, which had produced a sum just short of £8 in 1618.

As far as farm sizes are concerned, it is difficult to give an overall view. Both manor roll and tithe accounts seem to suggest five or six nucleated holdings, plus a similar number which had lands located in different places – these ten or twelve units constituting the main farms in the parish. Thus, although the cultivated acreage had increased by about 25% between 1618 and 1700, the basic pattern of farm location had probably not changed a great deal. Only two specific acreages of the larger farms are known: the 123 acres of Magdalen College's Akethorpe estate and the sixty acres which constituted the holding at Smithmarsh.[49] In the case of the former, the land was sometimes leased to a single individual, such as John Jex (merchant) during the 1720s, but at other times it was split between two or three different lessees.

Once the corn tithes began to be paid to the incumbent, in 1749, it can be seen that seven individuals produced the whole of the income deriving from grain production.[50] The particular men named are those who owned or rented the nucleated holdings and

---

[47] According to A. Young, *Annals of Agriculture* (London, 1795), p. 293, the letting price of arable land had increased to at least £1 10s 0d per acre by the end of the eighteenth century.

[48] P. Bowden, 'Agricultural Prices, Farm Profits, and Rents', in *Agrarian History*, iv, 684. The point is made that, because of the effects of inflation, many freeholders had actually ceased making payments of any kind by the middle of the seventeenth century.

[49] The Akethorpe estate also had forty acres situated in the adjoining parish of Gunton. The Smithmarsh holding (also referred to in note 46) does not feature as one of the nucleated ones in the 1618 manor roll, so it must have developed after this time – perhaps originating in part from land taken into cultivation as the seventeenth century wore on.

[50] Six of the seven produced 95% of the money paid to the minister.

who, by the standards of the parish at least, were farming on a considerable scale. A typical English farm of the seventeenth century has been described as being somewhere between fifty and 100 acres.[51] Lowestoft had only five or six units of that size between about 1600 and 1750, and these correspond with the nucleated holdings previously referred to. Even some of the more substantial farmers revealed in the tithe accounts probably worked no more than thirty to thirty-five acres. And at the other end of the spectrum were the small men, who moved from field to field and yard to yard, making a living as best they could and filling in slack times with labouring work of different kinds – men like James Tuck, who was exempted from paying some of his tithe in 1724 because he was poor.

There is evidence in the tithe accounts to show that crop rotation was being practised on larger farms by the first quarter of the eighteenth century. The payment of small tithes (sometimes referred to as *herbage*) by men such as John Peach, William Utting and William Woodthorpe show that turnips, clover and sown grass were being grown on a rotational system, with intervals of one, two or three years between each crop – years in which corn would have been produced, though there is of course no mention of the crop until 1749, when the great tithes began to be paid to the incumbent. With up to 700 acres devoted to grain (out of the 800 or so available for arable cultivation), such rotation could only have been partial on the annual cycle. However, it was certainly a feature of farming practice in Lowestoft – though without the emphasis on sheep, which characterised what was to become known as the Norfolk four-course model.

Of the five or six nucleated holdings previously referred to, only three were centred on a dwelling-house and buildings located out of town.[52] There was very little other building in the parish at large, which means that much of the farming operation must have been conducted from out of the built-up area on a daily basis, with carts and other equipment moving from their owners' premises out into the fields and back again. Some sense of this is conveyed in the trial of the Lowestoft witches at Bury St Edmunds, in March 1662, in evidence given by one of the chief accusers of the two women, John Soan (yeoman). He testified how one of his carts, on its way from his house and yard in Tyler's Lane (now Compass Street) to the North Field, during harvest time, had impacted on the window sill of Rose Cullender's cottage in Swan Lane (now Mariners Street). She had then cursed him for the damage caused, which led to a series of disasters that day involving the cart.[53]

---

[51] D. B. Grigg, *Population Growth and Agrarian Change* (Cambridge, 1980), p. 88. The actual sizes per county are as follows: fifty acres in Leicestershire, eighty to 100 in Lincolnshire, and fifty to sixty in Essex and Oxfordshire. Holderness, *Pre-Industrial England*, p. 51, cites a median farm size of thirty to sixty acres for the country as a whole.

[52] These were situated as follows: in the south-west corner of the former South Field (Smithmarsh), at the south-western extremity of the former South-west Field, and in that part of the South-west Field close to the junction of Beccles Way with the track across Skamacre Heath. Using the topography of today, they were located as follows: at the junction of Norwich Road and Rotterdam Road (Smithmarsh), on the site of the BP filling-station at the Normanston Drive/Gorleston Road roundabout, and at the top end of Normanston Park near the Normanston Drive/Fir Lane roundabout (referred to as 'Nomanstowne' in contemporary documents).

[53] E. Gillingwater, p. 370, and Geis and Bunn, *Witches*, pp. 92–3.

Both people involved in this trivial incident (which was ultimately fatal for one of them!) lived in that part of town which merged into the adjacent countryside. There was no hard edge on the western perimeter of Lowestoft, but an area where the houses progressively thinned out into Goose Green and the surrounding fields. At least one commentator has written of the need to record the history of the many town-dwelling yeomen and husbandmen of the seventeenth and eighteenth centuries.[54] Lowestoft had its fair share of them (men like John Soan) and their presence acted as an integrating factor, bringing urban and rural elements together in one location. The town may have looked to the sea for its main economic stimulus, but it would also have been aware of the value of its farmland. It has been argued that the historiographies of urban and rural England have diverged as each has been studied in greater depth.[55] The account of Lowestoft's agriculture in this chapter might well be said to have produced synthesis of urban and rural elements rather than separation.

Alimentary industry

Malting and brewing

Much of the barley grown in Lowestoft would have been used to make malt, the light soils in the parish producing the thin-skinned, mealy type of grain best suited for the malting process.[56] Altogether at least three or four separate malt-houses in different parts of town were in operation at one time or another during the period of study and a similar number attached to the town's breweries. There were five main brewing premises over the same timespan (at least three of which were operational at the same time), a number of inns and alehouses produced their own beer on site, and some of the merchants also had small household breweries in their yards. The fuel used to produce the heat required for both malting and brewing must have been either wood or coal, both of which were readily available from outside sources and well-established supply routes.

If the previous paragraph appears to suggest rather a large production capacity for a town of 1,500 to 1,800 inhabitants, it should be remembered that the consumption of beer by people in the pre-industrial era was large by the standards of today. It has been estimated that, during the seventeenth century, 50% of the national income was spent on food and drink and that 33% of that proportion went solely on beer – which represents about 16% of the overall amount.[57] With Lowestoft acting as market-centre for the hundred, it is likely that a proportion of the malt processed in town (and perhaps some

---

[54] H. R. French, 'Urban Agriculture, Commons and Commoners in the Seventeenth and Eighteenth Centuries: The Case of Sudbury, Suffolk', *AHR* 48, II (2000), 171–2.

[55] J. A. Chartres, 'City and Towns, Farmers and Economic Change', *HR* 64 (1991), 138–9.

[56] Mathias, *Brewing*, p. 403.

[57] Wilson, *England's Apprenticeship*, p. 22. The large *per capita* consumption of ale and beer must have been partly due to the amount of salt which was used to preserve and season all kinds of food and would have produced constant thirst. Furthermore, water supplies were usually tainted, so it was safer to drink alcoholic beverages where the water had been boiled as part of the brewing process and where the action of fermentation also probably helped to kill certain bacteria.

of the beer) was transported to neighbouring parishes. And apart from local consumption on land, the other main stimulus to the production of malt and the brewing of beer was the victualling of fishing and trading vessels.

Large quantities of drink were consumed on board, as may be seen in the petition of 1670 (cited in the previous chapter, page 192), whereby leading townsmen asked Parliament to exempt them from the 2s 6d duty payable on each barrel of strong beer brewed for use on fishing craft – thus helping to make the industry more profitable during a period of economic difficulty. It was claimed that, at the time, the town had twenty-five vessels regularly engaged in cod and herring voyages, with an annual consumption of nine tuns per boat. This works out at a total of 56,700 gallons. Thus, the maritime factor can be seen to have been important in the matter of creating a demand for beer – and it probably became even more so after the town was granted port status. Not only did the local trading fleet increase in size, but a greater number of vessels from other places began to call on a more regular basis than before – and some of the masters would have taken the opportunity to re-provision their craft. That there was money to be made from brewing is unarguable and those men involved in the industry were always among the wealthier local inhabitants.

Milling

Between 1550 and 1750, Lowestoft had a total of five windmills for grinding corn into flour and meal, not all of which were working at the same time. Ownership of the earliest one recorded was vested in the churchwardens (it formed part of an endowment intended to provide funds for the maintenance of the parish church) and it stood on a piece of high ground about half a mile west-south-west of the town. It had served the community on the town's earlier site and its successors continued to do so after the move to the cliff was completed. When the latest one blew down during a gale, in 1608, there was no attempt to replace it.[58] After its disappearance, four other mills were built at various times, though the exact date of construction of only one of them is known.

The earliest was the one which stood on the southern part of Goose Green, near to the common watering-place, and which acted as a replacement for the one destroyed. A court baron minute of 10 December 1645 shows that the site had been in use for a considerable length of time before Robert Tooly (grocer) redeveloped the plot and built a mill of his own there.[59] Thirty-three years or so later, a man called William Francis erected yet another mill on the site and it remained in the family's possession until his grandson, Thomas, sold it in 1715 to Francis Stamford of Pakefield.

In addition to this particular building, there was also a mill on the North Common to the north-west of the lighthouse, about 300 yards from the edge of the cliff, and another somewhere on the manorial waste at the southern end of the parish (next to the boundary with Kirkley, in what is now Mill Road). Both of these appear in the early years of the surviving tithe accounts and each of them paid an annual sum of 10s to the

---

[58] It stood near the present-day confluence of St Peter's Street, Normanston Drive and Rotterdam Road, occupying land in the Hill Road/Halcyon Crescent area.

[59] SRO(L) 194/A10/8, p. 87. The mill stood close to the present-day junction of Thurston Road and St Peter's Street, on a site now occupied by the *Plaisir House* sheltered accommodation unit.

vicar, plus *herbage* on any crops grown in the yards. The southern mill is not mentioned after 1713, and may therefore have ceased to operate, and there are no references of any kind to the mill on Goose Green. In 1713, Robert Chandler (baker) built a mill to the south of Church Way (now St Margaret's Road), within about 250 yards of the parish church, on which he, too, paid tithe. This means that, from the end of the seventeenth century to the middle of the eighteenth, Lowestoft was served at any one time by two or three working windmills.

As well as the grinding of wheat, barley and rye into various grades of flour and meal, production of oatmeal also took place. Some of this would have been processed in the windmills, but during the first half of the seventeenth century there was also a specialist manufacturer in the parish. The burial registration of Thomas Smyter (yeoman) in September 1657 refers to him as 'an oatmeal man', and among the bequests he made to his wife was 'the oat meal mill as it now standeth with the appurtenances thereunto belonging'. His son, Thomas, who lived in Great Yarmouth, was given the chance to purchase this piece of equipment, if he so desired, for the sum of £6. Both this valuation and the distance from Lowestoft of the place where Thomas Smyter Jnr lived would seem to suggest that the appliance was neither large nor a permanent fixture. It may well have been a small machine powered by horse – variants of which could be found on farms all over England well into the twentieth century. The grinding of oats for human consumption was not typical, as the grain was mainly used at the time as provender for horses.

Cheese-making

To refer to cheese-making as an industry is something of a misnomer, as the activity was probably conducted on a relatively small scale in the parish. There was a certain amount of dairy farming carried on and the presence of a *lactage* tithe at one point suggests that the money due was considered worth having as part of the minister's income – even though collecting it was not easy. It is not possible to assess the scale of dairying in Lowestoft, but the native Suffolk cow (later to develop into the Red Poll breed) was noted for high milk-yield and the county generally was famous for the quality of its butter. In fact, it was the success of the latter which was responsible for the bad reputation which Suffolk cheese acquired (it was known in the county as *bang* or *thump*). As more and more butter was exported to London during the seventeenth and eighteenth centuries, the milk was skimmed ever more intensively, until in the end the cheese was being made from milk with very little fat content at all.[60] All that could be said for it was that it kept well, which is no doubt why large quantities were purchased during the eighteenth century by Army and Navy victuallers and by the masters of London's workhouses![61]

No comment can be made regarding the quality of cheese made in Lowestoft, but its manufacture is ascertainable in three probate documents. The will of Bartholomew

[60] For further information on the export of Suffolk butter to the capital, see F. J. Fisher, 'The Growth of the London Food Market', *EHR* 1st series v, ii (1935), 51.

[61] J. A. Chartres, 'The Marketing of Agricultural Produce', in *Agrarian History*, v, ii, 446, 458–9 and 489.

Howard (yeoman), in May 1608, records the bequest to his wife of three cheese vats, a cheese press and two cheese shelves. This man owned at least five cows and a heifer and he was probably producing butter as well as cheese because his will also refers to three milk bowls and a churn. Just over 100 years after he died, the inventories of Robert Lilley (farmer) and Thomas Gardner (husbandman) both reveal cheese-making enterprises of sorts. Lilley had a dairy in his house at Smithmarsh, which accommodated various milk bottles and containers, while the chamber above held a quantity of cheese worth £2 10s 0d. Among various items listed in the backhouse was a cheese tub. Gardner had three cheese vats standing in his buttery and a cheese press was located in the backhouse.

Such evidence is slender, but both the inventories cited are two out of only five such documents to have survived for farmers of one kind or another throughout the whole period of study. Thus, there may well have been more cheese-making in the parish than appearances suggest. Whether it was a commercial undertaking, in the sense of there being a surplus of the product for sale elsewhere, must remain in doubt. Lowestoft was not a specialist dairying parish of the Suffolk wood-pasture region and its cheese-making was probably aimed at satisfying local demand alone.

Other industry

Leather production

There were two tanneries in Lowestoft during the first half of the seventeenth century. These had probably been operational for some time before that, and they stood next to each other, below the cliff, at the north end of town.[62] The more northerly of the two ceased to operate at some point after the mid-century owing to the deaths of its owners, Edward Browne Snr and his son Edward, and to the consequent sale of the property. The oldest son of Edward Jnr (another Edward) carried on the family trade a little further to the north, in a premises abutting onto Cart Score, but he died in 1669 at the age of twenty-five and the business did not continue long after his demise.[63] The reason for three tanneries being located below the northern cliff is to be found in the local geology. Tanneries needed a plentiful supply of water, and there was a spring-line near the base of the cliff (still ascertainable today) where the overlying glacial sands and gravels met the underlying impervious clay. The most southerly of the tanneries, which abutted onto a common score leading up to the High Street (later known as Lighthouse Score), remained in operation throughout the whole of the seventeenth century and was still functioning in the 1720s when John Tanner compiled his list of copyhold properties in town.

In addition to favourable geological conditions, a plentiful supply of hides must have been available both from within the parish itself and from further afield to make the

---

[62] Both sites are now occupied, respectively, by the houses situated at the bottom of Lighthouse Score and by the Sparrow's Nest bowling-green and garden.

[63] The site is now part of the Sparrow's Nest gardens.

tanning process viable. The Hundred of Mutford and Lothingland was good cattle country, especially in those parishes which had extensive areas of grazing marsh alongside the rivers Waveney and Hundred and also beside the freshwater broad at Oulton.[64] Thus, Lowestoft not only had its own animal population to call upon, but that of the surrounding area. As local market town, it must have drawn in a considerable gathering of people every Wednesday – prominent among whom, if the leet court records are to be believed, were butchers from a number of communities in north-east Suffolk.[65] Their activities probably produced an extra source of raw material, because beasts slaughtered for food produced hides, as did milk–cows once they were past their ability to breed.

Finally, the last requirement for a successful leather industry was a plentiful supply of oak or ash bark from which to make the tanning agent. Lowestoft did not have a great deal of woodland itself, but there was a plentiful supply from places in the rest of the hundred, as well as from the neighbouring ones of Blything and Wangford. It is very likely that the sources of billet wood for the fish–curing operation in Lowestoft were also the ones which provided the bark needed for the tanning process. No evidence exists to show exactly how much leather was manufactured in the town, but the number of people involved in leather trades generally appears to suggest that it was not an inconsiderable amount.

Altogether, there are six curriers, sixteen tanners, nine tawers, four cobblers, thirty-seven cordwainers, two corvisers, twenty shoemakers, eleven glovers and four knackers (one of whom was also referred to as a collar-maker) recorded in the occupational data. In broad terms, and allowing for differing shades of meaning attaching to words at different times, *cobbler*, *corviser*, *cordwainer* and *shoemaker* may be taken as broadly synonymous with each other. This means that the first half of both the seventeenth and eighteenth centuries seem to have had a greater number of people involved in the production and repair of footwear than either the second half of the sixteenth or seventeenth – though whether this represents an economic state of affairs or vagaries in the sources cannot be conclusively decided.[66] Similarly, the number of curriers, tanners and tawers actually producing leather was also at its maximum during the first half of the seventeenth century – something which may represent another facet of the community falling back onto the land during the period of maritime difficulty previously referred to.

With regard to production of leather and leather goods generally, it is likely that Lowestoft made both the raw material and the finished items not only for its own inhabitants, but for those of neighbouring communities. Among the manorial officers elected each year at the leet court were two searchers and sealers of leather (both of whom were usually people connected with the trade), whose duty it was to ensure that the commodity manufactured in the town had been cured in the proper way and met

---

[64] The River Hundred still forms the southern boundary of the hundred.

[65] They usually feature in the documentation because of various kinds of trading irregularity.

[66] During the last two decades of the second half of the seventeenth century, the parish registers are less consistently detailed with regard to occupational data than they are for the rest of the time.

the required standards for its various uses. This quality control was regarded as being of some importance and one of the trading irregularities which was frowned upon when detected on the local market was the sale of boots or shoes made from horse-pelts rather than from the hides of cattle.

Linen production

With an average area of only one and a half acres under cultivation for hemp (as revealed in the tithe accounts), the quantity of fibre produced annually in the parish during the first half of the eighteenth century was small: no more than sixty stones in weight, if late eighteenth-century estimates of the crop's yield are valid.[67] The light soils would have produced the finer type of fibre suitable for linen-making rather than the coarser variety used for twine and canvas. Unfortunately, there are no figures available to show how much raw material was needed to make one yard of linen cloth, so there is no way of converting Lowestoft's annual quantity of hemp grown into yards' length of the finished product. Of the nine weavers who were recorded in the parish registers during the second half of the sixteenth century, none is referred to as being concerned with linen – and the presence of at least one dyer in town at this time would seem to suggest a connection with woollen textiles. Similarly, the burial of a shearman early on during the seventeenth century is indicative again of activity connected with wool rather than linen.

Having said that, the number of references in wills and inventories (especially the latter) connected with hemp or linen, or with the equipment used to produce fibre and spun thread, certainly suggest that production of cloth was a feature of the local economy – though it is not possible to assess the scale. Between 1560 and 1730, there are forty documents in the surviving probate material which contain references to raw hemp, to linen yarn and to finished cloth, as well as to *pashells, heckles, tow-combs* and *spinning-wheels*. Six of the people referred to were widows, the rest men, and the occupation groups concerned included merchants, craftsmen, seafarers, husbandmen and labourers – a feature which would, once again, seem to reflect the mixed nature of people's interests.

The presence of a *brake-house* in town, the building in which rotted hemp stems were crushed between rollers as part of the process to produce fibre, would seem to suggest an operation of reasonable scale.[68] Of the twenty weavers who feature either in the parish registers or probate documents between 1600 and 1670, four were definitely producing linen cloth and two of them are mentioned in a monograph on the East Anglian linen industry.[69] When Thomas Betts made his will in May 1616, he left his wife two dwelling-houses and £5 to each of his four sons. Forty-five years later, in August 1661, John Smith bequeathed a house to each of his two sons and another to his

---

[67] Young, *General View of Suffolk*, p. 146. The writer says that, on average, hemp yielded thirty-six to thirty-eights stones of fibre per acre, with an overall range of twenty-five to sixty stones.

[68] The building stood to the north of Rant Score, in a yard to the rear of what is now No. 67, High Street. John Tanner refers to it in his list of copyhold properties and it belonged to the Durrant family, husbandmen, brewers and lesser merchants.

[69] Evans, *Linen Industry*, p. 87.

daughter. Further evidence of his substance is suggested by the fact that, at the time the will was made, the older son John (aged thirty-two) was already well established as a grocer and the younger one Samuel (aged thirty) as a yeoman. These two examples serve to show that money could be made from linen-weaving and place a man in the more affluent levels of local society.

Conclusion

As a final word, it is probably appropriate to comment on the close relationship between agriculture and industry which has featured in this chapter. Land has been referred to as 'the single greatest flywheel of the economy',[70] and even though Lowestoft looked primarily to the sea for the larger part of its wealth, the soil nevertheless remained of considerable importance in its economy. Production of food and drink, manufacture of textiles and leather goods, and creation of tools and equipment of various kinds relied upon links with agriculture both in the immediate area and in the hinterland. There was no separation between industry and farming in the pre-industrial period because the former relied largely on the latter for raw materials. This has been widely observed over the whole of England and Lowestoft was no different in this respect from thousands of other communities – but it had the additional advantage of being able to draw upon both fishing and maritime trade as further sources of prosperity.

---

[70] P. Mathias, *The First Industrial Nation*, 2nd ed. (London, 1983), p. 29.

– 10 –

Parochial and Manorial Administration

Parochial officials

The two most important officers were the churchwardens, who were appointed annually and were responsible for administering certain public business on behalf of the parish.[1] They were drawn from the upper levels of local society, especially the merchants and tradespeople, but there was also a representation from among the more substantial craftsmen. One of their tasks was to see that the nave and tower of the parish church were kept in good repair (the chancel was the minister's responsibility) and they were further charged with maintaining the fabric of the almshouses and three public wells, as well as arranging apprenticeships for poor children and assisting with administration of the town's charitable lands. It was also their duty to ensure that the steps in certain of the scores did not deteriorate, that the Denes and Church Green were kept properly drained and free of noxious weeds, that all fences around these two common greens and around the churchyard were attended to, and that the parish boundary markers (known as *butts*) were properly maintained.[2] Any negligence in these matters was dealt with in the annual leet court and the requisite fines imposed.

In addition to two churchwardens, eight other parish officials feature in documentation of the second half of the seventeenth century and the early part of the eighteenth. First were the four overseers of the poor, elected annually by the vestry,[3] whose task was to supervise collection of the local rate and make the various payments. Then there were the surveyors of highways: men, once again, drawn from the upper levels of local society. No information is offered as to the procedure which led to their appointment, whether it was by the local vestry or by justices of the peace, but their presence is detectable in two sources. The first is the overseers' accounts book for 1656–91, where their names are recorded for the years 1673–77 and 1680–82, and the second is the leet court documentation. It is noticeable that, during the 1720s

---

[1] The vicar's warden was chosen by the incumbent during Easter week; the people's warden was elected by the parishioners on Whit Monday.

[2] Care of the two areas may not always have been their responsibility, but it was certainly part of their remit during the eighteenth century. See Reeve, 'Lowestoft and Lothingland', iv, 1–5 (SRO(L), 193/3/4).

[3] The Lowestoft vestry was an open one, consisting of incumbent and leading townsmen.

particularly, the two surveyors (*supravisores*) were sometimes presented for failing to maintain roadways in parts of the parish and for neglecting to see that certain drain-heads were kept clear of rubbish.[4]

Finally, the list of parochial officials was completed by the posts of parish clerk and sexton. The former, requiring some degree of literacy for effective administration, was filled by quite a wide variety of men possessing the necessary skills: draper, schoolmaster, tailor, cordwainer and fisherman, to name but five. Their standard of education varied a good deal, if various surviving records and documents are any indicator. Most singular are the parish register entries of the 1660s, written by Thomas Breathet (cordwainer): his handwriting is best described as 'esoteric' and his spelling as 'phonetic'. In fact, it is not difficult to ascertain a strong dialect intonation in the way that certain individual words are rendered. The post of sexton, being generally concerned with maintenance of the churchyard and the digging of graves, required no educational refinement, and the men who performed the function seem to have come largely from a lesser artisan background.

Relief of the poor

The parish rate

The largest administrative task by far to demand both the attention and the time of the parochial authorities in Lowestoft was relief of the poor. This weighty responsibility has been the subject of a previously published essay and must now be given due consideration here.[5] Overseers' accounts books have survived for the period 1656–1712 and they reveal much about the implementation of the Poor Law Act of 1601.[6] Four overseers were elected annually, which was double the number appointed in some other communities,[7] and it would seem that this practice had been in operation for a considerable time. The financial year ran from April to April and each of the overseers was responsible for collecting the poor-rate and making the various disbursements for a period of three months. At the end of the year, the four respective accounts were properly audited and signed by justices of the peace.

The overseers were drawn from the more substantial levels of local society, as was the case with all other offices in the parish, and the likely reason for there being four of them (rather than two) is that spreading the work-load in this manner made the task less onerous for those involved. The choice of men able to perform the duties required from among the merchants, the tradespeople, the seafarers and the more affluent craftsmen was quite a wide one – and once someone had fulfilled his quarterly

---

[4] The pit used by the surveyors to supply sand and gravel for road maintenance can still be seen. It lies immediately next to Normanston Drive, just north of the junction with Lakeland Drive.

[5] D. Butcher, 'The Relief of Poverty in a Pre-Industrial Suffolk Town: The Case of Lowestoft', in *Counties and Communities: Essays on East Anglian History Presented to Hassell Smith* (Norwich, 1996), pp. 241–57.

[6] SRO(L), 01/13/1/1 and 2.

[7] G. W. Oxley, *Poor Relief in England and Wales, 1601–1834* (Newton Abbot, 1974), p. 43.

commitment, he was not likely to be called upon again for at least another twelve or thirteen years, or even longer.[8]

The amount of poor-rate paid by parishioners, in accordance with statute, was based upon ownership of property in the parish, where such means of assessment was relevant, and on a person's financial situation where no real estate was held. One interesting feature of the system is that the richest people in the town were not necessarily the ones who paid the most. For instance, Samuel Pacy (merchant), who was the wealthiest man in Lowestoft during the second half of the seventeenth century, did not pay as much as his uncle Thomas (yeoman and brewer) – the difference being that Thomas Pacy owned more real estate in the parish than his nephew. The system employed seems to have been flexible in operation and productive of funds, and it confirms the statement made by one commentator that parish poor-rates were capable of raising increasing sums of money during the seventeenth and eighteenth centuries.[9]

From £56 2s 4d in 1656, the amount raised annually in Lowestoft had risen to £181 3s 6d by 1712. There were occasions when the total slipped back to below that of the previous year, but generally speaking the trend was strongly and noticeably upwards.[10] This was not due to any progressive fall in the number of people requiring relief, but to the increasing population and prosperity of the town, which made it possible for more money to be raised. The average annual contribution had risen from 6s 2d per head in 1656 to 15s 9d by 1712, while the average benefit received *per capita* during the same period rose from £2 2s 9d to about £4 10s 0d. The money due was collected from the wealthier parishioners on a weekly basis and on a quarterly one from the less affluent, while payments to those in need were always made weekly. An overall view of the system's operation is best achieved by a summary of the finances of six single years, taken at ten-year intervals.[11]

1656–7

Receipts: £56 2s 4d (174 contributors: 73 weekly, 101 quarterly)

Annual contributions:	Gentry, merchants and yeomen, 2s to 10s
	Tradespeople, 6d to 2s
	Seafarers, 3d to 2s
	Craftsmen, 3d to 6d

Payments: £53 8s 8d (25 recipients, on average; no extra spending)

| **Rates of weekly payment:** | Poor men (3), 4d to 8d |
| | Widows (8), 6d |

---

[8] If a mariner or fisherman were chosen to serve, he would have had to suspend his normal activities. There is no evidence of surrogates standing in to do the work.

[9] Clark, *Transformation of Towns*, p. 31.

[10] An increase of about 150% has been noted in the east Suffolk village of Cratfield (some twenty miles or so south-west of Lowestoft), where disbursements rose from £22 16s 8d in the second quarter of the seventeenth century to £54 9s 11d by its end. See L. A. Botelho, *Old Age and the English Poor Law* (Woodbridge, 2004), pp. 137–8.

[11] The decadal approach cannot be strictly adhered to because of certain incomplete accounts. The years to be considered are as follows: 1656–7, 1666–7, 1676–7, 1686–7, 1695–6 and 1707–8.

Spinsters (5), 4d to 6d

Children (9), 6d to 2s[12]

1666–7

Receipts: £75 15s 10½d (147 contributors: 56 weekly, 91 quarterly)

Annual contributions: Gentry, merchants and yeomen, 2s 6d to £1 1s 3d

Tradespeople, 1s to 4s

Seafarers, 4d to 1s 4d

Craftsmen, 4d to 1s 6d

Payments: £67 4s 2d (26 recipients, on average; £1 9s 9d extra spending)

Rates of weekly payment: Poor men (5), 4d to 1s 6d

Widows (12), 3d to 9d

Spinsters (2), 6d

Children (7), 1s to 1s 6d

1676–7

Receipts: £92 11s 8d (183 contributors: 70 weekly, 113 quarterly)

Annual contributions: Gentry, merchants and yeomen, 2s to 19s

Tradespeople, 1s to 4s 9d

Seafarers, 4d to 1s 6d

Craftsmen, 4d to 1s 1d

Payments: £67 15s 2d (32 recipients, on average; £16 6s 0d extra spending)

Rates of weekly payment: Poor men (6), 3d to 1s 6d

Widows (18), 4d to 1s

Spinsters (5), 3d to 4d

Children (3), 1s to 2s

1686–7

Receipts: £55 11s 6½d (225 contributors: 70 weekly, 155 quarterly)

Annual contributions: Gentry, merchants and yeomen, 3s to 9s 3d

Tradespeople, 1s to 4s

Seafarers, 6d to 1s 6d

Craftsmen, 6d to 1s 6d

Payments: £51 12s 2d (16 recipients, on average; £2 3s 0d extra spending)

Rates of weekly payment: Poor men (4), 6d to 1s 6d

Widows (8), 6d to 2s

---

[12] The children's allowance was for those boys and girls farmed out for someone to look after, usually because the parents were dead. The amount paid varied according to their age, with older ones being more expensive to keep. The task of looking after orphan children was usually undertaken by widows (with or without children of their own), who would have found the weekly allowance a means of boosting their income.

Spinsters (1), 2s 6d

Children (1), 2s

Married women (2), 1s to 2s[13]

1695–6

Receipts: £116 13s 11½d (237 contributors: 84 weekly, 153 quarterly)

Annual contributions: Gentry, merchants and yeomen, 6s 6d to 17s

                                 Tradespeople, 1s to 4s

                                 Seafarers, 6d to 2s

                                 Craftsmen, 6d to 2s

Payments: £112 0s 8d (33 recipients, on average; 14s 6d extra spending)

Rates of weekly payment: Poor men (6), 1s to 2s

                                 Widows (11), 1s to 2s 6d

                                 Spinsters (4), 1s to 1s 6d

                                 Children (5), 2s

                                 Married women (7), 1s to 2s 6d

---

1707–8

Receipts: £141 3s 5d (236 contributors: 73 weekly, 163 quarterly)

Annual contributions: Gentry, merchants and yeomen, 3s to £1 5s 0d

                                 Tradespeople, 1s to 4s

                                 Seafarers, 6d to 3s 6d

                                 Craftsmen, 6d to 2s 3d

Payments: £93 6s 3d (23 recipients, on average; £44 3s 9¼d extra spending)

Rates of weekly payment: Poor men (2), 2s

                                 Widows (7), 6d to 2s 6d

                                 Spinsters (7), 6d to 1s 6d

                                 Children (7), 1s 3d to 2s

The six years cited above are sufficient to demonstrate the basic structure of the system of poor relief in Lowestoft and most of the discernible trends (the notable increases in collections and extra spending for 1676–7 and for 1707–8 seem to have been largely due to the overseers purchasing stocks of materials for the poor to work on). The town's growth in population during the last quarter of the seventeenth century was not spectacular, but it can be seen in the increased number of

---

[13] The years 1682–87 show a fall both in the amount of money raised and the amount disbursed. The decrease resulted from fewer people requiring relief, but there is no apparent reason for the temporary improvement, other than the town flourishing commercially in the years immediately following the gaining of port status.

contributors.[14] Interestingly, the number of recipients did not increase in a similar fashion, which may have been at least partly the result of greater prosperity resulting from the awarding of port status. In fact, apart from one point during the 1680s, when it dropped for a time, the total number of people in receipt of poor relief in Lowestoft stayed much the same, varying between about twenty-three and thirty-five people annually. This was only about 1.75% of the town's population at any one time, which is a noticeably lower proportion of the deserving poor than has sometimes been cited for communities during the second half of the sixteenth century.[15] The figure may well serve to reinforce the opinion that the problem of the poor was less critical by 1700 than it had been 100 years before, largely owing to effective implementation of poor law legislation and refinement of its methods.[16] Unfortunately, there are no statistics relating to Lowestoft from the Elizabethan and Jacobean periods on which to base any comparisons and contrasts. The only piece of evidence which suggests that the town may have had a problem with poor people is that cited in Chapter 3, in the section on population mobility, when the annual leet court of 1582 attempted to prevent residents giving shelter to the migrant poor by imposing prohibitive financial penalties. The reference is a frustrating one, because it stands in isolation from any corroborative material, there being no surveys extant for Lowestoft of the kind which exist for Ipswich, Norwich, Salisbury and Warwick.[17]

The categories of people granted relief in Lowestoft during the second half of the seventeenth century and the early years of the eighteenth, as shown in the six representative years above, are predictable enough and represent those groups least able to fend for themselves. There must have been considerably more people just above them in the social and economic hierarchy who were not in sufficiently dire need to merit relief but whose situation was far from comfortable.[18] There is no way of ascertaining their numbers accurately, but family reconstitution material suggests that 25%–27% of the town's population had a residency period of three years or less and many of those people would have been among the least fortunate members of society. With regard to the recognised indigent or deserving poor in Lowestoft during the years covered by the overseers' accounts, the majority were widows (56%), followed by poor men (20%), spinsters and married women (13%) and children (11%).[19] The overall annual payments

[14] Botelho, *Old Age*, p. 49, records the opposite happening in Cratfield during the second half of the seventeenth century. Here, the number of contributors fell, increasing the burden on those having to pay.

[15] Clark and Slack, *Towns in Transition*, p. 121. The figure given here is 4% to 5%.

[16] *Ibid.*, p. 124.

[17] J. Webb (ed.), *Poor Relief in Elizabethan Ipswich*, SRS, ix (Ipswich, 1966); J. F. Pound (ed.), *The Norwich Census of the Poor, 1570*, NRS, xl (Norwich, 1971); P. Slack (ed.), *Poverty in Early Stuart Salisbury*, Wiltshire Records Society, xxxi (Devizes, 1975); Beier, 'Social Problems', in Clark, *Country Towns*, p. 60.

[18] P. Slack, 'Social Problems and Social Policies', in *The Traditional Community Under Stress* (Milton Keynes, 1977–8), p. 86. The book referred to is volume 4 of the OU's *English Urban History, 1500–1870*.

[19] There were very few married women in receipt of relief. Such ones as there were usually had husbands who were either sick or incapacitated.

received during the 1670s (amalgamating these four categories) were c. £2 10s 0d per capita on average, far more generous than those disbursed in York (£1 11s 0d), and those received during the late 1690s (c. £4 0s 0d per capita) were better than the sums paid out in Norwich.[20] Regrettably, there is no way of accessing any prior negotiations which must have taken place before grants were made.[21]

It is always dangerous when attempting to convert statistics into something with the feel of humanity about it, yet the impression derived from study of the Lowestoft overseers' accounts is one of care being shown to the least fortunate members of society. Katherine Garret, for instance, described as a beggar in her burial registration of September 1665, had been drawing 8d per week from the parish for at least nine years. Even more intriguing is the case of Prudence and Robert Grene, the children of John Grene (husbandman). Prudence was baptised in November 1632, but her brother's christening is not recorded. In September 1672, at an age when most of her contemporaries would have been married for at least fifteen years (had they lived that long!), she began to draw a weekly allowance of 9d for Robert, payment which had increased to 1s 6d by the end of the century.[22] Her will of July 1704 made reference to this payment in the request that Dorothy Hudson, her executor, wife of Roger Hudson (tailor), should take care of Robert and receive the parish allowance. The circumstances behind that particular little family drama can only be guessed at.

As well as regular disbursements to the long-term poor, there were also 'contingency payments' made to all kinds of people on a short-term basis, according to particular need (these form a noticeable part of the 'extra spending' shown in the decadal breakdown above). Mary Bentley, for instance, drew 1s 9d a week during her husband's illness in 1666, and there are numerous other references to people being 'in distress', 'in want' or 'in sickness', with varying amounts of money granted – though specific details of individual misfortune are unfortunately never recorded. In 1675, an unnamed woman who had broken her leg at the house of John Hunt received a payment of 2s 6d and somebody else (also unnamed) received the sum of 14s for acting as 'a keeper for old widow Bollard and minding her' – the woman receiving this care being the relict of a seafarer.

Specialist medical care also features from time to time, with payments made to local doctors for success in curing the sick, while the end of life was given due dignity for those who could not afford it in the provision of burial clothes, at about 3s per set (such as those which clad Henry Atkins, a sawyer), and of coffins, at about 6s or 7s each. By 1681, the widow Bollard (previously referred to) had recovered sufficiently from her indisposition to 'wind' the corpse of Robert Emeris (shoemaker) in a five-yard length of

---

[20] Slack, 'Social Problems', p. 94, table 5. The Norwich figure given (£3 17s 0d) is actually for the year 1700.

[21] S. Hindle, *On the Parish? The Micro-Politics of Poor Relief in Rural England, c. 1550–1750* (Oxford, 2004), p. 452.

[22] Prior to this, from December 1659, Robert Grene had been cared for by Richard Brissingham, who kept *The Dolphin* inn at the northern end of the High Street. Brissingham seems to have specialised in looking after needy and aged men (as well as orphaned children), because he had three or four of them in his charge at any one time and drew their parish allowance. There is nothing to suggest why Robert Grene became dependent on the parish.

cotton shroud (cost 5s) and be given 1s for her service.[23] Nor did the care stop at local people. During 1675, a sum of 1s was given to 'an officer that came beyond Sea', while the following year 'a traveller with a pass' was given 6d to help him on his way – not the first time that this had happened, and not to be the last. Finally, 'two men that came out of Turkey' were each given 6d in 1676, though without any indication of their origins or how they came to be in town.

In studying the Lowestoft accounts, it is clear that the overseers were sufficiently prudent not to spend more on relief than was able to be raised from local contributions. There were always a few pounds left over to form a credit balance. Furthermore, given the way that individual allowances to those in need rose over the course of time, the suggestion which has been made that poor relief may sometimes have provided a mild stimulus to urban demand for goods and services is perhaps correct.[24] The spending power of the deserving poor in Lowestoft did increase in real terms; and while the payments made cannot be termed generous, they were better than those which many other communities were prepared to disburse. Another factor to be borne in mind in the whole matter of relieving poverty is that the cancellation of trade debts in favour of people unable to repay what they owed has been judged to have been of greater importance than the collection of the poor rate itself.[25] Indeed, it has been claimed that the passing of the formative Poor Law Act of 1601 was an attempt to combat the rising number of defaults by providing a minimum, predictable income (known to everyone in a community), in the form of a cash dole, to reduce the amount of trade credit which needed to be extended to the poor.[26]

The attitude of those who contributed to the maintenance of people less fortunate than themselves is impossible to assess. Comment has been made how, by the late seventeenth century, wealthy inhabitants of parishes had, in the administration of poor law, an effective means of disciplining the poor, many of whom were seen as potentially and actually criminal.[27] The system of relief became more a means of maintaining social order and preventing civil unrest than of extending Christian charity to people in need.[28] And even the state of poverty itself was sometimes construed as criminal by a peculiarly Puritan interpretation of God's favour manifesting itself in the rewards which personal industriousness could bring.[29] While such ideas may have been current in post-Restoration England, it is wise not to generalise too readily concerning their effect. There is no evidence in the Lowestoft documentation to suggest whether or not poor law administration was manipulated in such a way as to exercise social discipline and control. The account books, in so far as figures

---

[23] This is an interesting departure from legislation of the time which required that people be buried in woollen shrouds – a measure introduced in order to boost the native textile industry.

[24] Clark and Slack, *Towns in Transition*, p. 109.

[25] Muldrew, *Economy of Obligation*, p. 305.

[26] *Ibid.*, p. 311.

[27] J. A. Sharpe, *Crime in Early Modern England, 1550–1750* (London, 1984), p. 91.

[28] Slack, 'Social Problems', pp. 98–9.

[29] G. Taylor, *The Problem of Poverty* (London, 1969), pp. 19–20.

can say anything, seem to suggest that the system was operated with a little more humanity than was the case in a number of other places.[30]

The apprenticing of poor children

This task fell to the churchwardens, as mentioned previously. In all likelihood, the work had occupied them from early on in the overall period under review, but there are no relevant surviving records until 1656 – the year that the surviving overseers' accounts begin. From then onwards, the placing of orphan boys and girls with employers can be seen as part of the provision made to relieve both their predicament and that of the parochial authorities and it constituted part of the extra spending incurred over and above the regular weekly payments made to the needy. In 1699, apprenticeship details began to be recorded in a separate book.[31] Between that year and 1730, eighty-nine youngsters (sixty boys and twenty-nine girls) were found employers, either because their parents could not support them or because their fathers had died and left the family in reduced circumstances. It has been claimed that the role of apprenticeship in alleviating poverty has been exaggerated, simply because survival of records has made it seem more important than it really was.[32] However, the eighty-nine children who were bound to different masters would have represented a considerable saving on the local poor-rate. It cost somewhere between about £1 and £2 to apprentice a boy or girl within the town (it was more expensive to arrange employers further removed), whereas annual expenditure on their upkeep if fostered out was between £3 and £5.

Most of the placements were made within the town itself (seventy-three altogether), but the sixteen children who could not be provided for within the community were placed in service elsewhere. Seven of them went into nearby parishes: Oulton (a boy and a girl), Corton (a boy), Blundeston (a girl), Kirkley (a boy and a girl) and Kessingland (a boy). Another six were sent to places within a ten-mile radius of Lowestoft: Barnby (a girl), Benacre (a boy), Shadingfield (a girl), Beccles (a girl), Great Yarmouth (a boy) and Thorpe-next-Haddiscoe (a girl). Two more were found homes further away in Norfolk (a boy being sent to Norwich and a girl to Bunwell), while the last one of all (a girl) went to an employer in London. On the evidence of children detectable in the family reconstitution process, the age range of boys and girls who were bound apprentice varied between nine and fourteen years.

Within Lowestoft itself, any man who declined to take an apprentice was fined the sum of £4 (no women are mentioned as employers). There were fifty-four refusals in all, from forty-nine different people, and the occupational groups they were drawn from

---

[30] Hindle, *On the Parish?*, p. 452, comments on the danger of interpreting overseers' accounts in such a way.

[31] SRO(L), 01/13/1/3. The document in question is a book containing settlement orders and apprenticeship details. Rutledge, *Yarmouth Apprenticeship Indentures*, 18, 21–2, 25, 29–30, 39–40, 46–7 and 54, records details concerning the apprenticing of Lowestoft boys to masters in the Norfolk town. Of the eleven cases cited, all of them falling between 1584 and 1628, seven of the boys were from families where the father had died. There are also two examples of Yarmouth boys being apprenticed to Lowestoft masters.

[32] Oxley, *Poor Relief*, p. 75.

constituted a substantial cross section of the middling and upper levels of local society. Merchants, yeomen, grocers, drapers, brewers, doctors, innkeepers, mariners, butchers, bakers, blacksmiths, locksmiths, carpenters, sailmakers and husbandmen were all represented. Presumably, the £4 fine was not considered excessive by the people who had to pay it (they may even have thought it economic, compared with the expense of taking on a boy or girl), while the authorities were also probably satisfied with the level of imposition. It was, after all, two to four times the amount that had to be to be paid in order to bind youngsters to masters in the town, but a good deal less than was required to place them in another parish (according to the surviving information, this ranged from £6 5s 6d to £11 12s 0d). Just for the record, it is worth pointing out that a number of the men who refused to take on apprentices had taken them, or did take them, on other occasions.

The almshouses

The town had at least two sets of almshouses in use before the end of the sixteenth century. The better-documented of them was a building on the north side of Fair (or Fairstead) Lane, which occupied the second plot to the west of the junction with Old White Horse Lane (otherwise known as West Lane).[33] Reference to it is made in a rental of June 1545 and it seems to have had its origins in the second half of the fifteenth century, because the document (drawing on old information) mentions it as once having been connected with John Manyngham, vicar from 1456–78.[34] There is also a leet court minute of 1585 connected with it, when the churchwardens were fined 3d for not sufficiently maintaining the road surface outside.[35] The building had three units within it, each consisting of a downstairs room with chamber above.

During the early years of the eighteenth century the property was amalgamated with the one immediately to the west to provide four units, and the town's residential capacity for the elderly infirm was further increased in 1715 by the purchase of the house which stood next on the west to this consolidated property. The sum of £80 needed for the acquisition was provided by James Hocker (labourer), who had died of smallpox in December 1710 and who, having no immediate family, had left his whole estate (amounting to £120 in value) to charitable uses in the town. The dwelling purchased from this bequest provided another structure of four downstairs rooms with chambers above, which should have given the vestry eight units for the accommodation of elderly people.[36] However, two of the first set of four had been destroyed by fire in 1707 and were not rebuilt until twenty or so years later, at which time the block in which they were situated served the parish as a small workhouse until the union building at Oulton opened in 1765.

In addition to the properties in Fair Lane, there was another almshouse unit on the

---

[33] Fair Lane was also known as Almshouse Lane, after the charitable housing. It is now called Dove Street. Old White Horse Lane, or West Lane, is now part of Lowestoft's inner relief road, Jubilee Way.

[34] SRO(L), 194/A10/71.

[35] SRO(L), 194/A10/4, p. 111.

[36] Botelho, *Old Age*, p. 12, defines the term 'elderly' as applying to people of about 50 years of age.

freehold land west of the High Street, at its southern end.[37] This is also referred to in the rental of 1545, and it provided at least two dwellings, but no evidence has been discovered to give even a tentative estimate of its founding date. Thus, civic almshouse provision during the late sixteenth century and throughout the seventeenth totalled at least five units, while by 1715 it had risen to at least eight. Both complexes were administered by panels of trustees, but the churchwardens were also involved in the overall jurisdiction.[38] Other members of the town's elderly deserving poor (who formed the majority of those in receipt of relief) must have lived mainly either in rented accommodation or in homes shared with relatives. There is no evidence of such people 'clubbing together' to provide themselves with shelter under one roof, as has been observed in at least one other Suffolk community.[39]

As well as parochial almshouses, there was also a privately endowed facility for four needy women on the south side of Bell Lane at its southern extremity, where it abutted onto Goose Green.[40] It had four downstairs rooms, with chambers above, and was called 'St Martin's Hospital' in honour of the man responsible for its foundation. Martin Brown was the second son of Edward Browne (tanner), his baptism being recorded in the parish registers in May 1646. His mother and father had both died by the time he was three years old, leaving him, his older brother Edward (aged five) and his younger brother Thomas (aged five months) in the care of their paternal grandfather (also named Edward and also a tanner). When Edward Snr died in October 1652, the youngest child had already been dead for nearly seven months and the two surviving children were committed to the care of their mother's brother, Martin Folkes (gentleman) of Rushbrooke, near Bury St Edmunds.

Both boys were well endowed with money and property from their mother's and their grandfather's wills, and at some point Martin was apprenticed to a merchant in Rotterdam. He became a notable trader there himself, a process aided by marrying his employer's widow, and he lived in the city for the rest of his life. However, he obviously retained an interest in the place of his birth and it is likely that he visited it from time to time during the course of business and also to maintain family contact with his relatives, the Wildes, and with his brother's widow, Susan Church (née Pacy). He was the largest contributor to the fund for the rebuilding of the Town Chapel in 1698 (he gave £50) and, when he died, he left money for the building of almshouses in his native town.[41]

---

[37] It occupied a site in the vicinity of what are now shops at nos 113–115, High Street.

[38] There were bequests of money made in three wills of the second half of the sixteenth century for the repair and building of almshouses: those of Joone Wiseman (1566) William Wylde Snr (1569) and Alice Rivers (1578). In addition to these, the will of Thomas Annot (1577) makes specific reference to the provision of two almshouses, but they do not seem to have been constructed.

[39] Botelho, *Old Age*, p. 123. Payment of poor people's rent is regularly recorded in the Lowestoft accounts.

[40] The site today is occupied by a children's play-area, at the junction of Crown Street West with Thurston Road.

[41] For the subscription list, see NRO, PD 589/112: the Lowestoft Town Book. Martin Brown's donation is recorded on p. 56.

These were duly erected in 1716 on the site of a cottage which had been purchased and cleared away. James Wilde (merchant) supervised the work and also acted as trustee of the almshouses themselves.[42]

The town lands

There were two separate lots of town land, with a combined area of 106 acres. The larger of the holdings, some seventy-seven and a half acres (including some dole land and a windmill), was the accumulation of various bequests made over a long period towards repair and maintenance of the parish church. The smaller one, of twenty-eight and a half acres, was land purchased with the £60 left by William French (merchant) in April 1529 to finance the gift of 1d per week to each of thirteen poor people – the money to be drawn from the rents produced. Both lots of land were dispersed in different parts of the parish and the location of a number of plots changed over the years as various sales and transfers took place. The total acreage, however, remained the same.[43]

According to the memorandum book of the Rev. John Arrow (vicar from 1760–89), there was trouble over the implementation of William French's will and it was some time before the lands were purchased.[44] Later, the property came under control of the powerful Jettor family via the re-marriage of French's daughter, Agnes. The Jettors are said to have made weekly payments to the thirteen poor people, but to have kept surplus money deriving from an increase in rental values and to have conveyed the lands to their own heirs as part of the family inheritance (this must have occurred during the 1540s or 50s). Eventually, an appeal was made to the Court of Chancery, which decreed that a proper enfeoffment of the lands be made and the property administered in accordance with the donor's wishes. After Robert Jettor had been convicted of recusancy in May 1560, two local men, George Chandler (innkeeper) and Isaac Rivet (yeomen), seized French's lands for their own use, only to be thwarted by the townspeople, who once again appealed to Chancery.[45] The memorandum book records that a new enfeoffment took place on 3 January 1585, when Edmund Jettor and others appointed John Arnold (merchant), John Wild (merchant) and Matthew Fullwood (merchant and scrivener) and others to be trustees.

A more serious misuse of revenues deriving from both lots of town land came to light in 1615, though it was not the kind of malversation for direct personal advantage noted elsewhere – in Salisbury and Winchester, for instance.[46] The money had been used to

[42] E. Gillingwater, p. 299, says that Brown left a fortune of over £30,000 when he died, half of which went to his widow's family and half to the heirs of Martin Folkes.

[43] A churchwardens' map of 1761 shows the distribution of the lands. See SRO(L), 61/2.

[44] NRO, PD 589/92, p. 80.

[45] The fines imposed on the Jettor family can be found in volumes xviii, lvii and lxi of the Catholic Record Society's printed series.

[46] P. Slack, 'Poverty and Politics in Salisbury, 1597–1666', in Clark and Slack, *Crisis and Order*, p. 179. The writer cites a Chancery inquisition of 1599 which found that £938 worth of bequests was not being used for the intended purposes and that the money was often being diverted to the undeserving. A. Rosen, 'Winchester in Transition, 1580–1700', in Clark, *Country Towns*, p. 160, notes that charitable funds were often used to provide loans to aldermen and to local gentry, with flexible repayment dates.

defray expenses incurred by the town in certain legal cases, especially that of 1597 with Great Yarmouth concerning herring-trade rights. That suit alone was said to have cost £120, and over £210 worth of funds had been misapplied in helping to defray these and other costs (the latter including a lawsuit defending the town's free grammar school). The matter was made public at an inquisition held in town on 4 September and considerable detail concerning the proceedings is preserved in the form of transcriptions made by John Arrow.[47] The prime mover in the misdirection of money was found to be Thomas Warde (yeoman), a prominent person in the town's affairs, and a number of the lessees of the lands in question were also adjudged to have been aware of what was going on. They included William Bentley (the vicar), John Arnold, William Wilde, Edmund Hill and William Lucas (all merchants), Simon Page (weaver), Robert Coe (yeoman), John Tyler (scrivener), Thomas Dobson (boatman) and Adam Game (husbandman?).

By the time the inquisition was held, Bentley, Wilde, Hill, Page and Dobson were all dead. The rental value of the lands was said to be £20 per annum from William French's bequest and £40 per annum from the rest. Little could be done about malpractice of the past, but the local gentlemen who headed the enquiry took care to see that nothing similar would occur in future.[48] The concluding decretal order is reproduced in the parish tithe accounts book and among its requirements was the setting-up of a new body of twenty-four feoffees from among 'the most Honest & best sufficient Inhabitants of the said town'.[49] Predictably, the men were drawn from those ranks of society which filled all other public offices and they were to serve until their deaths. When only four of the twenty-four were left alive, a new panel of trustees was to be appointed – a practice which continued until 1768.

Among other directives issued were these: a maximum of £20 per annum was to be spent on poor relief, inclusive of William French's 13d a week (which amounted to £3 0s 8d); a further £10 was to be disbursed annually on apprenticing poor children and supplying a stock of materials with which to set poor people to work; and up to £20 a year was to be devoted to church repairs.[50] The new seven-year leases that were prepared yielded anything between £69 and £92 per annum during the period covered in this book. The income was kept separate from the poor-rate contributions and, as far as can be ascertained, was used for its intended purposes.

---

[47] NRO, PD 589/92, pp. 1–12. The inquisition had its origins in the Act of Charitable Uses (1601), which gave the Lord Chancellor the power of appointing commissions to enquire into abuses.

[48] The commission was composed of the following men: Sir Thomas Playters (of Sotterley), John Wentworth Esq. (of Somerleyton), Nicholas Garnies Esq. (probably of Ringsfield), Thomas Feltham and George Bonham.

[49] NRO, PD 589/80, pp. 57–9. The decree was made on the day of the enquiry itself and confirmed by Lord Chancellor Ellesmere on 10 July 1616.

[50] The stock of materials referred to would probably have been hemp fibre, which people would have spun into either twine or linen thread (depending on its type and quality) in their own homes.

Private bequests and donations

In attempting to establish basic motivation for charitable giving in England, the following comment has been made: 'It perhaps simplifies a process far too much to say that men of the Middle Ages gave alms as an act of piety while men of the Sixteenth Century gave, and much more generously, under the dictate of social need.'[51] The nature of bequests by Lowestoft people during the late mediaeval period is not part of this chapter's remit, but the surviving wills of those people who lived during the second half of the sixteenth century certainly show a considerable number of legacies aimed at the resident poor of the parish. Altogether, cash bequests totalling £396 6s 5d were made between 1565 and 1599, and there were often donations of goods in kind to accompany the money. The following 130 years saw £249 15s 4d bequeathed, which may say something about people's generosity or the relative needs of the town at the time they were living. The upturn in the amounts of cash left for charitable uses during the first half of the seventeenth century, noted as a trend nationally, is not reflected in the Lowestoft figures.[52] Between 1600 and 1649, eighteen testators out of a total number of 129 left only £25 13s 4d to the poor.

The sum of £396 6s 5d bequeathed between 1560 and 1599 came from forty-five testators out of 102 in all. Fifteen of them were merchants and fourteen were widows (largely the relicts of merchants and seafarers). The other sixteen consisted of the following trades and occupations: five seafarers, three tradespeople (two butchers and a merchant tailor), three craftsmen (housewright, carpenter and thatcher), two labourers, one professional (a surgeon), one yeoman and one man simply referred to as 'Mr'. The smallest bequest to the poor of the parish was that of 1d, made in February 1578 by Robert Wylde (sailor); the largest was the £100 left by Thomas Annot (merchant) in October 1577. The latter gift was to be disbursed at the rate of £5 per annum for a period of twenty years. Annot also left funds for the provision of two almshouses (which seem never to have been built), the endowment for a free grammar school and a further sum of £100, which was to be split up into £25 amounts and loaned to four honest men at 1% interest.

Other bequests took note of poor people's particular needs. Ann Girling (widow) left her house, yard and barn near the market place so that the rents could be used to provide wood billets for domestic fuel. Margaret Coldham (merchant's widow) had the same intention when she ordered her executors to spend £40 on the purchase of lands to provide an income for buying wood and coal. Margaret Jettor (gentleman's widow) left all her faggot wood to the poor of the parish, as well as 20s in cash, while Robert Lawer wished some of the money from the sale of his house to be spent on providing a chaldron of coal (two and a half tons) and 1,000 wood billets each Christmas for a period of ten years. Some people left money to be spent on food and drink, which was to be distributed on the day of burial, thereby maintaining a link with mediaeval times, when such practice had been common. Most interesting and varied of all was the legacy of Joone Wiseman (widow). When she made her will in October 1566, she left £6 to

[51] W. K. Jordan, *Philanthropy in England, 1480–1660* (London, 1959), p. 146.
[52] *Ibid.*, p. 246.

be spent on blind and sick people, three new smocks to be given by her executor where he considered greatest need to be, and nine shrouds to be kept by him for people who had no winding-sheet when they came to be buried.[53]

The much smaller sum donated for the first half of the seventeenth century has already been referred to. The largest single bequest was £5 6s 8d from Edward Sparrow (yeoman) and the smallest was the 6s 8d bequeathed by John Knightes (innkeeper). Sparrow's legacy was to be spent partly on three barrels of beer (he owned *The Spreadeagle* inn!) and 240 penny-loaves, with the handout of these victuals and any remaining cash to be made at the Town Chapel on the day of his burial. There were three merchants and four widows among the total of eighteen donors and their collective contributions were worth £4 and £6 respectively. The other benefactors' social and occupational groupings were as follows: two gentlemen, three yeomen (including Edward Sparrow), a minister, a brewer, a tanner, an innkeeper (John Knightes), a sailor and a carpenter.

The reason for such a small overall sum being bequeathed for charitable uses during the first half of the seventeenth century is not entirely clear. It may have had something to do with the effect on the town's population of two serious plague outbreaks in 1603 and 1635 and the depressed state of the fishing industry at the time. It is also possible that if poor-rate collections had been introduced to the town soon after the Act of 1601, this might have had a diminishing effect on bequests made to those in need. Many people would not have been prepared to pay twice!

There was something of a recovery in the amount of charitable giving after 1650 – not in the number of donors, but in the total sum donated. Even so, the sum of £98 10s 0d bequeathed by the sixteen testators (out of 144 in all) was still well short of the sixteenth-century figure. In fact, over half the amount came from one man. James Wilde (merchant) left £50 in August 1682, to be used as thought best by his widow, his children and the leading townspeople.[54] Of the sixteen donors, six were merchants, two were widows (of merchants), and the other eight were made up as follows: two gentlemen, a draper, a doctor, a tanner, a yeoman, a mariner and a single man, who seems to have been working for one of the town's brewers. Richard Gilbert was no mere servant, because he made cash bequests totalling £58 in his will, 10s of which was to be divided among ten poor widows in the town.[55] One of the gentleman, Henry Coe (he belonged to a local family of merchants and yeomen, and had grandified himself), showed a concern for conventional religious observance in his bequest He left £5 in his will of October 1680, to be distributed among 'such of the poor of the town of Lowestoft aforesaid as come constant to divine service at Church'. The payment of the money was to be left to the discretion of his daughter and executrix, Thomasine Arnold, wife of a brewer.

---

[53] Her executor was William Nashe, the vicar, father of the Elizabethan writer Thomas Nashe.

[54] The money was eventually used to fund a bread charity for the poor, the income being raised from rents on a messuage below the cliff at the north end of town (purchased from the legacy). The area is now occupied by the Lowestoft Maritime Museum and the Sparrow's Nest bowling greens.

[55] He left an identical amount to the same number of husbandless women in Kirkley and Pakefield.

The final phase, from 1700 to 1730, saw only four people out of 132 (whose wills have survived) make charitable bequests. The legacy of James Hocker (labourer) has already been referred to in the section concerning almshouse provision, and his £120 was the largest one-off amount. John Hayward (mariner) did not leave a finite sum, but he made provision in March 1717 for his son, Robert, to disburse £2 12s 0d per annum out of the rents from family property 'for as long as ever they the said Churchwardens and Trustees shall think fit to accept'. The money was to be spent at the rate of 1s a week on fourteen loaves of bread, which were to be given away each Sunday afternoon after divine service to fourteen poor people chosen by the churchwardens.

Very different in tone was the bequest made by Joseph Pake (surgeon). When he died in April 1713, he left £2 to the poor of the parish, but he seems to have been unsure about his standing in the local community – or, at least, with some elements of it. The money bequeathed was to be paid out at the discretion of the churchwardens and overseers, but with this proviso: 'if any of the poor shall molest or disturb my funeral, or trouble the house, such of them shall have no share or part of the said money.' This does not suggest a man at peace with either his less fortunate neighbours or himself – unless, of course, he was worried about his burial day being disrupted by people wanting a share of the legacy there and then.[56] Nevertheless, it is tempting to speculate as to his behaviour towards the lower orders.

The last bequest made to the poor during the first three decades of the eighteenth century was that of James Wilde (merchant) in November 1723. He was the trustee of St Martin's Hospital almshouses, previously referred to, and when he died he left 5s to each of the four female occupants. He also made a directive to the churchwardens to the effect that they were to replace the present inmates, as vacancies arose, with widows and old maids who were judged to be most in need of accommodation.

Charitable donations: causes beyond the parish

It would be inappropriate not to take the opportunity of demonstrating awareness on the part of Lowestoft's inhabitants of the wider world beyond the town and of the needs existing there. Stuck into the pages of a woollen burials register (which was later used as vicar's day-book) is a list of briefs which were the subject of public collections made at Sunday morning service between 1681 and 1698.[57] There are twenty-six appeals listed, with a combined amount raised of £76 18s 10¼d. Fires in various English parishes, from Devon to Yorkshire, account for seventeen of the funds launched, but the biggest single raiser of money by far was an appeal made on behalf of Irish Protestants who had fled

---

[56] Somewhat ironically, perhaps, Joseph Pake's grave-slab, in the middle of the chancel of St Margaret's Church, has its inscription end with the following words: *Liberius frui Coepit Charissima Sui Memuriae relicta* – 'He begins to experience the reward of a greater freedom, most dear in the memory of those left behind'.

[57] NRO, PD 589/3.

into England.[58] This is the only entry which is not dated (it fell somewhere between 1 June 1685 and 7 May 1691, which perhaps identifies it with the siege of London-derry in the summer of 1689), and it produced a total of £38 4s 6d. Two other collections made in the cause of Protestantism were those of 4 September 1681 and 2 July 1682. The former raised £3 8s 10d for the relief of churches in Lower Poland, while the latter brought in £5 14s 8d for the assistance of Huguenot refugees who had crossed the Channel to settle in England.

The collection and payment of tithe

An important matter of local financial administration, at least as far as the vicar was concerned, was that of tithe. The Lowestoft incumbent was entitled to the parish *small tithes*, which were those of *herbage* (all field crops other than corn), *lactage* (milk and dairy products), pigs and poultry, and to half of one share of the profits made by each fishing vessel in operation – all of which have been previously discussed.[59] The total value of the vicarage was declared to be £10 1s 0d in 1566 and it was never a particularly productive living because even by 1707 the combined value, together with that of the parish of Kessingland, some five or six miles distant, did not exceed £100.[60] In order to boost the minister's stipend, it was obviously the custom to raise sums of money periodically for his 'encouragement' (this is the word used) by means of public subscription, and two of the lists have survived, bound into the pages of the tithe accounts. The first one, of 4 June 1705, shows that £12 10s 6d was collected for James Smith and the second, of 10 February 1711, reveals a sum of £12 10s 3d gathered on behalf of his successor, John Tanner.

There is no way of ascertaining when modus payments became established in Lowestoft, rather than payments in kind, but it was probably before the middle of the sixteenth century.[61] The only time that details concerning the payment of tithe in the parish become really clear is after 1698, when a surviving book of accounts enables

---

[58] It is therefore surprising that the town of Bungay, devastated by fire in March 1689, does not appear in the list of appeals. Briefs were formal documents requiring verification by the Lord Chancellor who, if satisfied with the validity of the claim, authorised their issue. They were then printed and distributed over a specified area. See S. Porter, *The Great Fire of London* (Stroud, 1996), pp. 5–6.

[59] The great (or rectorial) tithes in Lowestoft consisted of grain alone. Hay was not produced in sufficient quantity to be included (as was the case in many parishes), nor was timber.

[60] The parishes had been united in 1691, and a letter bound into the pages of the tithe accounts, from the Rev. James Smith (vicar during the early 1700s) to Thomas Tanner, Chancellor of Norwich diocese, mentions the joint valuation. See NRO, PD 589/80, p. 81. Thomas Tanner (later Bishop of St Asaph) was the older brother of John Tanner, vicar of Lowestoft from 1708 to 1759. He was a noted antiquarian, whose vast collection of documents has long been housed in the Bodleian Library.

[61] R. J. P. Kain and H. C. Prince, *The Tithe Surveys of England and Wales* (Cambridge, 1985), p. 15. Reference is made to cash payments having been fixed by the mid sixteenth century, or even earlier. The inquiry into the Lowestoft vicarage valuation, in 1566, suggests that cash values were being discussed rather than payments in kind.

most aspects of the system to be understood. The herbage tithes, which are recorded every year in considerable detail, yielded the vicar an annual income of somewhere between £22 and £32, depending on the quantity of crops grown and the variability of the weather. Tithe of lactage was difficult to collect, ceasing to become a factor after about 1708, and tithe of pigs and poultry was always a somewhat spasmodic and random affair. Thus, the other main source of income was the fishing tithes, which fluctuated between about £17 and just over £35 a year – making a regular annual income ranging from £39 to £65.[62] Occasionally, even as late as the first decade of the eighteenth century, some parishioners settled their account with the vicar by the payment of goods in kind. The most interesting and varied of such settlements is to be seen in the year 1700, when Edward Daines (brewer) discharged a debt of £15 18s 3d to the Rev. William Whiston by giving him 10s in cash, three bushels of wheat, three bushels of malt, two bushels of coal, three standard-sized anchors, one half-anchor and an old horse.[63]

In 1719, the Rev. John Tanner found himself with the opportunity to increase the value of the living at Lowestoft. To be specific, the rectorial tithes of corn (or *great tithes*, as they were known, because of their value) had become available for purchase from certain members of the Church family, whose origins had been in the adjoining parish of Kirkley, but whose links with Lowestoft were well established before the end of the seventeenth century. The impropriation of Lowestoft had passed from St Bartholomew's Priory, Smithfield, at the Dissolution of the Monasteries, into the hands of Sir Richard Rich and afterwards to a London family called Burnell.[64] Members of this family had enjoyed the income deriving from possession of the corn tithes for three or four generations, before disposing of them to another owner – who may or may not have been a member of the Church family.[65]

The sale of the corn tithes was forced upon female members of the Church family by James Mighells of Lowestoft (retired vice-admiral and Comptroller of the Navy) to meet the payment of debts owing to him by their deceased father, William Church of Kirkley (yeoman). A Chancery decree of 20 May 1718 authorised the sale to take place and John Tanner acted decisively to raise the necessary money. A local subscription fund was inaugurated and money collected not only in the town itself, but in various parts of

---

[62] There was also annual income of 16s 8d from the tithe paid on two parish windmills. According to E. Gillingwater, pp. 265–7, valuation of the vicarage in Queen Anne's reign (1702–14) was £43 16s 6d.

[63] The anchors were probably ones which had been recovered from inshore waters by salvors. They would have had good second-hand value either for re-use or for scrapping.

[64] Kain and Prince, *Tithe Surveys*, p. 10, refers to the way in which, after the Reformation, impropriations could be sold or leased at will. From the thirteenth century onwards, St Bartholomew's Priory had appointed vicars in Lowestoft (in collaboration with Norwich diocese) and taken the corn tithes. Once Henry VIII's reforms had taken place, the Bishops of Norwich became solely responsible for appointing vicars to Lowestoft.

[65] The Burnells were related to a local family called Baispoole (or Baspole). The manor roll of 1618 shows a Richard Burnell owning two houses on the east side of the High Street, at its northern end, which he had inherited from these relatives. He sold them three years later. The houses stood immediately to the north of No. 27 High Street.

Plate 21. *The tithe barn: the rearward section of the building, as seen, is the barn itself – the front part being of nineteenth-century construction. The barn dates from c. 1500 and retains its lower, aisled timber-framing; the roof is a later replacement (also nineteenth-century), but its queen-post structure may be a copy of the earlier trussing.*

Norfolk and Suffolk from among his clerical acquaintances.[66] A sum of £523 15s 6d was raised and this was augmented with a £200 payment from Queen Anne's Bounty. The actual cost of the tithes was £1,000, according to an account of Tanner's preserved in the tithe book (p. 60), and various fees and charges added another £251 5s 1d. The discrepancy between the amount of money donated and the total sum required was made up by Tanner mortgaging the tithes to the Diocese of Norwich (a process assisted by his older brother, Thomas, the diocesan chancellor) and by taking out a personal loan himself for £100 from Mary Baas, the widow of a local schoolmaster. As well as the tithes themselves, the purchase also included a late mediaeval barn and the plot on which it stood (Plate 21).[67]

All the various transactions were carried out between January and December 1720, but John Tanner did not clear himself of the debts he had incurred with both the mortgage and the £100 loan until Michaelmas 1745. The repayment of interest on the money borrowed amounted to £431 9s 6d over the twenty-five-year period, and it was not until four years later that Tanner began to receive the corn tithe income. The extra

[66] NRO, PD 589/92, pp. 66–7. The Rev. John Arrow's memorandum book reproduces the list in full.

[67] The messuage was one acre in size (on the western edge of town), with other buildings situated on it as well. The barn is still standing, on the northern side of Crown Street West – an aisled construction of c. 1500, with its ground-floor timber frame largely intact. It is currently used as a car-repair workshop.

£70 generated enhanced his stipend considerably and he enjoyed the revenues for the last ten years of his long incumbency. As with most of his other works in Lowestoft, the purchase of the rectorial tithes had been carried out not for his own personal advantage but for the benefit of his successors.

Manorial organisation

The courts of Lothingland Half-hundred

Before any attempt is made to view the operation of manorial bureaucracy in Lowestoft, the town needs to be placed in the context of its surrounding area. The organisation of the Lothingland half of the local hundred was complex, with each individual manor having its own court baron, but with most of the leets zoned into four geographical areas based on physical proximity (Map 6).[68] The four areas devised were as follows: North Leet (Belton and its outlier Browston, Bradwell and Fritton), South Leet (Oulton, Flixton, Blundeston and Lound), East Leet (Lowestoft, Gunton, Corton and Hopton) and West Leet (Somerleyton, Ashby and Herringfleet). Gorleston, with Southtown, had its own leet (probably originating in its mediaeval status as paramount manor for the half-hundred) and so did Burgh Castle – a hang-over, most likely, from the twelfth and thirteenth centuries, when the Norman fortification built there had been the centre of a local jurisdiction. One implication of the zoning is that the leets may not have been under the control of the individual manorial lords, but of the lord of the half-hundred – who also happened to be the Lowestoft lord. The two titles had been held in tandem for a considerable length of time and probably reflect the town's rise to pre-eminence in its local area.

The court for North Leet met annually at Belton on the first Tuesday in Lent, those for the South and West (which were joined together) at Blundeston on the first Monday in Lent, while the East Leet convened at Corton on the first Thursday in Lent. The Lowestoft jurors were sworn in at the East Leet assembly, but they probably attended only for admiralty business (when relevant) because the town had its own individual leet court held on the first Saturday in Lent – a situation which must have come about when the town grew to be larger than the other local communities and when its lordship became linked to that of the half-hundred.[69] Gorleston and Southtown had a leet on the second Wednesday in Lent, while Burgh Castle's was held on the first Friday in Lent.

In addition to the annual leets, a general court for the half-hundred was held three times a year as follows: Gorleston, on Holy (Maundy) Thursday; Lound Wood Head, on the Thursday after the feast of St John the Baptist (24 June); and Lothingland Mouth on the Thursday after the feast of St Faith the Martyr (6 October). It dealt with the admission of chief tenants from the various local manors, with matters of complaint, with the non-attendance of jurors at the various leets, and with occasional cases of

---

[68] In broad terms, the manors can be conveniently equated with parishes – though there were cases where the former transcended parish boundaries.

[69] The local admiralty courts, or water leets, were referred to at the end of Chapter 8. Salvage and wreck never constituted much of the business handled in the Lowestoft leet, because of the local tidal pattern (see note 132, page 200 above).

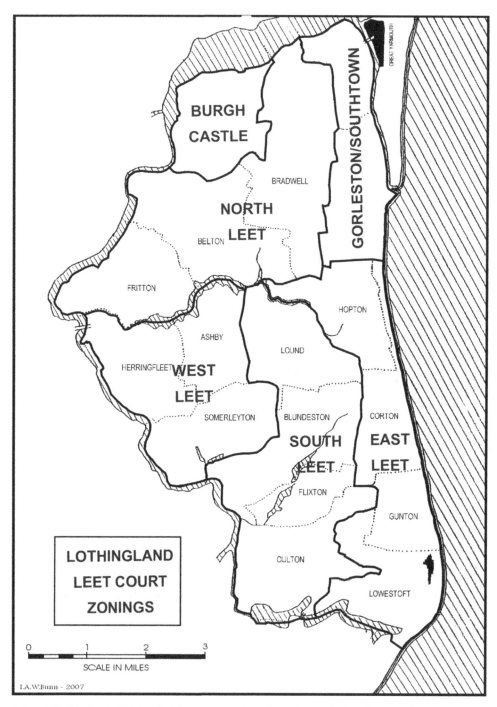

Map 6. *Lothingland Half-hundred leet court zonings. Historic complexity of manorial organisation in the jursidiction was one factor behind the geographical amalgamation of local leets. Another was the overview of proceedings thereby created for the lord of the Half-hundred.*

misdemeanour not dealt with there. Two other general courts were held annually, at Gorleston and Bradwell respectively, which considered matters of complaint and the non-attendance of jurors, and a similar body met at six-weekly intervals at Gunton Score on Lowestoft's northern boundary.[70] The opinion has been expressed that general hundred courts had originally been set up to handle all kinds of undifferentiated business and that the appearance of specialisation was the result of an uneven rate of decay in the various functions.[71] The Lothingland courts do not appear to fit this notion and their function seems to have been specifically worked out.

Finally, there was the six-monthly *tourn*, held at Mutford Bridge (the crossing-point between Lake Lothing and the freshwater broad at Oulton) for both halves of the hundred – Mutford and Lothingland having a significant geographical divide created by these two stretches of water. It met on a Wednesday in April or May and a Thursday in October, and the business it dealt with consisted mainly of the election of officers and the hearing of cases of misdemeanour either not dealt with in the various leets or referred by those courts to the tourn. Matters of salvage and wreck of the shore came under the jurisdiction of the Gorleston and Southtown leet, of the East Leet, and of the special water leet held annually in either Kirkley or Pakefield some time between the end of November and the middle of March.[72]

Court baron and court leet

Originally, over the whole of England, the court baron had been a private court of the lord, in which he sought to assert his rights over tenants and the tenants attempted to maintain their privileges against him. The main business was to declare and enforce the ancient customs of the manor, as well dealing with the surrender of lands and tenements and with the hearing of complaints and the settling of disputes.[73] Throughout the years covered by the surviving Lowestoft manor court minute books, which are relevant to the timespan covered in this book, the court baron was largely concerned with matters of complaint (up until the middle of the seventeenth century) and with the transfer of customary property within the manor. After c. 1660 the presence of two chief tenants and the steward was sufficient for the business to be conducted and the court only sat when there were transactions to be recorded.

In order to comply with the custom of the manor, anyone selling or otherwise conveying a copyhold messuage had to surrender it into the hands of one of the chief tenants in the presence of two of the other copyholders. Failure to do this could result

[70] Gunton Score has long been known as The Ravine. All matters of complaint dealt with in the general courts are indicated by having the plaintiff's name written first, followed by a v (*versus*) and the name of the defendant. Many of the cases would probably have been of trespass and debt. 'Trespass on the case', as it was known in full, concentrated on the contractual nature of credit agreements, whereby the plaintiff sought to demonstrate the social harm done by the defendant breaking his or her promise to repay the money borrowed.

[71] S. and B. Webb, *English Local Government: The Manor and the Borough* (London, 1908), p. 52. This book is still probably the best work on the English manorial system.

[72] Occasionally, they turn up in the Lowestoft court baron and court leet material.

[73] Webb and Webb, *English Local Government*, pp. 13–17, has an excellent exposition of the original functions of the court baron.

in forfeiture of the property and reversion to the lord. The transaction was always conducted out of court and then duly entered in the rolls at a meeting of the baron. This procedure involved quite a wide range of townspeople in the business of property transfer, but women were not part of the process (even though a number of them were copyholders). During the later part of the sixteenth century, on the evidence of wills, it was common practice for the surrender of copyhold houses and land (when they were being transferred by bequest) to be made at the time when the testator's intentions were being declared. A number of surviving documents record the practice, but it seems to have died out early in the seventeenth century. Acknowledgement of the surrender was actually written on the bottom of the will, together with the names of the chief tenant receiving it and those of the two copyholder witnesses. Sometimes, these three people also acted as witnesses to the will itself, presumably because they were present at a time when it was convenient for them to perform that function.

During the mediaeval period, all adult males over the age of sixteen who had been resident in a parish for a year and a day were supposed to attend the annual leet. The view of frankpledge was usually taken, and then the court proceeded to consider the cases of nuisance brought before it. Even in the later years of the seventeenth century a roll-call of the inhabitants was supposed to be made, with people answering their names, but this practice was not much adhered to. The Lowestoft leet was held on the first Saturday in Lent in one of the town's leading inns, the previous day having been spent by the jurors on a tour of inspection of the manor's environs (after they had been sworn in at the East Leet assembly, on the Thursday). The preliminary business included the swearing of the homage, the formal acknowledgement of the death of any chief tenant during the preceding year, the election of the chief tenant responsible for collecting the lord's rents (due at Michaelmas), and the fining of any absentee jurors and officers. After these matters, the court went on to consider the cases of misdemeanour and nuisance which had been brought before it.

It has been claimed that most leet courts were defunct by 1650, but Lowestoft's definitely did not experience such decline.[74] It remained active throughout the whole of the seventeenth century and for much of the eighteenth, holding its last session on 3arch 1770. The matters dealt with fell largely into the following categories: highway and footpath offences; hazards to public safety; damage to, or interference with, property boundaries and drainage channels; misuse of the common greens; insufficient control of livestock; pollution of ponds; neglect of certain obligations and duties by the manorial or parochial authorities; market and trading irregularities; breaches of the peace; and gambling. Some of the offences were dealt with, year in and year out, right through into the eighteenth century. Others seem to have been a problem only at certain times – or, at least, to have been so regarded.

The chief tenants and the chief pledges

The jury which sat at the leet each year consisted of those *chief tenants* of the manor who resided in the parish, together with the *chief pledges* (any of the former who lived outside

---

[74] Sharpe, *Crime*, p. 83.

the parish were eligible to collect rents, but not obliged to attend the leet). There were twenty-two full chief tenements (or *chieves*, as they were usually known) and a further thirteen *half-chieves*.[75] The people who held them were were usually referred to as *chevers*, rather than chief tenants, and it was their duty (in addition to attending baron and leet) to collect the lord's rents, which were then paid over to the steward. Again, as with the implementation of poor relief, this responsibility was worked out on a rotational basis, with one of the chieves or two of the half-chieves being designated each year. Thus, if a person owned a number of chief tenements (as was often the case), he or she would find himself or herself performing the task more often than someone who only had one.[76]

The chieves and half-chieves themselves were freehold plots spread through the parish (which was synonymous with the manor), anything between one eighth of an acre and half an acre in size. The holders of these seem originally to have been responsible for the collection of rents from areas of twelve or thirteen acres in extent, which were not necessarily concentrated in the immediate vicinity of the individual chief tenements. Those people who held half-chieves performed the same function on six acres or so.[77] Many of the names by which these holdings were known were those of people or families who had held the land about 300 years earlier. The Lothingland hundred rolls of 1273–4 reveal fifteen of them (one of which cannot be conclusively confirmed), while the subsidy list of 1327 has seven (three of which appear in the earlier source).[78] The remainder are recognisable as the names of people who must at some stage have owned the particular pieces of land, but no information has yet revealed itself as to when.

The manor roll of 1618 shows that the great majority of chief tenements and half-chieves were concentrated in the hands of the major owners of agricultural land in the parish. To be specific, this meant the lord of the manor, the Lowestoft charitable trustees, and William Canham, John Grenewood, William Grenewood and Thomas Jenkinson (Oulton), Robert Jettor (Flixton), and John Utber, Francis Whayman, Gislam Wolhowse and Francis Wrott (Gunton). All of these nine individuals were gentlemen who either lived in the parish or just outside. By the middle of the seventeenth century there had obviously been a considerable turnover in the ownership of the chief tenements as various pieces of land changed hands. The lord of the manor and the Lowestoft town trustees were still represented, and so were the heirs of Robert Jettor and William Canham, but other people had bought themselves in – men such as James Smiter (tailor and son of a yeoman), Edward Browne (tanner), John Gardiner (yeoman) and John Wilde (merchant). Such practice was to be the case throughout the rest of the seventeenth century and during the first half of the eighteenth. The chief tenants of the manor of

---

[75] The thirty-five holdings were described by only thirty-two different names, Harymans, Holetts and Reynolds each being used for different tenements.

[76] The chief tenants were usually men, but women also held this position and were not debarred from collecting rents. It was also the duty of chief tenants to attend half-hundred courts and collect escheats.

[77] Reeve, 'Lowestoft and Lothingland', iv, 156–86 (SRO(L), 193/3/4). This unpublished manuscript of c. 1810, compiled by a steward of the manor, contains useful information concerning the chief tenements. There is also a surviving chief tenements list of c. 1550 to consult: SRO(L), 194/A10/70.

[78] Lord John Hervey, *Lothingland Rolls*, p. 9 and SGB, ix, 95.

Lowestoft were always the more substantial members of the community, people who could afford to purchase real estate; and while this did not necessarily mean the very wealthiest in all cases, it ensured that control of the chief tenements remained within what may be termed the office-holding levels of society.

One interesting feature is that, in the later years of the sixteenth century, merchants seem to have constituted a substantial proportion of chief tenants (men such as William Davye, William Grene, John Grudgfild and Richard Rooke). So just how the chieves came to be dominated by the nine gentlemen named in the paragraph above is debatable. It may have been due in part to the normal pattern of sale or inheritance, but it may also have had something to do with the plague outbreak of 1603. This had a marked effect on the town's population and it may have caused a vacuum in the property market by killing off a number of established landowners and their families. In the years that followed the outbreak a lot of land probably changed hands because both owners and their immediate heirs had died, and also perhaps because others had decided to sell up and move away.[79] At least three of the chief tenants who feature in late sixteenth-century documentation did not survive the epidemic, and there may have been others, too.

The men who served as chief pledges and who formed a majority of the leet jury were, predictably, drawn from the more substantial levels of local society. There were about twenty to twenty-four of them altogether (though not all of them presented themselves as they were supposed to do) and they probably had their origin in the office of head of the *tithing groups* which had once been so important a part of the whole mechanism of *frankpledge*. Whatever the case, nothing is known of the procedure(s) whereby they became chosen as part of the local administration. All that can be ascertained is that there may have been some kind of rota system in operation, giving men of suitable status the opportunity to serve as leet jurors and thereby play their part in the ordering of the local community.

Officers appointed

The offices held under the manorial jurisdiction were as follows: steward, bailiff, constable, ale-taster (or ale-founder, as it was often termed), leather searcher and sealer, swine-reeve and afferator. There had also been a pinder at one stage, but the post does not seem to have survived much beyond the end of the sixteenth century. Certainly, there is no mention of it in the main sequence of court books beginning in the year 1616. There is no clear indication as to how the first two appointments referred to above were made, but the other five were all elected by the leet jurors and the people chosen served a term of one year.

The position of steward must, in theory at least, have been an influential one within manorial bureaucracy (especially in areas where there was no resident lord), yet the court books give no real sense of this. A sequence of men who held the position over the years is ascertainable, but little is known about them other than their being classified as 'gentlemen'. None of them features in the family reconstitution material, and up until

[79] Unfortunately, no court books have survived for the earliest part of the seventeenth century, so it is not possible to form a firm opinion as to what happened.

the present time the place of residence of only one has been established (they must, presumably, have lived at not too great a distance from the town).[80] Their attendance at the meetings of both the court baron and the leet seems to have been variable, though it is noticeable that the last two men identified seem to have put in more appearances than their predecessors. The office of bailiff was actually two separate posts: the chief tenant elected each year to collect the lord's rents and the man who acted as court bailiff. It was the duty of the latter to inform those people who had infringed any of the local manorial laws of the nature of their offence(s) and to summon them before the leet.[81] His period of jurisdiction often ran for a number of years before he was eventually replaced.

As far as the offices of constable, ale-taster, leather-searcher, swine-reeve and afferator are concerned, the people chosen to fill them all came from the upper and middle sections of local society – a feature which should come as no surprise and which has been observed in other places.[82] There were four constables elected annually, but there is nothing specific to show whether they served the whole year together or performed a three-month period of duty in the manner of the overseers. A single surviving court minute book for the 1580s shows that two constables had been chosen each year at one time, but thirty years later the number had doubled. The leet records refer to these men as under-constables (*subconstabularius*), which may imply that they were subordinate either to the constable of the hundred (or had been at some point in the past) or to the chief constables of the Beccles quarter sessions division. It was their responsibility to maintain the peace and carry out any acts of public administration required of them, including tax collection.[83]

The two ale-tasters were responsible for ensuring that alcoholic drink brewed in town was of a satisfactory standard and that its sale was conducted honestly. It was required that those serving in this post had no connection with either the brewing or victualling trades, and members of various occupation groups performed the function.[84] With the post of

---

[80] Robert Lulman (1704–9) lived in Great Yarmouth. The other men identified are as follows: John Randall (1616–53), Thomas Plumstead (1668–79), Thomas Godfrey (1680–1704), Robert Lowde (1709–25) and Richard Allin (1726 onwards).

[81] John Brissingham, who held the post for a time during the second half of the seventeenth century, was fined 5s at the 1673 leet for not informing wrongdoers of their offences in sufficient time.

[82] J. A. Sharpe, 'The People and the Law', in B. Reay (ed.), *Popular Culture in Seventeenth Century England* (London, 1985), pp. 255–6. The writer is discussing rural communities, but his comments regarding the status of the various parish officers is true, in general terms, of Lowestoft – a community which combined urban and rural characteristics. See also K. Wrightson and D. Levine, *Poverty and Piety in an English Village: Terling, 1525–1700* (New York, 1979), chapter 5; K. Wrightson, 'Two Concepts of Order: Justices, Constables and Jurymen in Seventeenth Century England', in J. Brewer and J. Styles (eds), *An Ungovernable People: The English and Their Law in the Seventeenth and Eighteenth Centuries* (London, 1980), pp. 41–4; and Moxon, pp. 214–6.

[83] J. Kent, 'The English Village Constable, 1580–1642: The Nature and Dilemmas of the Office', *JBS* 20, ii (Spring, 1981), 40–5. Tax-collecting is specifically referred to here as duty sometimes falling upon constables. The Lowestoft officers certainly supervised the collection of the Ship Money rate in 1636 (NRO, PD 589/178) and may have performed public service of this nature at other times.

[84] It was probably considered prudent not to place regulation of brewing and consumption in the hands of people involved in the trade. Vested interest can be a powerful incentive to defraud.

searcher and sealer of leather, it was different. Again, two men were chosen for the year, but they were nearly always specialist leather-workers of some kind (cordwainers were the ones most commonly elected). It was obviously an area in which some expertise was called for, in order to determine whether hides had been cured in a correct and legal manner, and it was perhaps deemed wise not to leave the assessment solely in the hands of tanners.

After 1620, two swine-reeves were appointed annually, to make sure that regulations were being enforced concerning the stricter control of pigs and ringing of their snouts. It was an office that continued for nearly fifty years before being changed into the new one of fen-reeve, where the duties were primarily concerned with maintenance of fences and boundaries in the parish at large – and not just on the low-lying, marshy areas, as might be inferred from the title. Finally, the two afferators were appointed from among chief tenants of the manor resident in the parish, having as their task the duty of fixing the level of fines to be paid by those people who broke the laws of the manor (it cannot have been a particularly onerous task, as the fines hardly varied from year to year). In most cases, the various offices were spread equitably, so as not to burden the same men year after year, and even mariners took their turn as constable in spite of being at sea for a good part of the year.[85]

Misdemeanour, nuisance and crime

Leet court offences

As the Lowestoft leet records are so voluminous, the only realistic way of presenting an over-view of the court's business is to use five-year blocks of material spaced by intervals of twenty years. It was not possible to adhere rigidly to this principle because of volumes withdrawn for conservation at the time the sampling was carried out and because of missing years where certain stewards appear not to have written up the minutes. The different time-blocks chosen are as follows: 1582–5, 1618–22, 1649–53, 1669–73, 1689–93 and 1709–14.[86] The main sequence of records begins in 1616, with just one isolated volume surviving for the 1580s.

The commonest of all offences dealt with by the leet were those relating to the state of roadways and footpaths in town. Each occupant was responsible for keeping the street surface outside his or her house level and consolidated, and failure to do this resulted in a 3d fine.[87] If the neglect continued, the offender was presented in the following year's

---

[85] They served only rarely in any other manorial capacity, which may mean that the constable's period of duty was indeed for three months only. All other posts lasted for a year and seafarers seem to have been kept clear of these.

[86] SRO(L), 194/A10/4, 5, 8, 11 and 12, 13 and 14, 16. There are no leet records extant for either 1586 or 1713. All the presentments are to be found in the eight minute-books cited.

[87] Allen, 'Aldeburgh', Appendix 2, reveals that the standard fine in this Suffolk coastal community was 3s 4d, the penalty being fixed by a local byelaw. W. T. Jackman, *The Development of Transportation in Modern England* (London, 1966; originally pub. Cambridge, 1916), pp. 37–41, says that 'paving' regulations were common during the sixteenth century, but with variation from town to town. The Latin word *pavire* is used a great deal in the Lowestoft leet records; it means 'to ram down' (i.e. to pack down, or consolidate).

leet and the fine increased to 6d. There are cases of serious neglect, where the sum of 3s 4d was imposed, but it made no difference to those able to afford the penalty. It is very noticeable in the Lowestoft leet records how the wealthier members of the community (including the jurors) took no action over the state of the street outside their homes, but just went on paying the fines year after year.

The same holds true of the other main highway offence: the noisome depositing of rubbish, and of animal manure and human sewage, in the streets, scores and pathways. Again, a fine of 3d was imposed in the first instance, with increases following in subsequent years if no remedial action was taken. As with failure to keep the street surfaces level and passable, the random deposition of excrement was a practice that was widespread throughout the town and knew no social bounds. So was the dumping of domestic rubbish and trade waste of all kinds – such as the 'neats' scalps' (cattle heads) thrown into the street by six local butchers (Thomas Mewse, John Roden, William Whelpdale, Gilbert Wilson, John Foxe and William Meeke) and referred to in the leet records of 1584. The obstruction of roadways and footpaths in the wider parish, however, was usually the fault of particular landowners. Failure to ensure that hedges and fences were properly maintained, that stiles and footbridges were kept in good repair, and that access-points were free from obstruction carried a basic 3d fine.

Allied to specific highway infringements was risk to public safety along the various streets, footpaths and rights of way. Things which were construed as constituting a danger to the public were varied in nature and giving a selection of them is the best way of creating some sense of conditions at the time. Thus, in 1584, John Foxe (butcher) was fined 3d for not carrying out essential repairs to his slaughterhouse in Bier Lane (or Almshouse Lane/Fair Lane) – a building that was considered a potential danger to passers-by.[88] The following year saw William Becke (mariner), William Porter and William French (merchant) each fined 3d for not keeping their chimneystacks in good repair. At the leet of 1618, Hugh Calver (husbandman) was fined 6d for digging a claypit in the king's highway (location unspecified), while in 1619 Robert Haltwaye had a penalty of 3d imposed for not making a cover for the entrance to his cellar, next to the street. The following year, Peter Durrant (husbandman and alehouse keeper) was fined 3d for leaving a ladder standing in the High Street, both day and night.

Even relatively inaccessible places came under scrutiny. Richard Mason was fined 3d in 1653 for hanging up a brewing copper, without a chain, in his stable – something which was considered hazardous. More immediately obvious as a possible risk were the three pits which Robert Mighells (mariner), Henry Ward (merchant) and William Barber had failed to fill in adjacent to their respective barns. They were fined 3d each at the leet of 1670 for neglecting to carry out the work. Two years later, Titus Calfe (mariner) was fined 3d for erecting a shed on the Denes – a building which not only caused an obstruction, it was claimed, but also represented a fire-risk.[89] Finally, in 1690, the

---

[88] The name Bier Lane suggests this must have been the roadway once used to convey deceased townspeople to the parish church for burial.

[89] Calfe's construction may have been put up as a store for fishing equipment or items of wreck. Various attempts made over the years to build sheds on the Denes all fell foul of the manorial rules.

brothers James and John Wilde (merchants) were each fined 6d for not maintaining a railed fence round their well at the bottom of the cliff, close to the Denes, thus causing risk to passers-by.

Damage to fences features from time to time in the records, especially in the late sixteenth century, with 3d fines imposed on people of various stations in life (including women) for being 'common breakers of their neighbours' fences'. There is no hint given as to whether the damage was accidental or deliberate, however. The term 'fences' encompassed both railed constructions and hedges, and there are many references in the leet's proceedings to fines being imposed on property owners for not maintaining them in the proper fashion. Failure to do so, of course, not only caused inconvenience to passers-by, but possible physical risk as well.

The obstruction of watercourses, both within town and in the parish at large, was another common offence. A lot of the problems were caused by rubbish and manure of different kinds being dumped in ditches and culverts. In the days before large-scale drainage works of the modern kind, arrangements for dealing with surface water were of great importance.[90] Any blocking of ditches and gullies was soon likely to cause flooding and the local authorities clearly faced a problem in seeing that people kept them clear. Again, the standard 3d fine was applied for the first offence, with increases thereafter. Just as with road maintenance, however, the wealthier inhabitants seemed quite happy to take little action and go on paying the fines.

Another matter to occupy the attention of the leet was the use, and misuse, of common greens in the parish, with the three closest to town (Denes, Goose Green and Church Green) concerning the authorities most of all because of their easy accessibility. All the greens were 'common' in the sense that people had access to them, but the services provided had to be paid for. The main one related to the grazing of livestock and it was a facility that was strictly controlled. Thus, in 1582, Roger Rant (baker) and Robert Wrote (gentleman) were each fined 3d for pasturing more sheep and cattle on the Denes than they were entitled to. Also, at the same court, an ordinance was passed preventing any of the townspeople turning geese out onto any of the commons other than Goose Green, which was situated on the western edge of the built-up area (Plate 22). Anyone disobeying the order (which was presumably made because of the adverse, fouling effect which geese had on pasture) was to be fined 2d for each offending bird.

Apart from specific infringement of grazing regulations, the other main offences relating to commons were the depositing of manure and rubbish of different kinds and the digging of pits to extract sand and gravel. Once again, a fine of 3d was the usual penalty exacted for first offence. The illegal taking of rabbits was regarded much more seriously (these being the property of the lord), as may be seen in the case of Charles Boyce, a substantial

---

[90] The scores were an important means of taking flood-water from the High Street to a lower level and some had gulleys on either side of the footway, down which the excess ran. During the course of excavations to the rear of Nos 72 to 80, High Street, in 2001–2, an old drain running across the gardens was uncovered. It was rectangular in shape and built of high-quality seventeenth-century bricks butted up without mortar joints. It followed a south-west/north-east alignment and had obviously once taken water away from the top of the rather narrow Wildes Score by diverting it to the much broader Rant Score, which had deep gulleys on either side of it.

Plate 22. *Goose Green/St Margaret's Plain: the last remaining part of the old common green is preserved today as a car park and children's play-area.* The First and Last *public house, seen in the middle of the picture, stands on the site of a much earlier building known as 'the house on the green' – this latter being an outlier from the town itself.*

yeoman, who lived in the adjoining parish of Gunton. He was fined 5s in 1712 for this act of lesser poaching, which had taken place somewhere out on the Denes.

Apart from regulating use of the greens, the leet court was also the instrument whereby people were punished for damage or nuisance caused by straying animals. Pigs seem to have been the biggest cause of trouble, with their wandering nature and habit of rooting up the ground wherever they went.[91] In 1584, a ordinance was passed forbidding anyone to allow pigs to roam either in the streets or out onto the common greens. The animals were to be confined to their owners' yards and failure to comply with the regulation was to result in a fine of 3s 4d. The following year, access to the greens was allowed once more, but not free passage around the streets. Problems obviously continued for the next three decades or more, because in 1620 the order was given for all pigs in the parish to have their snouts ringed. Two swine-reeves were appointed annually to make sure that the practice was adopted and a 3d fine was imposed for every animal which did not comply. Stray sheep and cattle do not seem to have caused too much of a problem in the parish, but there are a number of references to horses being on the loose. Most frowned upon were those infected with mange or scab. Fines of up to 10s, such as those imposed in 1618 and 1620 respectively on Thomas Bleasbye (husbandman) and William Rising (yeoman), show how seriously the misdemeanour was regarded.[92]

[91] T. S. Willan, *Elizabethan Manchester*, CSP, xxvii (Manchester, 1980), 40–1. Pigs were a great preoccupation with the leet court in pre-industrial Manchester.

[92] As pointed out in this section's first paragraph, the post of pinder does not seem to have continued beyond the end of the sixteenth century, so the task of rounding up stray animals probably fell to anyone who was prepared to do it.

The pollution of certain of the parish's ponds did not go unnoticed either, because of their importance as providers of water for livestock. Linen production was a secondary industry in Lowestoft, but the preliminary rotting-down of hemp was not allowed in the most commonly frequented drinking-pools – especially the one known as 'the common watering-place', or 'the watering', a large pond just to the west of the town's built-up area at the southern extremity of Goose Green.[93] Fines of 3d were imposed by the leet court in 1584 on Robert Wilkeson, Thomas Towne (ploughwright), John Warde (tawer and tanner) and Giles Palmer (gentleman) for putting bundles of hemp into it. Among the other offences connected with this particular pond were the depositing of dead animals and of quantities of waste straw. William Arnold (brewer) and Thomas Brissingham were fined 3d each for the first offence in 1652 (pigs being the animals in question), while Robert Mighells (mariner) had the same penalty imposed for the second some twenty years later.

A number of the day-to-day misdemeanours cited so far (especially dumping of rubbish and disposal of waste) would have been carried out by servants and other employees. However, the lower orders hardly feature in the leet court records, as they would have simply done as they were told, and it was their employers who bore the responsibility and therefore paid the fines. With general disregard for a number of manorial regulations being apparent, it is no surprise to find that failure to carry out certain duties was also punished fairly regularly by the court. The fining of jurors for non-attendance at the leet was quite common, and this was not always a matter of simple neglect. The court also had to contend with the wilful refusal of certain chief tenants and chief pledges to undertake their responsibilities and perform service. Such a one was William Rising (merchant), who was fined 2s 6d in 1709 for not only declining to serve as juror, but also for giving false excuses as to his behaviour.

At other times, the elected officers neglected to carry out their duties. Two of them, Joseph Smithson (merchant) and William Mewse (butcher) were fined 10s each at the 1691 leet for having failed to perform the function of ale-taster during the previous year. Nor were they alone in their dereliction of duty. In 1673, John Brissingham, the court bailiff, was fined 5s for not informing wrongdoers of the nature of their offences in sufficient time, thereby making the leet's corrective function more difficult. He was in good company, because the lord himself, Philip Hayward of Carlton Colville (gentleman), was indicted three years running, in 1671–3, for not maintaining a steelyard in the market place. The first occasion resulted in a fine of 3d, the two subsequent ones 20s each. This was not the only example of a lord's neglect. In 1712 and 1713, Sir Richard Allin of Somerleyton Hall was indicted for allowing the pound to fall into disrepair.[94] No fines are mentioned, but his additional failure in 1712 to provide the ale-tasters with a suitable set of measures for the carrying-out of their duties resulted in his being amerced 3s 4d.

---

[93] The location today is where Thurston Road meets St Peter's Street. As well as watering livestock, the pond was also the site of the town's ducking-stool.

[94] It stood on Goose Green, close to the present-day junction of Factory Street with Thurston Road.

Of regular appearance in the leet throughout the whole of the period covered were the Lowestoft churchwardens. They had a whole series of 3d penalties imposed for not maintaining the street surface outside the parish almshouses, for not repairing steps in certain of the scores, for not keeping the communal Green Well in good repair, and for not cleaning out watercourses on Church Green.[95] More seriously regarded was their neglect of the parish boundary markers, or *butts*, during the late sixteenth century and the first three decades of the seventeenth (this particular offence carrying fines of 3s 4d or 6s 8d). The butts were large stones or pieces of masonry set at regular intervals along the boundaries, and they had to be kept visible. Allowing them to become overgrown with vegetation was not favourably regarded.[96]

As well as scrutinising the kind of public responsibility outlined in the preceding paragraph, the leet also had an important part to play in trying to control various trading irregularities, both in the town's shops and alehouses and at the weekly market. No market officials were elected by the leet and no one is ever specifically referred to in this capacity, so perhaps the conduct of the market came under the jurisdiction of the court itself, with its elected constables made responsible for ensuring fair trading. Butchers, both from within Lowestoft itself and from further afield, feature most prominently in the records for breaches of honest dealing, involving themselves in all kinds of dubious practice.

In 1583, for instance, John Foxe and John Roden were fined 4d each for selling the flesh of 'draught animals', though whether in their shops or on the market is not made clear. Nor is it stated whether the offending meat derived from oxen or horses! The following year, Foxe received the much stiffer penalty of 10s for purveying beef from old, inferior animals which might have died from natural causes. In 1618 and 1619, there were instances of butchers regrating certain items in the market, thereby infringing both local and national regulations. For instance, a man from Beccles, called Burkine, was fined 6s 8d for buying a side of beef from someone else and then re-selling it, while a townsman called Silvester was fined the same amount for handling a cowhide in identical fashion. Two years later, in 1621, five Beccles men (Abraham Todd, John Balye, Richard Wake, ? Jackson and John Clarke – the last of whom was a mason) and one townsman (John Oarrman) were each fined 6s 8d for slaughtering bulls not purchased in Lowestoft and selling the meat on the market. This restriction on the purchase of stock for killing was obviously intended to benefit local farmers and dealers. Two years later, in 1623, John Balye appeared once again – this time being fined 6s 8d for selling unwholesome meat. The regularity with which the same butchers appear in the leet records at this time suggests they believed that the money to be made from dishonest practice was worth the risk of being caught and getting fined.

---

[95] The Green Well stood at the junction of Back Lane, West Lane, Gun Lane and Frary Lane, taking its name from proximity to Goose Green. Its location in today's terms is best defined as lying just beyond the western end of Wesleyan Chapel Lane, beneath the south-bound carriageway of Jubilee Way.

[96] References to neglecting the butts are also to be found in the tourn minutes. Evans, 'South Elmham', p. 43, records identical dereliction of duty in the Suffolk community of Flixton (near Bungay) during the reign of James I. The fines imposed there rose from 3d to 3s 4d between 1612 and 1618.

A reminder of the cruelty once experienced by animals destined for slaughter is to be seen in references to various butchers who were fined for selling meat from bulls which had not first been baited by dogs.[97] One of them, Abraham Sallers from Beccles, was found guilty of the offence in 1710 and had a fine of 10d imposed. The most common offence regarding meat, however, during the later seventeenth century and the first part of the eighteenth, was the inflation of cuts of veal by means of a blow-pipe. The joints had certain blood-vessels plugged with fat at one end while air was inserted in the other, which was then also plugged. By this means, the meat was made to appear plumper and more succulent than it really was. Two members of the Sallers/Sallows family from Beccles and a man called Thomas Copping, from Wenhaston, were fined 2s 4d each in 1689 for carrying out the practice, while the following year sums of 3s 4d were imposed on four offenders – one of whom was Abraham Sallows (als. Sallers) and another Abraham Nollard, from Wenhaston.

Bakers were also regular offenders in the matter of fair trading. The assize of bread seems to have been contravened fairly regularly, with the customer being sold underweight loaves both in shops and on the market. At the leet of 1584, Roger Rant, John Parker and Richard Smyth of Lowestoft, and Richard Smyth of Beccles were fined 2s 6d, 12d, 6d and 2s 6d respectively for carrying on their trade of 'common bakers' less than honestly. Nearly thirty years later, in 1621, John Draper, William Mingaye, Peter Button and Robert Husskyne (all of Lowestoft) were each fined 6s 8d for identical offences.

Nor was short measure confined to those people involved in making and selling bread. Various alehouse keepers in town seem to have been equally dishonest – though the eleven who were indicted in 1618 (including a woman) and amerced 6d each did constitute an unusually large number to be dealt with in one session. At the other end of the timescale under consideration, a man called Thomas Palmer was fined the sum of 5s in 1706 for refusing to allow the ale-taster to sample his product (unfortunately, no clue is offered as to the kind of adulteration which had been carried out). Interestingly enough, the regular appearance of butchers, bakers and alehouse keepers for their various acts of dishonesty mirrors exactly what happened in the Leicestershire town of Ashby-de-la-Zouche.[98]

Among the various other 'weights and measures' offences recorded in the court books are ones relating to goods both specified and unknown. Margaret Coldham (merchant's widow) was fined 6d in 1584 for selling cloth that had been measured by a *yardwand*. The following year, Samuel Puckle (merchant tailor), William Purse, William Bamforthe and Peter Butcher (servant of Samuel Puckle's father, Robert) were all fined 3d each for doing the same thing. The particular infringement here must have related to the thirty-six-inch measurement being used instead of the forty-five-inch *ell*, but Peter Butcher's indictment is unusual because members of the lower orders scarcely feature in the leet records at all. It may well have been that he was cut or two above the normal type of factotum or menial.

---

[97] This was considered essential to tenderise the flesh and improve its flavour. Small animals and poultry were often treated more abominably at the kitchen stage, when a number of preparations were carried out while they were still alive. See, Pullar, *Consuming Passions*, p. 150.

[98] Moxon, pp. 222–4. Apart from non-attendance at court, trading irregularities constituted most of the offences dealt with.

In 1649, Richard Mighells (cooper) had a 12d penalty imposed for refusing to let parish officials (it does not say who) inspect the measures he was using to make barrels of the required sizes and volume. Twenty-three years later, in 1672, an outsider from Frostenden, William Gayde, was fined 2s 6d for using an under-sized pint measure on the market, but the liquid dispensed is not named. Nor are the underweight goods which Thomas French sold in his shop and for which he was fined 5s in 1706. It was in this year also that Robert Nalborow of Great Yarmouth had an identical punishment imposed for selling shoes made from horse-hide to market customers. Finally, no account of commercial skulduggery would be complete without the presence of a miller; and the imposition of a 6d fine on Edward Taylor in 1584, for taking an excessive toll of grain for services rendered, would seem to fit perfectly with the way that millers were expected to behave.[99]

With most of the various kinds of trading irregularity having been described, it is time to turn to consideration of breaches of the peace. These seem to have been confined largely to the Elizabethan and Jacobean period (when such matters were high on the national agenda because of central government's concern with civil disorder), with physical assault being the most common offence. A standard fine of 3s 4d (a week's wages or more for a skilled craftsman) was imposed on guilty parties, with an increase to 6s 8d the following year if no improvement in behaviour had resulted. Brawling was not confined to any particular occupational or social grouping and merchants were as likely to 'draw blood' (the official phrase used) on each other or on other men as were seafarers, tradesmen and artisans. Even the occasional gentleman was not above becoming involved in fisticuffs.

Verbal abuse sometimes went hand in hand with physical violence, apparently, with men such as Philip Hales (boatwright) and Oliver Graye (mason) being termed 'common brawlers and scolders of their neighbours' – offences which resulted in each of them being fined 3s 4d in 1619. The term 'scold' is an interesting one when used in connection with men, but as one observer has pointed out, although the archetype was female, male examples were also to be found.[100] Public recognition of the problems which could be caused by an uncontrolled tongue are to be seen in a pronouncement of 1582: 'Item we do further ordain that this Township of Lowestoft shall provide an Able ducking stool and to be placed in A place convenient before the feast of the nativity of St John Baptist [24 June] next upon pain of xls.' The device was almost certainly erected beside the common watering-place on Goose Green.

Apart from the specific matter of launching attacks upon one's neighbours with intemperate words, other kinds of abuse were not favourably regarded either. Sometimes, the insults and threats were directed at manorial officers in the execution of their duties. Thomas Burges (smith) was fined 3s 4d in 1585 for abusing and threatening chief

---

[99] Millers were proverbial in mediaeval and pre-industrial England for dishonesty – a reputation based on their habit of taking more than a just amount of grain or meal as their payment. Even before the fourteenth century had ended, Geoffrey Chaucer was able to have his Reeve, from *The Canterbury Tales*, say of Roger, the miller of Trumpington, 'A thief he was for sooth of corn and meal'.

[100] Sharpe, *Crime*, p. 89.

pledges when they visited his house, though the purpose of the visit is not revealed. In 1649, Thomas Bacheller was fined 12d for swearing at Thomas Gardner (blacksmith) and William Harweld (or Harrold), the ale-tasters, while in 1706 Thomas Spratt (mariner) had a 2s 6d penalty imposed for swearing at and mocking chief pledges. Three years later, the same sum was exacted from Simon Holliday (yeoman) for his having abused certain of the jurors in the execution of their duties.

In addition to incidents where manorial representatives suffered verbal attacks from fellow townsmen, there are also examples of people being fined for general abuse directed at all and sundry. Richard Hewes (mariner) was fined 3s 4d in 1582 for his use of bad language, and the impression of general rowdyism on his part is reinforced by his being presented two years later for firing off a gun in the street. He was fined 12d for that particular offence. Altogether different from the examples of verbal aggression, but probably no less disruptive in its effect on the immediate locality, was the case of Stephen Harte, who was fined 4d in 1584 for being a 'common eavesdropper' around the houses of his neighbours.

The last offence of any note to occupy the attention of the leet, again during the Elizabethan and Jacobean periods, was gambling.[101] In 1582, Thomas Hadenham, John Parker and John Medley were fined 6d each for allowing illegal games to be played inside their houses. The three men may have been alehouse keepers, but no positive information is given regarding their status and nor are the offending games identified. Any moral objections to gambling in the thinking of the time were probably the result of conventional Christian attitudes to a pursuit that was seen to have no merit, but there was also the practical matter of the disorder it could lead to among its adherents when disputes arose.

In 1618, the alehouse was specifically named as the venue for the playing of illegal games, when Henry Westgate (mason), Thomas Neale (husbandman), Robert Frarye (blacksmith), Thomas Ferney (cobbler), Robert Oxe (blacksmith), Robert Ottle, Ellis Roope and John Warde were all fined 6s 8d each for being participants. Nor did the proprietors go unpunished. Edward Westgate (father of Henry and owner of the *Old White Horse* inn), Thomas Bleasby (husbandman), Henry Cobb (innkeeper) and John Murcock (yeoman) were also fined 6s 8d each. The only reference to card-playing is recorded in a year not part of the sampling process used. It occurred in 1635, when Michael Bentley was fined 40s for allowing Robert Haltwaye and Joseph Bird (mason) to use his house for the purpose. Haltwaye and Bird were fined 6s 8d each for the offence and a further 3s 4d each for fighting. Thus, it would seem that the game ended in dispute.

It may perhaps be inferred from the amount of occupational data appended to the names of people mentioned in this section that the minute books themselves reveal such information. They do not. Occupations or social groupings are only divulged occasionally throughout the whole sequence of surviving records. Gentlemen are often accorded the courtesy of having their status given, but an occupation is usually only written down to distinguish between people who had the same name as each other.

---

[101] Evans, 'South Elmham', p. 43. Reference is made here to dice and backgammon, the playing of which resulted in two men each being fined 3s 4d at the leet court of 1553.

Where trading irregularities are concerned, the people selling unwholesome meat or underweight loaves are obviously thereby identified as butchers and bakers, but they are not always described as such. Most of the occupational information given derives from the major sources named in Table 16 (page 59).

A comparison of leet activity in the Jacobean and early Georgian periods leads to some very interesting contrasts, which manifest themselves in Tables 41 and 42. Though the number of indictments had doubled by the 1720s, the number of people presented remained practically the same – and this in spite of a population increase from something well under 1,500 people (the result of the 1603 plague epidemic) to 1,850 or so. Moreover, it can be seen that the gambling, the brawling, and the cursing and swearing had disappeared – reflecting not so much a change in society as less concern for such

Table 41. *Leet presentments, 1618–22*

Offence	1618		1619		1620		1621		1622		1618–1622	
Highway neglect	2	8	4	7	4	16	3	17	4	14	17	62
Safety hazards	4	4	3	3	3	3	1	1	2	2	13	13
Boundaries/drainage	1	1	4	4					2	3	7	8
Livestock control	1	1	1	11	2	14					4	26
Common greens												
Water pollution												
Dereliction of duty	1	1									1	1
Trading irregularity	1	11	3	11	3	12	4	15	2	8	13	57
Breaches of the peace			4	13					1	1	5	14
Gambling	2	12									2	12
	12	38	19	49	12	45	8	33	11	28	62	193

(Note that the left-hand columns show the number of charges, the right-hand ones the number of people presented.)

Table 42. *Leet presentments, 1718–22*

Offence	1718		1719		1720		1721		1722		1718–1722	
Highway neglect	8	10	18	25	8	10	12	18	4	4	50	67
Safety hazards	1	1	3	3	1	1	3	4	12	13	20	22
Boundaries/drainage	4	9	5	6	3	3	2	8	11	14	25	40
Livestock control			1	1							1	1
Common greens	5	15	3	3	4	4	2	2	7	15	21	39
Water pollution												
Dereliction of duty	1	2	3	8	3	7			5	8	12	25
Trading irregularity					1	1					1	1
Breaches of the peace												
Gambling												
	19	37	33	46	20	26	19	32	39	54	130	195

behaviour being shown by the authorities.[102] On the other hand, both trading irregularities and the lack of control of livestock seem to have genuinely diminished, with far fewer presentments than before.[103] Neglect of highways of one kind or another remained the chief offence, though the number of people involved showed little change from a century earlier. However, there were noticeable increases in offences relating to public safety, to boundaries and surface-water drainage, to damage done to the common greens (such acts consisting largely of the deposition of rubbish and muck, the digging of clay and sand, and various types of encroachment), and to dereliction of manorial and parochial duties – all of which may point to a weakening of manorial control as the community became more committed to maritime pursuits and more urban in nature. The only offence which is not to be found in either of the five-year periods compared is the pollution of ponds because, although this did occur from time to time, it was never a major problem.

Tourn offences

The Mutford and Lothingland tourn was probably a court of the lord of the hundred originally, rather than of the sheriff, though the post-Easter and post-Michaelmas meeting times matched those of old-style Sheriff's Tourn.[104] Its jurors consisted of chief tenants from the various local manors and, in dealing with a variety of petty offences, it was a mirror-image of the individual leets. It was a survival from an earlier period, which probably continued to operate because it had a particular usefulness at local level.[105] Records of its activities are only extant for the years 1588–1612, but they serve as a useful complement to the Lowestoft material (largely filling in the gap which exists in the sequence of court books between 1586 and 1615).[106] Moreover, since the tourn

---

[102] There had been a general tightening-up of the moral climate in England during the first half of the seventeenth century, but attitudes changed greatly after the Restoration. See D. Underdown, *Revel, Riot and Rebellion: Popular Politics and Culture in England, 1603–1640* (Oxford, 1985), pp. 8–43.

[103] Fewer livestock offences may indicate that fewer people kept animals than had been the case a century earlier. This may, in turn, reflect Lowestoft's increased maritime specialisation during the later part of the seventeenth century and the early decades of the eighteenth.

[104] J. Richardson (ed.), *The Local Historian's Encyclopedia* (New Barnet, 1974), p. 165. The Sheriff's Tourn was held in order to review frankpledge for the hundred, to see that the tithing groups were up to strength and to deal with minor criminal cases.

[105] F. W. Maitland, *Select Pleas in Manorial and Other Seignorial Courts*, SS, vol. ii (London, 1889), xxvii–xxxviii. The writer says that the leet court and the tourn were both 'royal police courts' which were co-ordinate with each other. Both had the power to deal with trespass and nuisance, but not with felony, which had to be referred to a higher authority.

[106] SRO(L), 192/4 and 194/C1/1. These two volumes, covering the years 1588–94 and 1595–1612, are the only remaining books which contain an account of the activities of the tourn and of other courts in Lothingland Half-hundred. Lowestoft leet court material is available in such quantity because the town had its own separate leet and details of proceedings, along with those of the court baron, happen to have survived. Most of the other parishes in the Half-hundred (manors and parishes being more or less synonymous by the sixteenth century) had their leets zoned geographically in the manner described earlier in this chapter. And, in having the minutes of their proceedings written up in one composite volume along with tourn business, this means that records only exist for the years 1588–1612.

dealt with misdemeanours identical to those handled in the various leets, the question arises as to why there was such duplication. Perhaps the court acted as a kind of safety net for the area, whereby cases which had escaped the attention of jurors in local leets, or which had been deferred for some reason, were brought to adjudication at either of the six-monthly tourns.

The number of cases considered relating to Lowestoft and to the other parishes in the Lothingland Half-hundred certainly fluctuated a good deal, which reinforces the notion of the tourn being used as a back-up agency. Its basic fine was 4d, which made it one penny more than the Lowestoft leet, and the higher penalties were usually multiples of this (the most common ones were 12d and 3s 4d). On some occasions there was no Lowestoft misdemeanour considered at the tourn, whereas at other times there were as many as nine or ten individual cases. It is not possible to ascertain whether such fluctuations are reflected in corresponding 'highs' and 'lows' in leet presentments because the two sets of records do not overlap. There are few references in the tourn material to the offenders' places of origin, but it is possible to identify Lowestoft people because of the family reconstitution process.

As far as any account of the town's basic system of justice is concerned, the tourn is most useful as a provider of detail not given in the leet. The 'illegal games' mentioned in its various entries, for instance, turn out to include both dice and shove-ha'penny (the latter being referred to as *slide-groat*), while bowls was also on the proscribed list.[107] The objection to these activities was probably that money was being wagered on the outcome, but there is also the possibility that they were being played during church service times. Regarding the matter of assault, there are instances of men not only attacking each other, but assaulting women as well – such as the cases recorded in May 1593, when William Copping was fined 20d for striking Katherin, the wife of Jeremiah Marks, and in October 1595, when John Munds (cordwainer) had a 3s 4d penalty imposed for hitting Elizabeth Godfreye.

There are occasional references in the leet minutes to the illegal keeping of dogs – a matter which is clarified in the tourn records by specific mention of mastiffs. People were obviously not allowed to keep these animals because of their aggressive nature.[108] More information is also afforded regarding sale of beer by unlawful measure: a number of alehouse keepers were fined at the tourn for selling their drink in 'small cans little more than a pint' (presumably, a quart should have been the correct quantity). Finally, the offence of scolding and hurling abuse can be seen, on the evidence of the tourn records, to have been considered serious not only because of its disruptive effect on the community, but also because of the bad example it set other people. In October 1588, Christopher Harrold was fined 9d for allowing his wife Elizabeth to be the common scold of the neighbourhood, while in April 1594, George Rugge (shopkeeper?) was amerced 12d for being a 'railer and slanderer', thereby disturbing the peace and setting a bad example to his wife.

---

[107] Games of bowls may well have been games of skittles.

[108] Moxon, p. 201. A local manorial ordinance in Ashby-de-la-Zouche forbade the owners of mastiffs to allow their dogs to roam the streets unmuzzled.

Table 43. *Tourn presentments, 1607–11*

Offence	1607		1608		1609		1610		1611		1607–1611	
Highway neglect	2	3	2	8	2	1			1	3	7	15
Safety hazards												
Boundaries/drainage			1	1	3	3	1	1	3	3	8	8
Livestock control					2	2			3	3	5	5
Common greens												
Water pollution												
Dereliction of duty	1	1					2	2	1	1	4	4
Trading irregularity	4	5	1	5							5	10
Breaches of the peace	3	3							1	1	4	4
Gambling												
	10	12	4	14	7	6	3	3	9	11	33	46

(As before, the left-hand columns show charges, the right-hand ones people presented.)

If the last five full years of tourn offences are analysed (so as to provide the nearest possible comparison in terms of time with the leet indictments presented in Table 41), the degree of similarity regarding the type of misdemeanour dealt with is clearly seen. Table 43 shows that six of the ten standard offences occupied the attention of the jurors during the period in question, though another three (hazards to public safety, water pollution and gambling) do appear at other times. The only cases not to feature at any point are those concerning damage done to the common greens by digging holes for clay and sand or for dumping rubbish – though there are a number of references to pigs rooting up the ground (a matter classified under livestock control). The cross section of society represented by the offenders is exactly the same as that detectable in the leet material: the people indicted range from gentlemen down to husbandmen, with the lowest orders of society not visible at all. Six of the forty-six men who appear in the indictments categorised in the table also appear in the leet presentments for 1618–22, while others are detectable in other years.[109] The impression derived is that the punitive action taken by the manorial courts generally had little effect upon the transgressors.

Quarter sessions cases
With so much material available for the study of misdemeanour and nuisance, the ability to assess the degree of felony among Lowestoft's inhabitants is made a great deal more difficult by fewer records and by the difficulty of accessing those that do exist There are

---

[109] The six in question were Thomas Betts (linen weaver), Oliver Graye (mason), Philip Hales (boatwright), William Mayhewe (mariner), Thomas Powle (husbandman) and Francis Whayman (gentleman). The offences were as follows: jury default (Betts and Powle); allowing pigs to root up the Denes (Gray); depositing muck in the High Street (Hales); not keeping the street surface outside his house in good order (Mayhewe); and allowing pigs to wander on one of the common greens (Whayman). Their leet transgressions were these: not maintaining the street surface outside his house (Betts and Powle); brawling and hurling abuse (Graye and Hales); not maintaining his fences next to The Denes (Mayhewe); and not cleaning out his ditches on Skamacre Heath (Whayman).

a number of bundles of indictments relating to the Norfolk Assize (the county of Suffolk forming part of that circuit) during the seventeenth century at the Public Record Office, Kew. However, they are not indexed and there has not been time to sift through them to see if Lowestoft people feature there.

A certain, limited amount of information is to be had from quarter session records.[110] Suffolk had four centres for the holding of sessions (Ipswich, Woodbridge, Bury St Edmunds and Beccles), thus covering its area of jurisdiction on a regional basis, and order books for a period of over 100 years relevant to this study (1639–1747) have survived.[111] Unfortunately, there are no accompanying indictments and their absence makes it very difficult to gain any real idea of either the nature of crimes committed by Lowestoft people or of the amount of criminal behaviour. The town did not begin to stage quarter sessions of its own until 1748 (alternating with those held at Beccles), and it probably became the venue for petty sessions at about the same time.[112] Both sittings were held in the so-called 'Shire House', a building on the northern side of Swan Lane at its western end. It had originally been erected by Sir Thomas Allin (local merchant and seafarer, who became one of the leading admirals in Charles II's navy) and was the house identified in the 1674 Hearth Tax as having eleven fire-places.[113] The town also got its own bridewell, or lock-up, at about the same time as it was granted sessions – a small building erected on Goose Green (not far from the Shire House), leading to the area becoming known as 'Cage Green' during the later part of the eighteenth century and thereafter.

Thus, effectively, for practically the whole of the period under review in this book, Lowestoft had no real status as a centre for legal matters. Beccles, with its quarter sessions and petty sessions, its courthouse and its gaol, was very much the focal point of law enforcement locally where felony was concerned. Furthermore, the position of Lowestoft was further diminished, legally speaking, by its never having a resident Justice of the Peace. There was a justice for Lothingland Half-hundred, but he never lived in Lowestoft and the next nearest JP was to be found in Beccles.

One problem with quarter sessions order books as a source of information is that, in the absence of indictments, there is no way of ascertaining how many of these latter became the subject of orders made in the books. At least one leading commentator on social behaviour during the sixteenth and seventeenth centuries has expressed the opinion that justices usually made an order only when they thought that exemplary punishment was required.[114] Thus, the fact that only two cases of felony involving

---

[110] Quarter sessions were so called because they were held four times a year: Easter, Midsummer, Michaelmas and Epiphany. They dealt with crimes below the level of seriousness of those handled at the assizes, as well as a whole range of local administrative matters (including licensing, wage-fixing, road and bridge repair, taxes and the committal of lunatics).

[111] SRO(I), series B105. Micro-film copies of the documents are also available: Acc. 11/M1 (1639–83) and Acc. 11/M2 (1683–1747). These may be accessed in SRO(L).

[112] SRO(L), Acc. 11/M3 (1748–84). E. Gillingwater, p. 419, says that quarter sessions were first held in 1756. Petty sessions (deriving from the French *petit*) were legal proceedings supervised by local Justices of the Peace, which dealt with a number of minor acts of criminality and with the hiring of servants.

[113] SGB, xi, 198.

[114] The authority in question is Keith Wrightson., who expressed this opinion during the course of correspondence with the writer of this book some years ago.

Lowestoft people are recorded in the order books need not be particularly surprising. Furthermore, it is also possible to detect, in both instances, the exemplary nature of the punishment meted out, both in terms of its effect upon the criminals themselves and upon any potential transgressors.

The first case appears on 9 January 1688, when Elizabeth, wife of Thomas Clarke (mariner), was convicted of stealing one pound's weight of candles from John Aldred (grocer). Her punishment was 'to be whipped from the middle upward and publicly whipped in the Market place of Lowestoft until her body be bloody'. After the flogging had been carried out (by one of the constables), she was to be released – but she and her husband had to pay 2s 4d gaol fees for the time she had spent in the lock-up at Beccles. Seven years after this incident, in 1695, John Trussell was convicted of petty larceny. What he had stolen is not recorded, but he admitted his wrong-doing and, on agreeing to join the Royal Navy, was exempted from corporal punishment. His period of service was not specified, but it was to be without pay and he was to sail under the command of a Captain Pacy. This may have been John Pacy, one of the sons of Samuel Pacy deceased, Lowestoft's wealthiest merchant.

The majority of Lowestoft cases recorded in the order books during the later part of the seventeenth century and the first three or four decades of the eighteenth are concerned with removal orders. Next in number are those which record social or moral offences of one kind or another. Thus, on 5 October 1696, Alice Garnett, having been committed to the Beccles quarter sessions as a disorderly person, was to 'Remain in Gaol till next sessions the Inhabitants of Lowestoft by consent are to pay 2s a week for her maintenance'. The next year, on 11 January, John Ditcham (mariner) was ordered to be detained in the Beccles gaol until he had admitted his parental responsibilities with regard to the bastard son fathered on Mary Carre of Kirkley. Ditcham was contesting paternity at the time and already had a wife and two-year-old son. A second child (a daughter) was baptised in March 1697 and three further children were born to him and his wife, so he apparently managed to resolve his difficulties one way or another with regard to Mary Carre.

On 12 July 1714 Thomas Denney (alias Johnson and Drake), Edmund Grimston and Samuel Mingay were sentenced to remain in gaol 'till they severally find sureties for their good behaviour and respective appearances at next sessions', but there are no further references to them. Grimston was the twenty-year-old son of Edward Grimston, a Lowestoft innkeeper, who kept *The George* on the east side of the High Street, opposite the market, but the other two wrongdoers are not traceable in the family reconstitution material. Denney's two aliases suggest that he was a shady character who used alternative names for his own particular purposes. There is nothing equivocal, however, about the entry of 6 April 1730, which declared Edward Dixon to be an 'Incorrigible and Lewd Vagrant' and ordered him to be 'whipped publicly at the market place in Lowestoft between the hours of 12 and 1 on Wednesday next [being market day] till bloody and then passed away'.

Visitation material

One potentially rewarding source for research into all kinds of social and moral transgression within a community is to be found in ecclesiastical court records. The

Suffolk Archdeaconry material is limited in extent, while that of Norwich Consistory is massive. Neither collection is indexed, so accessing it for information relating to people from a particular community is rather like tying a rope to the handle of a bucket, throwing that bucket into a lake and drawing it back to land in the hope that it contains a fish. With all the other areas of study that had to be pursued in order to produce an integrated picture of life in Lowestoft, there was not time to investigate ecclesiastical court material in order to find out what kind of anti-social and, particularly, what kind of immoral behaviour its people indulged in.[115]

However, a good idea of the kind of things which would probably have been uncovered may be had from three bishop's visitations conducted during the first half of the seventeenth century. The first of these, carried out in 1606, certainly bears out what at least one commentator has said about such reports of the late sixteenth and early seventeenth centuries concentrating on morality rather than belief.[116] The Lowestoft details consist entirely of eight cases of adultery or fornication (the former being regarded as the more serious offence), and one of harbouring – this being the act of allowing an immoral person (usually a pregnant woman) to live in one's house, thereby effectively condoning the offence.[117] Furthermore, remarks which have been made about people of the time not being able to rely on the silence of friends and neighbours when it came to matters of sexual misdemeanour are demonstrably confirmed.[118] The various men and women accused of loose living were mainly exposed by 'common fame' (rumour and gossip). From what can be learned about them from the occupational data, the families they came from were mainly in the middle levels of local society, with seafarers and craftsmen featuring prominently.

The visitations of 1629 and 1633 both fix upon an offence which is said to have been rampant (among others) in Winchester during the first half of the seventeenth century: trading commercially on Sundays[119] The former of the two records refers specifically to butchers' shops being kept open on the Sabbath (those belonging to William Mewse and Thomas Durie), while the latter concentrates on other forms of business activity.[120] Particularly prominent are cases of people identified as ferrying barrels of pickled herrings out to trading vessels lying offshore. The mariner and the merchant engaged in this traffic (Peter Peterson and Francis Knights) are to be expected, but a tailor (John Sanderson) and a tanner (Richard Brethett) were also involved. Their activity probably

---

[115] Sharpe, *Crime*, p. 27, refers to the following matters being dealt with by church courts prior to 1642: sexual misdemeanour, drunkenness, Sabbath-breaking, defamation and disorderly behaviour.

[116] NRO, VIS/4. Spufford, *Contrasting Communities*, p. 257, makes reference to the emphasis on moral matters, citing R. A. Marchant, *The Church Under the Law* (Cambridge, 1969), pp. 240–1, which shows concentration on cases of sexual immorality.

[117] P. Hair, *Before the Bawdy Court* (London, 1972), pp. 236 and 246, refers to both sexual misconduct and harbouring. The Lowestoft harbouring case concerned a man called John Goddarde, who had given shelter to a pregnant single woman, Ann Bottwright. Whether he was performing a simple act of Christian charity or whether he was the father is not made clear.

[118] Laslett, *World We Have Lost*, pp. 137–8.

[119] NRO, VIS/6. A. Rosen, 'Winchester in Transition,', p. 161.

[120] Hair, *Bawdy Court*, p. 247, refers to all kinds of Sunday working.

serves to illustrate further the mixed nature of the local economy. In addition to the conveying of cured fish, there was also buying and selling of fresh herrings and mackerel taking place. The indictment against one of the men involved, John Bunn, has a colloquial and somewhat modern ring about it: he is described as 'scouting about after herrings'.[121]

The 1633 visitation also refers to a local brewer, Francis Ewen, barrelling beer on Sundays in contravention of traditional observance, while two other men, Hill Tidman and Thomas Meldrum, were noted for persistent absence from church. In 1629, a different kind of Sabbath-breaking had been noted in the playing of dice (probably for side-bets) during Sunday service-time by a brewer and a husbandman (Philip Bitson and Thomas Kipping) and in the excessive drinking during service-time by another husbandman (William Manfrey).[122] Both these offences had probably been committed regularly rather than being one-off aberrations.

Most ironic of all was the case of Thomas Hawes, boatwright by trade and the oldest child of Robert Hawes, the vicar of Lowestoft (his birth had pre-dated his father's appointment in 1610). He was noted, in 1633, as living incontinently with Elizabeth Hales, the twenty-seven-year-old daughter of Philip Hales, another boatwright and the man who had been fined at the leet of 1619 for being a common brawler and scolder of his neighbours. Perhaps the indictment caused the couple to get married, because in October a son (Robert) was baptised and duly registered as legitimate offspring. It may be presumed that Hawes senior was pleased to have the grandchild named after him, but even more relieved that his son had made an honest woman of Elizabeth Hales. The marriage, perhaps significantly, seems to have taken place outside Lowestoft, because it is not to be found recorded in the parish registers.

Regulation of the community: governors and governed

In the absence of a body of material relating to felony, and with ecclesiastical court records left largely unexplored, the leet court business in Lowestoft will be used as indicator of attitudes towards the regulation of local society. There were two differing views of the role of the law current in pre-industrial England. The first one saw the whole code as 'a cultural and ideological force so widely diffused in English society as

[121] Handling herrings on Sundays during the autumn was still a perceived problem over a century later. There is a surviving proclamation made by the Rev. John Tanner on 20 September 1747, in response to complaints received concerning the 1746 fishing season, which is to be found in Lowestoft parochial material lodged in the Norfolk Record Office (NRO, 589/86). It reads thus: 'When I first came to this place, To the Best of my Remembrance, No Body carted Herrings on the Lord's Day after Nine o' clock in the Morning, Nor till half an Hour after Four in the afternoon. And I earnestly desire that those Hours may be observed now, That I may not Leave a worse custom in the parish than I found. I must take the Liberty to add, That if these Hours be not observed, and I have any complaint and proof of Any one's carting after Nine o' clock in the morning & before Half hour after Four in the afternoon, I shall think myself Obliged to apply to the Magistrate for their being punished.'
[122] Hair, *Bawdy Court*, p. 251, makes reference to the following forbidden Sabbath pursuits: ball-games, dice and cards; while p. 249 mentions excessive drinking.

to inform the notions and actions of the population at large'; the second regarded it as 'more obviously the embodiment of the ideas and aspirations of the groups which ruled that population'.[123] The use of the law, by better-off members of society, as a means of controlling the lower orders has been admirably demonstrated with regard to the Essex village of Terling. The collation of assize, quarter session and ecclesiastical court material has been used to show how the various cases brought before these bodies were attempts by the richer villagers to control the poorer ones.[124]

Such manipulation of the law was practised in other communities of the time, and it has even been seen as a vital element in the mood of England generally during the first half of the seventeenth century.[125] The argument would seem to be that, in an age of mounting population pressure and more clearly defined social stratification, local officials and other people belonging to the levels of society from which those officials were drawn became more aware of the cultural gap between themselves and the poor. With that heightened awareness came a sense of greater need to control the lower ranks lest they should prove a threat to the established order.

It has already been noted, earlier in this chapter, that administration of poor law in Lowestoft does not seem to have been carried out in such a way as to make it a means of social control. And as for the function of the leet court, which one observer has said 'still represented a link in the chain of institutions upon which law and order depended in this period' (i.e. the first half of the seventeenth century), it can only be said to have sat in judgement on itself.[126] As has been seen, the jurors were either chief tenants or chief pledges and the various officers of the court were appointed from among the merchants, the tradespeople and the more substantial craftsmen. And who were the offenders requiring to be disciplined? – people from the same levels of society and even, on occasions, jurors and officers themselves![127]

A limited number of examples will serve to demonstrate the typicality. At the session of 1620, William Rising (yeoman), one of the newly elected parish constables, was fined 10s for allowing a mangy horse to roam about on one of the common greens. In 1652, Richard Brissingham, John Sone (yeoman) and Thomas Harvey (gentleman), all jurors of the leet, were each fined 3s 4d for not maintaining the road surface outside their houses, as they had been ordered to do the previous year. There is no surviving record for 1651, but it is interesting to note that William Arnold (brewer), who had been elected as one of the four constables for that particular year, was fined 3d in 1652 for throwing dead pigs into the common watering-place on Goose Green. In 1690, John Wilde (merchant) was fined 3d for blocking a footway with two posts and a rail and 6d

---

[123] Sharpe, *Crime*, p. 143.

[124] Wrightson and Levine, *Poverty and Piety*, pp. 118–19, tables 5.1 and 5.2.

[125] Wrightson, 'Concepts of Order', pp. 41–4, looks at the manipulation of the legal process. Underdown, *Revel, Riot and Rebellion*, pp. 8–43, considers the philosophy behind its implementation.

[126] J. A. Sharpe, 'Crime and Delinquency in an Essex Parish, 1600–1640' in J. S. Cockburn (ed.), *Crime in England, 1500–1800* (London, 1977), p. 92.

[127] Conversation with John Ridgard, an authority on late mediaeval Suffolk manor courts, has revealed that the situation was exactly the same.

for not fencing off a well. As he had been appointed afferator at the previous leet, he was in the ironic position of fixing the rate at which he was to be fined. And he wasn't the only one to be in that position over the years! Finally, in 1710, all four of the parish constables who had just completed their year of office had 3d fines imposed for highway offences. John Wilde, William Balls and Edward Colby (all merchants) were penalised for not maintaining the road surface outside their houses, while John Peach (yeoman and brewer) was found guilty of two misdemeanours: depositing muck on the Queen's highway and not keeping a ditch and footpath near his malt-house in sufficiently good order.

None of the offences cited here was particularly serious in the hierarchy of crime, but the regularity with which such misdemeanours were committed by some people, over a number of years, suggests a community of petty offenders who knew what the local ordinances were, but who seemed quite content to go on paying the fines. Even the vicar, Henry Youell, was amerced 3d on two separate occasions (1669 and 1670) for throwing the contents of his privy into the street – though no doubt it was a servant who performed the task rather than the clergyman himself. The propensity of certain parish constables in Kelvedon, Essex, for indulging in all kinds of illegal and immoral activities has been commented on.[128] In the absence of any kind of evidence drawn from ecclesiastical court material, it cannot be claimed that their Lowestoft counterparts did not indulge themselves in such anti-social behaviour. Yet, at the same time, the manorial records overall do not suggest anything worse than general nuisance, the committing of which seems to have been accepted almost as part of the pattern of life itself.

The people who broke the laws most frequently (overwhelmingly, in fact) were from those sections of society responsible for upholding and enforcing the code.[129] No stigma seems to have attached to the many lapses from the required standard of public conduct. People obviously flouted the rules because it was convenient to do so or because there was no great pressure within the community to behave otherwise. Even the most worthy citizens were guilty of infringement. No family did more good for the inhabitants of Lowestoft over the years than the Wildes, but they were just as capable of depositing muck in the streets, blocking footpaths and allowing watercourses to flood as those people with a less philanthropic disposition.

Any picture of the Lowestoft leet as an instrument of social control shows that, at best, it had only a limited effect with the kind of order it sought to impose and that it dealt almost exclusively with the better-off members of society. There was no question of the court being used by the more affluent to regulate the conduct of the poor, because it was primarily an agency which dealt with misdemeanours of the property-owning classes. The humblest members of society did not possess real estate, had little or no livestock, were not able to rent land on any scale, and probably could not afford to drink or gamble to any great extent. Therefore, given the nature of the ten main offences discernible in the minute books, the lower orders did not really have the

---

[128] Sharpe, 'Crime and Deliquency', pp. 95–7.

[129] Moxon, pp. 216–19, refers to the minor law-breaking committed by officials in Ashby-de-la Zouche.

opportunity to appear before the jurors. Even brawling in the street, on the evidence of the records, does not seem to have been practised by them.

The court existed as the means of regulating the conduct of the manor's inhabitants (and therefore of the parish, because both areas were identical in size) – but only those inhabitants who were of some substance. Its failure to raise standards of behaviour in certain matters of public responsibility probably suggests not so much weak manorial control in itself (through an absentee lord) as the inability or unwillingness, on the part of the guilty, to change codes of established practice. The fact of the various offences being indictable under the laws of the manor showed that the authorities acknowledged the anti-social nature of such behaviour, but the fines imposed were not sufficiently punitive in many cases as to deter offenders from committing the same acts over and over again.[130]

Conclusion: urban government by manorial and parochial means

Throughout the period of study covered by this book, Lowestoft was (by the standards of the time) a market town of respectable size – though not a large one. During the last seventy years of the 200 covered, it was also a place of increasing maritime specialisation. It had no charter (and therefore no corporation) and governed itself by a combination of parish vestry and manor court, with the leet being the latter's main instrument.[131] The combination of these two agencies was certainly not uncommon in small towns during the early modern period and attention has long been drawn to the way in which they often acted as substitutes for the governing institutions established by a charter of incorporation.[132]

One market town of similar size to Lowestoft which seems to have been controlled largely by manor courts is Ashby-de-la-Zouche, in Leicestershire. The baron and the leet were combined in this particular community, meeting twice a year, in the spring and the autumn, and their influence may well have been reinforced by the presence of a resident lord[133] – something which Lowestoft never experienced during the whole of its history (at least, not until the second half of the nineteenth century, when the title had largely ceased to have any significance). Non-residency on the part of the lord had the advantage, through separation caused by distance, of preventing – or, at least, of watering down – possible conflict caused by a clash of interests with tenants.[134] From what can

---

[130] Evans, *Beccles*, p. 22. Comment is made that neither the town's land leet nor its water leet was wholly successful in attempts to regulate the conduct of local people. The period assessed covered the years 1649–59.

[131] Lowestoft did not receive a charter of incorporation until 1885, when a 17,500 population and flourishing maritime activity drew official recognition of its importance as Suffolk's second town.

[132] Clark and Slack, *Towns in Transition*, p. 22; Jack, *Towns*, p. 75.

[133] Moxon, pp. 192 and 340–56.

[134] Jack, *Towns*, p. 76.

be ascertained, it would seem that, as long as the rents were collected and paid over, Lowestoft's lords were content to let the chief tenants and other leading townsmen run their community without interference.

Much closer to Lowestoft lay the neighbouring market town of Beccles – again, a community of similar size, but one which had been granted a charter in the year 1584. Here, the instruments of government were twofold: the corporation itself and two manorial courts (land leet and water leet). The former, consisting of thirty-six members, concerned itself with the administration of the extensive area of marshland and common adjoining the town, with relief of the poor, with supporting the town's free grammar school and with assisting the parish church in various ways.[135] The latter two dealt largely with infringements of local ordinance, at least six of which were the same as the offences handled by the Lowestoft leet.[136]

The emphasis placed on the Lowestoft court, in the absence of any institutions established by charter, may help to explain why it remained active over such a long period of time. Its regulation of the community was a combination of the attempted and the actual, and its influence seems to have been supplemented by the tourn for at least some of the total period of study. Altogether, the manorial bureaucracy was responsible for the creation of fifteen official posts (steward, rents bailiff, court bailiff, four constables, two ale-tasters, two leather searchers, two hog-reeves or fen-reeves, and two afferators), while the parish vestry contributed another ten (parish clerk, two churchwardens, sexton, four overseers and two highway surveyors). In addition to this twenty-five, there was also (by the end of the seventeenth century/beginning of the eighteenth) what may be termed the *de facto* position of town clerk.[137] The model of government may have been essentially rural in origin, even perhaps in nature, but it appears to have been adequate for the demands made upon it. Those people elected or appointed to office were the ones who administered local government – not only in the sense of having executive power, but also through belonging to those levels of society from which officialdom was recruited.

In the sense that Lowestoft's rulers were drawn from the better-off sections of the population, it may be tempting to view the governing elite as oligarchical – a feature which is said to have been typical at the time in English towns.[138] However, such a view needs qualification, because membership of the elite was not restricted to a limited number of the wealthiest men of all and office-holding was spread across various occupational and social groups – with the exception of labourer and servant. In Ashby-

---

[135] Evans, *Beccles*, pp. 57–8 and 59–63.

[136] *Ibid.*, p. 23. The six offences referred to were failure to maintain the road surface, depositing rubbish in the streets, blocking water-courses, polluting ponds, dereliction of duty and trading irregularities.

[137] The term is encountered in the burial entry of John Evans (January 1706). He was a scrivener of some kind, first detectable in a baptism entry of February 1682, who obviously performed various kinds of public service in the town (including keeping the poor law accounts). His period of residence coincided with the increasing maritime specialisation evident in Lowestoft and the growth of population deriving from this. His literacy skills were obviously valuable in helping to cope with an ever-increasing amount of bureaucracy and paperwork.

[138] Clark and Slack, *Towns in Transition*, pp. 127ff.

de-la Zouche, over a five-year period, no less than seventy-one men held some kind of manorial position – a number which represented about one-third of the town's families.[139]

In Lowestoft, at any point during the seventeenth century, a similar five-year period would have produced about sixty men who held manorial and parochial office, while during the first half of the eighteenth it had risen to about seventy.[140] The former figure, on the evidence of the family reconstitution data, represents about 23% of family heads during the first half of the seventeenth century and about 17% during the second. The latter accounts for 16%. Such proportions are, of course, worked out on a relatively short timespan. If the period of office-holding analysis is extended to twenty-five years (bearing in mind that the levels of society involved were usually not those which formed the town's transient population), then something like 40% of family heads in Lowestoft are seen to have served in some kind of official capacity between 1650 and 1699 and 33% between 1700 and 1730.[141] This degree of involvement in the regulation of the community hardly suggests that a local oligarchy was the controlling factor in the town's affairs.

What is difficult to ascertain, in terms of hard evidence, is the overall influence of substantial, long-stay families detectable among merchants, retailers, wealthier craftsmen and seafarers. 'Ruling families' have been identified in both Ipswich and Northampton,[142] and there is no doubt that Lowestoft had its equivalents. The Arnolds, Ashbys, Barkers, Durrants, Jexes, Mighells, Pacys, Risings, Utbers, Wards and Wildes all exercised considerable authority in the town because of their wealth and because they had been resident for so long.[143] Of lesser standing than these twelve, but also of some importance, were the Canhams, Coes, Daynes(es), Feltons, Ferneys, Fishers, Fowlers, Frarys, Hawes(es), Kitredges, Landifields, Mewses, Munds(es), Neales, Spicers and Uttings. Any marriages which took place among members of the various long-stay families must have helped to reinforce their position as leaders of the community, but there are no real signs of deliberate exclusiveness on their part.[144] In fact, people

[139] Moxon, p. 361. The period of study covered in this work is 1570–1720.

[140] This increase was largely due to the town's growth in population. It was quite common for a man to hold more than one office during a five-year period and it was not unknown for some individuals to serve in two capacities (or even three) during the same year.

[141] This compares closely to the city of Gloucester during the early modern period, where it has been estimated that 42% of the ruling elite were related either by marriage or by blood. See P. Clark, 'The Civic Leaders of Gloucester, 1500–1800', in Clark, *Transformation of Towns*, p. 318.

[142] A. Everitt, 'The Market Towns' in Clark, *Early Modern Town*, p. 186. This particular essay was first published as 'The Marketing of Agricultural Produce', in Thirsk, *Agrarian History*, iv, 467–506. I. Archer, 'Politics and Government, 1540–1700', in P. Clark (ed.), *The Cambridge Urban History of Britain, Vol. II, 1540–1840* (Cambridge, 2000), 243, says that 'urban dynasties' were rare in chartered towns of the early modern period.

[143] Members of the Arnold, Barker and Wilde families are to be found in the 1524 lay subsidy. The Arnolds and Wildes are also present in that of 1568, as are the Ashbys, Mighells and Wards. The Allens (or Allins) have not been placed in the list of influential families because they ceased to have any real part in the town's affairs after about the middle of the seventeenth century.

[144] There is no evidence of pronounced or deliberate inter-marriage among the influential families, except perhaps in the case of some of the seafarers. However, those marriages which did take place within the wealthier levels of local society served to preserve the position of the parties concerned.

moving into the town were soon accepted into the office-holding classes, as long as they were of sufficient means to merit a place there.[145] In a very small number of cases, they did not remain in Lowestoft for long, but they were made part of its governing structure during their period of residence.

Some examples of the acceptance of newcomers into the ruling establishment during the earlier part of the eighteenth century may now be given for the purposes of example. Leake Bitson (merchant) does not feature in any documentation until 1714. In that year, he appears as one of the chief pledges at the leet and was also elected ale-taster. He had three children baptised between September 1714 and May 1717, and he himself died before the third one was christened. Edward Morgan (innkeeper) had only been in town about a year, when he was made one of the chief pledges in 1712. A year later, he was appointed as one of the four constables, and this was followed by his election as fen-reeve in 1720. He died in 1732. Humphrey Overton (also an innkeeper) appears in the leet records of 1709 as one of the chief pledges. He was appointed constable the next year, overseer in 1711, and the parish register records the baptism of three of his children between October 1710 and March 1713. After the latter date, there is no further sign of him, so he had presumably moved on to new premises somewhere else.

John Peach (yeoman and brewer) is first detectable in the tithe accounts of 1708. The following year, he appears in the leet records as chief pledge and constable. Much later on, in 1736, 1737 and 1747, he served as churchwarden,[146] and he died in February 1749. James Primrose (baker) is detectable in the leet of 1707 as both chief pledge and constable (he also took an apprentice in the same year), and four of his children appear in the parish registers between January 1707 and April 1711. His wife, Margaret, died in the latter month and year (perhaps of childbirth complications) and he himself left Lowestoft at some point after this, eventually re-marrying in Beccles in April 1714.

Inclusion in the process of governing the community was not limited solely to the elected offices. If an incomer bought one of the chief tenements, the purchase entitled him to serve as juror on the leet and take his turn as collector of the lord's rents. It was not necessarily the richest people who owned these pieces of freehold land – especially during the latter part of the period covered in this book – and thus an influential position was able to be held by someone of lesser means than the wealthiest members of local society.

In the final analysis, it was probably the case that the most powerful people in town were the members of families which had been resident for generations and which derived their influence not only from accumulated wealth, but also from the accumulation of local custom and tradition, backed by a reputation for financial probity and credit-worthiness (social trust, in early modern times, being almost as much of a commodity as goods traded).[147] At the same time, their control of the community in

---

[145] Jack, *Towns*, p. 70, notes that what may be termed urban oligarchies were self-perpetuating but not impermeable.

[146] H. D. W. Lees, *The Chronicles of a Suffolk Parish Church* (Lowestoft, 1949), pp. 214–15.

[147] Muldrew, *Economy of Obligation*, pp. 5 and 58.

which they lived was not absolute and they were prepared to share the process of government with any newcomers deemed to be suitable. What is more, there is no suggestion that they were forced to do this because of an inbuilt inability to regenerate and maintain the hierarchical structure from within their own ranks.[148] There seems to have been genuine recognition that, among the incomers entering the town, were those suitable to be involved in the ordering and conduct of its affairs.

[148] I. Archer, 'Politics and Government', in Clark (ed.), *Cambridge Urban History*, II, 243. It is stated here that, in the chartered towns discussed, the urban elite was 'unable to replenish itself from its own ranks'. This resulted from one-third of office-holders failing to produce male heirs, from sons failing to follow their fathers' occupations and from family wealth being spread too widely in the pattern of bequests. Lowestoft was not affected by the first two characteristics and its pattern of bequest (largely, a combination of primogeniture and partible inheritance) does not seem to have disadvanataged beneficiaries.

– 11 –

Literacy, Education and Religious Belief

Aspects of literacy

Introduction

Even today, there would probably be argument (or at least discussion) among specialists in the field as to what literacy means. The same holds true for historians. And even if the two basic criteria of a person's being able to read and write are accepted as evidence of it, the question then arises as to what level of proficiency in each skill identifies the truly literate man or woman. At least one commentator has remarked on the imprecision shown by historians regarding the word and has pointed out further that the level of literacy skills considered appropriate in any historical context has rarely been adequately specified.[1] In the final analysis, it seems that the only convenient means of measuring people's standard of literacy in previous centuries is their ability (or lack of it) to sign their own names. Such proficiency is deemed to satisfy almost all the requirements of a universal, standard and direct method of assessment.[2]

Regarding source material suitable for investigating of people's ability to sign their names, it has been pointed out that the best results are derived from documents requiring large numbers of individuals to sign or make a mark. Two classic examples are the Protestation Oath of 1642 and the Association Oath of 1696 – the former being a signed protest organised by Parliament against the danger of 'arbitrary and tyrannical government', the latter a declaration of loyalty to the Crown affirmed by all holders of public office. Both of them have severe under-representation of women and the former also suffers from uneven geographical survival of the signatories.[3] Other productive sources include wills, allegations and bonds for marriage licences, and the depositions of witnesses in ecclesiastical court proceedings. Lowestoft has no existing documentation for either of the oaths referred to; its marriage licence data has not as yet been fully investigated; and, as stated in the previous chapter, the ecclesiastical court material would have been too time-consuming to access. Therefore, the survey of literacy carried out has been based on wills and inventories. This means, once again, that the lower orders

---

[1] R. Schofield, 'The Measurement of Literacy in Pre-Industrial England', in J. R. Goody (ed.), *Literacy in Traditional Societies* (Cambridge, 1968), p. 313.

[2] *Ibid.*, p. 319; Cressy, *Literacy*, p. 53.

[3] Schofield, 'Measurement of Literacy', p. 319.

cannot be reached – the fate of that particular class in so much of the study of history during the early modern period.

In concentrating solely on surviving probate material, it is possible (in the case of testators) that the rate of literacy shown in the ability to sign or in the necessity of making a mark may be an under-estimate of the true state of affairs. One investigator found that literacy rates based on the ability to sign a will were lower than in comparable samples of ecclesiastical court depositions and speculated that this may have been due to the fact that wills were often signed when the testator was close to death.[4] However, the signatures of testators alone are not the only consideration: there are those of the many witnesses to be taken into account as well. And in a town such as Lowestoft, with limited geographical area and a relatively small population, it is possible to ascertain from the family reconstitution process which of the witnesses were resident and which of them lived out of town. It would be interesting to be able to prove a link between the relatively high number of people able to sign their names and the influence exerted by the town's schools. As things stand, however, the effect of these institutions can only be presumed.

Signatures on wills

Out of a total of 507 wills which have been analysed for the years 1560–1730 416 bear the signatures, initials or marks of the testators, thirty-six are nuncupative and unsigned, and a further fifty-five are standard copies which have no identifying marks of any kind by the testator (though twenty-six of them are witnessed).[5] Of the 416 documents which are either signed or marked by the testator, 216 have signatures, eighteen have initials and 182 bear marks. Initials were only classified as such if both were used; a single initial has been treated as a mark. The 216 wills which were properly signed represent 42.6% of the total number of 507 and 52% of the 416 which were authenticated by the testator. Both proportions are considerably higher than those established for an area of rural High Suffolk and for two Cambridgeshire country parishes.[6] The difference noted is probably the result of the differing nature of urban and rural communities in terms of social and economic structure, whereby the need for literacy was more pronounced in towns than in the countryside. The Lowestoft inhabitants' ability to sign their names may be compared with that of the citizens of Ipswich, Suffolk's biggest town. In Lowestoft, 43% of testators possessed the skill during the first half of the seventeenth century (as opposed to 37%) and 54% showed it during the early years of the eighteenth (as opposed to 57%).[7]

Another point deserving attention, which has drawn comment from historians using probate material for various purposes, is the quality of handwriting evident in the signatures of both testators and witnesses. No claim is made that good handwriting

---

[4] D. Cressy, 'Literacy in Seventeenth Century England: More Evidence', *JIH* 8 (1977), 149–50.

[5] Forty-five of the wills which are not signed date from the second half of the sixteenth century.

[6] Evans, 'South Elmham', p. 242, shows 30% of testators as signing wills; Spufford, *Contrasting Communities*, p. 202, has the ability to sign as only 15% in Willingham and 17% in Orwell.

[7] Reed, 'Ipswich', p. 233, table 1.

means a high (or even reasonable) standard of literacy, because well-educated people, even today, are capable of producing an inferior script.[8] Nevertheless, in assessing a large number of signatures from a single body of documents, certain inferences may be drawn from the overall quality of calligraphy. For instance, facility in using a pen becomes apparent – and if a person handled a pen with ease, then he or she might well have been confident in putting words onto paper. Furthermore, a good handwriting style may also be taken as evidence of thorough training in the art of writing or of regular practice at it. And people who write regularly are usually those who have some degree of literary attainment. Thus, while legible, well-formed handwriting may not be conclusive in itself of a high standard of literacy, it can probably be accepted as a general indicator of proficiency.

The great majority of signatures of testators in the Lowestoft wills show an impressive level of calligraphic skill. Over 90% of them are well-formed, and it is probably reasonable to assume that at least some of the inferior signatures were the result of physical weakness rather than general ineptitude.[9] Having said that, for every inferior signature appended to a will where the preamble refers to the testator's sickness or infirmity, there are four or five others with identical preambles but with good handwriting. Witnesses' signatures are less equivocal because those people were presumably in good health (or, at least, not seriously ill) when they signed the document before them. Over 95% of witnesses' signatures are well-formed, but there is much greater variability in the initials and marks, with an overall tendency for the standard of penmanship to be lower than that evident in the signatures. This is not surprising, bearing in mind that it was largely the illiterate members of society who used either initials or marks as their means of formal identification, and these would have been the very people not used to handling pens on a regular basis.[10]

There are two kinds of initials used in the wills: those representing both Christian name and surname and those which opted for one or the other. It is noticeable that the quality of handwriting is better on the part of testators and witnesses who used both initial letters of their names than it is on the part of those who used one letter only. There are eighteen examples of testators who used both initials and sixteen examples of witnesses who did the same (two of the former presented them as monograms, as did one of the latter). A further twenty-six testators used their Christian name initial only and another four the initial letter of their surnames. The preponderance of Christian name initial over that of the surname is also to be seen in the witnesses' marks: there are thirty-six examples of the former and thirteen of the latter. In both types of initials used for either signing or witnessing wills, the malformation of certain letters is noticeable:

---

[8] Cressy, *Literacy*, p. 16, notes that professional scriveners, during the sixteenth and seventeenth centuries, often exhibited a poor standard of handwriting.

[9] There are seventeen inferior signatures written by testators (out of a total of 216), sixteen of which appear on wills where the preamble declares the person to be sick or infirm.

[10] Cressy, *Literacy*, p. 59, states that initials are regarded as indicating illiteracy. But it is possible that literate people used initials when it suited them. Then are ten examples of Lowestoft testators (nine men and a woman) who signed their own wills, but made a mark when acting as witnesses.

M and W were sometimes written upside-down; E, N and S were sometimes rendered back to front. In nearly every case where initials were written, capital letters were used.

The marks employed (in other words, those symbols which do not have anything to do with the initial letters of the testators' or witnesses' names) fall into three categories: personal marks of varying shape and type (a number of these may be interpreted as imitations of mediaeval merchants' marks), trade tools or representations, and imitations of a cursive hand. The first group contains a wide variety of different crosses, circles, lines and strokes, with varying facility in the operation of the pen.[11] Actual trade tools or symbols are very limited in number, but interesting nevertheless.[12] There are seven examples of testators using such a mark and they are as follows: William Barnard (shipwright, 1580), an adze; Hugh Calver (husbandman, 1593), a three-tined fork; John Besecke (mariner, 1597), a beacon; John Landefield (mariner, 1617), a beacon; Robert Beeteson (husbandman, 1623), a scythe; John Stroud (mariner, 1636), a beacon; Thomas Neale (husbandman, 1649), a pick or mattock. In addition to these, there are two instances of witnesses employing the same technique: Thomas Burges (smith, 1575), outlined a three-tined fork, while Thomas Graye (mason, 1603) drew a spade.[13]

Finally, there are the attempts by a minority of people to imitate proper handwriting. There are twenty-two examples of this particular practice (fifteen testators and seven witnesses), and just over half of the exponents were women. This is not a sufficiently large majority (on an admittedly small number to begin with) to make any assumption that certain women were trying to compensate for their lack of educational opportunity by pretending that they were able to write, any more than it is to submit a similar claim on behalf of the men who did it. What the practitioners did, in all cases, was to pen an irregularly undulating line that looked like a cursive hand at first glance, but did not bear closer scrutiny as genuine writing.

As might be expected, the ability of a person to sign his or her name has a pronounced social and economic factor about it, with the greatest degree of literacy evident among the wealthier levels of Lowestoft's population. Not only could such people afford to pay for the education that was available (either by meeting the costs involved or by not having to see their children become wage-earners at an early age), they also needed to acquire the basic skills of reading and writing in order to conduct business interests more efficiently. This latter point held for tradespeople and craftsmen as well, while seafarers would have seen the benefits of being able to read charts and cargo manifests and sign their names on customs documents. The increase in literacy

[11] Evans, 'South Elmham', p. 245, notes how the quality of marks (as well as that of signatures) varies in the wills made in this particular part of rural Suffolk.

[12] Cressy, *Literacy*, p. 59, refers to the use of trade tools as marks on documents and says that such practice was often adopted by artisans and craftsmen during the sixteenth and seventeenth centuries. Evans, 'South Elmham', p. 245, also makes passing reference to 'trade marks' as a way of signing wills, though without giving any specific details.

[13] Of the various trade symbols used by Lowestoft people, the beacon is the most interesting because it is a copy or variant of the symbol used on contemporary maps and charts (Plate 7). This suggests that the mariners who employed it as their personal mark were familiar with it. And this, in turn, means that they may have been able to interpret a chart without being able to read in the conventional sense.

Table 44. *Literacy statistics: wills (testators)*

Occupational/ social group	1560–1599 S	I	M	1600–1649 S	I	M	1650–1699 S	I	M	1700–1730 S	I	M	1560–1730 S	I	M
Merchants, yeomen & gentry	11		4	18		8	26		6	14	1	1	69	1	19
Professional & medical	1			3			2			4			10		
Tradespeople & retail	2			9		5	12		4	6		4	29		13
Seafarers	2		5	5	2	7	12	3	13	26	3	9	45	8	34
Craftsmen	7			5		15	12	1	7	6	2	3	30	3	25
Husbandmen		1	2			4			1			4		1	11
Labourers				1								2	1		2
Occupation unknown	1		2	1			4		2	2		1	8		5
Women	4		7	3	1	18	3	3	19	14	1	29	24	5	73
Total	**28**	**1**	**20**	**45**	**3**	**57**	**71**	**7**	**52**	**72**	**7**	**53**	**216**	**18**	**182**

S signature **I** initials (both) **M** mark (including single initial)

among the sea-going fraternity in Lowestoft is particularly noticeable after 1700, by which time the town was becoming much more of a specialist maritime community. With growing numbers of menfolk involved in coastal and overseas trade, there would have been increased need for masters and mates to be able to read and write in order to deal with the documentation which came their way.

Tables 44 to 47 present the literacy statistics derived from the 416 surviving wills which are signed, and perhaps the most interesting feature revealed is the relatively high rate of female literacy from the second half of the seventeenth century onwards. This is not so pronounced among testators as among witnesses, and it can be clearly seen how women became the single most important group of people to authenticate wills during the first three decades of the eighteenth century. Such a development may have been due in some measure to the town's burgeoning maritime life, which resulted in substantial numbers of men being absent from home for weeks at a time (especially on trading voyages) – though it does not explain where the women learned to write. As far as the ability of witnesses to sign their names is concerned, Tables 45, 46 and 47 include only those people for whom it was possible to prove residency in town by the family reconstitution exercise.[14] A large proportion of witnesses in the 'Occupation unknown' category who were able to sign belonged to families in the first four occupational and social groupings.

In order to arrive at an accurate analysis of people's ability to write their names based

---

[14] The number of witnesses who seem to have lived out of town was very small. There are only about twenty examples between 1560 and 1730 (thirteen men and seven women) and it is possible that some of these people were resident in Lowestoft. Parish registration did not record everyone living in the place – nor did other local bureaucratic systems, such as poor law administration and the manor courts.

Table 45. *Literacy statistics: wills (witnesses)*

Occupational/ social group	1560–1599			1600–1649			1650–1699			1700–1730			1560–1730			Adjusted		
	S	I	M	S	I	M	S	I	M	S	I	M	S	I	M	S	I	M
Merchants, yeomen & gentry	16		2	26		1	26		1	15		1	83		5	75		5
Professional & medical	2			13			5			19			39			36		
Tradespeople & retail	1			10		7	14		1	18		1	43		9	39		9
Seafarers	6			8		1	12			25		1	51		2	45		2
Craftsmen	13	1	2	12	1	14	10	1	2	12		1	47	3	19	42	2	19
Husbandmen						3	1			1			2		3	2		3
Labourers						3				2		1	2		4	2		4
Occupation unknown	16		8	21	4	15	20	2	4	13		3	70	6	30	69	6	30
Women	4		3	1	1	8	17	2	28	53	4	29	75	7	68	74	7	66
Total	58	1	15	91	6	52	105	5	36	158	4	37	412	16	140	384	15	138

Table 46. *Literacy statistics: wills (testators and witnesses)*

Occupational/ social group	1560–1599			1600–1649			1650–1699			1700–1730			1560–1730			Adjusted		
	S	I	M	S	I	M	S	I	M	S	I	M	S	I	M	S	I	M
Merchants, yeomen & gentry	22		6	39		8	44		6	26	1	2	131	1	22	115	1	22
Professional & medical	3			14			6			20			43			41		
Tradespeople & retail	2			18		10	22		5	21		4	63		19	57		19
Seafarers	8		5	10	2	7	24	3	11	45	3	10	87	8	33	81	8	33
Craftsmen	17	1	1	15	1	22	17	2	7	16	2	4	65	6	34	62	6	34
Husbandmen		1	2			6	1		1			4	1	1	13	3		6
Labourers				1		3				2		3	3		6	3		6
Occupation unknown	17		10	22	4	15	24	2	6	15		4	78	6	35	78	6	35
Women	8		10	4	2	25	20	5	45	66	5	54	98	12	134	96	12	133
Total	77	2	34	123	9	96	158	12	81	211	11	85	569	34	296	536	33	288

on the evidence available in wills, it is necessary to make adjustments within Tables 45 and 46. In the case of the former, the final column takes account of those people who acted as witnesses in two of the individual sub-periods and who must not, therefore, be counted twice so as to inflate the overall total. The same principle applies in the latter table: the amalgamation of testators and witnesses has to take account of the men and women who signed their names or made their marks in both capacities. Furthermore, the calculations have to apply to both the individual sub-periods used and also to the

Table 47. *Literacy statistics: wills (% of testators and witnesses able to sign their names)*[15]

Occupational/ social group	1560–1599	1600–1649	1650–1699	1700–1730	1560–1730	Adjusted
Merchants, yeomen & gentry	78.5	83.0	88.0	89.6	85.1	83.3
Professional & medical		100.0		100.0	100.0	100.0
Tradespeople & retail		64.3	81.5	84.0	76.8	75.0
Seafarers	61.5	52.6	63.2	77.6	70.0	65.8
Craftsmen	89.5	39.5	65.4	72.7	61.9	60.8
Occupation unknown	63.0	53.6	75.0	78.9	65.5	65.5
Women	44.4	13.0	28.6	52.8	40.2	39.8
All men classified	75.0	63.1	76.5	82.6	74.0	72.5

Note: blank spaces are the result of too few people signing documents to constitute a reliable sample.

overall timescale. Hence, there is a final column for the adjusted totals, whereby people who were witnesses in one sub-period and testators in another are amalgamated to produce figures which are as reliable as possible with regard to the data used.

Analysis of literacy rates in Norwich diocese between 1580 and 1700, based on ecclesiastical court depositions, found that 56% of tradespeople and craftsmen and only about 11% of women were able to sign their names.[16] Table 47, in providing a summary statement of the overall pattern of literacy on the part of those people who signed wills, either as testators or witnesses, is able to demonstrate that Lowestoft people in these categories had a notably higher ability. In fact, if tradespeople and craftsmen are grouped together for a period covering the late sixteenth century to the beginning of the eighteenth, the rate of literacy is about 60%–65% and that of women about 25%. It is, however, possible that the better literacy rate for women may be exaggerated above the norm because of the particular documentation used. Women who made and who witnessed wills were likely to have been members of the more affluent social and occupational groups, whereas those appearing in ecclesiastical court depositions would have been drawn from a wider cross section of society, including the less fortunate.

Percentages of literacy among the various social and occupational groups in Lowestoft may seem to suggest a decline in people's ability to sign their names during the first half of the seventeenth century. It is tempting to view this as further evidence of the town's decline at this time – but there may be another explanation. If Table 46 is scrutinised, it

---

[15] Husbandmen and labourers have been omitted from this table because their numbers, either as testators or witnesses, are not large enough to create representative percentages of literacy for their respective categories.

[16] Cressy, *Literacy*, p. 119, table 6.1. The writer presents the information as percentages of people unable to sign their names. For the purposes of comparison here, emphasis has been placed on literacy rather than illiteracy.

can be seen that the varying (and variable) survival rate of the wills themselves may be responsible for inflating the degree of literacy measurable from the signatures of testators and witnesses between 1560 and 1599. For instance, nearly all of the nineteen craftsmen recorded were able to sign their names – a trend which does not observe the pattern evident in the other three sub-periods. And there was quite a high degree of female literacy resulting from a good survival rate of wills relating to women from merchant and yeomen families. There were probably other anomalies and variables, too, and perhaps the safest response to the data in all four tables is to look at the long-term trend revealed: one of increasing rates of literacy among most of the social and occupational groups listed.

Signatures on inventories

The statistics derived from a study of appraisers' signatures and marks on the ninety-five surviving inventories which are undamaged and complete are not the same as the results yielded by the wills – though there is still the same bias, in terms of numbers, towards the better-off social and occupational groupings. To have amalgamated the inventory material with that of the wills would have had a distorting effect on the picture of literacy given. There is a complete absence of either labourers or women in the documents and there is a great preponderance of signatures over initials and marks. Labourers, of course, did not feature strongly in the will material and their absence from inventories need not be surprising: given their economic and social status, their services were not likely to have been required in assessing the value of goods belonging to wealthier people.[17] The absence of women was probably due to their social position at the time and even inventories taken of women's possessions do not include a single female assessor.

The pronounced dominance of signatures over marks, which can be clearly seen in Table 48, is probably the result of the best-educated people in the various social and occupational groupings being in demand as assessors simply because of their ability to read and write. Again, as with the wills, an impressive level of facility is evident in the signatures and the documents themselves are generally well written too. Only those people whose residency in Lowestoft could be proved were considered for inclusion in the table (there were only about ten assessors all told who could not be traced in the family reconstitution data) and, once again, adjustments were made in the final column to take account of those people (three only) who acted as appraisers in two of the individual sub-periods. As was the case in the earlier tables, most of the people in the 'Occupation unknown' category who were able to sign their names belonged to families in the first four occupational groupings.

---

[17] Husbandmen comprise the other group which has a very limited presence in will material, and the same is true of inventories. The reason for this is the low survival-rate of documents – and in the case of inventories, of course, the people best qualified to assess the value of agricultural equipment and stock were men involved in farming themselves. Thus, if few husbandmen's inventories have survived, there will not be many men from that occupational group in evidence as assessors.

Table 48. Literacy statistics: inventories

Occupational/ social group	1560–1599			1600–1649			1650–1699			1700–1730			1560–1730			Adjusted		
	S	I	M	S	I	M	S	I	M	S	I	M	S	I	M	S	I	M
Merchants, yeomen & gentry	7			10			10			14			41			39		
Professional & medical	1			2			3			3			9			9		
Tradespeople & retail	1	1		7			5			10			23	1		22	1	
Seafarers	3			4			2			14			23			23		
Craftsmen	4			6			2			5		1	17		1	17		1
Husbandmen						1				2			2		1	2		1
Labourers																		
Occupation unknown	7	1		4	2	3	2			3			16	2	4	16	2	4
Women																		
Total	23	1	1	33	2	4	24			51		1	131	3	6	128	3	6

The writers of wills and inventories

It has been possible to identify the scribes responsible for drawing up 86% of the Lowestoft wills between 1560 and 1730. There seem to have been 188 people involved as writers of the 507 surviving documents, 121 of whom are known by name (the occupations of ninety-seven of these are also known). The work of ascertaining the identity of the writers was assisted by the abbreviation scr. (scriptor) being appended to some of the names, but more especially it derived from an exercise in comparing and matching handwriting styles. The use of copy-books at the time as a means of training people to write was not ignored (in theory at least, pupils who were taught from the same book might all have finished up writing very similarly), but there is enough individuality detectable even within definite graphological styles to be able to distinguish one writer from another.

The men who emerge as writers provide no major surprises, with schoolmasters and clergymen featuring prominently among the 'informal scriveners', as they have been termed.[18] Nevertheless, a considerable variety of people is revealed as participating in the process and there also are sixteen instances of a testator drawing up his own will.[19] It is

---

[18] Cressy, Literacy, p. 15.

[19] Evans, 'South Elmham', p. 246, records only one example. The Lowestoft testators who wrote their own wills are as follows, in date order: Peter Beddyngfelde (tailor), December 1586; John Gouldesmith (draper), April 1594; Abraham Turnpeneye (shoemaker), April 1617; John Wild (merchant), January 1641; Arthur Ashby (naval captain), July 1666; James Reeve (doctor), February 1679; James Wilde (merchant), August 1682; Robert Knight (gentleman), September 1689; Richard Rootsy (mariner), March 1696; John Buxton (mariner), January 1711; Joseph Pake (doctor), September 1712; Thomas Mighells (merchant), August 1723; James Wilde Snr (merchant), November 1723; Abraham Freeman (surgeon), September 1724; Thomas Sayer (mariner), November 1726; William Botson (schoolmaster), May 1728.

Table 49. *Writers of wills and inventories, 1560–1730 (inventories bracketed)*

Occupational/ social group	1560–1599 Scribes	Docs	1600–1649 Scribes	Docs	1650–1699 Scribes	Docs	1700–1730 Scribes	Docs	1560–1730 Scribes	Docs
Gentleman	2	11	4	8	3	5	6(5)	13(7)	9	24
Merchant	3(1)	4(2)	2(2)	8(2)	3(3)	8(3)	3(1)	17(6)	14(11)	33(14)
Clergyman	2	13	5	12	2	2	3	6	12(1)	44(6)
Doctor					1	1			4	7
Yeoman	2(1)	11(4)	1(1)	16(2)	(1)	(1)	13(1)	36(1)	3(3)	27(7)
Scrivener	1	1	4(3)	37(3)	6(1)	28(3)	2(1)	21(3)	24(5)	102(7)
Schoolmaster	1(1)	17(5)	2(1)	16(2)	1	31	2(2)	21(8)	6(3)	85(10)
Parish clerk					1	6	2(1)	2(1)	3(2)	27(8)
Customs officer							1(1)	1(1)	2(1)	2(1)
Tradesman/retail	4	15	3(1)	6(1)	2(1)	4(1)	2	2	10(3)	26(3)
Seafarer	1	1			3	3			6	6
Craftsman			1(1)	1(1)			1	1	2(1)	2(1)
Husbandman					1	1			1	1
Labourer							1	1	1	1
	16(3)	73(11)	22(9)	104(11)	23(6)	89(8)	36(12)	121(27)	97(30)	387(57)
Occ. unknown	3(1)	3(1)	2(2)	2(2)	14	38	5(2)	5(5)	24(5)	48(8)
Identity and occ. unknown	22(3)	26(3)	22(8)	23(8)	17(10)	17(10)	6(14)	6(14)	67(35)	72(35)
Total	41(7)	102(15)	46(19)	129(21)	54(16)	144(18)	47(28)	132(46)	188(70)	507(100)

noticeable in Lowestoft that, as time went on and literacy became more widespread, more and more townsmen became involved in the writing of wills. The increase, although not dramatic, is nevertheless detectable, as Table 49 shows. The rise in the number of professional scriveners involved in writing wills, especially after 1700, does not reflect a growth in the presence of lawyers practising in Lowestoft. An increasing number of local seafarers (often those serving in the Royal Navy) based themselves in Wapping and Stepney and their wills were invariably drawn up by scriveners or notaries public who lived there. Nowhere, in any of the Lowestoft probate material, are women to be found as writers of wills.

When it comes to writers of inventories, it is possible to identify twenty-five of the seventy scribes as resident in the town. Between them, they drew up fifty-five of the 100 surviving documents (there are five damaged ones, but in three cases it is possible to recognise the handwriting). Their identities provide no surprises and sixteen of them were people who, at one time or another, wrote wills for local testators. There is, as to be expected, close correlation between the occupational groupings in both sets of data and the rise in rates of literacy, especially during the first three decades of the eighteenth century, is once more reflected in a greater number of people drawing up inventories – a feature also observable among those men for whom occupation and place of residence cannot be established.

Table 50. *Book ownership and the ability to make a signature*

| Occupational/ | Ability to sign | | |
social group	Signature	Mark	Not known
Gentleman	3(1)		1
Merchant	12(1)	1(1)	1(1)
Naval officer	1		
Clergyman	3		
Doctor	1		
Schoolmaster	2		
Customs officer	1		
Tradesman/retail	4(1)	1(1)	
Seafarer	8	3(1)	1
Craftsman	5	2(1)	2(1)
Farmer			1
Labourer		1	
	40(3)	**8(4)**	**6(2)**

The ownership of books

The presence of books in houses, as an aspect of household contents, has already been touched upon in Chapter 6, but it can also serve as an indicator of literacy within the community. A total of fifty-four people (forty-five men and nine women, all of the latter being widows) between 1581 and 1730 are seen to have owned books of one kind or another – the former year providing the earliest evidence in the surviving probate material. Forty-one inventories and fourteen wills make reference to books, with only one pair of those documents relating to the same person: Margaret Coldham, a merchant's widow (1584). Table 50 presents the data regarding the ownership of books and relates it to the ability of the owners (or the lack of it) to sign their names. The people represented are predictable in the main, because they emanate from levels of society with the money to purchase books and with the ability to read them. The nine women are shown bracketed in their respective categories. It needs to be said, of course, that a person's inability to sign his or her name does not necessarily mean that he or she was unable to read. Of the two literary skills, reading is usually learned first and is probably the more widely practised.[20] It is possible, even today, for someone to read in a rudimentary fashion, yet not be able to form letters correctly in the written mode.

The books most frequently referred to by name, in both wills and inventories, are Bibles. There are sixteen individual references altogether, but their presence in a house did not necessarily mean that the occupant was able to read. Bibles were prized not only for their value as Holy Writ, but for their financial worth (the Lowestoft ones ranged in

---

[20] MacFarlane, *Reconstructing Historical Communities*, p. 191, makes this point unequivocally with regard to literacy in the pre-industrial era.

value from 2s to 6s 8d) and for their presumed magical properties. In any attempt to divine the future by 'book and key', a Bible was a necessary part of the equipment – and, in some cases, rank superstition rather than the ability or the desire to read it may have been the reason for having a Bible.[21] Lowestoft's Bible-owning citizens consisted of three merchants and a merchant's widow, a retired naval officer, a victualler, a butcher's widow, a hatter's widow, four seafarers (one of whom was a Nonconformist), a farmer, two cordwainers and a blacksmith. The dates of ownership, in sequence with this list, are as follows: 1581, 1588, 1590, 1585, 1669, 1710, 1648, 1645, 1613, 1696, 1711, 1712, 1711, 1590, 1602 and 1596.

Apart from the Bible, few other books are mentioned by name. John Foxe's *Book of Martyrs* (published in 1563) occurs once and there are occasional references to prayer books and psalters, collections of homilies, theological treatises, statute books and navigational works. John Collins's collection of volumes was referred to in Chapter 6 (page 120). Given his legal training, some of the books would have been law works and others possibly classical texts. It would be interesting, however, to know whether any of the 'ninety small books' listed in his inventory (November 1671) were literature of the time or of an earlier period. One of the frustrations of working through probate inventories is to see collections of books merely itemised as such, but the assessors' concern was to estimate monetary value, not itemise individual titles.

Four of the people in Table 50 (including a married couple) not only had books in their houses, but were carrying on a shop trade in them as well. Allen Coldham (merchant) died in January 1583 and his wife, Margaret, carried on running the business after his decease.[22] Her inventory of January 1585 shows that she and her husband had been involved in large-scale trade in cloth and drapery, a considerable one in groceries and a specialist dealing in books. The volumes listed are six grammar books, six service books (Church of England liturgy, almost certainly), eight psalters, two small works of Cato, one book of governance and virtue, twenty-two English primers, five copies of Ovid's works, eleven catechistic books of Calvinist doctrine and eighteen alphabet books. Obviously, there must have been a demand for such diverse literature and, in the case of the two classical authors, some of it may have been generated by the town's free grammar school. Furthermore, given the relatively high number of English primers and alphabet books, it is possible that this institution was educating its pupils in their mother tongue as well as in Latin. Stocks of pens, ink and paper are also listed among the items in the Coldhams' shop, which reinforces the idea of education and literacy being serviced by their enterprise.

Nearly 140 years later, the inventory of Thomas Utting (grocer) reveals that he, too, was conducting a retail trade in books in addition to the various foodstuffs and items of hardware in his shop. The document dates from June 1723 and shows that part of his stock-in-trade consisted of twenty-four New Testaments, forty-eight horn books and

---

[21] Cressy, *Literacy*, pp. 50–1, refers to the use of Bibles for curing illness, for warding off evil spirits and for divination. The point is made that owners of the book may not have been able to read it.

[22] They emanated from Great Yarmouth, but came to Lowestoft at some point during the second half of the sixteenth century. Allen Coldham had held office in Yarmouth, as one of the town's four bailiffs, in 1559.

seventy-eight primers.[23] It was a quantity of books sufficient to suggest regular trade in such reading matter – one which was probably stimulated by demand from local schools. About six years later, in March 1729, 'a parcel of horning book primers' was listed among all the other items being offered for sale in the shop of Richard Ward (labourer and woolcomber): scissors, lengths of ribbon, buttons, pins, pen knives, etc. There is also a reference to thirteen 'bound books' noted among the contents of his wash-house, but whether they were for sale or not is unclear. There is no such uncertainty regarding the horn books; they were intended to teach children to read.[24]

Conclusion

The degree of literacy evident in the sub-sections above suggests that, in the middle and upper levels of society at least, there was a marked competence on the part of Lowestoft people to sign their names – a feature which also included women – especially after 1700. Reasons have been given for the advantages of being literate in a maritime and trading community, and it is perhaps significant that the East Anglian coast has been noted as an area with quite a high rate of literacy among its inhabitants.[25] In that case, it is not surprising to find that Lowestoft conforms to an overall pattern. Alternatively, it may also be the case that market towns had a marked degree of literacy among the populace, because investigation has shown that 61% of the adult males (over the age of sixteen years) in seven Suffolk communities were able to sign their names to the Association Oath of 1696.[26] Had the documentation for Lowestoft survived, it is likely that the town would have shown a rate of literacy equal to this, if not in excess of it.

Over the county as whole, the same investigation showed that the ability to make a proper signature was 47%; in the Hundred of Mutford and Lothingland, the area for

[23] D. W. Sylvester, *Educational Documents, 800–1816* (London, 1970), pp. 79–82, gives descriptions of both horn book and primer, though they relate to the 1530s. The former was a sheet of paper containing the alphabet and perhaps the ten digits and the Lord's Prayer, which was protected by a layer of translucent horn and mounted on a wooden frame with a handle – thus enabling it to withstand rough use by children. The latter was a book which contained the alphabet, the *in nomine patris* etc., the Lord's Prayer, the Hail Mary, the Nicaean Creed and the Ten Commandments – the last five items all being printed in both English and Latin. During the post-Reformation period, the primer shed its Roman Catholic trappings and became increasingly an instruction manual for teaching children to read.

[24] A number of long-stay families in Lowestoft had quite a high proportion of members who, over the years, were able to sign their names and were probably also proficient at reading. They included the Arnolds (mariners, merchants and brewers), Barkers (shipwrights, coopers and merchants), Canhams (lesser gentry and mariners), Coes (yeomen, merchants and mariners), Durrants (brewers and mariners), Frarys (blacksmiths), Haywards (mariners and merchants), Mighells (merchants and mariners), Pacys (fishermen, mariners and merchants), Spicers (mariners and merchants), Uttings (brewers and merchants), Wards (merchants and mariners) and Wildes (merchants).

[25] Roger Schofield (of the Cambridge Group for the History of Population and Social Structure), during the course of conversation with the writer, once referred to 'a crescent' of pronounced literacy along the coastal fringe of Norfolk and Suffolk.

[26] Cressy, *Literacy*, p. 99. The towns in question were Beccles, Ixworth, Nayland, Newmarket, Southwold, Stowmarket and Woolpit.

which Lowestoft was the local centre, it was 38%.[27] Both rates are considerably lower than that in evidence in market towns. The rural nature of much of Suffolk no doubt served to bring down the county average below that of the towns. What, if any, were the advantages enjoyed by urban or proto-urban communities in promoting literacy, over and above the stimulus of trading activities? One factor is almost certainly to be found in the presence of schools.

Education

Annot's free grammar school

The single most important event in the process of public education in Lowestoft during the early modern period came in June 1570, when Thomas Annot (merchant) founded a free grammar school.[28] A summary of the original deed of gift is to be found in the Rev. John Arrow's memorandum book and the preamble particularly has an evocative quality about it.[29] As he considered the state of the town in which he lived, he saw that it was 'replenished with great numbers of youth who are very uncivil and ignorant for want of good Instruction and Education And the more for that they have within the said Town small or no trade to bring up their youth of the younger sort until they shall be trained and used to the Sea or other Service to preserve them from Idleness and other Misdemeanours…'

Thus it was that he dedicated the revenues from an estate in Wheatacre, Norfolk, to pay a salary of £13 6s 8d to a master who would instruct forty boys in 'the Rules and Principles of Grammar and the Latin Tongue and other Things incident and necessary to the said Art'.[30] Thus, the curriculum was not as wide-ranging as other contemporary grammar schools, such as the one at Ashby-de-la-Zouche, in Leicestershire, an institution of similar size where boys were taught both Latin and Greek and where, during the early part of the seventeenth century, Hebrew was introduced to older students.[31] However, its teaching of Latin would seem to place it on a higher level than some of the free

---

[27] Cressy, *Literacy*, p. 103. There were 215 usable parishes over the whole county, providing a total of 10,056 subscribers. In Mutford and Lothingland Hundred, only eleven parishes were able to be analysed, totalling 371 subscribers between them.

[28] This and other charitable works were alluded to in the previous chapter. He also left a tenement in the parish of Gisleham for the maintenance of the free grammar school in Woodbridge. There was, at one time, a funerary brass to Annot in the south aisle of St Margaret's Church, published by John Sell Cotman in *Engravings of Sepulchral Brasses in Suffolk* (1817). The figure had been ripped out (along with other parts of the memorial) during the 1640s, but a plate recording Annot's details had survived, along with a skeletal figure of Death carrying its dart, which was aimed directly at the side of the missing effigy. A reproduction of this can be found inserted into some re-bound copies of Gillingwater, between pp. 298 and 299.

[29] NRO, PD 589/92, pp. 13–14. Also see E. Gillingwater, p. 299.

[30] The foundation was not unlike that of 1560 at Moulton, Lincolnshire, where a yeoman left lands to endow a school. See J. Simon, *Education and Society in Tudor England* (Cambridge, 1966), p. 310.

[31] Moxon, pp. 243–4.

schools and lower forms of grammar school of the time, where the skills taught were largely concerned with basic literacy and with practical mathematics and accounts.[32]

It was intended that the forty scholars in Lowestoft be indigenous to the town, but if there were not enough to make up the number then a simple residential qualification would suffice. And if the full complement could not be mustered from among the youth of the town, then the number was to be made up from boys living anywhere in the local hundred. No records for the institution have survived, but it is known that the first schoolhouse stood immediately east of the churchyard in an enclosure belonging to the town trust (it is mentioned in the 1618 manor roll). It performed the function for the best part of 100 years, before falling into a state of disrepair. In 1674, part of the Town Chamber was fitted out as a replacement schoolroom and served this purpose from then on, throughout the rest of the seventeenth century and for much of the eighteenth. The commitment shown towards education on the part of the town fathers, in making premises available, is typical of the time – though Annot's School never benefited from the revenues deriving from charitable lands, as was the case in some other communities.[33]

After the death of Thomas Annot, in November 1577, the responsibility for paying the schoolmaster's salary fell first of all on his widow, Agnes, and then upon his step-daughter Christian and her husband, William French (merchant). The legal complications which ensued after the death of the founder, hinging upon certain of his heirs (and supposed heirs) disputing the legality of the original bequest, led to an expensive lawsuit in 1591. Most of the money spent on defending Annot's intentions was drawn from the town lands revenue – a fact referred to in the previous chapter. Eventually, after the dispute had dragged on for another seventeen years, a Chancery decree of 10 June 1608 was made to safeguard the school's existence.[34]

Another threat to its survival came much later, during the 1670s (resulting perhaps from the decrepid state of the original building), when Sir Thomas Allin (or Allen), a former townsman, tried to close it down in favour of a foundation of his own. Allin had been granted a baronetcy in 1669 for his services as a naval commander and, having made a considerable fortune from prize money, had purchased the Somerleyton estate in 1672.[35] Here he lived for the last thirteen years of his life (he was sixty years old when

[32] L. Stone, 'The Educational Revolution in England, 1560–1640', *P&P* 28 (July, 1964), p. 44.

[33] Simon, *Education and Society*, p. 376. The writer cites four examples of the practice in Leicestershire, in the towns of Hinckley, Lutterworth, Market Harborough and Melton Mowbray.

[34] E. Gillingwater, pp. 323–5, and NRO, PD 589/92, pp. 21–6. Both the published work and the Rev. John Arrow's memorandum book cast light on the matter. So does the will of William French (November 1593).

[35] Samuel Pepys noted of Allin, on the latter's own admission, that he loved 'to get and save' (see *DNB*, i, 333). Allin's career at sea was an illustrious one, nevertheless, both against Algerine pirates and the Dutch. In the earlier part of his life, he had been a Lowestoft merchant and boatowner, with family antecedents going back to the 1524 Subsidy. He was one of five top naval officers to emanate from the town during the second half of the seventeenth century and the first decade of the eighteenth (the other four being Richard Utber, John Ashby, Andrew Leake and James Mighells). In fact, no other community of similar size in England probably produced so many eminent fighting commanders. In addition to the men referred to, Arthur Ashby (older brother of John), Thomas Canham, William Whiting, John and Robert Utber (sons of Richard), Josiah Mighells (nephew of James) and Thomas Arnold all commanded vessels in the service of their country.

he acquired the property), setting himself up as a country gentleman. At some point during his retirement it seems that he formed the desire to leave a permanent memorial to himself in his native town and saw the opportunity to do this, using a large house on a freehold plot on the north side of Swan Lane, close to its western boundary with Goose Green (on land held, significantly, by the manor of Somerleyton).

This building was the one referred to in the previous chapter, which eventually became the so-called 'Shire House', where quarter sessions and petty sessions were held during the second half of the eighteenth century. Allin had probably constructed it as a town house for himself on acquiring the Somerleyton estate, but he never lived in it and, having bought his country seat, he tried to thrust it upon the people of Lowestoft as appropriate premises for the school that he wished to endow as a replacement for Thomas Annot's. He was not successful in his attempts, and nor was his son Thomas, who succeeded his father to both the baronetcy and the Somerleyton estate in October 1685. The reasons for the Allins' failure to assert their will are not clear, but there are two possibilities. It is likely that the leading Lowestoft townsmen, who seem to have been committed to Annot's school's success through allowing its re-location to the Town Chamber, wished to see it survive. Then there is the matter of possible resentment on their part towards one of their own kind who, having gained both fame and fortune, seemed desirous of perpetuating his own memory in the home town where he no longer chose to reside.[36]

It is clear that the first Sir Thomas was serious in his attempt to set up a school because he attempted to stop the salary of the master of Annot's foundation.[37] The man in question was called Henry Britten and a letter written by him in retirement at Wickham Market on 26 December 1701 describes how 'old Sir Thomas' made life awkward for him because of his refusal to resign from his post.[38] It also makes reference to how Allin's building was being used to house a school teaching writing and English, run by a man called John Evans – he who functioned as both scrivener and town clerk in Lowestoft during the later part of the seventeenth century and the earlier part of the eighteenth (he first appears in parish register material in February 1682). Sir Thomas wished to divert the salary of Annot's schoolmaster to the new educational venture, but Henry Britten stood his ground.[39] When, eventually, he did resign in 1696, both Sir Thomas Allin and his successor were dead and there appear to have been no further attempts to close down the free grammar school.

In 1716, the number of pupils was formally reduced from forty to sixteen, with the decision being taken that the master should only teach as many boys as he received pounds clear in remuneration.[40] This seems to have been in recognition of the fact that £16 per annum (the original salary had been augmented by £2 13s 4d by the Chancery

[36] Allin also purchased the Manor of Lowestoft, thereby becoming its lord (c. 1679).

[37] It is not known whether he was able to do this by acquiring the lands in Wheatacre bequeathed to provide funds for the master's remuneration or whether he became a feoffee of the trust.

[38] E. Gillingwater, pp. 326–7.

[39] The strong-mindedness of Britten, in refusing to resign, cannot have existed in isolation. He must have had support from the townspeople.

[40] NRO, PD 589/92, p. 13.

decree of 1608) was not a great deal of reward for instructing forty boys. The school continued in existence until the later years of the nineteenth century (though amalgamated by then with a National School) and it finished its days during the earlier part of the twentieth as Mariner's Score School – an all-age establishment for children who lived in the northern part of town.

Given the fact of some degree of commitment on the part of local people towards Annot's School, it is disappointing that no documentary evidence has survived to show specifically who was educated there. The remarks of the founder in considering the state of the young male population of Lowestoft in 1570 would seem to suggest that he was thinking of boys who belonged to the families of seafarers, and perhaps of lesser tradespeople and craftsmen, rather than of the merchant fraternity. In the event, it is not known who received formal education as a result of Annot's munificence and a certain amount of conjecture has to be employed in arriving at any notion of the foundation's effect on the town. As has been demonstrated in this chapter, there was quite a high degree of literacy among merchants, tradespeople, seafarers and craftsmen, and much of the proficiency was probably due to the influence of Annot's School. Furthermore, there are no references in any of the townspeople's wills to bequests of money left to either of the universities at Cambridge or Oxford – which may suggest that, whatever education was received by Lowestoft's boys and young men, it was contained within a local context.[41]

The master of Annot's School had to be a man of good character and a member of the Church of England. Any successful candidate for the post was recommended by the vicar of Lowestoft and his two churchwardens to the Chancellor of Norwich diocese. The Chancellor then made the appointment formally and granted the master's licence.[42] At least six of the men appointed were in holy orders and there may have been others who were also ordained. Unfortunately, the lack of documentation on the school does not allow all the serving masters to be named.

Stephen Phillipp, a clergyman, was the first of them and he performed his duties from the time of inception until his death in 1605. He became well integrated into the life of his adopted town through marrying into a family of mariners and blacksmiths (the Witchinghams) in July 1571 and by later becoming parish clerk.[43] He kept the registers from 1584 onwards, thereby reversing a trend ascertainable in Elizabethan times whereby parish clerks sometimes undertook to act as schoolmasters if they were competent to do

---

[41] The only evidence of a bequest to one of the universities is to be found in the will of Ann Hunt (gentleman's widow), in December 1671. She endowed a scholarship at Emmanuel College, Cambridge, in memory of her son, John Collins, who had studied law there and who had died the previous month. He was the young man previously referred to in this chapter, and in Chapter 6, regarding ownership of a large number of books. Neither he nor his mother was native to Lowestoft; they were simply living there at the time of their respective deaths.

[42] E. Gillingwater, p. 325.

[43] He may already have known the vicar at the time of his appointment, William Nashe, because Nashe too had married into the Witchingham family after the death of his first wife. Thomas Nashe, the Elizabethan writer and wit, was a child of this union. On the other hand, vicar and schoolmaster would have been quite closely connected through their work, so it is equally possible that Phillipp became acquainted with the Witchinghams through regular contact with the minister.

so.[44] He may well have assumed parochial duties in order to supplement his income (he and his wife produced eleven children, though only three of them survived), and he also acted as a scribe for probate material: thirty-two wills and seven inventories written in his exemplary hand have survived.[45]

His successor, Brian Warde, another ordained man, only served as schoolmaster in Lowestoft for about five years. His burial is not recorded in the registers, but his death must have occurred before 29 November 1612, the date on which his widow remarried. A son, Thomas, was baptised a week later on 7 December, so it would seem that Margaret Warde had delayed the child's christening, having first arranged herself a husband (one Edward Barnard, a widower himself) to ensure its well-being. She and her first husband had married as single people in September 1607. During his relatively brief time in Lowestoft, Brian Warde also acted as vicar for a five- or six-month period in 1610 between the death of John Gleson (June) and the arrival of Robert Hawes (December).

There is a gap of twelve years before the next master is detectable. Richard Linsye was in holy orders and, just like Stephen Phillipp and Brian Warde, he was also a married man. He and his wife had a daughter baptised in November 1624, followed by another daughter in 1626 and a son in July 1628. Linsye himself was buried in July 1641 and the only other documentary information relating to him is a surviving will of 1633 (that of Henry Wodshed, a yeoman), of which he was the scribe. No successor to him is identifiable and the next ascertainable appointment is that of Henry Britten in 1667. Britten does not feature at all in parish register entries, and if it were not for Sir Thomas Allin's attempt to divert the Annot bequest his period of service might have gone unrecorded. Again, he appears to have been ordained, because a court baron minute of the 1670s refers to him as 'clerk'.

He was succeeded in 1696 by the Rev. John Troughton who, in due course, was also to act as curate of the combined benefice of Lowestoft and Kessingland.[46] When Troughton resigned from the post in about 1705, Joseph Poolhouse became at least the sixth clergyman to fill it and he worked at his calling for twelve years, before being presented to the living of Carlton Colville. There is no record of an immediate successor, so he may have continued teaching for a while as well as ministering to his parish. In 1720, Henry Wilde was appointed – a man who, according to Edmund Gillingwater, had a talent for various Middle Eastern languages and who only remained in Lowestoft for about eighteen months before leaving to teach these foreign tongues in London.[47] The name of his successor has not been discovered, which effectively brings to an end what is known of Lowestoft's free grammar school during the period covered in this book.

[44] J. Lawson and H. Silver, *A Social History of Education in England* (London, 1973), p. 113.

[45] Phillipp's own will of November 1605 (written by an unidentified scribe) left his wife the dwelling-house in which they lived. This would seem to suggest that the Annot's School building, abutting the churchyard wall, did not incorporate accommodation for the master – or, if it did, that it was not adequate for the needs of Phillipp and his family.

[46] Lees, *Chronicles*, p. 169. The information derives from the memoirs of the vicar of the time, William Whiston.

[47] E. Gillingwater, p. 300. Wilde was apparently known as 'The Arabian Tailor' because of his linguistic abilities and his previous occupation. He was from Norwich originally and his exceptional talent came to the notice of Dean Prideaux at the cathedral.

Other schools

The establishment run by John Evans in the building erected by Sir Thomas Allin offered a less elevated curriculum than Annot's School, but would have performed a useful function nevertheless. A contemporary report of it as 'a writing school' identifies an emphasis on basic literacy and it may also have concentrated on simple numeracy as well, thereby equipping its pupils with what became known later as 'The Three Rs'. Establishments of this nature were also referred to as 'petty schools' and there are a number of descriptions of them to be found in studies of the early modern period.[48] At least one commentator has expressed the opinion that such centres of learning fell into two different categories: petty schools themselves, which taught children basic literacy, and free schools (or lower forms of grammar school) which provided instruction in reading, writing, practical mathematics and accounts, and which aimed at preparing boys for apprenticeship.[49] One thing which distinguished these places from the grammar schools proper was that the teaching was conducted in English vernacular, whereas the grammar schools used Latin and Greek as well as the native language. A number of Elizabethan teachers and educationalists (most notably, Richard Mulcaster) advocated not only use of the vernacular throughout all schools in England, but also urged standardisation of both grammatical usage and spelling in order to produce a truly uniform national tongue.[50] Their recommendations were not acted upon and it was another 100 years before a formal English grammar began to emerge. The logic and discipline of the new age of science and discovery demanded that the language become more ordered and such formal grammar as tended to emerge during the first half of the eighteenth century was based on Latin models, not English ones.[51]

The academic concerns of John Evans's school would have been of less elevated nature than those of Thomas Annot's, but it is no easier to ascertain who was taught there than it is to discover who attended the latter. Given the classical emphasis of the grammar school (which is certainly attested in its early days by the Latin texts present in Allen and Margaret Coldham's shop), it is tempting to see it as the venue for education of the sons of the wealthier members of the community, with Evans's place serving the children of lesser tradespeople and craftsmen. However, comment has already been made

---

[48] The word *petty* derives from the French *petit* and refers to the 'small skills' of reading and writing as opposed to the greater ones of learning Latin and Greek. Many grammar schools insisted on proficiency in the basic skills before a pupil was accepted. Two works which comment on the nature of petty schools in differing environments are Spufford, *Contrasting Communities*, p. 187, and P. Clark, 'The Cultural Role of Towns in the Late Sixteenth and Seventeenth Centuries', in *The Fabric of the Traditional Community*, p. 128 (the former dealing with schools in rural Cambridgeshire, the latter with one started in Canterbury in 1600). The town school's benefactor, Sir John Boys, referred to the idleness and dishonesty of many children at the time, which gives the preamble to his founding statement a similar tone to the declaration of Thomas Annot in Lowestoft thirty years before.

[49] L. Stone, 'Educational Revolution', *P&P* 28, 42–4.

[50] Simon, *Education and Society*, p. 400. Mulcaster's treatise was entitled *The First Part of the Elementarie which entreateth chiefly of the right writing of our English tongue* (London, 1582).

[51] R. McCrum *et al.*, *The Story of English* (London, 1986), p. 128; A. S. Collins, 'Language, 1660–1784', in B. Ford (ed.), *From Dryden to Johnson* (London, 1957), p. 136.

concerning whom Annot may have had in mind when making his endowment, so it is probably wise not to speculate too far. In any case, both schools are so far apart in their respective times of origin that they can in no sense be seen as rivals. Once they were both operative, it may well be that the people in Lowestoft who wished (and who could afford) to have their sons educated were provided with a choice between a classical education and a more utilitarian one.

There is, of course, no evidence to suggest how good a teacher John Evans was – though he ought, at the very least, to have been worthy of imitation in the matter of handwriting. His script is both elegant and flowing, as may be seen in any of the surviving thirty-one wills and four inventories which were written by him between 1685 and 1705 – to say nothing of the Overseers' Accounts for the late seventeenth century, which he kept in an exemplary fashion. He was probably involved in other official administrative business as well, because his burial registration of 3 January 1706 refers to him as 'Town Clerk'. The widely ranging employment of his literary skills was not so different from that of the master of Annot's School 100 years before, Stephen Phillipp; he, too, was in demand to perform a variety of tasks which drew upon his ability to read and write. What had changed was the situation appertaining to the increase in the amount of urban business, which had grown sufficiently to warrant its being dealt with by one competent official.

After John Evans died, the school he ran came under the direction of Robert Baas. He leased the building from Sir Richard Allin of Somerleyton Hall on 9 April 1706 and details of the agreement may be found in an early nineteenth century manuscript history of the town.[52] They reveal, among other things, that the master had his accommodation on the premises and that arithmetic was taught to the pupils, as well as reading and writing. Part of the agreement whereby Baas took over the school was that he should teach, free of charge, four poor boys from families receiving parish relief (in order to prepare them for apprenticeship). It seems to be implied in the wording of the information that this was the continuation of a practice already established, rather than something new. Baas performed his function until his death in December 1718 (he left a widow and at least three children) and the eighteen surviving wills and three inventories written by him show that he had an elegant hand. He was succeeded by William Botson, the son of a local mariner and a man whose handwriting was workmanlike rather than graceful. Three wills written by him have survived, one of them his own. He died a bachelor, at the age of forty-two, in March 1729, leaving the bulk of his estate to his sister Alice, his best suit of clothes to his younger brother Michael and one shilling to his other sister, Elizabeth.

In addition to the school run successively by Messrs Evans, Baas and Botson, there may also have been an earlier establishment of some kind in operation during the second half of the seventeenth century. Its proprietor was Thomas Tye, the preamble of whose will (April 1681) describes him as a scrivener, but whose burial registration the following month refers to him as a schoolmaster. Given the fact that John Evans and his family first appear in the parish registers in February 1682, it is possible that there are not two schools under discussion, but one. It is not known where Thomas Tye taught his pupils,

---

[52] Reeve, 'Lowestoft and Lothingland', iv, 273.

but at the time of his death he owned, and lived in, a substantial house on the freehold land at the northern end of the High Street. He also owned a copyhold property on the north side of Blue Anchor Lane, near the junction with the High Street, which his wife Susan ran as a public house.[53] The possibility exists that, during the latter stages of his life, he was using the building erected by Sir Thomas Allin in the manner that John Evans was later to do, but there is no evidence of his tenancy. The thirty-one surviving wills written by him, covering the years 1657 to 1680, show his handwriting to have been stylish and individualistic – especially in the flourishes on the capital letters and the very thick downstroke employed on the letter t.

The last of the schools to manifest itself in Lowestoft was another whose existence is revealed in the burial record of the person who ran it. Mary Roomer (widow) was laid to rest in January 1709. She is referred to in the registers as 'a good school dame', from which description it may be inferred that she was responsible for the instruction of younger children, including girls as well as boys. Her school, wherever it was located (possibly in her own house), probably differed a good deal from those (or that) of Thomas Tye and John Evans, having a level of teaching which was less demanding, less wide-ranging and almost certainly cheaper. Dame schools were, in fact, aimed at the poorer levels of society and domestic tasks such as knitting and sewing were sometimes taught, as well as very basic reading and writing.[54] Parents paid what they could afford in the way of having their children educated and attendance by pupils was often very spasmodic.

Thus, in the latter part of the seventeenth century and early years of the eighteenth, Lowestoft had one of each of the three main types of school present in pre-industrial England: a grammar school, a petty school and a dame school. Annot's free grammar school meant exactly what it said with regard to the tuition provided (it was a charitable foundation, with the master's salary provided for), but books and writing materials would have had to have been paid for by the scholars' parents, and the purchase of classical texts would not have been cheap. The other two schools in town would have made tuition charges as well, but no information has come to light concerning what the children's parents had to pay. In the case of the dame school, it may have been no more than 1d a day, but during the late seventeenth century that represented about 8% of a labourer's summer day-wage and 5% of a craftsman's (for the winter months, the proportion rose to 17% and 13% respectively) – these payments representing those made without the provision of food.[55]

Given these figures, it then becomes a question of which people could either afford to have their offspring educated or were prepared to make the sacrifices necessary to secure some kind of basic schooling for them. On the evidence of literacy data drawn

---

[53] It may have been called *The Blue Anchor*, after which the roadway itself was named.

[54] Lawson and Silver, *History of Education*, p. 181.

[55] I. Gillingwater, 'Lowestoft and Lothingland', ii, 1412–19 (SRO(L), 193/1/2). These pages contain the full range of wages fixed at the Beccles quarter sessions in April 1684. A labourer's daily rate was about 1s for the summer and 10d for the winter; a craftsman received 1s 2d to 1s 8d for the summer and 1s to 1s 2d for the winter. These were all earnings without the provision of food and drink. If victuals were provided, the wages paid were halved.

from wills and probate inventories, it would seem that the education available in Lowestoft was largely taken up by the merchants, the tradespeople, the seafarers and the craftsmen. It does not seem to have had much of an impact on the lower orders: the labourers, the servants and the poor. Apart from the known number of forty boys in Annot's School (reduced to sixteen in 1716), there are no other statistics available to reveal how much of the town's youthful population was being educated at any one time. However, with two or three other institutions in operation, it may have been as high as about 100 by the beginning of the eighteenth century. And, given the high rate of female literacy after 1700, the possibility has to be considered that girls were being educated in the petty schools as well as boys. If they were not, it has to be presumed that they acquired the ability to read and write within the home environment.

References in wills

Altogether, seventy-two of the surviving Lowestoft wills between 1560 and 1730 contain specific directions for the upbringing of children (14.2%) – a comparatively high proportion compared with at least one area of rural Suffolk, which showed only 5.2%, though this did relate to the period 1550–1640.[56] If Lowestoft wills for the years 1560–1650 are considered, then forty-seven documents out of a total number of 231 make reference to care of the young (20.3%) – a higher proportion than for the overall period of study and one which reflects a higher rate of adult mortality (much of it due to epidemics) than that which prevailed later on. Another difference between Lowestoft and rural High Suffolk is that, in ten of the fifteen documents relating to the latter, the references to the education and bringing-up of children were meant to be taken in a general, unspecified way and only in the other five referred specifically to actual learning. In Lowestoft, seventeen of the seventy-two wills that mention the upbringing of children contain references to education in the accepted sense of the word, while another six request apprenticeship or service for sons and daughters, and a further one makes provision for both modes of training.

These twenty-four documents are fairly evenly spread across a timespan of about 150 years (1569–1721) and a breakdown of the testators' occupations reveals that nine of them were from a maritime background (eight men and a widow), five were merchants, four were shipwrights or boatwrights, three were of yeoman level (two men and a widow), one was a brewer, one was a hatter and one the widow of a man of unknown status. The term 'education' was not used exclusively for sons, and in eleven cases daughters were also included in the request for learning of some kind to be imparted. Most interesting of all the educational references is that to be found in the will of William Meeke (yeoman) in June 1602. He requested that his executor, Harry Askewe, guardian of his oldest son Raphe (aged thirteen years), ensure that the boy learnt to both speak and write French. In terms of the pattern of educational references as a whole, it is interesting to note that over half of them emanated from

[56] Evans, 'South Elmham', p. 252.

people with maritime connections, nine being from sea-going families and a further four from men who built craft of different kinds.

In so far as children may be seen as providing testators with motivation to make a will, 159 of the 338 married men whose documents have survived (47%) had to provide for two or more sons or for under-age children.[57] It is not surprising, therefore, that there are regular references to the upbringing of children, often with the phrase 'in the fear of God' being used by way of qualification.[58] There were sixty married male testators altogether whose children were all under-age: fifty-three of them laid responsibility for the upbringing with their wives, four with their executors, one with his wife and a supervisor, one with his mother and brother, and one with his mother-in-law.[59] The six widows who made wills which include directions for the care of children placed responsibility on executors in four cases, on a brother and father-in-law in another and on three brothers in the last.

Religious belief and affiliation

The Established Church

In his late eighteenth-century history of the town, Edmund Gillingwater claimed that Lowestoft was 'as much distinguished in religious concerns for inviolable attachment to the establishment of the Church of England, as in civil affairs, for its unshaken loyalty to the sovereign'.[60] The sentiment is phrased in a rather high-flown manner, typical of the time, and while perhaps being true in general terms it does not take account of the Dissenting element in the town's population, which was certainly a noticeable feature by the middle of the seventeenth century. Roman Catholicism, on the other hand, seems to have had hardly any impact at all on the religious life of the community. It is true that the Island of Lothingland had a reputation among the Elizabethan authorities as being potentially dangerous, full of subversive supporters of Rome, but official worries focused very largely on the ten or twelve gentlemen and landowners named in the 1584 Defence Plat.[61]

---

[57] Spufford, 'Peasant Inheritance', in Goody, *Family and Inheritance*, pp. 171–2, reveals that 75% of male testators in the Cambridgeshire parish of Willingham between 1575 and 1600 fell into this category. Evans, *Linen Industry*, p. 5, establishes that it was 25% in the South Elmham area of Suffolk between 1550 and 1640.

[58] Dyer, *Worcester*, p. 247, notes this particular phrase as having been in common use in wills during the first half of the sixteenth century.

[59] In the six cases where children's upbringing did not involve the wife, five of the testators were widowed. The remaining case saw an executor given the responsibility.

[60] E. Gillingwater, p. 355.

[61] R. A. Houlbrooke (ed.), *The Letters of Bishop John Parkhurst*, NRS, xliii (Norwich, 1974), 159. In a letter of 23 January 1573, Parkhurst (who was Bishop of Norwich) refers to Lothingland as a locality which contained 'many stubborn people neither religious nor otherwise well disposed'. TNA: PRO, MPF 283, is the map drawn in 1584 to accompany an assessment of the area's defence capability. See Redstone, 'Lothingland', *PSIA* xx, 1–8.

The majority of Lothingland's population was neither recusant nor disloyal. In Lowestoft's case, the only prominent Roman Catholic family was the Jettors and they moved out of town shortly after the accession of Elizabeth I and went to live in neighbouring Flixton.[62] The type of Anglicanism adhered to by most of the townspeople, if the practice of certain of the ministers has any significance, was a middle-of-the-road observance free from either High Church excess or Calvinistic fundamentalism. William Bentley, for instance, who was vicar from 1574 to 1603, seems to have had no great feeling for liturgical ritual because he was noted in the 1597 bishop's visitation as not wearing the surplice at divine service.[63] On the other hand, both the preamble and the peroration of his will (the latter being a most unusual addition) contain a wonderful expression of his own personal faith in God, showing his acceptance of the saving grace extended to all men and his belief in the Holy Trinity.[64] There are no puritan overtones at all.

Nothing is known in either a doctrinal or liturgical sense about his two successors, John Gleson and Robert Hawes, but the man who followed them, James Rous (minister from 1639 to 1654), was another person of the middle way. The most significant event of his incumbency was being taken away to Cambridge by Oliver Cromwell in March 1643, when the latter visited Lowestoft to deal with certain Royalist sympathisers who had gathered in town.[65] On his release some months later, he returned home and continued his ministry. About a year after he had been arrested, Rous experienced the arrival of a puritan 'visitor', Francis Jessop from Beccles, with a commission from the Earl of Manchester to remove 'superstitious' inscriptions from inside St Margaret's Church. Most of the memorial brasses were ripped from their matrices and sold to a local merchant, Josiah Wilde, who had them melted down and

---

[62] Robert Jettor was convicted of recusancy on 8 May 1560, according to the memorandum book of the Rev. John Arrow: NRO, PD 589/92, p. 80. Either he, or his son Robert, became the most heavily fined of all the Suffolk recusants on 29 October 1586, when a penalty of £1,500 was imposed. See M. M. C. Calthrop (ed.), *The First Recusant Roll, 1592–93*, CRS, xviii (London, 1916), 314.

[63] J. F. Williams (ed.), *Bishop Redman's Visitation*, NRS, xviii (Norwich, 1946), 125.

[64] Bentley died towards the end of the plague outbreak of 1603. His will was written on 20 August by Stephen Phillipp, schoolmaster and parish clerk, and his burial entered in the register five days later.

[65] The Lowestoft episode is well recorded. Most of the royalists arrested by Cromwell were Norfolk and Suffolk gentlemen who had assembled in town to handle a quantity of arms, which had either been landed there or which was due to be shipped out. The only local men taken away by Cromwell, other than Rous, were Thomas Allin (merchant and mariner, and later to become a notable naval commander) and the brothers, Thomas and Simon Canham (mariners). All those arrested were eventually released from their period of imprisonment at Cambridge. See B. Schofield (ed.), *The Knyvett Letters, 1620–44*, NRS, xx (Norwich, 1949), 32–5, and R. H. Hill (ed.), *The Corie Letters, 1664–87*, NRS, xxvii (Norwich, 1956), 8. Both books contain certain information concerning the episode, having as their sources people who were involved in it and who are referred to by James Rous in his comments written in the Lowestoft register book (in a space following the baptisms performed during 1643). Also, see A. Kingston, *East Anglia and the Great Civil War* (London, 1897), pp. 93–5.

cast into a bell for the Town Chapel. Rous did not approve, as an account of the incident (which he wrote into a space at the end of the first register book) makes clear.[66] Not a great deal is known about the next three clergymen (Henry Youell, Joseph Hudson and Edward Carleton), whose ministries covered the years 1654–1698, but their successor, William Whiston, was a man destined to become famous on succeeding Isaac Newton as Professor of Mathematics at Cambridge. Some evidence of this bent is present on the inside cover of the tithe accounts book, where certain of his geometrical drawings and calculations may be seen. During his four-year incumbency at Lowestoft, he held morning and evening prayers every day in the Town Chapel, preached twice on Sundays in St Margaret's Church and held catechistic lectures in the evenings during the summer months.[67] These latter (held in the Town Chapel) were attended by Dissenters as well as Anglicans and were, in the opinion of Whiston himself, more effective than his sermons.[68] His ministry seems to have been both imaginative and vigorous (he once refused to sign a licence for a new alehouse, saying that if he were presented with a paper to pull one down he would certainly sign it) and there is no evidence of the unorthodoxy in matters of doctrine which was to become a feature of his time at Cambridge.[69]

He was succeeded by a Scottish non-juror. James Smith came to the town in 1702 and, while he may not have been happy about a Dutch protestant acceding to the English throne, he was no High Churchman either. His time in Lowestoft was comparatively short (he died in July 1708), but he enjoyed the confidence of the townspeople sufficiently to have a public collection made on his behalf in June 1705 to compensate for loss of income caused by meagre fishing tithes.[70] When he died, John Blaque, the parish clerk, wrote this tribute next to his burial entry in the register: 'That good and faithful minister of this town, Mr James Smith, aged 60 years, my extraordinary good master'. After James Smith came John Tanner, of whom much has been said throughout the pages of this book. He was the longest-serving of all the recorded Lowestoft parish priests and his incumbency (1708–59) was distinguished by sound common sense, the avoidance of extremes of behaviour, honest belief in Christian principles and concern for the well-being of all his parishioners.

[66] NRO, PD 589/1. Rous claims that Jessop's instructions were to remove from gravestones only those inscriptions which had *orate pro anima* on them. He also remarks that the latter was unable to read and therefore ripped up memorial brasses regardless of their legends. Among those removed were twelve in the middle aisle commemorating members of the Jettor family. Josiah Wilde is said to have paid Jessop 5s for the metal and Rous says that the bell was made from the brass without his knowledge (by the Norwich bell-founder, John Brend). He clearly disapproved of the whole business. The bell is still in existence. It hangs in Lowestoft Town Hall and sounds the curfew every evening at 8 p.m.

[67] Lees, *Chronicles*, pp. 169–70. The writer's information was drawn from Whiston's own autobiography, *Memoirs of the Life and Writings of Mr. William Whiston* (London, 1749).

[68] There was a marked degree of understanding and co-operation between the two congregations during the late seventeenth century and throughout the first half of the eighteenth, in marked contrast to what occurred in many other communities.

[69] Whiston embraced the Arian heresy, which denies the doctrine of the Holy Trinity by giving precedence to the Father over the Son. It also does not acknowledge the divinity of Christ.

[70] NRO, PD 589/80, p. 35. The subscription list is preserved in the pages of the tithe accounts book.

Nonconformity

The first official reference to any kind of Nonconformity in Lowestoft is to be found in the bishop's visitation of 1597, when a local woman, Joan Rivett, was revealed as having been excommunicated two years previously for non-attendance at church and for belonging to the Brownists.[71] She may well have had other co-religionists locally, but her name was the only one cited. It is possible, even likely, that a small body of Independent worshippers was present in town during the first half of the seventeenth century, because in the 1650s signs of organised Nonconformist observance are made manifest.

It would appear that the favourable religious climate of the time had allowed the Lowestoft congregation to come into the open. In February 1654, the Council of State examined the misdemeanours of Thomas Brecket (otherwise, Brethett) who, in company with other people, had disturbed 'several well affected' in their religious observances on Sunday, 22 January.[72] Brethett, a cordwainer by trade, was one of the four parish constables (he was also to serve as parish clerk for a time during the 1660s) and he seems to have been attempting to prevent Nonconformist worship from taking place in the Town Chapel.[73] In March 1654, the Council of State ordered the Suffolk justices to allow a certain Mr Alberry (presumably a preacher of some kind) and 'the rest of the honest people of Lowestoft' to have the freedom to use the chapel in town for their services and to be shielded from molestation.[74] It is to be conjectured that the Independent congregation enjoyed this privilege for the duration of the Protectorate.

Thomas Brethtett's interruption of Sunday worship occurred during what appears to have been an interregnum. James Rous last signed the register after a baptism entry for 17 August 1651. The first reference to his successor, Henry Youell, appears on 24 April 1655, when Youell's son George was baptised. Local Nonconformists were probably taking advantage of the absence of an incumbent to use the chapel-of-ease as a venue for their services – and Brethett, as a loyal Anglican, was determined to stop this. The Independents' presence in town certainly calls into question Edmund Gillingwater's statement concerning the 'inviolable attachment' shown to the Established Church, quoted above. It would also seem to contradict the long-accepted description of Lowestoft as 'a Royalist town'.

This particular title probably has more to do with the town's long-running commercial rivalry with Great Yarmouth than to politics. The latter was definitely a place of strong Parliamentary leanings and it seems the idea formed in people's minds that Lowestoft must therefore have been Royalist – a notion reinforced by the town's successful lobbying of the House of Lords in the immediate Restoration period to rid itself of Yarmouth's claim to precedence in the herring trade. Cromwell's visit in March 1643 also helped to

---

[71] Williams, *Redman's Visitation*, 125. The Brownists derived their name from Robert Browne, of Norwich, and later became known as Congregationalists.

[72] M. A. E. Green (ed.), *SPD, 1653–4* (London, 1879), 381–2, no. 76.

[73] The fact the Brethett was the only officer involved suggests that the four Lowestoft constables each served a three-month period of duty rather than all four of them working concurrently for the year.

[74] M. A. E. Green (ed.), *SPD, 1654* (London, 1880), 3, no. 5.

foster the myth, but most of the people arrested that day were not townsmen. The 'stand' made at the top of Rant Score against an overwhelming force of cavalry was a token of resistance only, in spite of three cannon being dragged up from the battery on Ness Point and placed to traverse the High Street and market place. A local merchant, Thomas Mighells, acted as intermediary between the opposing parties and matters were resolved without bloodshed. Many people in Lowestoft probably had no compelling loyalty either way in their country's great division and it is interesting to note that the father of two of the four Lowestoft men taken away to Cambridge that day seems to have had leanings towards the Puritan side. When William Canham (gentleman) made his will in May 1647, he left the sum of £5 to his fourth son, Simon – to be given to him 'when he shall have made his peace with the Parliament of England and return home to Lowestoft'.

It has been said that towns were places in which religious dissidents could find concealment,[75] but that is not true of communities the size of Lowestoft. There simply was not a sufficiently large population, nor a big enough area of building, to hide anyone. The local Nonconformists would have been well known in Lowestoft and, having had their time of freedom and independence during the Protectorate, they would have found their religious activities much more restricted after the Restoration. In fact, three of them appear in the Beccles quarter sessions records because of their unorthodoxy.[76] On 5 October 1663, John Smith (tanner), one of the parish constables, was summoned to appear at the next session to give evidence against Samuel Pacy, Thomas Porter and William Rising (all merchants) and against Edward Barker of Wrentham (dissenting minister). Three months later, on 11 January 1664, Pacy and the others were indicted for attending conventicles and were summoned to appear at the next summer assizes (it has not been established whether they appeared or not). Pacy had been one of the two main instigators of the accusation of witchcraft brought against two local women, Rose Cullender and Amy Denny, in March 1662 – a charge which cost them their lives.[77] He was a well-educated man by the standards of the time (as was his co-accuser, John Soan, a yeoman), but his learning and literacy did not liberate him from rank superstition – a characteristic he shared with many other people of his era.[78]

Eight years after Samuel Pacy and his associates were indicted for attending illegal religious gatherings, the changing climate of opinion saw the house of William Rising

[75] Jack, *Towns*, p. 45.

[76] SRO(L), Acc. 11/M1.

[77] Anon, *A Tryal of Witches* (London, 1682); E. Gillingwater, pp. 369–73; G. Geis and I. Bunn, 'Sir Thomas Browne and Witchcraft', *IJLP* 4 (1981), 1–11; Geis and Bunn, *Witches*. The first publication cited is a first-hand account of the trial at Bury St Edmunds; the second gives a somewhat cursory summary of events; the third examines the role of the philosopher and writer at the trial in his capacity of expert witness; and the final one is a detailed account of the trial itself and all the background events and people connected with it. The original indictment against the two women is TNA: PRO, A551 16/4/1.

[78] Lawson and Silver, *History of Education*, p. 143. The writers make the point that the diffusion of literacy 'did not mean the triumph of reason over ignorance and ancestral superstition', and they proceed to give examples, including executions for witchcraft. The persistence of traditional beliefs was probably due, in part, to the power of the oral tradition.

Plate 23. *A late eighteenth-century study of the Nonconformist Chapel: Richard Powles' drawing represents its essential simplicity, the only concessions to decoration being curved, pedimented gables and pilasters adjoining each of the outer, upper windows and framing the door-case. The chapel site has long been unoccupied and forms part of The Triangle market area.*

licensed as a place of Independent worship in June 1672.[79] The dwelling stood on the east side of the High Street (the site today of No. 67) and, prior to this, local Dissenters had used a barn belonging to the Pacy family, situated in Blue Anchor Lane and backing onto the market place. Twenty-three years after this concession, in 1695, a chapel was built on the west side of the High Street close to the market. The plot was donated by James Ward (merchant) and an inn called *The Spreadeagle* had once stood on it. Ownership of the chapel was originally vested in three trustees, which included Samuel Pacy Jnr, self-styled gentleman and oldest son of the man referred to above (the other two were Sir Robert Rich of Roos Hall, Beccles, and Thomas Neale of Bramfield), and by 1716 the number had increased to five.

The building's dimensions were thirty-eight feet by twenty-eight and a drawing done by Richard Powles in 1782 shows it to have been a two-storey, three-bay construction, with a shuttered window on either side of a central door, three unshuttered windows on the first storey, and Dutch gables at either end (Plate 23). Edmund Gillingwater

[79] F. H. Blackburne Daniell, *SPD, 1672* (London, 1899), 199, 202 and 222.

describes it as galleried inside, with the pulpit facing the entry-way, which is a typical Nonconformist layout, making the preaching place the focal point and thereby placing the emphasis in worship on God's word.[80] Gillingwater also says that, until it was built, the congregation was dependent for its existence on the Independent community in Great Yarmouth, being wont to visit their chapel in order to receive communion.[81]

Three of the ministers who served in Lowestoft during the later part of the seventeenth century and the earlier part of the eighteenth were of sufficient importance to be included in *The Dictionary of National Biography*. Most famous of all was Thomas Emlyn, later to become the country's first Unitarian minister, who led the Lowestoft congregation for an eighteen-month period in 1689–90 and who enjoyed a cordial relationship with the vicar of the time, Joseph Hudson, even going so far as to attend divine service in the parish church with fellow Nonconformists.[82] Such tolerance and understanding were unusual for the time and suggest good relations in Lowestoft between both Christian congregations. Thomas Emlyn was succeeded as pastor by his friend William Manning, of Peasenhall, who became responsible for the Lowestoft Dissenters on a part-time basis, until about 1698, when another full-time appointment was made.[83] This was the Rev. Samuel Baxter, who had a daughter buried in St Margaret's churchyard in January 1699, another small piece of evidence to suggest some degree of affinity between Anglicans and Nonconformists – though it is also worth saying that the latter had no burial ground of their own.

Neither Baxter nor his successor, Henry Ward, was as notable as their predecessors, but Samuel Say, the man who followed Ward, most certainly was. He was one of the longer-serving Independent ministers, functioning as pastor from 1707 until 1725.[84] His most enduring achievement was to keep a series of observations on the weather during his time at Lowestoft, and the document is among the many manuscripts in possession of the Bodleian Library.[85] After he had left, a Mr Whittick led the congregation for a period of eight years, before being succeeded by Thomas Scott. He stayed for five years, before his delicate health succumbed to the effects of the biting easterly winds and he left to seek a more congenial climate in Ipswich.[86] The man who followed him, James Alderson, was the longest-serving of all the Dissenting ministers, remaining in post from 1738 until his death in 1760. He was, if Edmund Gillingwater is to be believed, held in great esteem by his congregation.

It is not possible to calculate accurately the size of the Independent community in Lowestoft, but Edmund Gillingwater describes the number of Dissenters as having been

[80] E. Gillingwater, p. 356.

[81] *Ibid.*, p. 356. The Yarmouth congregation had a permanent minister, who was able to administer the sacrament. Nonconformity was strong in the Norfolk town, to the point where a leading Dissenter, William Bridge, had functioned as minister of the parish church for about twenty years, until his ejection in 1662 following the Act of Uniformity.

[82] *DNB*, vi, 775; E. Gillingwater, pp. 355–6.

[83] *DNB*, xii, 958; E. Gillingwater, pp. 361–2.

[84] *DNB*, xvii, 877; E. Gillingwater, pp. 362–3.

[85] Bodleian Library, Western Mss. 35448.

[86] E. Gillingwater, p. 366.

'very considerable' in about the year 1735 – which would, again, seem to call into question his description of the town as being so staunchly Anglican. Between September 1709 and March 1712, no less than sixteen families are positively identified as Nonconformist in their children's baptism entries in the parish registers, which means about ninety people if the adults and all their children living at the time are added together.[87] The figure must have been higher than this, because there would have been other Dissenting families not identified in the registration process, as well as similarly practising relatives of some of those that were.

In the sixteen identifiable Nonconformist families, no less than eight of the husbands were mariners or fishermen (Thomas Brame, John Goddle, Thomas Granger, James Kingsborough, Samuel Kitredge, John Landifield, Thomas Landifield and Thomas Salter), four were merchants (Samuel Church, William Rising, Francis Ward and James Ward), one was a tailor (George Middlemis), one a butcher (Thomas Mewse) and two were of unknown occupation (Francis Manfrey and John Smith). A further Dissenting family is detectable in the earlier part of 1709, where the husband (another John Smith) was a grocer. Conditions conducive to the development of Nonconformity in rural areas have been written about.[88] A study of the growth of Dissent in maritime parishes would probably be equally revealing, with independence of belief almost certainly being the result (at least, in part) of the liberating effect of life at sea and the contact made with continental influences.

As has been intimated earlier, the relationship between both ministers and members of the two religious communities in the parish seems to have been generally harmonious from the late seventeenth century onwards. Given the number of known Nonconformist families during the early eighteenth century, the proportion of Dissenters in the town's population was probably 10% or 12% (170–200 adults and children) and may even have been higher than this.[89] The families identified as Nonconformist in the baptism entries between 1709 and 1712 had been having their children christened by the Anglican rite prior to that time, but without their religious leanings alluded to in the entries. After 1711, most of them no longer feature in the parish registers and were therefore, presumably, having their children christened elsewhere – perhaps in the Independent Chapel in town.

The Established Church provided the burial ground for everyone, however, so Anglicans and Nonconformists alike were laid to rest in its soil and were thus unified in death. Further evidence of the co-operation which existed between both denominations

---

[87] There is no explanation as to why such identification took place for a period of two and a half years only. John Tanner, the vicar, had previously noted the inclusion in the register of three Nonconformist children not baptised by him: John, son of William Rising (merchant), September 1708; Sarah, daughter of Thomas Mewse (butcher), October 1708; and Daniel, son of John Smith (grocer), February 1709. There is no hint as to who had performed the rite and it may be that Tanner was anxious to regularise procedures at the start of his long incumbency. See NRO, PD 589/2.

[88] A. Everitt, 'Nonconformity in Country Parishes', *AHR* 18 (1970), 178–99.

[89] Terriers of the town lands in 1729 and 1735, which are preserved in the Lowestoft Town Book, refer to about 25% of the community's families being Dissenters (see NRO PD 589/112, pp. 62 and 71) – a proportion which is probably too high. The earlier source refers to these people as Independents, the latter as Presbyterians. The former title is the correct one.

may be seen in a letter written by the Rev. John Tanner, which is affixed to the inside of the front cover of the parish's third register book.[90] It is dated 28 July 1750 and is addressed to Mrs Rose Burwood, who wished to have her husband, David (a fisherman), buried early on a Sunday evening. Tanner did not insist on the coffin being brought into St Margaret's Church before the completion of the afternoon service's sermon (which was the custom). Instead, he agreed to begin his service later than that at the chapel and to wait for the funeral party's arrival after he had finished preaching: arrangements which were calculated to give Mrs Burwood ample time to complete all her final preparations.

In addition to the people who attended the Independent Chapel in town, there were also members of the Society of Friends among the local population. They were a much smaller fraternity than the other Nonconformists, but it is known that among their number were members of the Sowell family (mariners and fishermen).[91] It is possible that meetings were held locally in private houses, and there may even have been a chapel of some kind in neighbouring Pakefield, where it is known that a community of Friends existed.[92] There was certainly a meeting house at Worlingham, near Beccles, some seven or eight miles' distance from Lowestoft. Ann Landifield (née Utting), a mariner's widow, was laid to rest in the burial ground there in August 1722. Her interment is recorded in the Rev. John Tanner's day-book, but it was not transferred into the parish register of the time.

The apparent lack of friction between the two main religious communities in Lowestoft is perhaps not surprising in view of their close ties with each other. Both Anglicans and Nonconformists were often members of the same family groups, being closely related in some instances and more distantly in others. There were Nonconformist families which had a pattern of marriage within the denomination, but the feature was not universal and others belonging to the fellowship married into Anglican families. Then there was the community of interest experienced in making a day-to-day living: merchants were involved in maritime trade, in curing fish, in various kinds of farming, and in malting and brewing beer; mariners and fishermen went to sea together, making an often dangerous livelihood upon the waves, bound by that close and peculiar camaraderie which only the oceans seem able to produce. Thus, although there were doctrinal and liturgical matters to separate both sets of believers, other, perhaps more compelling factors served to bring them together.

When it came to the matter of holding manorial and parochial office, there was certainly no question of Nonconformists being debarred. They served as constables, ale-tasters, fen-reeves and the like, and they also performed the duty of churchwarden – though whether they were the vicar's choice or that of the people is not revealed. It may seem ironic that men who did not subscribe to the practice of the Established Church should act as its elected officers, but the duties of a churchwarden were wide-ranging

---

[90] NRO, PD 589/4.

[91] The terriers referred to in note 89 say that two or three families in the town belonged to the Society of Friends.

[92] R. J. Crozier, 'Notes on the History of the Friends' Meeting House, Pakefield', LA&LHS *Annual Report* 23 (Lowestoft, 1991), unpaginated.

and incorporated all kinds of parish business beyond the merely ecclesiastical. Among the townsmen of Nonconformist persuasion who served as churchwardens were the following people: William Rising Snr (1661 and 1678), Henry Ward Snr (1661), Richard Church (1668), Samuel Pacy Snr (1675), Samuel Pacy Jnr (1684 and 1685), William Rising Jnr (1698) and James Ward (1706, 1710, 1721 and 1722).[93]

It is interesting to note how, in the second half of the seventeenth century, a group of leading Dissenters all lived in the same part of town. It is not suggested that there was any kind of 'Nonconformist quarter', the physical extent of the town being no more than about sixty acres, but there may well have been an element of neighbourly influence in fostering and strengthening religious beliefs that were opposed to the official way of thinking. Samuel Pacy, Thomas Porter and William Rising, the three men indicted at the 1664 Beccles quarter sessions for attending conventicles, lived within 100 yards of each other on the east side of the High Street. On the west side, and opposite to the house owned by Pacy, lived Thomas Neale (husbandman), while immediately south of him were Christopher Philby (fisherman) and Henry Ward (merchant). The total distance between Rising's house and that of Ward was no more than 150 yards. The former residence was the one licensed for Independent worship in 1672, while it was on part of the Ward family's messuage that the Dissenters' Chapel was built in 1695.

Evidence has been found of support for radical religious ideas in major regional centres (Norwich and Ipswich among them) from the Reformation period onwards, and in smaller communities as well.[94] Furthermore, comment has been made on how commercial activity and links with the Continent fostered strong Protestant feelings in England, with certain major East Anglian towns (Colchester, Ipswich and Bury St Edmunds) identified as centres of reform.[95] Lowestoft, with its cross-North Sea trading links (especially with Holland and the Baltic), was at the forefront of traffic in both merchandise and ideas, and it should therefore come as no surprise that Nonconformity had taken hold before the sixteenth century had ended. And, in addition to the intellectual exchange facilitated by maritime trade, consideration also has to be given to the possible effect of the presence in town, during the 1570s, of the twelve Dutch refugee families noted in Chapter 3 (page 44).

The preambles of wills

In seeking to analyse the personal religious convictions of testators from the wording of preambles to their wills, attention has been drawn to the influence exerted by the people who wrote the documents.[96] It has been claimed that the best indicator of personal belief is to be found in the individual wording of certain preambles which depart from the usual stereotyped format.[97] Furthermore, at least one other

---

[93] Lees, *Chronicles*, pp. 212–14. The list of names reproduced is said to be drawn from a manuscript source (probably the Rev. John Arrow's memorandum book), but it makes no reference to anyone's religious leanings.

[94] V. Harding, 'Reformation and Culture', in Clark, *Cambridge Urban History*, II, 268.

[95] *Ibid.*, 268.

[96] Spufford, *Contrasting Communities*, p. 322.

[97] *Ibid.*, pp. 335–6.

commentator has declared that the problem of whose statement of faith is being made in a preamble can only be resolved in the few cases of testators who drew up their own wills.[98] A scrutiny of the Lowestoft probate material shows that this is not the case. It also contradicts a statement which has been made to the effect that, by the seventeenth century, wills had lost any value they might have once possessed as indicators of people's religious convictions.[99]

Study of the Lowestoft preambles reveals that, out of a total of 102 wills dating from between 1560 and 1599, no less than thirty (29%) have positive religious sentiments expressed. For the period 1600–1649, the number is twenty-nine out of 129 documents (22%). There then follows a noticeable decline in the characteristic during the second half of the seventeenth century and the first three decades of the eighteenth. Between 1650 and 1699, only fourteen documents out of 144 (10%) have any kind of recognisable religiosity in their preambles, while between 1700 and 1730 it is a mere eight out of 132 (6%). There are three main categories of expression: those which make reference to the Holy Trinity and are therefore high-church or quasi-Catholic (eighteen in number), those which mention God's Elect and must therefore be regarded as Calvinistic (fifteen), and those which have some other kind of obviously religious quality about them – such as thanks expressed to The Almighty for his sending sickness upon the testator to act as a corrective force (forty-eight).

The caveat referred to above concerning the writer of a will articulating his own religious beliefs in the preamble, rather than those of the testator, is probably a valid one in certain circumstances, at certain times, and in certain places, but it should not be taken as applying universally to all wills. It is clear from the Lowestoft documents, especially between 1560 and 1620 – a time of great religious change and debate – that the writers did pay due regard to the sentiments of the testators. What other explanation can be found for the fact that four of the most prolific scribes of the period can be seen to have written a Calvinistic preamble for one testator and one referring to the Holy Trinity for another? Robert Allen (draper and parish clerk), William Bentley (vicar), Stephen Phillipp (schoolmaster and parish clerk) and Thomas Warde (yeoman) all did this, while other writers of the time penned preambles which ranged from standard and rather neutral dedicatory declarations to ones which expressed deeply held convictions.

William Bentley's own profound exposition of faith, as he lay sick with plague in August 1603, has been previously referred to in this chapter (the will was written by his friend and fellow cleric, Stephen Phillipp). There are other statements which are equally evocative, and a few of them will serve to illustrate the point. Thomas Dameron (merchant), who died in December 1574, expressed the belief that he would 'be saved at the dreadful day of Judgement among the other faithful penitent sinners'. Hughe Evered (husbandman), who was buried in November 1592 one day after he had made his will, referred to his sickness in the following way: 'for the which loving correction of God I give unto him most humble and hearty thanks' (an echo there of the General Thanksgiving). Thomas Pereson (sailor), who was also interred the day after he had made his will, in February 1594, declared his faith in the redemption afforded to men by the

---

[98] Evans, 'South Elmham', p. 255.

[99] Reed, 'Ipswich', p. 285.

death of Christ, which enabled him to 'most willingly leave this present world with humble thanks unto his good majesty for so great mercies etc.'

Stephen Phillip (schoolmaster), who wrote so many wills for other people and for whose own testament the writer is unknown, died early in December 1605 and made the following observation: 'all flesh is grass and soon withereth and passeth away'. He then proceeded to commend his soul into the 'protection and defence of God the father, God the son and God the holy ghost, three distinct persons and one God'. Alice Eastgate (sailor's widow) left this world in March 1623, having expressed her hope to be 'made partaker of his heavenly kingdom with the Rest of his Redeemed children', while Phebe Waddelow (hatter's widow) passed to her eternal rest some time during the spring or summer of 1645, 'in full assurance of a joyful resurrection and reunion of my soul and body at the latter day'.[100]

These six examples could be multiplied a number of times to demonstrate the personal nature of Christian belief outlined in the preambles to wills made by Lowestoft testators. Moreover, they express feelings and convictions that are largely without meaning to many people in the society of today – such being the difference between an age of faith and the increasingly irreligious, post-Christian world.

---

[100] Her burial is not recorded in the registers, which was probably due to disruption of the registration process at this time.

– 12 –

Urban Status and Identity

The field of study constituting urban history is both complex and wide-ranging, combining a variety of sources and a number of disciplines. Economic and social history may unite in helping to explain and illuminate a community's existence and function, but integration with historical geography and demographic features is required in order to produce a deeper understanding of the human activity which created that entity. Moreover, once a community has been formed, it requires a governing process in order to operate effectively, and so politics of a local nature become part of any scrutiny of its development – placed wherever possible within the context of what national government allowed or believed was desirable. Nor should the religious practices of a previous era be ignored in attempting to understand the thinking of that time, because Christian beliefs and political creeds were once far more closely linked than it is possible to envisage in our current, post-Christian, world. Finally, the last two or three decades have seen a feminist agenda applied to the study of history, which has rightly raised awareness of women's role in society and their contribution to the historical process.

Consideration of the many different elements combining to produce the area of study that is urban history has led to warnings that there is a danger of fragmentation occurring.[1] This might be the case if each separate aspect of a community's development were pursued in isolation, without any attempt to integrate it with its fellows. But even the most elementary exercise in cross-referencing will enable some kind of synthesis to be made. Family reconstitution of parish registers provides the best means of drawing together the various concomitants and producing a coherent statement of a community's essence and function, simply because it provides an ideal platform on which to create historical reconstruction. In allowing the researcher to combine demographic features with details of family and neighbourhood relationship, population movement and occupational data, it creates considerable knowledge of the society under review – an understanding which is then enhanced by other documentation available for scrutiny.

The study of towns in the early modern period has led to the word 'urban' meaning different things to different historians – a feature alluded to in the Foreword. Differing interpretations of the word may be partly the result of academic semantics, but there is also the factor of the varying sizes and diverse economic structure of communities to be considered. The opinion has been expressed that that a community requires a population

---

[1] P. Corfield, 'New Approaches', *JUH* 23 (1), 95.

of at least 5,000 in order to be considered urban, the argument being that if identification of a town is pitched too low in terms of population, the study of urban England becomes merely 'a surrogate for a survey of all English history, and risks losing a distinctive urban flavour'.[2] Thus, the figure of 5,000, while not a totally satisfactory definition of urban in its own right, serves to at least to distinguish between the history of towns as opposed to that of village society.

The proposition is one that does not wholly accommodate the pre-industrial situation, when many communities with less than 5,000 inhabitants were nevertheless urban rather than rural in character. The questions have been asked, 'What is a town? How small is small? How big is big?' And the point has been made that no definition is completely satisfactory or all-embracing.[3] Moreover, whereas the mediaeval town was well defined within chronological and geographical limits, and the modern town is instantly recognisable through being large, industrial and expanding, it has been said that the early modern town, in being an attempt to bridge the gap, suffers from problems of definition.[4] One attempt to provide this has required that a town should show a concentration of population (albeit modest), possess a market, have a range of non-agrarian occupations and demonstrate a contemporary feeling of being urban.[5]

With the nature of urbanism being a topic of debate among present-day historians, it is wise to consider the opinion of an earlier writer. Gregory King, a late seventeenth-century commentator, regarded a settlement of 150–200 houses as constituting a town.[6] Lowestoft had 194 dwellings in its main built-up area in 1618, a total which had grown to about 380 by 1725 (400 or more if subdivisions are included) – numbers which place it comfortably within, and beyond, King's definition. The town's population totalled about 1,500 between 1560 and 1670 (it would have been lower than this after the epidemics of 1603 and 1635), rising to around 1,650 by 1700 and to just short of 2,000 by 1750. Such growth may not have been spectacular, but it fits a national pattern and contrasts with what was happening in northern Europe at the time.[7] Here, especially during the seventeenth century, many smaller towns saw their populations diminish and the only growth discernible was that which took place in a limited number of large regional centres.[8]

The criterion of a population of 5,000 in order for a community to be considered a town derives from the work of a well-known geographer.[9] However, it can be argued

[2] P. Corfield, 'Economic Growth and Change in Seventeenth Century English Towns", in *Traditional Community Under Stress*, pp. 36–7 and 67.

[3] A. Dyer, 'The Early Modern Town: Towards a Clearer Definition', *JUH* 26 (1) (November 1999), 77. This article is a review essay of two works: S. Jack, *Towns in Tudor and Stuart Britain*, and P. Clark (ed.), *Small Towns in Early Modern Europe* (Cambridge, 1995).

[4] *Ibid.*, p. 74.

[5] K. Lindley, 'Early Modern Britain: Regions, Themes and Types', *JUH* 28 (1) (November 2001), 122. This article is a review essay of P. Clark (ed.), *Cambridge Urban History*, II.

[6] Clark and Slack, *Towns in Transition*, p. 5.

[7] P. Clark, 'Introduction', in Clark, *Cambridge Urban History*, II, 3.

[8] P. Griffiths *et al.*, 'Population and disease, estrangement and belonging 1540–1700', in Clark, *Cambridge Urban History*, II, 197.

[9] E. Jones, *Towns and Cities* (Oxford, 1966), p. 5.

that the figure has been taken out of context, because it was used in a discussion of urban settlements in the twentieth century, not in the sixteenth, seventeenth or eighteenth. The whole of the passage in which the number appears is worth quoting for its flexibility of thinking, for its lack of dogmatism, and for its intuitive sense of the concepts which can foster an understanding of what an urban environment actually is. This is what it says:

> *In fact, the simple numerical index can be used on a world scale if enough allowance is made to clear possible contradictions among small settlements. Above 5,000 people there is less doubt that we are dealing with something urban, above 10,000 hardly any doubt at all. The recommendation of the U. N. on grading agglomerations by size is acceptable where the population is above 5,000. The difficulties arise at the point where a village is almost a town, or a town nearly indistinguishable from a village. At that point it is better to accept the local definition. A town is what is implied by the local people when they call a locality a town. If this differs from the criterion we use for statistical analysis, it is no less real. It may be much more meaningful than all the scholarly efforts at defining something too rich and varied to be caught by statistics. The latter have their uses, but it would be a pity if the humanity of cities were destroyed by academic niceties. Defining a town, whether in economic or legal terms, or merely by size, does not take us very much further towards understanding the nature of urbanism. It merely suggests some of the concomitants of urbanism without telling us which are universal or which are important. Is there a common factor, and if so, does it lie in the form of a city, or in its function, or in its society? There are almost as many answers to these questions as there are students interested in cities.*

In the case of Lowestoft, its inhabitants during the pre-industrial age certainly regarded it as a town and references to its urban identity are to be found in a range of contemporary documents, from manorial records to public petitions. The populace was concentrated into an area of about sixty acres, with a good deal of high-density housing in evidence (especially to the west of the High Street) and with house-sharing being practised to some degree throughout much of the period of study. The dwellings themselves cannot be regarded as wholly urban in type, in that there was none of the multi-storey development that was in evidence in places such as Chester and York (though there was common use of the roof-space as a second floor). Nor, among the larger houses, do there appear to have been any of the hall-less type identified in Norwich.[10] Most of Lowestoft's substantial homes were of the hall-parlour-buttery/kitchen variety, a rural type found over much of the Midlands and the southern half of the country during the post-mediaeval period.[11] Towards the end of the seventeenth century and during the first three decades of the eighteenth some surviving probate inventories suggest that the double-pile plan was beginning to manifest itself as

---

[10] Priestley and Corfield, 105.
[11] Barley, 'Farmhouses and Cottages', 197.

the type of house built – a factor which shows that at least some of the accommodation was becoming more unequivocally urban in design and showing an influence deriving from the capital city itself (albeit many decades later).[12]

The concentration of houses and people into a relatively small area is definitely an urban feature, and it was probably a major contributory factor to the town's high mortality rate – noted especially among infants less than a year old.[13] The fact that the population remained stable between 1560 and 1670 (dipping for a while because of two major epidemics), then rose modestly thereafter, was due in some measure to the steady influx of people coming into town from outside. A number of them (the majority) arrived from nearby parishes, others from places further removed, but the pattern of urban recruitment parallels what was happening in other communities.[14] Inhabitants living in an environment of restricted physical size is one of five characteristics cited as typical of the English pre-industrial town,[15] while the others are specialist economic function, complex social structure, sophisticated political order and distinctive influence beyond the immediate boundaries.

It would be difficult to argue that Lowestoft had a sophisticated political order (though the governing instruments of vestry and manor court certainly involved a considerable number of people in local administration), but it certainly shows evidence of the other three features. Its specialist economic interest was maritime in nature, with fishing and fish-processing generating wealth and with seaborne trade also making a valuable contribution to the local economy. But the town was more than mere fishing and trading anchorage; it also had a wide variety of non-maritime occupations. In fact, the number of individual trades and social groupings recorded for the town between 1560 and 1750 stands at 125, which reduces to 106 after the amalgamation of occupations which were synonymous with each other – a number far in excess of what has been identified as the norm for market towns during the early modern period.[16]

The variety and complexity of its occupational structure reflects Lowestoft's performance of a number of the functions identified as being signs of urbanism: it was the centre for the marketing and distribution of certain commodities; it was a place of both manufacture and consumption; and it provided specialist services in the medical, legal and finacial spheres of activity.[17] Much of its economic strength derived from its role as market town for the Hundred of Mutford and Lothingland, which made it the focal point for rural parishes lying to the north, south and west. The hinterland was agriculturally productive and well populated, making it the kind of area needed to

---

[12] Brunskill, *Vernacular Architecture*, pp. 104–5.

[13] Wrigley and Schofield, p. 178. The connection between high population density and high mortality is widely recognised as a feature of the pre-industrial era.

[14] Clark, 'The Migrant in Kentish Towns, 1580–1640', in Clark and Slack, *Crisis and Order*, p. 117; Clark, 'English Country Towns' in Clark, *Country Towns*, p. 4; F. Braudel, 'Pre-Modern Towns' in Clark, *Early Modern Town*, p. 59.

[15] Clark and Slack, *Towns in Transition*, p. 5.

[16] *Ibid.*, p. 5; S. Jack, *Towns*, p. 66.

[17] P. Slack, 'The English Urban Landscape', in *The Urban Setting* (Milton Keynes, 1977), p. 91. This particular book is Volume 1 of *English Urban History, 1500–1870*.

guarantee viability and success for the local market centre.[18] In serving its neighbourhood as the venue for the sale and purchase of goods, Lowestoft's commercial influence extended over most of the hundred, and the presence in town of retail shops is further evidence of its urban character.[19] Victualling was another feature of the place, with a substantial number of inns and alehouses offering their facilities to residents and travellers alike.[20] Lowestoft was a meeting place of lesser overland routes (ones which were important enough in a local context), while its maritime status as anchorage, landing place and fishing station fostered links with communities further removed in both England and continental Europe.

With regard to social structure, the town definitely showed some complexity in the way that its population was differentiated. The number of occupations cited two paragraphs above is sufficient to give a broad hint of the fact; and seven gradations can be identified within local society. The progression from top to bottom may be conveniently summarised thus: gentlemen; merchants, yeomen and the professions; substantial tradespeople and retailers, wealthier mariners and fishermen; substantial craftsmen; lesser tradespeople and craftsmen, husbandmen, lesser mariners and fishermen; journeymen and labourers; servants. There were certainly pronounced differences in wealth between one townsman and another, a situation which has been identified by at least two observers as a feature of urban communities.[21] However, such disparity did not necessarily observe the social order given above. For instance, the wealthiest merchants were usually better off than the members of gentry families, and certain craftsmen (especially shipwrights and linen weavers) were sometimes more affluent than some of the merchants and tradespeople.

Nor were there the sharp differences in status detected in other communities.[22] The first four levels of society outlined above were those from which churchwardens, overseers, leet jurors and manorial officers largely derived, and there seems to have been a blurring of distinction between them concerning election to public duty. The fifth tier was more clearly differentiated, with only limited interest in the process of local government, while the sixth and seventh categories were not involved at all. Further evidence of the fluidity which existed in the upper four levels of society can be seen in the number of men who, towards the end of the seventeenth century and during the first part of the eighteenth, either assumed the titles of 'Gentleman' or 'Mr' or were accorded such distinction in the parish registers. They had no real claim to such nomenclature, but in assuming it they can perhaps be classed as the kind of 'pseudo-gentry' identifiable in English society of the time.[23] In so far as social geography is ascertainable, in that certain classes of people lived in certain specific areas, all that can be safely said is that most of the

---

[18] Clark and Slack, *Towns in Transition*, p. 18.

[19] Corfield, *Impact of Towns*, p. 19.

[20] Everitt, 'English Urban Inn', in Everitt, *Perspectives*, pp. 94–129. There is a good discussion here of the function of inns during the pre-industrial era.

[21] Clark and Slack, *Towns in Transition*, p. 5.

[22] *Ibid.*, p. 5.

[23] A. Everitt, 'Kentish Family Portrait', in Chalklin and Havinden, *Rural Change*, pp. 170–1.

merchants and retailers dwelt on the High Street (especially the east side in the case of the former) and that the side-street area to the west was mainly populated by seafarers and artisans. The town was neither sufficiently large nor populous to show the well-defined occupational areas discovered in a place like Newcastle.[24]

There was no municipality in Lowestoft until borough status was granted in 1885. During the early modern period, its government was both parochial and manorial, a combination noted as typical of many market centres of the time.[25] However, it has been pointed out that self-government lay at the very heart of a town's identity[26] – and whether or not it was established by charter may not have mattered greatly to the people responsible for regulation of their particular community. With both vestry and the manor court lying in the control of the upper levels of local society, it may be thought that the administration of affairs was oligarchical in nature – but this was not the case. The number of men involved in governing the community was too large for it to be considered an oligarchy, with between 30% and 40% of all family heads holding some kind of office during a twenty-five-year period – a sharing of civic responsibility increasingly recognised as an urban characteristic.[27]

It has been shown how, in sixteenth-century Worcester, the ruling plutocracy consisted equally of people who had moved into the city, made money and joined the élite all in one lifetime and those who were the sons and grandsons of immigrants.[28] Lowestoft showed a similar capacity to absorb incomers into its ruling structure, but it retained a 'core' of dominant family groups which had been resident in town over a long period. The characteristic noted in some urban centres, whereby important families rarely stayed in a place beyond the third generation, did not apply to Lowestoft.[29] At least eight of its wealthiest and most important families in the 1730s had been living in town from the 1580s or earlier. Their members' sense of the past, bound by vertical ties of genealogy, would have been strong and, while it is hard to prove conclusively that they formed urban dynasties (for want of a better term), they must have exerted considerable influence on the people around them.

They would also, in conjunction with less affluent but equally long-established people, have created a strong sense of community. This is often marked in maritime towns and villages today, particularly ones which have a fishing industry; and pre-industrial Lowestoft had a further focus, other than the sea, on which to create a sense of its own identity. This was its rivalry with Great Yarmouth, a town seen as a threat to Lowestoft's independence and viability for over 300 years – a dark cloud on the northern horizon seeking to blot out the sun of commercial success by attempting to control not

---

[24] Langton, 'Residential Patterns', in *TIBG* 65, 1–27.

[25] Clark and Slack, *Towns in Transition*, p. 22.

[26] S. Jack, *Towns*, p. 70.

[27] Archer, 'Politics and Government', in Clark, *Cambridge Urban History*, II, 241–6. The writer deals largely with chartered towns, but the sharing of civic responsibility described relates to less elevated urban communities also.

[28] Dyer, *Worcester*, p. 186.

[29] *Ibid.*, p. 180; Hoskins, *Provincial England*, p. 76.

only the local herring fishery but traffic in all seaborne goods. And while Lowestoft may not have had a written account of its history to foster sense of place and civic pride, as Yarmouth had,[30] it certainly possessed a strong notion of its own identity, as may be seen in any of the documentation relating to the long-running dispute between both towns. Eventually, of course, Lowestoft did acquire its own, published, historical record (that written by the expatriate Edmund Gillingwater), but, coming as it did at the end of the eighteenth century, it celebrated a place which had changed radically from the one of even 100 years before.

Given the strong feeling of local identity, especially when combined with Christian conscience, it should come as no surprise to find that the relief of poverty was an important consideration for those in authority. Lowestoft had a well-developed and flexible system both for collecting the poor rate and making payments to those in need. As far as can be ascertained from the bare statement of figures in the overseers' accounts, there seems to have been no difficulty in collecting contributions and some of the disbursements appear to indicate understanding of the recipients' plight and even some degree of warmth towards them. Surviving documentation dates from 1656, but the need to alleviate distress was of much longer standing. The leet court minute of 1582 (referred to on page 41), which records the imposition of a heavy fine on anyone giving accommodation to immigrant families, shows that the town faced a problem common in the Elizabethan period: that of the indigent rural poor gravitating towards local towns in order to make a better life for themselves.

Another recognised urban feature, particularly associated with the second half of the sixteenth century, is that of education. Lowestoft had a free grammar school, which was established by private endowment in the year 1570 and which had its existence given official approval and encouragement in the provision of premises administered by local trustees. The presence of schools in market towns from the sixteenth century onwards has been identified as a distinctive feature of such communities,[31] and Lowestoft increased its educational capacity with the addition of at least two petty schools during the second half of the seventeenth century. One of the factors contributing to the town's having quite a high rate of literacy among its inhabitants must have been the existence of schools – and it was probably their concentration in towns, rather than in the countryside, which helped to create a higher degree of literacy in urban areas than was to be found in rural ones. Such a differential was not only a feature of England in the early modern period, but of Western Europe generally.[32]

Thus, in the light of all that has been said by way of summary and over-view, Lowestoft's urban status and identity is established. It may have been neither large in terms of population, nor extensive in area, but it had greater economic, social and topographical complexity than a village and its inhabitants certainly regarded it as a

---

[30] R. Tittler, *Townspeople and Nation: English Urban Experiences, 1540–1640* (Stanford, 2001), pp. 138–9. Chapter 5 is entitled 'Henry Manship Jnr: Constructing the Civic Memory in Great Yarmouth'. It deals with Manship's history of the town, completed in 1619 and eventually published in 1847.

[31] Clark and Slack, *Towns in Transition*, p. 23.

[32] Burke, 'European Context', in *Urban Setting*, pp. 71–2.

Plate 24. *A late eighteenth-century view of the town from The Denes: Richard Powles dedicated this to Robert Reeve, steward of the manor. It is the middle section of a larger drawing accommodated within the pages of Isaac Gillingwater's collection of illustrations. The cupola of the Town Chamber is just visible on the skyline towards the left-hand side of the picture.*

town. So, in all likelihood, did the people who went there to trade in one way or another, to say nothing of the casual visitor.[33] From the third quarter of the seventeenth century onwards, through until 1750, there was a rise in population from 1,500 inhabitants to 2,000 – an increase of 33% – much of which was probably due to the increase in maritime activity following the town being granted port status and becoming even more of a specialist maritime community than it had been before. It was the last two decades of the seventeenth century which also saw the adoption of the double-pile plan in house-building and the erection of a general purpose civic headquarters which incorporated market cross (for corn trading), town meeting-chamber, schoolroom and Anglican chapel-of-ease.[34]

Alongside the many urban features, however, there definitely existed a strong visual sense of Lowestoft's affinity with the surrounding countryside. Originally the settlement had probably been agricultural rather than maritime in nature, and the western edge of the relocated town merged gently with Goose Green and the fields that lay beyond. There was no hard line of demarcation to declare where the built-up area ended and the countryside began. Even the cliff's terraces were softened with the planting of trees and livestock was pastured on The Denes, so that a late eighteenth-century prospect of the town taken from the beach, or from a boat lying offshore, conveys something of a rural ambience (Plate 24). In a sense, the blurring of distinctions reflects the nature of some

[33] Thomas Baskerville, who visited in 1677, specifically refers to Lowestoft as 'a market town'. See HMC, 13, 266–7. Daniel Defoe, in his *Tour through the Eastern Counties* (1724), also calls it a town – though as a passing reference in comments made concerning the herring disputes with Great Yarmouth.

[34] P. Clark, 'Cultural Role', in *Fabric of Traditional Community*, p. 151, makes specific reference to the building of new town halls during the late seventeenth and early eighteenth centuries. As with other structures of the period, Lowestoft's urban headquarters had classical features in its design and its business chamber, in typical fashion, was situated above an arcade. See P. Borsay, *The English Urban Renaissance* (Oxford, 1989), p. 105.

small towns of the time because, in certain cases, there was little differentiation between them and large villages – a fact which has prompted one commentator to identify a network of about eighty 'micro-towns' scattered across the countryside of East Anglia.[35] Lowestoft is only mentioned as a significant new arrival in the hierarchy of towns proper (along with Wisbech) in about the middle of the nineteenth century – a classification based on the 1841 census count of 4,509 inhabitants.[36] Its admission is attributed (not wholly accurately) to its growth as a seaside resort, which did not take place on a large scale till after the arrival of the railway in 1847.

    Lowestoft had all the necessary elements to be considered a town long before the early Victorian period and the purpose of this book has been to show its development as an urban community, placed wherever possible in both local and national contexts – and, in some cases (in this final chapter) western European ones as well. The 200 years chosen for investigation broadly reflect the availability of suitable documentation with which to attempt reconstruction of the town and the lives of its inhabitants – this, in spite of claims that 'simple market towns' have been given little attention by historians because they left fewer records than their larger counterparts![37] But there is also the advantage of having been able to concentrate the study on a timespan which began during the reign of Edward VI and ended within a decade of the death of George II. During this period, Lowestoft evolved from its mediaeval past and was still comparatively unaffected at the end of it by the growing politeness in society, which was to alter the nature and appearance of the town during the fifty years which followed.

    It has been said that the early years of the eighteenth century saw a growing recognition, on the part of contemporary historians, of increasing civic pride and self-confidence as a feature of provincial culture.[38] Lowestoft had a strong sense of its past at this time, but it had still not developed any kind of significant role as a focal point for local polite society. However, by the time that Richard Powles produced his ink and wash study of the High Street (Plate 11), things had definitely changed.[39] Powles stood at a point opposite Lion Score (later Crown Score) and what he drew is of considerable interest. The scene clearly shows how a number of the houses had had their exteriors updated to keep abreast of the times and also how there had been one or two complete rebuildings in Georgian style. The growing sense of fashion is represented in another way, too. The bottom left-hand corner of the view shows the sign for the *Queen's Head* inn, which stood a little further to the west, in Tyler's Lane. It was this particular establishment which had begun to hold assemblies after about 1760, in a purpose-built annex abutting directly onto the stable-block of *The Crown*.[40] These gatherings were

---

[35] P. Corfield, 'East Anglia', in Clark, *Cambridge Urban History*, II, 35.

[36] *Ibid.*, 42.

[37] Goose, 'Pre-industrial economies', *UHY* 9, 28.

[38] J. M. Ellis, '"For the honour of the town": comparison, competition and civic identity in eighteenth century England', *UHY* 30, 3 (2003), 325.

[39] The drawing is to be found in I. Gillingwater, 'Drawings Illustrative of Lowestoft, Mutford and Lothingland' (SRO(L), 193/2/1).

[40] The site is still visible today from the overspill market-area (now a car park) created in 1703.

advertised in local newspapers and provide evidence of the growing 'politeness' of society, which was so much a feature of the period.[41]

The existence of a book club in town at this time is further proof that Lowestoft was developing a different cultural identity, but perhaps the most obvious and visible signs of change are to be found in its becoming a seaside watering place. The 1730s and 40s have been identified as the time during which the coastal resort began to emerge on a significant scale.[42] Lowestoft arrived a generation later, with its first bathing machines being placed on the beach in 1768. They were put there by Scrivener Capon, proprietor of *The Crown* inn, and modelled on ones in use at Margate.[43] The season was of six weeks' duration, in August and September, and the town enjoyed some success as a resort (though not on the scale of the second half of the nineteenth century), drawing in people not only from Norfolk and Suffolk but from greater distances as well.[44] Most notable of all was Charles Sloane, third Baron Cadogan, who built a fine cliff-top residence in 1789 at the northern end of the High Street (the present-day No. 3, *Beacon House*).[45] It was this influx of summer visitors which was partly responsible for the construction of a new turnpike road between Lowestoft and Great Yarmouth and for the provision of a mail-cart which passed through the town twice a day with letters to and from London, and a daily stage-coach to the capital.[46]

Perhaps the most lasting reminder of Lowestoft's taking its place in the Georgian age of elegance was the presence in town of a soft-paste porcelain factory – the third-longest-lived in England after Worcester and Derby. It had a lifespan in excess of forty years, from 1757 to c. 1800, and during that time produced a wide range of blue-and-white and polychrome pieces, which included tea, coffee and dinner wares, pastille-burners, inkwells, human and animal figurines, small plaques commemorating births of children, and personalised mugs and tankards with the owner's initials or name painted on.[47] Production was aimed at satisfying both local demand and that created by visitors arriving each year for the summer season. Hence, the named pieces particularly

---

[41] Borsay, *English Urban Renaissance*, pp. 118–308, refers to the assemblies held in inns on p. 157.

[42] Borsay, 'Early Modern Urban Landscapes', in Waller, *English Urban Landscape*, p. 118.

[43] E. Gillingwater, p. 51.

[44] One of the Norfolk visitors was James Woodforde, rector of Weston Longville, who recorded his excursion to the town (5 April 1786) in his diary and who was impressed by Lowestoft's urban quality. He breakfasted at *The Crown*, having arrived that morning from Southwold, spent two hours with his nephew and servant walking on the beach and Denes, then proceeeded to Yarmouth in the afternoon. See J. Beresford (ed.), *The Diary of a Country Parson*, 5 vols (Oxford, 1924–31), II, 236. The town's indigenous population also continued to increase after mid-century. E. Gillingwater, p. 54, tells us that a head-count taken by the vicar and churchwardens on 7 and 8 August, 1775, gave a total of 2,231 inhabitants. By 1801, the number had risen to 2,332.

[45] *Norfolk Chronicle*, 7 November 1789 and 10 July 1790.

[46] E. Gillingwater, p. 51.

[47] A number of authorities give the factory's starting date as c. 1757. However, local experiments in producing domestic wares may have begun earlier than this, because an entry in the vicar's day-book for a burial of 14 March 1756 reads thus: 'Ralph Bourne, Potman. Aged twenty-three years. He came from Burselm [*sic*] in Staffordshire'. Could it be that a journeyman potter from one of the Five Towns had been involved in a proto-enterprise in the town?

(especially when accompanied by the name of the town or village in which the person lived) assume the nature of an early souvenir industry. Then there were the items painted with the legend 'A trifle from Lowestoft', aimed at providing people with a memento of their stay at the seaside. The factory itself became something of a tourist attraction and among the many visitors was the young French aristocrat Francois de la Rochefoucauld. When he arrived in Lowestoft, in the late summer of 1784, he recorded the porcelain works' activities in his journal, as well as noting the town's sea-bathing facilities and involvement in fishing.[48]

The place in which he made his brief stay was a very different one from that described throughout the pages of this book.

---

[48] N. Scarfe (ed.), *A Frenchman's Year in Suffolk, 1784*, SRS, xxx (Ipswich, 1988), 215–17.

Bibliography

Primary sources

BL: Additional Mss. 56070: a map of the Lothingland coastline, c. 1580

BL: Harleian Mss. 595, no. ii, folio 168: Suffolk communicants' return, 1603

Bodleian Library: Western Mss. 35448: the Rev. Samuel Say's weather journal

MCA: 177/4: Akethorpe accounts roll, 1433–34

     73/4: Akethorpe accounts roll, 1438–39

     151/9: Akethorpe demesne rental, 1438–39

     FP 62: Akethorpe arrears accounts, post-1450

     FP 54: grants of land in Lothingland by Sir John Fastolf, 1455

     FP 105: Akethorpe terrier, post 1500

     Akethorpe terrier and map, 1843 (no archival reference number)

     Akethorpe map, 1848 (no archival reference number)

NRO: VIS/4: bishop's visitation of 1606

     VIS/6: bishop's visitations of 1629 and 1633

     PD 564/1: Corton parish register, 1579–1783

     PD 105/1: Kessingland parish register, 1561–1812

     PD 589/1: Lowestoft parish register, 1561–1649

     PD 589/2: Lowestoft parish register, 1650–1786

     PD 589/3: Lowestoft woollen burials register and vicar's day-book, 1678–1765

     PD 589/4: Lowestoft parish register, 1695–1767

     PD 508/1: Oulton parish register, 1564–1659

     PD 508/2: Oulton parish register, 1659–1729

     PD 508/3: Oulton parish register, 1723–1774

     PD 551/1: Pakefield parish register, 1678–1752

     PD 589/92: the Rev. John Arrow's memorandum book

     PD 589/112: the Lowestoft Town Book

     PD89/178: Lowestoft Ship Money return of 1636

     PD 589/86: proclamation by Rev. John Tanner concerning herring-carting on Sundays

     Registers of wills proved in the NCC

     NCC wills

     NCC inventories

     PD 589/80: Lowestoft tithe accounts book, 1698–1787

     TA 658: Lowestoft tithe apportionment and map of 1842

PRO: A551 16/4/1: assize indictments for criminal trial at Bury St.Edmunds, March
       1662
       C53/95: grant of the right to hold a market in Lowestoft (15 November 1308)
       C53/188: re-grant of the right to hold a market in Lowestoft (15 December
       1445)
       KR 59/4: muster roll of Mutford and Lothingland Hundred, 1535
       MPF 283: sketch map of Lothingland, drawn to accompany defence survey of
       1584
       PCC administration acts and bonds
       Prob II: PCC wills and will registers
       Prob 4: PCC inventories
       SP 1/80 f65v: Iceland fishing vessels' return, 1533
       SP 12/38/8/II: survey of east coast vessels suitable for expedition to Scotland,
       1544
       SP 12/39/17.1: national survey of maritime personnel, 1566
       SP12/171/61, 62 i and ii, 63: Lothingland defence survey of 1584
       SP 167/25: muster roll of Lothingland Half-hundred, 1584
       SP 28/171: Yarmouth customs watch on Lowestoft, 1640
       WO 30/48: national inns survey, 1686
SCC (Ipswich): compulsory purchase documentation, 1881–1926 (former WDC deed
       packets 140, 141, 171, 174 and 179)
SRO(I): SAC administration acts and bonds
       IC/AA1: SAC wills
       FE1: SAC inventories
       B105: Suffolk quarter sessions order books
SRO(L): Acc. 11/M1: Suffolk quarter sessions order books, 1639–83 (microfilm)
       Acc./M2: Suffolk quarter sessions order books, 1683–1747 (microfilm)
       Acc. 11/M3: Suffolk quarter sessions order books, 1748–84 (microfilm)
       192/4: Lothingland Half-hundred Court minute book, 1590–4
       194/C1/1: Lothingland Half-hundred Court minute book, 1594–1612
       194/A1/1, 2 and 3: Gunton Score Half-hundred court minute books,
       1667–1706
       194/A10/70: Lowestoft manorial chief tenements list
       194/A10/71: Lowestoft manorial chief tenements list and rental of 1545
       194/A10/4: Lowestoft manor court minute book, 1582–85
       194/A10/5–19: Lowestoft manor court minute books, 1616–1756
       454/1: the Rev. John Tanner's listing of copyhold properties (1725)
       454/2: The Rev. John Tanner's court baron extracts
       194/A10/72: Lowestoft manor roll of 1610
       194/A10/73: Lowestoft manor roll of 1618
       194/A10/122: Lowestoft manorial rental of 1675–76
       317/1/1/9 to 12: Mutford and Lothingland Hundred accounts, 1674–78
       194/B1/11: Mutford Half-hundred admiralty court membranes, 1558–76
       194/B1/15 to 23: Mutford Half-hundred manor court books, 1558–1704
       368: map of the local coastline, c. 1580 (a copy of BL Add. Mss. 56070)

61/2: churchwardens' map of the Lowestoft charitable lands, 1761

109/D2/1: Beccles parish register, 1586–1617

109/D2/9: Beccles parish register, 1586–1608

109/D2/10: Beccles parish register, 1608–1750

109/D2/2: Beccles woollen burials register, 1681–1764

153/D1/1: Southwold parish register, 1602–1751

M18/06/1: the Lowestoft Town Book (microfilm copy of NRO, 589/112)

01/13/1/1 and 2: Lowestoft Overseers Accounts, 1656–91 and 1691–1712

01/13/1/3: Lowestoft settlement and apprenticeship book, 1696–1785

WDC (Lowestoft): compulsory purchase documentation, 1881–1926 (deed packets 21, 25, 29, 30, 32–5, 68–73, 75–83, 86, 89, 94, 95, 110 and 126)

Printed primary sources

Ambler, R. W., Watkinson, B. and Watkinson, L. (eds), *Farmers and Fishermen: The Probate Inventories of the Ancient Parish of Clee, South Humberside, 1536–1742* (Hull, 1987).

Bailey, M. (ed.), *The Bailiffs' Minute Book of Dunwich, 1404–1430*, SRS, xxxiv (Woodbridge, 1992).

Brewer, J. S. (ed.), *Letters and Papers, Foreign and Domestic, Henry VIII*, iv (London, 1872).

Butcher, D. (ed.), *The Lowestoft Manor Roll of 1618*, HWC Publications (Lowestoft, 2004).

Calthrop, M. M. C. (ed.), *The First Recusant Roll, 1592–93*, CRS, xviii (London, 1916).

Daniell, F. H. Blackburne (ed.), *Calendar of State Papers Domestic, Charles II: 1672* (London, 1899).

Fowler, R. C. (ed.), *Calendar of Patent Rolls, Edward IV to Richard III, 1476–85* (London, 1901).

Fraser, C. M. (ed.), *The Accounts of the Chamberlains of Newcastle-upon-Tyne, 1508–11*, SANUT Record Series III (Newcastle, 1987).

Gairdner, J. (ed.), *Letters and Papers, Foreign and Domestic, Henry VIII*, vi (London, 1882).

Gairdner, J. and Brodie, R. H. (eds), *Letters and Papers, Foreign and Domestic, Henry VIII*, xiv (i), xv, xvi, xvii, xix (i) and xx (i) (London, 1894–1905).

Glasscock, R. E. (ed.), *The Lay Subsidy of 1334*, BA Records of Social and Economic History (Oxford, 1975).

Green, M. A. E. (ed.), *Calendar of State Papers Domestic, Parliament, 1653–4* (London, 1879).

Green, M. A. E. (ed.), *Calendar of State Papers Domestic, Parliament, 1654* (London, 1880).

Harris, G. G. (ed.), *Trinity House Transactions, 1609–1635*, LRS, xix (London, 1983).

Hervey, Lord John (ed.), *The Lothingland Hundred Rolls, 1273–74* (Ipswich, 1902).

Hervey, S. H. A. (ed.), *Suffolk in 1327*, SGB, ix (Woodbridge, 1906).

—*Suffolk in 1524*, SGB, x (Woodbridge, 1910).

—*Suffolk in 1674*, SGB, xi (Woodbridge, 1905).

—*Suffolk in 1568*, SGB, xii (Bury St Edmunds, 1909).

Hill, R. H. (ed.), *The Corie Letters, 1664–87*, NRS, xxvii (Norwich, 1956).

HMC 13th Report: vol. II of the Duke of Portland Mss. (London, 1892).

Houlbrooke, R. A. (ed.), *The Letters of Bishop John Parkhurst*, NRS, xliii (Norwich, 1974).

Isaacson, R. F. (ed.), *Calendar of Patent Rolls, Edward III*, 1340–3 (London, 1900).

—*Calendar of Patent Rolls, Edward III*, 1343–5 (London, 1902).

—*Calendar of Patent Rolls, Edward III*, 1345–8 (London, 1903).

Lemon, R. (ed.), *Calendar of State Papers Domestic, Elizabeth I: 1584–85* (London, 1865).

Oppenheim, M. (ed.), *The Naval Tracts of Sir William Monson*, NRS, v (London, 1914).

Pickering, D. (ed.), *Statutes at Large*, vi and vii (London, 1763).

Pound, J. F. (ed.), *The Norwich Census of the Poor, 1570*, NRS, xl (Norwich, 1971).

Powell, E. (ed.), 'Muster Rolls of Territorials in Tudor Times', *PSIA* xix (Ipswich, 1927).

Redstone, V. B. (ed.), 'The Island of Lothingland, 1584', *PSIA* xx (Ipswich, 1928–30).

Reed, M. (ed.), *The Ipswich Probate Inventories, 1583–1631*, SRS, xxii (Woodbridge, 1981).

Rumble, A. (ed.), *Domesday Book: Suffolk, Part One* (Chichester, 1986).

Rutledge, P. (ed.), *Great Yarmouth Apprenticeship Indentures, 1562–1665*, NNGS, xi (Norwich, 1979).

Scarfe, N. (ed.), *A Frenchman's Year in Suffolk, 1784*, SRS, xxx (Ipswich, 1988).

Schofield, B. (ed.), *The Knyvett Letters, 1620–44*, NRS, xx (Norwich, 1949).

Shaw, W. A. (ed.), *Calendar of Treasury Books, 1676–79*, v, i and ii (London, 1911).

—*Calendar of Treasury Books, 1679–80*, vi (London, 1913).

Slack, P. (ed.), *Poverty in Early Stuart Salisbury*, WRS, xxxi (Devizes, 1975).

Steer, F. W., *Farm and Cottage Inventories of Mid-Essex, 1635–1749* (Chelmsford, 1950; re-published Chichester, 1969).

Sylvester, D. W. (ed.), *Educational Documents, 800–1816* (London, 1970).

Webb, J. (ed.), *Poor Relief in Elizabethan Ipswich*, SRS, ix (Ipswich, 1966).

White, C. H. E. (ed.), *The Communicants' Return of 1603: Archdeaconry of Suffolk*, *PSIA* vi (Ipswich, 1888).

Willan, T. S., *Elizabethan Manchester*, CSP, xxvii (Manchester, 1980).

Williams, J. F. (ed.), *Bishop Redman's Visitation, 1597*, NRS, xviii (Norwich, 1946).

Secondary literature

Adair, R. L., 'Regional Variations in Illegitimacy and Courtship Patterns in England, 1538–1754' (unpub. PhD thesis, University of Cambridge, 1991).

Allen, M. E., 'The Development of the the the Borough of Aldeburgh, 1547–1660' (unpub. MA dissertation, University of Wales, 1982).

Anon, *A Tryal of Witches* (London, 1682).

—*General Instructions for the Collectors of the Duties upon English Salt* (London, 1721).

Arber, E., *An English Garner*, iii (London, 1877). This book contains the pamphlet *Britaine's Busse*, by E. S.

Archer, I., 'Politics and Government, 1540–1700', in P. Clark (ed.), *The Cambridge Urban History of Britain, Vol. II, 1540–1840* (Cambridge, 2000).

Ashby, M. K., *The Changing English Village: A History of Bledington* (Kineton, 1974).

Baker, A., and Butlin, R. H. (eds), *Field Systems in the British Isles* (Cambridge, 1973).

Barley, M. W., 'English Farmhouses and Cottages, 1550–1725', *EHR* 2nd Series 7 (1955), 291–306.

Barnard, J. E., 'The Barnard Shipyards', *SR* New Series 8 (1987), 1–17.
   —*Building Britain's Wooden Walls* (Oswestry, 1997).

Barringer, C. and Macdonald, F. (eds), *Aylsham in the Seventeenth Century* (North Walsham, 1988).

Beevor, H. E., 'Norfolk Woodlands from the Evidence of Contemporary Chronicles', *TNNNS* 2 (Norwich, 1924).

Beier, A. L., 'The Social Problems of an Elizabethan Country Town: Warwick, 1580–90', in P. Clark (ed.), *Country Towns in Pre-Industrial England* (Leicester, 1981).

Beresford, J. (ed.), *The Diary of a Country Parson*, 5 vols (Oxford, 1924–31).

Borsay, P., *The English Urban Renaissance* (Oxford, 1989).
   —'Early Modern Urban Landscapes', in P. Waller (ed.), *The English Urban Landscape* (Oxford, 2000).

Botelho, L. A., *Old Age and the English Poor Law* (Woodbridge, 2004).

Bowden, P., 'Agricultural Prices, Farm Profits and Rents', in J. Thirsk (ed.), *The Agrarian History of England and Wales*, vol. iv (Cambridge, 1967).

Braudel, F., 'Pre-modern Towns', in P. Clark (ed.), *The Early Modern Town* (London, 1976).

Brown, F. E., 'Continuity and Change in the Urban House: Developments in Domestic Space Organisation in Seventeenth Century London', *CSSH* 28 (1986), 558–90.

Brown, R. J., *English Farmhouses* (London, 1982).

Brunskill, R. W., *Illustrated Handbook of Vernacular Architecture* (London, 1970).

Burke, P., 'The European Context', in OU, *The Urban Setting* (Milton Keynes, 1977–8).

Burwash, D., *English Merchant Shipping, 1460–1540* (Toronto, 1947; Newton Abbot, 1969).

Butcher, D., *The Driftermen* (Reading, 1979).
   —*The Trawlermen* (Reading, 1980).
   —*Living from the Sea* (Reading, 1982).
   —*Following the Fishing* (Newton Abbot, 1987).
   —'The Development of Pre-Industrial Lowestoft, 1560–1730' (unpub. MPhil thesis, University of East Anglia, 1991).
   —*The Ocean's Gift* (Norwich, 1995).
   —'Aspects of Population Mobility in Pre-Industrial Lowestoft', in A. Longcroft and R. Joby (eds), *East Anglian Studies: Essays Presented to J. C. Barringer on his Retirement* (Norwich, 1995).
   —'The Relief of Poverty in a Pre-Industrial Suffolk Town: The Case of Lowestoft', in C. Rawcliffe, R. Virgoe and R. Wilson (eds), *Counties and Communities: Essays on East Anglian History Presented to Hassell Smith* (Norwich, 1996).
   —'The Herring Fisheries in the Early Modern Period: Lowestoft as Microcosm', in D. J. Starkey, C. Reid and N. Ashcroft (eds), *England's Sea Fisheries* (London, 2000).

Butcher, D. and Bunn I., *Lowestoft Burning*, HWC Publication (Lowestoft, 2003).

Campbell, B. M. S., and Overton, M., 'A New Perspective on Mediaeval and Early Modern Agriculture: Six Centuries of Norfolk Farming c. 1250–c. 1850', *P&P* 141 (November, 1993), 38–105.

Carter, A. *et al.*, *The Norwich Survey* (c. 1980).

Chalkin, C. W., 'The Making of Some New Towns, 1600–1720', in C. W. Chalklin and M. A. Havinden (eds), *Rural Change and Urban Growth* (London, 1974).

Chambers, J. D., 'Three Essays on the Population and Economy of the Midlands', in D. V. Glass and D. E. C. Eversley (eds), *Population in History* (London, 1965).
—*Population, Economy and Society in Pre-Industrial England* (Oxford, 1972).

Chartres, J. A., *The Internal Trade in England, 1500–1750* (London, 1977).
—'The Marketing of Agricultural Produce', in J. Thirsk (ed.), *The Agrarian History of England and Wales*, vol. v, ii (Cambridge, 1985).
—'City and Towns, Farmers and Economic Change', *HR* 64 (1991), 138–55.

Childs, W. R., 'Fishing and Fisheries in the Middle Ages: The Eastern Fisheries', in D. J. Starkey, C. Reid and N. Ashcroft (eds), *England's Sea Fisheries* (London, 2000).

Clark, P., 'The Migrant in Kentish Towns, 1500–1800', in P. Clark and P. Slack (eds), *Crisis and Order in English Towns, 1500–1700* (London, 1972).
—'The Early Modern Town in the West', in P. Clark (ed.), *The Early Modern Town* (London, 1976).
—'The Cultural Role of Towns in the Late Sixteenth and Seventeenth Centuries', in OU, *The Fabric of the Traditional Community Under Stress* (Milton Keynes, 1977–8).
—'English Country Towns, 1500–1800', in P. Clark (ed.), *Country Towns in Pre-Industrial England* (Leicester, 1981).
—'The Civic Leaders of Gloucester, 1500–1800', in P. Clark (ed.), *The Transformation of English Provincial Towns* (London, 1984).
—'Introduction', in P. Clark (ed.), *The Cambridge Urban History of Britain, Vol. II, 1540–1840* (Cambridge, 2000).

Clark, P. and Slack, P., *Crisis and Order in English Towns, 1500–1700* (London, 1972).
—*English Towns in Transition, 1500–1700* (Oxford, 1976).

Clarkson, L. A., *The Pre-Industrial Economy in England* (London, 1971).

Clay, C. G. A., *Economic Expansion and Social Change*, 2 vols (Cambridge, 1984).

Cobbe, H., 'Four Manuscript Maps Recently Acquired by the British Museum', *JSA* 4, viii (October, 1973), 646–52.

Coleman, D. C., 'London Scriveners and the Estate Market in the Later Seventeenth Century', *EHR* 2nd Series 4 (1951–2), 221–30.
—*The Economy of England, 1450–1750* (Oxford, 1977).

Collins, A. S., 'Language, 1660–1784', in B. Ford (ed.), *From Dryden to Johnson* (London, 1957; vol. 4 of *The Pelican Guide to English Literature*).

Collins, J., *Salt and Fishery, a Discourse Thereof* (London, 1682).

Cooper, E. R., *Memories of Bygone Dunwich*, 2nd edition (Southwold, 1948).

Copinger, W. A., *The Manors of Suffolk*, 7 vols (Manchester, 1905–11).

Corfield, P. J., 'A Provincial Capital in the Late Seventeenth Century: The Case of Norwich', in P. Clark and P. Slack (eds), *Crisis and Order in English Towns, 1500–1700* (London, 1972).

—'Economic Growth and Change in Seventeenth English Towns' in OU, *The Traditional Community Under Stress* (Milton Keynes, 1977–8).

—*The Impact of English Towns, 1700–1800* (Oxford, 1982).

—'New Approaches for Old Towns?', *JUH* 23, i (November, 1996), 94–107.

—'East Anglia', in P. Clark (ed.), *The Cambridge Urban History of Britain, vol. II, 1540–1840* (Cambridge, 2000).

Cotman, J. S., *Engravings of Sepulchral Brasses in Suffolk* (London, 1817).

Cressy, D., 'Literacy in Seventeenth Century England: More Evidence', *JIH* 8 (1977), 141–50.

—*Literacy and the Social Order* (Cambridge, 1980).

Crozier, R. J., 'Notes on the History of the Friends' Meeting House, Pakefield', LA&LHS *Annual Report* 23 (1991), unpaginated.

Davis, D., *A History of Shopping* (London, 1966).

Davis, R., *The Rise of the English Shipping Industry in the Seventeenth and Eighteenth Centuries* (Newton Abbot, 1962).

Dean, D. M., 'Parliament, Privy Council and Local Politics in Elizabethan England: The Yarmouth-Lowestoft Fishing Disputes', *Albion* 22, i (Spring, 1990), 39–64.

Deane, P. and Cole, W. A., *British Economic Growth, 1688–1959* (Cambridge, 1962).

Defoe, D., *Tour through the Eastern Counties* (London, 1724).

Drake, M. (ed.), *Population in Industrialisation* (London, 1969)

Durbidge, P., 'A Limited Excavation of the Drying Area at Wilde School, Lowestoft', LA&LHS *AnnualReport* 36 (2004), 16–33.

—'A Second Limited Excavation in the Grounds of the John Wilde School, Lowestoft', LA&LHS *Annual Report* 37 (2005), 21–43.

Dyer, A. D., *The City of Worcester in the Sixteenth Century* (Leicester, 1973).

—'The Early Modern Town: Toward a Clearer Definition', *JUH* 26, i (November, 1999), 74–82.

Dymond, D., 'The Parish of Walsham-le-Willows: Two Elizabethan surveys and Their Mediaeval Background', *PSIA* 33, ii (1974), 195–211.

Ekwall, E. (ed.), *The Oxford Dictionary of English Place Names*, 4th edition (Oxford, 1960).

Ellis, J. M., '"For the Honour of the Town": Comparison, Competition and Civic Identity in Eighteenth Century England', in *UHY* 30, 3 (December, 2003), 325–37.

Elton, G. R., *Star Chamber Stories* (London, 1958).

E. S., *Britaine's Busse*, (London, 1615). See Arber, E. above.

Evans, E., 'Tithes', in J. Thirsk (ed.), *The Agrarian History of England and Wales*, vol. v, ii (Cambridge, 1985).

Evans, G. E., *The Horse in the Furrow* (London, 1960).

Evans, J. T., *Seventeenth Century Norwich* (Oxford, 1979).

Evans, N., 'The Community of South Elmham, Suffolk, 1550–1640' (unpub. MPhil thesis, University of East Anglia, 1978).

—'Tithe Books as a Source for the Local Historian', *LH* 14, i (February, 1980), 24–7.

—'Occupations in Parish Registers: A Note', *LH* 15, vi (May, 1983), 361.

—*Beccles Rediscovered* (Beccles, 1984).

—*The East Anglian Linen Industry* (Aldershot and Brookfield, Vermont, 1985).

Everitt, A. M., 'The Marketing of Agricultural Produce', in J. Thirsk (ed.), *The Agrarian History of England and Wales*, vol. iv (Cambridge, 1967).

—'Nonconformity in Country Parishes', *AHR* 18 (1970), 178–99.

—'The English Urban Inn' in A. M. Everitt (ed.), *Perspectives in English Urban History* (London, 1973).

—'Kentish Family Portrait', in C. W. Chalklin and M. R. Havinden (eds), *Rural Change and Urban Growth* (London, 1974).

—'The Market Towns', in P. Clark (ed.), *The Early Modern Town* (London, 1976). This essay is the same as that published in *Agrarian History*, iv, above.

Eversley, D. E. C., 'Population History and Local History', in E. A. Wrigley (ed.), *An Introduction to English Historical Demography* (London, 1966).

—'Exploitation of Anglican Parish Registers by Aggregative Analysis', in E. A. Wrigley (ed.), *An Introduction to English Historical Demography* (London, 1966).

Fisher, F. J., 'The Growth of the London Food Market, 1540–1640', *EHR* 1st Series 5 (1935), 46–64.

French, H. R., 'Urban Agriculture, Commons and Commoners in the Seventeenth and Eighteenth Centuries: The Case of Sudbury, Suffolk', *AHR* 48, II (2000), 171–99.

Gee, J., *The Trade and Navigation of Great Britain* (London, 1729).

Geis, G. and Bunn, I., 'Sir Thomas Browne and Witchcraft: a Cautionary Tale for Contemporary Law and Psychiatry', *IJLP* 4 (1981), 1–11.

—*A Tryal of Witches* (London and New York, 1997).

Gentleman, T., *England's Way to Win Wealth* (London, 1614). Reprinted in *Harleian Miscellany*, iii (London, 1744 and 1809).

Geological Survey, *Quarter Inch Geological Survey Map* (London, 1931).

Gillingwater, E., *An Historical Account of the Ancient Town of Lowestoft* (London, 1790).

Gillingwater, I., 'A History of Lowestoft and Lothingland', 3 vols (unpub. manuscript of c. 1800) – SRO(L), 193/1/1, 2 and 3.

—'Drawings Illustrative of the History of Lowestoft, Mutford and Lothingland' (a collection of drawings of c. 1807, possibly intended to embellish the text immediately above) – SRO(L), 193/2/1.

Glass, D. V., 'Two papers on Gregory King', in D. V. Glass and D. E. C. Eversley (eds), *Population in History* (London, 1965).

Godden, G. A., *The Illustrated Guide to Lowestoft Porcelain* (London, 1969).

Goody, J. R., 'Inheritance, Property and Women: Some Comparative Considerations', in J. R. Goody, J. Thirsk and E. P. Thompson (eds), *Family and Inheritance: Rural Society in Western Europe, 1200–1800* (Cambridge, 1976).

Goose, N., 'English Pre-Industrial Urban Economies', *UHY* 9 (1982), 27–30.

Gough, J. W., *The Rise of the Entrepreneur* (London, 1969).

Gough, R. ed. P. E. Razzell, *The History of Myddle* (Firle, Sussex, 1979).

Grassby, R., *The Business Community of Seventeenth-Century England* (Cambridge, 1995).

Gray, H. L., *English Field Systems*, vol. xxii (Harvard, 1915).

Gray, M., *The Fishing Industries of Scotland, 1790–1914* (Oxford, 1978).

Gregg, P., *Black Death to Industrial Revolution* (London, 1976).

Griffiths, P., Landers, J., Pelling, M. and Tyson, R., 'Population and disease, estrangement and belonging, 1540–1700', in P. Clark (ed.), *The Cambridge Urban History of Britain, Vol. II, 1540–1840* (Cambridge, 2000).

Grigg, D. B., *Population Growth and Agrarian Change* (Cambridge, 1980).

Hair, P. (ed.), *Before the Bawdy Court* (London, 1972).

Harding, V., 'Reformation and culture 1540–1700', in P. Clark (ed.), *The Cambridge Urban History of Britain, Vol. II, 1540–1840* (Cambridge, 2000).

Hey, D. G., *An English Community: Myddle Under the Tudors and Stuarts* (Leicester, 1974).

Hindle, S., *On the Parish? The Micro-Politics of Poor Relief in Rural England, c. 1550–1750* (Oxford, 2004).

Hipkin, S. A., 'The Economy and Social Structure of Rye, 1600–1660' (Unpub. PhD thesis, University of Oxford, 1985).

Hodgson, W. C., *The Herring and its Fishery* (London, 1957).

Holderness, B. A., *Pre-Industrial England* (London, 1976).

——'Credit in English Rural Society before the Nineteenth Century, with Special Reference to the Period 1650–1720', *AHR* 24, ii (1976), 97–109.

——'East Anglia and the Fens', in J. Thirsk (ed.), *The Agrarian History of England and Wales*, vol. v, i (Cambridge, 1984).

Hoskins, W. G., 'English Provincial Towns in the Early Sixteenth Century', in W. G. Hoskins, *Provincial England* (London, 1963). Article first published in RHS *Transactions* 5th Series 6 (1956), 1–19.

——'An Elizabethan Provincial Town: Leicester', in W. G. Hoskins, *Provincial England* (London, 1963). Article first published in J. H. Plumb (ed.), *Studies in Social History: A Tribute to G. M. Trevelyan* (London, 1955).

——'The Rebuilding of Rural England, 1570–1640', in W. G. Hoskins, *Provincial England* (London, 1963). Article first published in *P&P* IV (1953), 44–59.

Howell, C., 'Peasant Inheritance Customs in the Midlands, 1280–1700', in J. R. Goody, J. Thirsk and E. P. Thompson (eds), *Family and Inheritance: Rural Society in Western Europe, 1200–1800* (Cambridge, 1976).

Husbands, C., 'Regional Change in a Pre-Industrial Economy: Wealth and Population in England in the Sixteenth and Seventeenth Centuries', *JHG* 13, 4 (1987), 345–59.

Jack, S. M., *Trade and Industry in Tudor and Stuart England* (London, 1977).

——*Towns in Tudor and Stuart Britain* (London, 1996).

Jackman, W. T., *The Development of Transportation in Modern England* (Cambridge, 1916; republished London, 1966).

Jenkins, J. T., *The Herring and the Herring Fisheries* (London, 1927).

Jones, A. G. E., 'Plagues in Suffolk in the Seventeenth Century', *N&Q* CXCVIII (1953), 384–6.

——'Shipbuilding in Ipswich, 1700–1750', *MM* 43 (1957), 298–304.

Jones, E., *Towns and Cities* (Oxford, 1966).

Jones, E., 'England's Icelandic Fishery in the Early Modern Period', in D. J. Starkey, C. Reid and N. Ashcroft (eds), *England's Sea Fisheries* (London, 2000).

Jordan, W. K., *Philanthropy in England, 1480–1660* (London, 1959).

Kain, R., and Prince, H. C., *The Tithe Surveys of England and Wales* (Cambridge, 1985).

Kent, J., 'The Village Constable, 1580–1642: The Nature and Dilemmas of the Office', *JBS* 20, ii (Spring, 1981), 26–49.

Kerridge, E., 'Turnip Husbandry in High Suffolk', in W. E. Minchinton (ed.), *Essays in Agrarian History*, vol. i (Newton Abbot, 1968).

Kingston, A., *East Anglia and the Great Civil War* (London, 1897).

Kussmaul, A., *Servants in Husbandry in Early Modern England* (Cambridge, 1981).

Laithwaite, M., 'The Buildings of Burford: A Cotswold town in the Fourteenth to Nineteenth Centuries', in A. Everitt (ed.), *Perspectives in English Urban History* (London, 1973).

—'Totnes Houses, 1500–1800', in P. Clark (ed.), *The Transformation of English Provinicial Towns* (London, 1984).

Langton, J., 'Residential Patterns in Pre-Industrial Cities: Some Case Studies from Seventeenth Century Britain', *TIBG* 65 (July, 1975), 1–27.

Laslett, P., *The World We Have Lost*, 2nd ed. (London, 1971).

—*Family Life and Illicit Love in Earlier Generations* (Cambridge, 1977)

—*The World We Have Lost Further Explored* (London, 1983).

Laslett, P. and Wall, R., *Household and Family in Past Time* (Cambridge, 1972).

Lawson, J. and Silver, H., *A Social History of Education in England* (London, 1973).

Lees, H. D. W., *The Chronicles of a Suffolk Parish Church* (Lowestoft, 1949).

Lindley, K., 'Early Modern Urban Britain: Regions, Themes and Types', *JUH* 28, 1 (November, 2001), 120–9.

Lloyd, D. W., *The Making of English Towns* (London, 1984).

Lloyd, N., *A History of English Brickwork* (London, 1925).

Lucas, R., 'Dutch Pantiles in the County of Norfolk: Architecture and International Trade in the Seventeenth and Eighteenth Centuries', *JSPMA* 32 (1998), 75–94.

McCrum, R., Cran, W. and MacNeil, R., *The Story of English* (London, 1986).

McCulloch, J. R., *Early English Tracts on Commerce* (Cambridge, 1952).

MacFarlane, A., *Reconstructing Historical Communities* (Cambridge, 1977).

Mackenzie, D., 'Ring a ring o' rosies', in *NS* 172, no. 2318 (November, 2001), 35–7.

McKeown, T. and Brown, R. G., 'Medical Evidence Related to English Population Changes in the Eighteenth Century', *PS* ix (1955), 119–41. This article is also to be found in M. Drake (ed.), *Population in Industrialisation* (London, 1969).

Maitland, F. W., *Select Pleas in Manorial and Other Seignorial Courts*, SS, vol. ii (London, 1889).

Manship, H., Jnr, 'Great Yarmouthe, a Booke of the Foundacion and Antiquitye of the said Towne and of Diverse Specialle matters concerninge the same' (Great Yarmouth, 1619). This manuscript was published in 1847 by C. J. Palmer.

Marchant, R. A., *The Church Under the Law* (Cambridge, 1969).

Marshall, W., *The Rural Economy of Norfolk, Comprising the Management of Land Estates and the Present Practice of Husbandry in the County* (London, 1787).

Mathias, P., *The Brewing Industry in England, 1700–1820* (Cambridge, 1959).

—*The First Industrial Nation*, 2nd ed. (London, 1983).

Metters, G. A., 'The Rulers and Merchants of King's Lynn in the Early Seventeenth Century' (unpub. PhD thesis, University of East Anglia, 1982).

Michell, A. R. 'The Fishing Industry in Early Modern Europe', in E. E. Rich and C. H. Wilson (eds), *The Cambridge Economic History of Europe*, vol. 5 (Cambridge, 1977).

—'The Port and Town of Great Yarmouth and its Social and Economic Relationships with its Neighbours on Both Sides of the Sea, 1550–1714' (unpub. PhD thesis, University of Cambridge, 1978).

Mitchell, I., 'The Development of Urban Retailing, 1700–1815', in P. Clark (ed.), *The Transformation of English Provincial Towns* (London, 1984).

Moxon, C. J. M., 'Ashby-de-la-Zouche: A Social and Economic Survey of a Market Town, 1570–1720' (unpub. PhD thesis, University of Oxford, 1971).

Mulcaster, R., *The First Part of the Elementarie which Entreateth Chiefly of the Right Writing of our English Tongue* (London, 1582).

Muldrew, C., *The Economy of Obligation* (London and New York, 1998).

O'Day, R., *Economy and Community* (London, 1975).

Overton, M., 'Agricultural Change in Norfolk and Suffolk, 1580–1740' (unpub. PhD thesis, University of Cambridge, 1980).

——'The Diffusion of Agricultural Innovations in Early Modern England: Turnips and Clover in Norfolk and Suffolk, 1580–1740', *TIBG* new series 10, 2 (1985), 191–221.

Oxley, G. W., *Poor Relief in England and Wales, 1601–1834* (Newton Abbot, 1974).

Page, W. (ed.), *The Victoria County History of Suffolk*, 2 vols (London, 1907).

Palliser, D. M., 'Dearth and Disease in Staffordshire, 1540–1670', in C. W. Chalklin and M. R. Havinden (eds), *Rural Change and Urban Growth* (London, 1974).

——'A Crisis in English Towns? The Case of York, 1460–1640', *NH* 14 (1978), 109–25.

——*Tudor York* (Oxford, 1979).

Parker, V., *The Making of King's Lynn* (Chichester, 1971).

Patten, J., *English Towns, 1500–1700* (Folkestone, 1978).

Peck, L. L., *Consuming Splendor* (Cambridge, 2005).

Pennell, S., 'Consumption and Consumerism in Early Modern England', *HJ* 42, 2 (1999), 549–64.

Pevsner, N., *The Buildings of England: Suffolk*, 2nd edition (London, 1974).

Philanglus, *Britannia Languens or A Discourse of Trade* (London, 1680). This pamphlet is reproduced in J. R. McCulloch, *Early English Tracts on Commerce* (Cambridge, 1952).

Phythian-Adams, C. (ed.), *Societies, Cultures and Kinship, 1580–1850: Cultural Provinces and English Local History* (Leicester, 1993).

Porter, S., *The Great Fire of London* (Stroud, 1996).

Portman, D., *Exeter Houses, 1400–1700* (Exeter, 1966).

Postgate, M. R., 'Field Systems of East Anglia', in A. R. H. Baker and R. A. Butlin (eds), *Field Systems in the British Isles* (Cambridge, 1973).

Pound, J. F., 'The Social and Trade Structure of Norwich, 1525–1575', *P&P* 34 (1966), 49–69.

——'The Validity of the Freeman's Lists: Some Norwich Evidence', *EHR* 2nd Series 34 (1981), 48–59.

Priestley, U. and Corfield, P. J., with Sutermeister, H., 'Rooms and Room Use in Norwich Housing, 1580–1730', *JSPMA* 16 (1982), 93–123.

Pullar, P., *Consuming Passions* (London, 1971)

Rackham, O., *Trees and Woodland in the British Landscape* (London, 1976).

——*The History of the Countryside* (London, 1986).

——*Woodlands* (London, 2006).

Razzell, P. E., 'Population Change in Eighteenth Century England: A Reappraisal', *EHR* 2nd Series xviii (1965), 312–32. This article is also to be found in M. Drake, *Population in Industrialisation* (London, 1969).
    —*The History of Myddle* (Firle, Sussex, 1979). The writer acted as editor of this version of Richard Gough's classic work.
Reed, M., 'Ipswich in the Seventeenth Century' (unpub. PhD thesis, University of Leicester, 1973).
    —'Economic Structure and Change in Seventeenth Century Ipswich', in P. Clark (ed.), *Country Towns in Pre-Industrial England* (Leicester, 1981).
Reeve, R., 'A History of Lowestoft and Lothingland', 4 vols (unpub. manuscript of c. 1810) – SRO(L), 193/3/1, 2, 3 and 4.
Rich, E. E. and Wilson, C. H. (eds), *The Cambridge Economic History of Europe*, 5 vols (Cambridge, 1977).
Richardson, J., *The Local Historian's Encyclopedia*, 1st and 3rd editions (London, 1974 and 2003).
Robinson, R. 'The Common North Atlantic Pool', in D. J. Starkey, C. Reid and N. Ashcroft (eds), *England's Sea Fisheries* (London, 2000).
Rosen, A., 'Winchester in Transition, 1580–1700', in P. Clark (ed.), *Country Towns in Pre-Industrial England* (Leicester, 1981).
Sandon, E., *Suffolk Houses* (Woodbridge, 1977).
Schofield, R., 'The Measurement of Literacy in Pre-Industrial England', in J. R. Goody (ed.), *Literacy in Traditional Societies* (Cambridge, 1968).
Scott, S. and Duncan, C., *Biology of Plagues: Evidence from Historical Populations* (Cambridge, 2001).
Sharpe, J. A., 'Crime and Delinquency in an Essex Parish, 1600–1640', in J. S. Cockburn (ed.), *Crime in England, 1500–1800* (London, 1977).
    —*Crime in Early Modern England, 1550–1750* (London, 1984).
    —'The People and the Law', in B. Reay (ed.), *Popular Culture in Seventeenth Century England* (London, 1985).
Short, B. M., 'The South-East: Kent, Surrey and Sussex', in J. Thirsk (ed.), *The Agrarian History of England and Wales*, vol. v, i (Cambridge, 1984).
Shrewsbury, J. F. D., *A History of the Bubonic Plague in the British Isles* (Cambridge, 1970).
Simon, J., *Education and Society in Tudor England* (Cambridge, 1966).
Simpson, A., *The Wealth of the Gentry* (Cambridge, 1961).
Slack, P., 'Poverty and Politics in Salisbury, 1597–1666', in P. Clark and P. Slack (eds), *Crisis and Order in English Towns, 1500–1700* (London, 1972).
    —'The English Urban Landscape', in OU, *The Urban Setting* (Milton Keynes, 1977–8).
    —'Social Problems and Social Policies', in OU, *The Traditional Community Under Stress* (Milton Keynes, 1977–8).
Smith, S., *Lowestoft Porcelain in Norwich Castle Museum*, 2 vols (Norwich, 1975 and 1985).
Souden, D., 'Migrants and Population Structure of Later Seventeenth Century Cities and Market Towns', in P. Clark (ed.), *The Transformation of English Provincial Towns* (London, 1984).

Spufford, M., *Contrasting Communities* (Cambridge, 1974).

—'Peasant Inheritance Customs and Land Distribution in Cambridgeshire from the Sixteenth to the Eighteenth Century', in J. R. Goody, J. Thirsk and E. P. Thompson, *Family and Inheritance: Rural Society in Western Europe, 1200–1800* (Cambridge, 1976).

Starkey, D., Reid C. and Ashcroft, N. (eds), *England's Sea Fisheries* (London, 2000).

Stephen, Sir L. and Lee, Sir S., *The Dictionary of National Biography*, vols i, vi, xii and xvii (Oxford, 1917; reprinted 1967–8).

Stone, L., 'The Educational Revolution in England, 1540–1640', *P&P* 28 (July 1964), 41–80.

—*The Family, Sex and Marriage in England, 1500–1800* (London, 1977).

Supple, B. E., *Commercial Crisis and Change in England, 1600–1642* (Cambridge, 1970).

Tawney, R. H. (ed.), *A Discourse Upon Usury* (London, 1925 and 1962). The book was originally written by Thomas Wilson and published in 1572.

Taylor, A. Clifton, *The Pattern of English Building* (London, 1962).

Taylor, G., *The Problem of Poverty, 1660–1834* (London, 1969).

Theobald, J., 'Agricultural Productivity in Woodland High Suffolk, 1600–1850', *AHR* 50, I (2002), 1–24.

Thick, M., 'Market Gardening in England and Wales', in J. Thirsk (ed.), *The Agrarian History of England and Wales*, vol. v, ii (Cambridge, 1985).

Thirsk, J., 'The Farming Regions of England', in J. Thirsk (ed.), *The Agrarian History of England and Wales*, vol. iv (Cambridge, 1967).

—'Enclosing and Engrossing', in J. Thirsk (ed.), *The Agrarian History of England and Wales*, vol. iv (Cambridge, 1967).

—'Farming Techniques', in J. Thirsk (ed.), *The Agrarian History of England and Wales*, vol. iv (Cambridge, 1967).

—'The European Debate on Customs of Inheritance, 1500–1700', in J. R. Goody, J. Thirsk and E. P. Thompson (eds), *Family and Inheritance: Rural Society in Western Europe, 1200–1800* (Cambridge, 1976).

Thompson, E. P., 'The Grid of Inheritance', in J. R. Goody, J. Thirsk and E. P. Thompson (eds), *Family and Inheritance: Rural Society in Western Europe, 1200–1800* (Cambridge, 1976).

Tittler, R., 'The English Fishing Industry in the Sixteenth Century: The Case of Great Yarmouth', *Albion* 9, i (Spring, 1977), 40–60.

—'Henry Manship Jnr.: Constructing the Civic Memory in Great Yarmouth', in R. Tittler, *Townspeople and Nation: English Urban Experiences, 1540–1640* (Stanford, 2001).

Tranter, N. L., 'Demographic Change in Bedfordshire, 1670–1800' (unpub. PhD. thesis, University of Nottingham, 1966)

Underdown, D., *Revel, Riot and Rebellion: Popular Politics and Culture in England, 1603–1640* (Oxford, 1985).

Unger, R. W., 'The Netherlands Fishery in the Late Middle Ages: The False Legend of Willem Beukels of Biervliet', *Viator* 9 (1978), 335–56.

Weatherill, L., 'A Possession of One's Own: Women and Consumer Behaviour in England, 1660–1740', *JBS* 25 (1986), 131–56.

—*Consumer Behaviour and Material Culture in Britain* (London, 1988; 2nd edition 1996).

Webb, S. and B., *English Local Government: The Manor and the Borough* (London, 1908).

Whiston, W., *Memoirs of the Life and Writings of Mr. William Whiston* (London, 1749).

Wight, J. A., *Brick Building in England* (London, 1972).

Willan, T. S., *The English Coasting Trade* (Manchester, 1937 and 1968).

—*The Inland Trade* (Manchester, 1976).

Williams, N. J., 'The Maritime Trade of the East Anglian Ports, 1550–1590' (unpub. PhD thesis, University of Oxford, 1952).

—*The Maritime Trade of the East Anglian Ports, 1550–1590* (Oxford, 1988). This book is the published form of the thesis cited immediately above.

Wilson, C., *Profit and Power* (London, 1957).

—*England's Apprenticeship, 1603–1763* (London, 1965).

Wilson, F. P., *The Plague in Shakespeare's London* (Oxford, 1963).

Wilson, T., *A Discourse Upon Usury* (London, 1572).

Woolgar, C. M., 'Take This Penance Now and Afterwards the Fare will Improve: Seafood and Late Mediaeval Diet', in D. J. Starkey, C. Reid and N. Ashcroft (eds), *England's Sea Fisheries* (London, 2000).

Wrightson, K., 'Two Concepts of Order: Justices, Constables and Jurymen in Seventeenth Century England', in J. Brewer and J. Styles (eds), *An Ungovernable People: The English and Their Law in the Seventeenth and Eighteenth Centuries* (London, 1980).

Wrightson, K. and Levine, D., *Poverty and Piety in an English Village: Terling, 1525–1700* (New York, 1979).

Wrigley, E. A., 'Family Limitation in Pre-Industrial England', *EHR* 2nd Series 19 (1966), 82–109.

—*An Introduction to English Historical Demography* (London, 1966).

—'Marital Fertility in Seventeenth Century Colyton', *EHR* 2nd Series 31 (1978), 419–28.

Wrigley, E. A. and Schofield, R. S., *The Population History of England, 1541–1871* (London, 1981).

—'English Population History from Family Reconstitution: Summary Results, 1600–1799', *PS* 37 (1983), 157–84.

Wrigley, E. A., Davies, R. S., Oeppen, J. E. and Schofield, R. S., *English Population History from Family Reconstitution, 1580–1837* (Cambridge, 1997).

Yelling, J. A., *Common Field and Enclosure in England, 1450–1850* (London, 1977).

Young, A., *Annals of Agriculture* (London, 1795).

—*A General View of the Agriculture of the County of Suffolk* (London, 1797 and 1813; republished Newton Abbot, 1969).

Name Index (people and places)

Numbered Christian names give chronological order, without always showing family ties
References to counties pre-date the boundary changes of 1891 and 1974
Illustrations and their captions are indicated by bold type

Subject Index

Illustrations and their captions are indicated by bold type

Printed and bound by CPI Group (UK) Ltd, Croydon, CR0 4YY

09/06/2025

14685720-0003